Financial Exclusion

How Competition Can Fix a Broken System

By
Robert E. Wright

Financial Exclusion:
How Competition Can Fix a Broken System

ISBN: 978-1-63-069170-7

Financial Exclusion

How Competition Can Fix a Broken System

By
Robert E. Wright

 | AMERICAN INSTITUTE
for ECONOMIC RESEARCH

Dedicated to the spirit
of singer-songwriter
Johnny Cash, who wore
black clothes to mourn
the plight of the poor
and beaten down, who
live on the hopeless and
hungry side of town.

Contents

Acknowledgments

If the book is not as amusing as the last new novel the writer cannot help it. He has done the best he could … with the dry and stubborn materials he had to handle. — William Gouge, *The Fiscal History of Texas* (Philadelphia: Lippincott, Grambo, and Co., 1852), iv.

Andrew Smith of the University of Liverpool provided incredibly useful early advice on how to tackle such an enormous and important subject. Arizona's Price Fishback provided detailed feedback and important source material that saved me from numerous errors, great and small. UVA's Ron Michener also read a complete draft and offered several important correctives. Jan Traflet of Bucknell's Freeman College of Management read and expertly commented on early drafts of three chapters and did such a good job that we are currently working together on a biography of corporate gadfly and NBC radio personality Wilma Soss. Susie Pak of St. John's offered important advice on organization as well as Korean barbeque. Stephen Campbell also offered useful advice on several chapters, while Mira Wilkins gave encouragement during a particularly difficult period. Dave Nichols turned me on to Navajo Pawn. Finally, several anonymous reviewers provided useful criticisms. I don't know who they are, but they do (Although I often ignored some of your advice, thank you!). Finally, Augustana University's Mikkelsen Library outdid itself again, fulfilling all of my reasonable requests, and several unreasonable ones, with dispatch. Granted, Katrina Stierholz and the other good folks who run the FRASER database at the St. Louis Federal Reserve lightened the load considerably by supplying researchers like myself with a steady stream of digitized archival sources related to U.S. financial history. Any and all errors remaining within these pages, though, remain my soul's sole responsibility.

CHAPTER ONE

Introduction: Defining and Mitigating Financial Exclusion, Discrimination, and Predation

Trade between two societies is maximized when there is no discrimination, and it decreases with all increases in discrimination.
— Gary S. Becker, *The Economics of Discrimination*, 2nd ed.
(Chicago: University of Chicago Press, 1971), 22.

This book is about financial exclusion, discrimination, and predation, i.e., bad behaviors committed by legitimate financial institutions with help from government regulators and regulations. Its main goal is to persuade readers, via an historical narrative informed by economic theory, that the best way to combat financial discrimination is through the encouragement of new entrants, not top-down regulation.

An equally long, and probably more interesting, book could be written about scammers and grifters on both sides of financial transactions, from wildcat banks, Ponzi schemes, and fly-by-night insurers to consumers who kite or counterfeit checks, defraud insurers, and "loadups" who

1

purposely run up debt before leaving the country or filing for bankruptcy. Yet most of the time, consumers pay their bills in as timely a manner as they can and file only legitimate insurance claims. Similarly, most of the time most financial services companies behave lawfully and even ethically. But sometimes they do not and that is a major problem for those preyed upon, excluded from access entirely, or discriminated against. As the head quote from Nobel economist Gary Becker indicates, such practices are also a major problem for the overall economy and some believe they even threaten democracy.[1]

Financial discrimination should not be confused with financial predation. Predation occurs when a financial services company does business with an applicant that objectively it ought *not* to in order to secure some strategic economic advantage over its customer. Loans to sharecroppers (black and white) in the postbellum South, for example, were sometimes predatory contracts that tied workers to landlords in quasi-feudal arrangements. Many types of mortgages, from FHA-insured loans in the 1970s to the notorious subprime mortgages of the late 1990s and the first half of the first decade of the Third Millennium, also should not have been made, and ended up hurting borrowers, their neighbors, and, ultimately, the global economy. Many farm loans made in the late 1970s, by contrast, were just incompetent, not predatory, as the lenders suffered large losses, or even went bankrupt, along with their borrowers.[2]

---

1 Gregory Squires, "The New Redlining," in *Why the Poor Pay More: How to Stop Predatory Lending*, ed. Gregory D. Squires (Westport, Conn.: Praeger, 2004), 8; Sheri J. Caplan, *Petticoats and Pinstripes: Portraits of Women in Wall Street's History,* (Denver: Praeger, 2013), 31; Clifton R. Wooldridge, *The Grafters of America,* (Chicago: Monarch Book Company, 1906); Hillel Black, *Buy Now, Pay Later,* (New York: William Morrow and Company, 1961), 23–27, 43, 53–54, 63–66, 128; Daniel Aaronson, Daniel Hartley, and Bhashkar Mazumder, "The Effect of the 1930s HOLC 'Redlining' Maps," Federal Reserve Bank of Chicago Working Paper WP 2017–2 (August 3, 2017), 2; Mehrsa Baradaran, *How the Other Half Banks: Exclusion, Exploitation, and the Threat to Democracy* (Cambridge: Harvard University Press, 2015).

2 Kyle Smith, *Predatory Lending in Native American Communities,* (Fredericksburg, Va.: First Nations Development Institute, 2003), 4, 9–10; Squires, "The New Redlining," 1–4; Stephen Ross and John Yinger, *The Color of Credit: Mortgage Discrimination, Research Methodology, and Fair-Lending Enforcement,* (Cambridge: The MIT Press, 2002), 19–21; Arthur Raper and Ira De A. Reid, *Sharecroppers All,* (Chapel Hill: University of North Carolina Press, 1941); Clarence Page, "Foreword: Loan Sharks in Pinstripes," in *Why the Poor Pay More: How to*

Consumers sign predatory contracts because they do not realize that they will be expropriated. Predators take pains to hide their intentions and have much more experience with the intricacies of the financial system than do consumers, most of whom suffer under myriad irrational ways of thinking catalogued over the last few decades by behavioral economists like Dan Ariely, Richard Thaler, and Vernon L. Smith. But over two hundred years ago another Smith, first name Adam, noted that most people believe that they possess superior abilities and/or luck, an "overweening conceit" as he put it. In short, many predatory contracts are signed out of simple human hubris.[3]

Financial discrimination occurs when a financial services company does *not* do business with an applicant (make a loan to, provide insurance coverage for, etc.) that objectively it ought to. In its most extreme form, as during the long reign of Jim Crow, members of certain groups lacking in political or economic power were completely, or almost completely, excluded from participation in specific parts of the financial system. Financial exclusion is relatively easy to discern from the historical record. As public opinion and laws increasingly disdained exclusion, however, more subtle and less detectable forms of discrimination arose. I deliberately occluded the subject of the sentence immediately prior to this one because the origins of the newer forms of discrimination remain unclear. If "Mr. Charlie," "Bobo," and "the Man" ever met in a smoke-filled back room and worked it all out, they did not leave a clear paper trail of their

Stop Predatory Lending, ed. Gregory D. Squires (Westport, Conn.: Praeger, 2004), viii; Dan Immergluck, *Credit to the Community: Community Reinvestment and Fair Lending Policy in the United States*, (New York: M. E. Sharpe, 2004), 110, 224. Jack M. Guttentag and Susan M. Wachter, *Redlining and Public Policy*, (New York: Salomon Brothers Center, 1980), 45; Osha Gray Davidson, *Broken Heartland: The Rise of America's Rural Ghetto*, (New York: Free Press, 1990), 15, 35, 55.

3 Richard H. Thaler, *Misbehaving: The Making of Behavioral Economics*, (New York: Norton, 2016); Dan Ariely, *Predictably Irrational: The Hidden Forces that Shape our Decisions*, Rev. Ed. (New York: Harper 2010); Nava Ashraf, Colin F. Camerer, and George Loewenstein, "Adam Smith, Behavioral Economist," *Journal of Economic Perspectives* 19, no. 3 (2005): 131–45; Robert Schafer and Helen F. Ladd, *Discrimination in Mortgage Lending*, (Cambridge: MIT Press, 1981), 9; Richard L. Peterson, "An Investigation of Sex Discrimination in Commercial Banks' Direct Consumer Lending," *Bell Journal of Economics* 12, no. 2 (1981), 548.

meeting.[4] It is more likely that the new forms of discrimination, which were most virulent at the economic margins, evolved spontaneously because laws and regulations changed more quickly than incentives and social attitudes did.

Throughout U.S. history, many groups have faced financial preda- tion, exclusion, and discrimination, including Arabs; atheists; Asians; Catholics; Eastern Europeans; Irish; Jews; Mexicans, Puerto Ricans and other Hispanics; members of the LGBTQ and transvestite com- munities; the physically disabled; the aged; minors; "fuglies" (fat and/ or ugly people);[5] and members of specific occupational groups including

---

4 I have not been able to canvas all extant bank records but I have broadly sampled them and most do not provide crucial details of decisions. For example, the Community Savings Bank of Rochester, New York noted in its minutes only that "103 loans [were] approved in the amount of $748,178.64, ... There were 20 mortgage loan applications rejected." The more detailed board reports that must have existed at one time are no longer extant or in private hands but even those materials would probably be insufficient to establish discriminatory practices. Regular Board Meeting, May 28, 1951, Agendas/Minutes: Board Meetings; Mortgage Loan Applications, East Side Bank, University of Rochester. Others, like Dean Chavers, have also failed to find direct evidence of conspiracy. Dean Chavers, *Racism in Indian Country*, (New York: Peter Lang, 2009), 56.

5 Rowena Olegario, *A Culture of Credit: Embedding Trust and Transparency in American Business*, (Cambridge: Harvard University Press, 2006), 119–38; Susie Pak, *Gentlemen Bank- ers: The World of J. P. Morgan*, (Cambridge: Harvard University Press, 2013); Jeffrey A. Adler, *Yankee Merchants and the Making of the Urban West: The Rise and Fall of Antebellum St. Louis*, (Cambridge: Cambridge University Press, 1991), 81; Charles Abrams, *Forbidden Neighbors: A Study of Prejudice in Housing*, (New York: Harper & Brothers, 1955), 179, 183; John Sibley Butler, *Entrepreneurship and Self-Help Among Black Americans: A Reconsideration of Race and Economics*, (Albany: State University of New York Press, 1991), 20–22; Karen Brodkin, "How Jews Became White," in *Race, Class and Gender in the United States* 5th ed., ed. Paula S. Rothenberg (New York: Worth, 2001), 40; Rita Chaudhry Sethi, "Smells Like Racism," in *Race, Class and Gender in the United States* 5th ed., ed. Paula S. Rothenberg (New York: Worth, 2001), 108; Richard Sterner, Lenoir Epstein, and Ellen Winston, *The Negro's Share: A Study of Income, Consumption, Housing and Public Assistance*, (New York: Harper & Broth- ers, 1943), 200–1; BFCU Proposal to Philadelphia Corporation for Aging, November 7, 1983, Hispanic Federation for Social and Economic Development, Administrative Series, Box 4, Folder 13, Historical Society of Pennsylvania; Black, *Buy Now*, 39–40, 124–27; Committee on Banking, Housing, and Urban Affairs, U.S. Senate, 103rd Congress, 2nd Sess., "Homeowners' Insurance Discrimination," May 11, 1994, (Washington: GPO, 1994), 6; Thomas Demeco, Mortgage Loan Applications, East Side Bank, Rush Rhees Library; Daniel S. Hamermesh, "Ugly? You May Have a Case," *New York Times*, 27 August 2011; Christina Jenq, Jessica Pan, Walter Theseira, "What Do Donors Discriminate On? Evidence from Kiva.Org," (Working Paper, May 2011).

miners, farmers,[6] and lawyers.[7] When choosing managers, Andrew Carnegie discriminated against college graduates in favor of mercantile clerks because he believed the latter had greater capacity. Most creditors in Carnegie's time also discriminated against older borrowers on the presumption that they had less reason to protect their reputations as they would soon be retired or dead. Lenders also discriminated against single men because they did not have as much incentive to do well, or any help from a spouse or children. Even corporations, qua corporations, faced discrimination in nineteenth century credit markets because many lenders believed that limited liability and deteriorating management and corporate governance standards would conspire to render the probability of bankruptcy a high one.[8] "Go to any bank and ask why the discrimination is made," an early credit expert explained, "and they will tell you that they prefer to deal with individuals, for obvious reasons, and the merchant or manufacturer, applied to for credit by them, will render the same verdict."[9]

Canvassing the historical record, one is left with the distinct impression that at least some members of every group faced, or thought they faced, some sort of financial discrimination at some point or another. Their stories are all important but four groups have confronted particularly interesting and intense discrimination in financial markets and institutions:African-Americans, American Indians, poor whites, and women. Their experiences with discrimination therefore compose four discrete chapters of this book, each of which must reference terms that some readers may find troubling. Following scholars like Jacqueline Jones and Dean Chavers, I believe that race is a social construct with no basis in biological reality. The same can be said of ethnicity, class, and even,

---

6 "They have not had the same freedom to get credit on their real estate as others have had," Woodrow Wilson claimed. As quoted in W. Gifford Hoag, *The Farm Credit System: A History of Financial Self-Help*, (Danville, Ill.: Interstate Printers & Publishers, 1976), 214.

7 Reputedly because they "know so damned much." Black, *Buy Now*, 50.

8 Olegario, *Culture of Credit*, 107, 156; Peter R. Earling, *Whom to Trust: A Practical Treatise on Mercantile Credits*, (New York: Rand McNally & Co., 1890), 147.

9 Earling, *Whom to Trust*, 145.

to some extent, gender. Those concepts, however, are very real in terms of their effects on individuals and that is the sense in which they are used here. Bigoted ways of identifying members of different socioeconomic, religious, racial, and ethnic groups are used only when quoting or paraphrasing contemporaries to reveal their racial prejudices. Despite their obvious shortcomings, common synonyms, like "blacks" for African-Americans and "Indians" for American Indians, are sometimes employed, merely to avoid tedious repetition.[10]

In her recent book, *A Dreadful Deceit*, Jones challenged scholars to identify who benefits from racism and how.[11] The answer often depends on the structure of the market. Competition tends to destroy exclusion, discrimination, and predation by driving predatory, exclusionary, and discriminatory service providers out of business or, at the very least, providing the individuals being excluded, discriminated against, or preyed upon with viable alternative sources of supply.[12] "Trade," as one late nineteenth century author put it, "distinguishes between neither race, color, nor religion."[13] "The almighty dollar," African-American banker Maggie Walker argued, "is the magic wand that knocks the bottom out of racial prejudice."[14] "Profit is still a more powerful motive than discrimination," claimed Joseph Barr, president of American Security and Trust Company.[15]

Throughout history, though, most U.S. credit markets were not competitive and "Wall Street," the brokerage and investment banking sector, recently combined with national megabanks, has long displayed

---

10 Jacqueline Jones, *A Dreadful Deceit: The Myth of Race from the Colonial Era to Obama's America*, (New York: Basic Books, 2013), x, xvii; Chavers, *Racism*, 2.

11 Jones, *Dreadful Deceit*, xi.

12 Jones, *Dreadful Deceit*, xi; George C. Galster, "Use of Testers in Investigating Discrimination in Mortgage Lending and Insurance," in *Clear and Convincing Evidence: Measurement of Discrimination in America*, eds. Michael Fix and Raymond J. Struyk (Washington, DC: Urban Institute Press, 1993), 288.

13 Earling, *Whom to Trust*, 89.

14 Caplan, *Petticoats*, 63.

15 As quoted in Louis Hyman, *Debtor Nation: The History of America in Red Ink*, (Princeton: Princeton University Press, 2011), 201.

signs of oligopoly at some margins. America harbored thousands, and later tens of thousands, of commercial banks but few did business outside of a limited geographical area. Many states did not allow banks to branch at all. When states began to allow intrastate branching, some, like South Dakota, put severe geographical restrictions on new branches. Others, including New York, allowed incumbent banks to oppose new branches proposed by their competitors! In 1951, for example, the Community Savings Bank of Rochester, New York signaled that it would oppose any more banking institutions on Ridge Road West. "This area," it told the state banking regulators, "is now adequately served by three commercial bank branches and one savings bank branch."[16]

Less formal ways of limiting competition also existed. During the Depression, savings banks in Rochester met and entered into "a gentleman's agreement ... whereby none of the four savings banks would make application to write life insurance without notifying the other savings banks of their intentions."[17] They soon agreed to enter the business simultaneously and after the war, and much inflation, they tried to increase the maximum policy they could write from $3,000 to $5,000, only to arouse the ire of the traditional life insurers, who argued that savings banks deceived the public into believing that their policies were backed by more assets than they actually were.[18]

Because of the market power of individual banks, market discipline did not lead, as the Treasury Department put it in 1978, "to automatic improvement of the credit situation."[19] A dearth of competition meant monopoly profits, which can take the form of higher profits or

16 Regular Board Meeting, September 12, 1951, Agendas/Minutes: Board Meetings, Rush Rhees Library.

17 J. H. Zweeres (president) to Arthur A. Barry (trustee), December 15, 1938, Business Correspondence East Side Bank, Rush Rhees Library.

18 Charles Carson to Board of Trustees, March 6, 1947, Business Correspondence, Community Savings, Rush Rhees Library.

19 Treasury Department Study Team, *Credit and Capital Formation: A Report to the President's Interagency Task Force on Women Business Owners*, (April 1978), 52.

non-market preferences, like the expression of racial hatred or gender bias. The market for consumer loans was especially uncompetitive because financiers long duped regulators into believing that competition in lending was "destructive" and hence should be limited. I say duped because competition generally decreases profits but, as economist George Benston showed, "banks can remain quite viable even when the level of competition intensifies greatly."[20]

An equally important question to that posed by Jones is who does exclusion, discrimination, and predation hurt? Discrimination in any form is unfair in its own right but it is also economically damaging. For the latter reason, especially, it is of pressing policy concern. Governments, free governments anyway, should not be in the business of telling X that it has to do business with Y, unless, that is, X's unwillingness to do business with Y hurts Z, and perhaps everybody else too. Financial exclusion, discrimination, and predation appear to constitute such a case. Government action to reduce discrimination is therefore justified not only out of fairness but also to eliminate the social costs inherent in the under-consumption of loans, insurance, and other financial services.[21]

For all its faults and foibles, the financial system is absolutely indispensable to the nation's overall economy as well as its many sub-economies. Finance is so important that denying people equal access to the system is a surefire way of keeping them impoverished, which is morally reprehensible, fiscally imprudent, and ultimately economically damaging. That is why the main goal of the World Bank's Financial Inclusion initiative is to increase the poor's access to financial services worldwide.[22]

---

20 George J. Benston, "Savings Banking and the Public Interest," *Journal of Money, Credit and Banking* 4, no. 1 (1972), 37, 137–39.

21 George J. Benston, *Regulating Financial Markets: A Critique and Some Proposals*, (Washington, D.C.: AEI Press, 1999), 37, 50; Henry Hansmann, *The Ownership of Enterprise*, (Cambridge: Harvard University Press, 1996), 24–25; Immergluck, *Credit to the Community*, 5; Aaronson, Hartley, and Mazumder, "The Effect of the 1930s HOLC," 2.

22 http://www.worldbank.org/en/topic/financialinclusion

Suffrage and citizenship, important as they have been, are insufficient to ensure equal economic opportunities for all. The great abolitionist Lewis Tappan suggested that to ensure their well-being African-Americans needed "a musket in one hand and a ballot in the other"[23] but what they really needed was a home mortgage like that of their white neighbors and, if entrepreneurially inclined, equal access to business finance and insurance. Until everyone has equal access to bank loans, investment funds, insurance, and home mortgages, large income and wealth disparities will continue to blemish America's otherwise enviable record of prosperity and prevent it from achieving yet greater heights.[24]

Thankfully, achieving equal access is not as difficult as it may first appear. The chapters that follow document the fact that from colonial times to this very day, African-Americans, Amerindians, poor whites, and women did not have equal access to the mainstream U.S. financial system sketched in Chapter 2. Seldom were they excluded altogether; a recent claim that "access to consumer credit had for decades been limited to white men" is a gross exaggeration.[25] But members of minority groups often paid more, or received less, than they objectively should have. In the limit, some businesses contracted with them only to prey upon their vulnerabilities. I chose those specific groups in order to focus on four key variables: race, system of political economy, class or socioeconomic status, and gender. Financial services companies have also denied equal access to individuals due to age, ethnicity, marital status, weight and physical appearance, religion, and other personal characteristics

---

23 Olegario, *Culture of Credit*, 41.

24 Branko Milanovic, *The Haves and the Have-Nots: A Brief and Idiosyncratic History of Global Inequality*, (New York: Basic Books, 2012); Thomas Piketty, *Capital in the Twenty-First Century*, (Cambridge: Harvard University Press, 2014).

25 Enrico Beltramini, "Consumer Credit as a Civil Right in the United States, 1968–1976," in *The Cultural History of Money and Credit: A Global Perspective*, eds. Chia Yin Jus, Thomas Luckett, and Erika Vause (New York: Lexington Books, 2016), 81. As if to make my point, Beltramini offers no evidence for his claim but rather describes mechanisms of discrimination instead of outright exclusion.

but the underlying issues remain largely the same and the same policy recommendations apply.[26]

The final two chapters again survey U.S. financial history, but this time from the perspective of attempts to reduce discrimination. In the process, those chapters show that self-help, combined with free entry, is the best way for market forces and governments to work together to reduce financial exclusion, discrimination, and predation in America. In other words, what Americans of all colors, creeds, income levels, genders, races, sexual preferences, and so forth need are their own financial institutions, not easy credit from financial giants that pose systemic risks to the world economy.

Aficionados will quickly perceive that this conclusion is consistent with the path breaking work of economist Gary Becker in *The Economics of Discrimination*, which showed that in a competitive market discrimination by individual suppliers (lenders or insurers in our case) cannot injure customers (loan and insurance applicants) because the latter will be able to obtain what they need elsewhere. The key is establishing and maintaining a sufficient level of competition and information flow so that search and other transaction costs are not prohibitive and market power (over prices, by suppliers) is minimized.

Scholars well-versed in the economics of discrimination know that the Becker model is far from universally accepted. Economic sociologists like William A. Darity and heterodox economists from the left of the political spectrum are particularly skeptical. Most critiques, however, pick around the edges rather than confront the big insight of the model, which is that discrimination is unprofitable and hence can be eliminated by competition. I, like the Nobel committee and numerous neoclassical economists, therefore find Becker's model more theoretically sound than alternative theories.

Even more importantly, though, I find much empirical evidence for Becker's model in the historical record in the form of discrimination-induced financial innovation. So have the few economists who have

---

26 Squires, "The New Redlining," 1–23.

actually statistically tested the predictions of Becker's model. Other economists, leaders in the public choice school of thought, have shown that some forms of discrimination, like racial segregation on streetcars, stemmed from government fiat and not competitive markets. Becker's skeptics are therefore urged to read on and to keep an open mind.[27]

---

27 William A. Darity, Jr. and Samuel L. Myers, Jr. *Persistent Disparity: Race and Economic Inequality in the United States Since 1945*, (Cheltenham: Edward Elgar, 1998); Deborah M. Figart and Ellen Mutari, "Rereading Becker: Contextualizing the Development of Discrimination Theory," *Journal of Economic Issues* 339, no. 2 (2005): 475–83; Kerwin Kofi Charles and Jonathan Guryan, "Prejudice and Wages: An Empirical Assessment of Becker's The Economics of Discrimination," *Journal of Political Economy* 116, no. 5 (2008), 775; Jennifer Roback, "The Political Economy of Segregation: The Case of Segregated Streetcars," *Journal of Economic History* 46, no. 4 (Dec. 1986): 893–917.

CHAPTER TWO

A Whitewashed History of America's Financial System

This chapter presents a general, some might say whitewashed, textbook history of the U.S. financial system, from about 1750 to the present, with little attention paid to issues of exclusion, discrimination, or predation until the end. Readers conversant with the broad sweep of U.S. financial history can safely skip, or skim, it, but most readers will need to peruse the chapter in order to have sufficient background context to understand fully the more specialized chapters on the financial exclusion of African-Americans, American Indians, white trash, and women to follow.

Financing Prosperity

Credit is the vital air of modern commerce. It has done more, a thousand times, to enrich nations than all the mines of the world. It has excited labor, stimulated manufactures, pushed commerce over every sea, and brought every nation, every kingdom and every small tribe among the race of men to be known to all the rest; it has raised armies, equipped navies and, triumphing over the gross power of mere numbers, it has established national superiority on the foundation of intelligence, wealth and well-directed industry. — Peter P. Wahlstad and Walter S. Johnson, Credit and the Credit Man (New York: Alexander Hamilton Institute, 1917), 9.

Time was, many economists did not consider the financial system — the complex interaction of money, depository institutions, insurers, and markets for debt (notes, bonds, mortgages) and equity (shares in businesses) — all that important. Some viewed finance as merely an ancillary service that, while convenient, was hardly as important as sectors in the "real" economy like agriculture, mining, and manufacturing. A few even considered finance as little better than gambling, a way of redistributing existing resources but not a means of creating new wealth. It was thought that, at best, the financial system followed where the real economy led it, expanding as real economic sectors dictated.

In recent decades, however, increasing numbers of economists have found considerable merit in the finance-led growth hypothesis. According to that theory, a financial sector of sufficient size and competence is a necessary cause of modern economic growth, or sustained inflation-adjusted increases in per capita output. Finance, in other words, makes possible advances in the real economy, where brains, sweat, and steel interact in ways that are palpable but only seemingly fundamental. No economy, proponents of the theory showed, ever experienced modern economic growth without the prior establishment of an effective financial system comprised of a stable unit of account, financial intermediaries, financial markets, and effective mechanisms for reducing, sharing, and spreading risks.[28]

Moreover, economies that suffered major financial shocks, like the United States during the early 1930s, when thousands of banks experienced depositor runs and bankruptcy, also suffered major declines in output. Fear of repeating that experience explains why U.S. and European

---

28 For an excellent review of the literature, see Ross Levine, "Finance and Growth: Theory and Evidence," in *Handbook of Economic Growth, Vol. 1A,* ed. Philippe Aghion and Steven N. Durlauf (New York: Elsevier North Holland, 2005): 865–934.

taxpayers allowed their respective governments to bail out large financial institutions like Wells Fargo, AIG, and Northern Rock during the panic caused by the implosion of subprime mortgage and mortgage-backed securities markets in 2007–9.[29] In short, many now believe that the financial sector is to the economy what oil is to an engine, a seemingly minor detail until you try running the engine without enough lubricant and the thing, though perfect in every other respect, seizes up and shuts down. No wonder that boosters claim that finance "made civilization possible"[30] and created "the foundation of modern society"[31] while even critics admit that finance "has not only meant more material comfort for more people, but more jobs through increased production."[32]

More concretely, the financial system helps businesses to run more efficiently (same output from less input), freeing up inputs (people, land, machines) for other uses. Advances in food production, for example, freed up farmers to perform other services, while factory automation did likewise for common laborers and their children, many of whom became doctors, lawyers, professors, computer programmers, and so forth.[33]

Theory suggests that the financial system provides the real economy with two crucial services: intermediation and risk management. Intermediation is a fancy technical term for linking savers to spenders. Savers are economic entities (individuals, businesses, nonprofits, and governments) that in some period of time, like a quarter or a year, take in revenues

29 Robert E. Wright, ed. *Bailouts: Public Money, Private Profit*, Social Science Research Council (New York: Columbia University Press, 2010); Robert E. Wright, "Government Bailouts," in *Handbook of Major Events in Economic History*, ed. Robert Whaples and Randall Parker (New York: Routledge, 2013): 415–27.

30 William Goetzmann, *Money Changes Everything: How Finance Made Civilization Possible*, (Princeton: Princeton University Press, 2016).

31 As quoted in Lendol Calder, *Financing the American Dream: A Cultural History of Consumer Credit*, (Princeton: Princeton University Press, 1999), 37.

32 Hillel Black, *Buy Now, Pay Later* (New York: William Morrow and Company, 1961), 211.

33 W. Gifford Hoag, *The Farm Credit System: A History of Financial Self-Help*, (Danville, Ill.: Interstate Printers & Publishers, 1976), 7; Russell Roberts, *The Choice: A Fable of Free Trade and Protectionism*, 3rd ed. (New York: Pearson, 2006); Claudia Goldin and Lawrence F. Katz, *The Race Between Education and Technology*, (Cambridge: Belknap Press, 2010).

that exceed their expenditures. Spenders are economic entities that make expenditures that exceed their revenues. They are able to run a deficit by trading with savers, borrowing the savers' excess revenues in exchange for promises of future repayment. In textbooks, the spenders are usually portrayed as entrepreneurs, innovators with good business ideas but no means of bringing them to market. But because both savers and spenders freely agree to such trades, economists assume that both parties are enriched by such exchanges regardless of the reasons underlying them. Economists have a good point, unless, of course, one party tricked the other into exchanging for something they had not bargained for, as happens in cases of financial predation.[34]

In the absence of fraud, savers and borrowers will agree on a price, called the interest rate, at which both will be satisfied, the saver with delaying consumption and the borrower with anticipating it. Perhaps the borrower is an entrepreneur who needs to acquire resources from which she can produce goods that she believes will have value in some market. Or maybe he wants to buy a seaside condominium now, instead of waiting until he can save the entire purchase price. Whatever the reason underlying the transaction, the borrower must compensate the lender for present resources with the promise of greater resources in the future. The amount of that compensation, again usually called the interest rate, varies over time as the supply of, and demand for, loanable funds fluctuates with income/wealth levels, business conditions, and expectations of changes in major macroeconomic variables like exchange, tax, and inflation rates.

Unfortunately, savers and spenders have ample incentive to try to trick each other. A spender (borrower), for example, might use a loan to buy lottery tickets instead of a hot dog stand as promised, an example of what economists call moral hazard. A saver (lender) might lend with the intention of seizing collateral worth far more than the value of the loan, an example of financial predation. Lenders might not grasp adverse selection, the fact that applicants for loans (and insurance) become ever riskier

---

34 All this general information can be found in standard texts like Robert E. Wright, *Money and Banking*, 3rd ed. (Boston: Flat World Knowledge, 2017).

the higher the interest rate or insurance premium charged because less risky applicants would not consent to pay so much. Loans based on trust might work in some tight-knit communities but loans between strangers had better be based on collateral security and legal forms rendered as iron-clad as possible. Even finding acceptable counterparties can be extremely costly in terms of time, effort, and money (e.g., for advertising).

While even in advanced economies individuals make many loans to other individuals, such exchanges tend to comprise a relatively small percentage of all loans and an even smaller percentage of the total funds lent in any given place and year. (The person-to-person loans that are made tend to be highly collateralized, like mortgages with a low loan to value ratio, and/or between relatives, friends, business associates, co-religionists, or others with much information about each other.) Lending and borrowing simply is not that easy for most entities to do and that is one major reason why the financial system is so important. Financial markets allow savers (a.k.a. bondholders and stockholders) and spenders (a.k.a. issuers or borrowers) to find each other, and a fair (a.k.a. market) price for uniform contracts (a.k.a. financial instruments or securities), relatively quickly and cheaply. Investment banks reduce transaction costs by vouching for issuers while other specialized financial firms, called brokers (which profit from commissions), dealers (which profit from differences between seller's ask and buyer's bid prices), and specialists (which work on securities exchanges), help to maintain the secondary markets where bondholders and stockholders (or, more generically, investors) buy and sell evidences of debt or equity stakes with each other.

Financial institutions called intermediaries also link savers to spend-ers, but more indirectly than financial markets do. Depository institu-tions, like credit unions, savings banks, and commercial banks, use the savings of depositors (savers) to fund loans to businesses, governments, nonprofits, and households (generically, "entities") that need to balance their revenues with their expenditures (generically, "spenders" or "bor-rowers"). They do not just introduce borrowers and savers, they offer their own products (loans and deposits, respectively) to each other, using short-term deposits to fund long-term loans. Insurers, including life, health, and property and casualty insurers, are also intermediaries because they indirectly link savers (policyholders) to spenders (entities that borrow from insurers either directly or through the insurers' purchases of financial instruments in the financial markets). Insurers offer contingent contracts (contingent on a loss) to policyholders to fund their loans to entrepreneurs. All types of intermediaries use their specialized expertise to reduce adverse selection and moral hazard. Economies of scale keep unit costs much lower than with personal saver-to-spender transactions. Search costs are also much lower because savers and spenders need only find an appropriate intermediary, not each other.

Insurers are also major components of the second major function of financial systems, risk management, which entails reducing and sharing risks in the most efficient manner possible. That typically entails mitigating risks through behavioral or technological changes and then sharing residual risks. So, for example, mutual fire insurance companies in the nineteenth century charged high premiums to induce insured companies to improve construction standards, install firefighting technologies, and train employees in firefighting and escape techniques and by doing so greatly decreased the incidence of catastrophic blazes. Damaging fires, however, still occurred on occasion. Via so-called reinsurance, insurers spread those risks across all policyholders of the same risk class by diverting premiums from insured companies lucky enough to avoid conflagrations to those unlucky enough to suffer a major fire despite taking state-of-the-art precautions.[35]

Similarly, life insurers sought to keep their insureds alive as long as possible by giving them free health advice and screenings and encouraging them, through higher premiums, to avoid specific dangerous occupations, hobbies, and geographical areas (e.g., malarial areas in the tropics). Of course some people still died young due to accidents, unknown genetic defects, and so forth. Life insurers essentially paid their

---

35 Robert E. Wright, "Insuring America: Market, Intermediated, and Government Risk Management Since 1790," in *Encuentro Internacional Sobre la Historia del Seguro*, ed. Leonardo Caruana (Madrid: Fundacion MAPFRE, 2010).

beneficiaries with the premiums of those lucky enough to live long lives, the beneficiaries of whom they were able to pay by saving, i.e., by investing premiums in financial markets (e.g., for bonds and mortgages) and intermediaries (e.g., banks).

Insurance benefits the economy the most when it is based on accurate expectations of loss and assignment of policyholders into appropriate risk classes. The law of large numbers is a powerful tool in the hands of skilled and unfettered actuaries because it allows them to predict the number of losses (deaths, fires, accidents) in each class but not the specific policyholders who will suffer a loss. That allows insurers to calculate rational premiums, i.e., premiums that will allow them to pay all claims and expenses and still earn a profit, especially when risks are uncorrelated, as they often are. When risks are correlated, however, like when fires easily spread to adjacent buildings, or people die from contagious diseases, the calculation of rational premiums becomes more difficult. Many fire insurers, for example, failed in the aftermath of massive conflagrations that destroyed large swaths of many American cities in the nineteenth century.[36]

Insurers that take on more risk than they want can sell their excess risk. Traditionally, they reinsured with other direct writers or through specialized reinsurance companies, including Swiss Re and Munich Re, but financial markets can also help insurers to manage risks. Catastrophe bonds (cat bonds), for example, help to soften the blow to property and casualty insurers if a large earthquake or hurricane strikes before the bonds mature. Likewise, XXX bonds provide funds for life insurers shocked by unexpected spikes in mortality due to catastrophe or epidemic. Other alternative risk transfer mechanisms (ARTM) also work through markets rather than traditional insurance intermediaries.

Investors purchase cat bonds for their relatively high yields and their random nature, i.e., the fact that they are uncorrelated with financial market risks like interest rate and stock market fluctuations. If claims are

---

36 Sara E. Wermiel, *The Fireproof Building: Technology and Public Safety in the Nineteenth-Century American City*, (Baltimore: Johns Hopkins University Press, 2000).

higher than expected, bondholders can lose principal. Since the mid-1990s, the market has grown very quickly; by the end of 2004, cat bonds covered some $4 billion of risks related to earthquakes and hurricanes in North America, windstorms in Europe and Japan, and earthquakes in Japan. Cat bonds held up extremely well during the subprime mortgage disaster of 2007, bolstering the perception that they can be used to hedge (protect) against financial market shocks.[37]

Insurers may have systematically underestimated improvements in life expectancy and hence have seriously underpriced life annuities, policies that pay fixed sums each year that the annuitant (policyholder) remains alive. This is not the first time insurers underpriced annuities but they can now profit from life expectancy improvements by selling mortality-contingent bonds in the global capital market. By late 2007, about $20 billion of XXX or death bonds were outstanding. Issuing companies receive the present value of the expected profits to arise from a pool of life insurance policies.[38]

Insurance and ARTM may sound mundane, and hence unimportant, but risk management has saved economic entities from untold losses by reducing the probability of damaging events. Just as importantly, risk management has provided economic entities with incentives to undertake risky projects that they otherwise would not dare contemplate.

37 Richard Bernero, "Second-Generation OTC Derivatives and Structured Products: Catastrophe Bonds, Catastrophe Swaps, and Life Insurance Securitizations," in *Securitized Insurance Risk: Strategic Opportunities for Insurers and Investors*, ed. Michael Himick (Chicago: Glenlake Publishing Co., 1998); Robert Hartwig and Claire Wilkinson, "An Overview of the Alternative Risk Transfer Market," in *Handbook of International Insurance: Between Global Dynamics and Local Contingencies*, ed. J. David Cummins and Bertrand Venard (New York: Springer, 2007).

38 Erik Banks, *Alternative Risk Transfer: Integrated Risk Management Through Insurance, Reinsurance, and the Capital Markets*, (Hoboken, N.J.: John Wiley and Sons, 2004); Bernero, "Second-Generation OTC Derivatives"; Leora Friedberg and Anthony Webb, "Life Is Cheap: Using Mortality Bonds to Hedge Aggregate Mortality Risk," *The B.E. Journal of Economic Analysis & Policy* (2007); Charles Kindleberger, *Manias, Panics, and Crashes: A History of Financial Crises*, 4th ed. (New York: John Wiley & Sons, 2000); Ian McDonald and Liam Pleven, "'Cat Bonds' and Insurer-Inspired Issues Weather the Credit Storm," *Wall Street Journal*, 23 August 2007.

While risks sometimes result in losses they also spur the innovations and trades that drive economic growth.

Scholars now know that finance is crucial to economic growth because, holding other factors constant, nations with more and better finance, as measured by per capita deposits, average interest rates, and other objective statistics, are richer than those with less and worse finance. And financial capacity comes first. Canada, for example, lagged the United States economically until it underwent a financial revolution in the mid-nineteenth century, after which it rapidly caught up. Parts of nations, or former nations, that have more and better finance grow richer than the other parts. Consider, for example, North and South Korea and East and West Germany. Consider also the southern U.S., which for many decades after the Civil War stagnated both financially and economically. Within the South, as we will learn in Chapter 7, Arkansas had both the worst financial system and the worst economic performance.[39]

In short, modern economies cannot do without a robust financial system to link savers and spenders and to manage risks. That means that policymakers have to handle the financial system with care. If too many regulatory and tax burdens are imposed upon it, the financial system could wither and perhaps even die. That does not mean, of course, that policymakers should stand idly by while financiers discriminate against African-American, American Indian, poor, and female borrowers and insureds, or anyone for that matter, but it does mean that they need to be careful about how they respond to evidence of discrimination. So far, their regulations have not palpably reduced financial discrimination but they have imposed significant costs on financial intermediaries and the overall economy. It is time for a more effective approach, one with a proven track record for reducing discrimination, the encouragement of institutions of self-help. In short, if X will not lend to or insure Y on

---

39 Robert E. Wright, *One Nation Under Debt: Hamilton, Jefferson, and the History of What We Owe*, (New York: McGraw Hill, 2008), 241–46; Livio Di Matteo and Angela Redish, "The Evolution of Financial Intermediation: Evidence from 19th-Century Ontario Microdata," *Canadian Journal of Economics* 48, no. 3 (2015): 963–87; John A. James, "Financial Underdevelopment in the Postbellum South," *Journal of Interdisciplinary History* 11, no. 3 (1981): 443–454.

the same terms as Z, members of Y need to be able to form their own intermediaries and risk managers to meet their needs. That technique has worked before, many times, and may work again, and without endangering the health of the financial system or the overall economy. Of course, free entry combined with self-help is *not* a panacea as it cannot overcome systemic racism, but then again neither can government fiat. But it has done, and can do, much more at far less cost than top-down dictates.

The Evolution of Small Business Finance

Credit has been extended by the importer to the country shopkeeper; and through him, to the farmer and mechanic, who being thereby enabled to pursue their labors, have drawn produce from the surface and bowels of the earth, which has not only defrayed the cost and charges, but enriched the industrious. — Robert Morris as quoted in Wilbur C. Plummer, "Consumer Credit in Colonial Philadelphia," Pennsylvania Magazine of History and Biography 46, no. 4 (1942), 402.

Businesses are legal entities that try to earn profits. Typically, non-financial businesses are spenders in their early stages but later on they may become savers, at least some of the time, if they are successful. Businesses take a number of forms ranging from sole proprietorship (owned by a single person) to general partnership (owned by two or more people jointly responsible for the entity's debts) to limited partnership (owned by one or more general partners plus one or more silent or investment-only partners responsible only for the sums invested) to joint-stock corporation (owned by one or more stockholders who own transferable shares of the business, typically with some limitation of their liability for the business's debts) to mutual corporation (owned by customers, typically depositors or policyholders).

For practical purposes, the focus here is on small businesses generally organized as sole proprietorships or general partnerships. While a few corporations were owned and controlled by members of minority groups or associated with the poor, they were not all easily recognized as such, especially in financial markets. As noted above, corporations were subject to some forms of discrimination but corporations are not really people, no matter what the Supreme Court says. They are legal entities. So I exclude corporate finance from the discussion here in order to concentrate on businesses more or less coeval with the individuals who own and operate them.[40]

While many of the details have changed over the 250 or so years of U.S. history, the fundamental outline of small business finance has changed little.[41] Business credit was generally considered a good thing, a technology, according to two authors writing for the Alexander Hamilton Institute, that made "the capital of others available in the present, when one's own command of capital lies in the future."[42] For good or ill, most business at the wholesale and retail levels was done on trade credit. As Peter Earling put it in his 1890 treatise, *Whom to Trust*, "as a matter of fact we do not do business for cash. We do it on credit almost wholly."[43]

Aside from tapping friends and family members for funds, small business owners have always had four major short-term financing options: markets, intermediaries, leasing, and trade credit. Larger and more widely known small businesses can sell "commercial paper," basically short-term IOUs like promissory notes, drafts, and bills of exchange, directly to investors. Such instruments tend to be "zeroes" or non-coupon. That means that they do not promise periodic interest payments but rather a lump

40 Those interested in the history corporate finance should consult Jonathan Baskin and Paul Miranti, *A History of Corporate Finance*, (New York: Cambridge University Press, 1999) and Robert E. Wright and Richard Sylla, eds., *The History of Corporate Finance: Development of Anglo-American Securities Markets, Financial Practices, Theories and Laws*, 6 vols. (London: Pickering and Chatto, 2003). For the many problems with the Supreme Court's views of corporations, see Naomi Lamoreaux and William Novak, eds., *Corporations and American Democracy* (Cambridge: Harvard University Press, 2017).

41 Wilbur C. Plummer, "Consumer Credit in Colonial Philadelphia," *Pennsylvania Magazine of History and Biography* 46, no. 4 (1942): 385–409.

42 Peter P. Wahlstad and Walter S. Johnson, *Credit and the Credit Man*, (New York: Alexander Hamilton Institute, 1917), 21.

43 Peter R. Earling, *Whom to Trust: A Practical Treatise on Mercantile Credits*, (New York: Rand McNally & Co., 1890), 18.

sum (face value or principal amount) due on a specific future redemption date. The small business owner issues the "paper" by selling it in the
open market or to a note broker for a sum less than its face or principal
value. The difference between the sale price and the promised lump sum
payment is an implicit interest rate that varies with money market conditions (i.e., short-term market interest rates) and perceptions about the risk
of default (non-payment on the specified maturity date). The paper can
trade multiple times before redemption, appreciating towards the face
value if market interest rates and default perceptions remain constant.
Yields on such notes were typically in the low double digits to reflect
default risk. By the Great War, commercial paper houses specializing in
the sale of business paper had representatives, if not full-blown branches,
in every large city in the nation.[44]

Most small business owners, however, were not large or widely
known enough to be able to sell their own paper into the market at reasonable rates, so they turned to other sources of funds. Often, that meant
borrowing from friends, family, co-religionists, and others who felt they
could trust the borrower because they knew much about the condition
of his (or her as we will see in Chapter 6) business, could exert extra-legal
pressures on the borrower to repay the loan (God or Mom will get you if
you don't pay me back), and so forth.

Just as often, small business owners could obtain short-term credit
from their suppliers, who would fill orders for raw materials or inventory
today but not expect payment for some days, weeks, or months thereafter. Companies, like wholesalers, that regularly extended trade credit to
small business owners typically had access to formal financial intermediaries like commercial banks. Although they usually charged explicit interest

44 Rowena Olegario, *A Culture of Credit: Embedding Trust and Transparency in American Business,* (Cambridge: Harvard University Press, 2006), 27; Lance E. Davis, "The Investment Market, 1870–1914: The Evolution of a National Market," *Journal of Economic History* 25, no. 3 (September 1965), 372–73.

only on past due accounts, they of course built credit charges into their prices, offering discounts for cash.[45]

In the eighteenth and nineteenth centuries, credit came down to the "three Cs" of character, capacity, and capital. The first was a measure of moral hazard, of the likelihood that a borrower would default on purpose out of avarice or bad habits like drinking or gambling. The second basically meant business ability, or the likelihood that a borrower would default out of well-meaning incompetence. The third was a measure of incentive, of "skin in the game" as Warren Buffett would later call it. The notion was that borrowers with the largest percentage of their own money at risk would be the most prudent with other people's money. Various historians have made a mash out of the three Cs but they were, and remain, essential components of any objective model of credit decision-making. What led to discrimination was not the three Cs model itself but assuming, for whatever reason, that members of some group did not have sufficient character, capacity, and/or capital to obtain credit.[46]

By the 1890s, executives and corporate sales agents could charge traveling and lodging expenses using the "Traveletter System," an early forerunner of the corporate credit card. (They could also use American Express or other travelers' checks but those were just a means of payment rather than a source of credit.[47])

Between 1890, when credit man Peter R. Earling complained of "the total absence of literature and lack of information" about business credit, and the Great War, business credit decision-making ostensibly evolved into a science.[48] At the very least, it had been professionalized in corporations and larger trading firms. While Earling's treatise discussed the credit

---

45 Donna Rilling, "Small-Producer Capitalism in Early National Philadelphia," in *The Economy of Early America: Historical Perspectives and New Directions*, ed. Cathy Matson (University Park: Pennsylvania State University Press, 2006), 317–34; Plummer, "Consumer Credit," 394; Calder, *Financing*, 70, 175.

46 Olegario, *Culture of Credit*, 80–118; Black, *Buy Now*, 46.

47 Black, *Buy Now*, 14–15; Robert E. Wright and Richard Sylla, *Genealogy of American Finance*, (New York: Columbia University Press, 2015), 18–19.

48 Earling, *Whom to Trust*, 12.

risks posed by single men, women, and the aged in highly sexist (though positive) and ageist terms, a major textbook on credit published by the Alexander Hamilton Institute in 1917 said almost nothing about race, class, or gender and reduced business credit decisions to the analysis of ostensibly objective factors like: [49]

- *Ability and willingness to pay.*
- *Business ability, native and acquired.*
- *Technical ability.*
- *Knowledge and experience.*
- *Buying methods.*
- *Manufacturing.*
- *Equipment.*
- *Advertising.*
- *Location.*
- *Age.*
- *Evidence of financial ability.*
- *Outside ventures.*
- *Distribution of due dates.*
- *Cooperation with mercantile agencies.*
- *Insurance.*
- *Payment methods.*
- *Financial strength.*
- *Convertibility of assets.*
- *Liquidating values.*
- *Capital – how acquired.*
- *Moral Character.* [50]

That list is essentially the three Cs on some serious steroids.

---

49 Olegario, *Culture of Credit*, 174–78; Earling, *Whom to Trust*, 86–88, 148–152.

50 Wahlstad and Johnson, *Credit*, 47–66.

Most such information could be garnered from the credit-seeker itself, mercantile credit agencies, banks, competitors, and suppliers. As the twentieth century progressed, increased reliance was placed on payment histories and formal financial statements, especially ones audited by major accounting firms.[51]

According to the Hamilton Institute text, professional credit men prided themselves on steering "a middle course" so that they did not accept many bad risks but also did not needlessly turn away many good ones. Credit was about the use of reason, not emotion. "The ability to examine facts dispassionately and to form conclusions based strictly upon the evidence at hand" was an "indispensable" trait for "a credit man. ... An open mind, an unbiased judgment, and firmness in executing his policies" were paramount, the authors asserted. So the credit professional should deny the credit applications of "the intemperate, the gambler, the manifestly incompetent, the shiftless and the idler."[52]

For example, a banker declined to discount for a small woolens jobber the $275 note of a large mercantile house that one of the mercantile credit agencies claimed was worth a quarter million dollars and was a "good pay." When pressed, the banker explained that he had not discriminated against either party. Rather, the transaction was obviously tainted. "That the big house should buy of the small jobber at all is noteworthy. Under normal conditions such a house would have larger and better sources of supply" and normally would buy such a small order on open account, or with cash, instead of giving its note. The banker was right about something being amiss as the big house soon toppled and the proprietor committed suicide.[53]

Despite such close scrutiny, some small business owners were able to obtain short-term loans directly from banks. While big, urban banks have a well-deserved reputation for ignoring the little guy, so-called

---

51 Wahlstad and Johnson, *Credit*, 69; Olegario, *Culture of Credit*, 178–90; Mark Stevens, *The Big Eight*, (New York: Collier Books, 1981).

52 Wahlstad and Johnson, *Credit*, 176, 182, 267.

53 Wahlstad and Johnson, *Credit*, 181.

community banks, smaller banks that serve rural areas, suburbs, or specific urban neighborhoods, were often an important source of financing
for small business owners. They would not, and by virtue of their business practices could not, extend reliable long-term credit to anyone, but
they could help businesses to finance short-term (30 to 270 day) projects
or to weather seasonal business fluctuations or temporary reversals of
fortune (bad luck).

If banks could not help, factors might be able to. Unlike banks,
which usually lent money on the basis of a business's general credit
and strength, factors outright purchased the business's accounts receivable. In other words, they paid the small business owner a fixed sum in
cash for the right to collect the debts owed to it. Obviously, the factors
offered to pay the business owner somewhat less than the total accounts
receivable. The discount fluctuated with the market interest rate, the
default risk on the debt, and the time until the debts fell due. Small business owners could also obtain short-term chattel loans from pawn shops
or finance companies that accepted personal property (like furniture,
office machines, or horse or engine-powered vehicles) as collateral, i.e.,
goods that would become the property of the lender if the loan was not
repaid.[54]

By the twentieth century, sales finance companies would, much
like factors, purchase retail time-sales contracts. Unlike factors, they
would also make wholesale inventory loans to retailers, essentially
taking a borrower's entire inventory as collateral. Similarly, small businesses that needed to borrow for a year or more could turn to chattel
mortgages where tools or other moveable property was posted as
collateral, though few borrowers not in desperate straights resorted to
such contracts.[55]

---

54 Wright and Sylla, *Genealogy*, 50, 93–97, 116, 174, 256–58, 313.

55 Martha L. Olney, *Buy Now, Pay Later: Advertising, Credit, and Consumer Durables in the
1920s,* (Chapel Hill: University of North Carolina Press, 1991), 106; Plummer, "Consumer
Credit," 396; Earling, *Whom to Trust,* 153–56.

Small businesses could also finance their operations via leases, the market, or intermediaries. Instead of buying property outright, certain types of businesses could simply lease land for a fixed dollar fee or for a share of revenues. In the Early Republic, brick makers, marble quarriers, and lime burners, among others, found it better to lease than to buy outright. After removing and working up the raw materials, the business/leasee moved on and the owner put the land to an alternative use. In the twentieth century, leasing agreements and lease-buyback arrangements became very important sources of finance in some sectors. Shortly after World War II, for example, the Mayflower Doughnut Corporation and the Attic Linen Shop rented their facilities rather than owning them. The former was nearly in partnership with its landlord, promising it 7 percent of gross sales and at least $1,000.[56]

The most common instrument for obtaining long-term loans was a mortgage collateralized with real property, typically the business owner's home, shop, or both (as they were often in the same building throughout much of the nation's history). The lender, or mortgagee, could be a wealthy individual, a non-profit organization, or a financial intermediary like a savings bank or life insurer. The borrower, or mortgagor, gave up ownership of the collateral, the real estate, if s/he failed to repay the loan as promised. Sometimes mortgages were used to fund major projects, like new construction or the expansion of an existing business, but sometimes they merely consolidated and collateralized pre-existing unsecured debts or even legal judgments.[57]

---

56 Rilling, "Small-Producer Capitalism," 317–34; Clyde William Phelps, *The Role of Fleet Leasing in Motor Vehicle Fleet Plans of Business Firms*, (Baltimore: Commercial Credit Co., 1969); John Finnerty and Douglas Emery, *Debt Management: A Practitioner's Guide*, (Boston: Harvard Business School Press, 2001); Bernard Goldstein, *A Documentary Guide to Commercial Leasing*, (Philadelphia: American Law Institute, 1985); Executive Committee Meeting, February 4, 1946, August 11, 1947, Agendas/Minutes: Exec. Committee Community, Rush Rhees Library.

57 Rilling, "Small-Producer Capitalism," 317–34. Bruce Mann, *Republic of Debtors: Bankruptcy in the Age of American Independence*, (Cambridge: Harvard University Press, 2009).

Mortgage Markets from the Colonial Period to Fannie Mae

We do not have a choice whether or not to discuss history. History has
    always been invoked in contemporary controversies. The only
    choice is between discussing what actually happened in the past
    and discussing notions projected into the past for present purposes.
    — *Thomas Sowell, Black Rednecks and White Liberals (San*
    Francisco: Encounter Books, 2005), 276.

Individuals and married couples could mortgage real property to
finance the purchase or improvement of a home. Sometimes, as noted
above, such mortgages were bound up with a small business like a grocery, an artisanal shop, or a farm. As more Americans became employees
instead of self-employed, however, consumer and small business mortgages became more distinct conceptually, though they continue to over-
lap to some degree to this day.

The American colonists regularly bought and sold real estate to make
room for children, move closer to friends and family, take a new job,
build up a business, or simply show off their prosperity. Like Americans
throughout history, colonists were enticed by rising real estate prices but
could rarely afford to pay for their acquisitions with cash. Three types of
mortgages were available to them: 1) government ones that amortized
over ten or so years, much like modern mortgages, leaving nothing due at
the end of the term; 2) private, interest-only (IO) mortgages callable by the
lender after at most a few years that left the principal untouched; 3) private
perpetual interest-only mortgages called ground rents. Despite leaving the
principal intact indefinitely, ground rents were gilt-edged securities, as safe
as British, and later U.S., government bonds because they had much lower
loan to value (LTV) ratios, 10 to 80 percent generally, than the subprime
IO mortgages of the 2000s typically did. Unlike today, lenders (called
ground lords) had substantial recourse, including writs that empowered
sheriffs to enter the property and take away and auction off goods to the
value of the debt owed. If necessary, the ground lord could take title to the

land and imprison the debtor until all debts and damages had been repaid. Few borrowers ever defaulted, however, because the contract was perpetual and the principal non-callable. In other words, if the borrower kept up the interest payments the ground lord could never insist upon repayment of the principal. (Instead, ground lords could sell the right to receive the ground rent stream to the borrower or a third party at a negotiated price that was a function of prevailing interest rates.)[58]

Those who borrowed from some of the government loan offices were also protected from untimely calls and balloon payments at the end of the contract. For 40-odd years, Pennsylvania's provincial government subsisted almost entirely on a liquor tax and the profits from its General Loan Office, which made 50 percent loan-to-value uncallable amortized loans at 5 percent to thousands of safe Pennsylvania borrowers. Some other colonies enjoyed similar institutions. New Jersey's first loan office, for example, also lent at 5 percent and spread repayment of principal and interest into 12 equal annual installments. Its second and third loan offices increased the term to 16 years. Government mortgages, however, were available to only a fraction of those who wished to borrow and ground rents were generally available only in the urban areas of Pennsylvania, Delaware, Maryland, and New Jersey.

Short-term, interest-only callable private mortgages supplied the balance of the demand for colonial real estate financing. In contrast to ground rents and amortized government mortgages, they were a disaster waiting to happen. If mortgages are not callable, as with ground rents, colonial government mortgages, and most mortgages today, borrowers cannot be evicted from their properties, no matter how low the market value sinks, so long as they continue to make scheduled payments.

---

58 Frank A. Kaufman, "The Maryland Ground Rent – Mysterious But Beneficial," *Maryland Law Review* 5 (December 1940): 1–72; Charles Stein, *The Maryland Ground Rent System* (Baltimore: Wyman Park Federal Savings and Loan Association, 1952). For more on ground rents, see Robert E. Wright, "Ground Rents Against Populist Historiography: Mid-Atlantic Land Tenure, 1750–1820," *Journal of Interdisciplinary History* 29, no. 1 (1998), 23–42; Robert E. Wright, *The First Wall Street: Chestnut Street, Philadelphia, and the Birth of American Finance*, (Chicago: University of Chicago Press, 2005).

Similarly, those with long-term fixed rate mortgages need not worry about facing higher payments if interest rates increase. Colonists who borrowed on callable mortgages, by contrast, faced both risks. If real estate values fell, lenders could call for the principal on the grounds that their mortgages were under-collateralized, that the properties pledged to support the loans were no longer of sufficient value, in other words. If interest rates increased, lenders could also call simply to reinvest the principal at higher rates. (Usury laws or interest rate caps were in place but when it came to mortgages they were as about as effective as drug laws are today.)

Due to the collapse in trade and the money supply that followed the French and Indian War and new postwar Imperial policies, the colonial real estate market, which had experienced a large bubble during the war, collapsed. Private lenders called in their mortgages en masse but of course few borrowers could repay or refinance so lawsuits and imprisonment for debt spiked. The colonists, largely correctly, blamed British policymakers for the fiasco. They were so bloody angry about the Stamp Act because it came at a time when they were losing their homes, farms, and shops due to British macroeconomic policies, particularly restrictions on paper money issuance and trade. "I must observe," one colonist noted in 1768, "that it is not the Stamp Act or New Duty Act alone that had put the Colonies so much out of humour tho the principal Clamour has been on that Head but *their distressed Situation had prepared them so generally to lay hold of these Occasions* [emphasis added]." Thus did the bursting of a real estate bubble, poorly handled, help launch the independence movement.[59]

After the Revolution, some states continued to operate loan offices but, shorn of their ability to lawfully issue money by the new Constitution, they petered out over time. (More on these in Chapter 6.) Individu-

---

59 As quoted in Ron Michener and Robert E. Wright, "The Real Estate Crash of 1764 and the Coming of the American Revolution," Crisis and Consequence Conference, Hagley Museum & Library, Wilmington, Del., 5 November 2010.

als continued to lend on mortgages.[60] In 1817, for example, Marylander Littleton Teackle noted that in his state "freeholders found no difficulty in borrowing what money they wanted for the cultivation and improvement of their estates, as the rich landowners and lawyers, and other persons who had money, were glad to lend it to them at the legal interest of six per cent on mortgage of their land."[61] By the early twentieth century, however, the most important mortgage lenders in terms of total dollars lent were institutional: non-profit charities, benevolent societies, and academies and colleges that had excess funds (i.e., endowments) to invest, as well as savings banks, life insurers, building and loan associations (later called Savings and Loans), trust companies, specialized mortgage companies, and state-chartered commercial banks. (Commercial banks chartered by the federal government, so-called national banks, could not invest in mortgages until the 1910s.) Mortgage brokers and "loan correspondents" also arose to help lenders and borrowers find each other, for a fee of course. Most mortgages remained short-term and/or callable and interest-only, resulting in a large balloon payment at the end of the term that was usually refinanced in whole or in large part, with conservative LTVs of around 50 percent.[62]

---

60 D. M. Frederiksen, "Mortgage Banking in America," *Journal of Political Economy* 2, no. 2 (1894), 209.

61 Littleton Teackle, *An Address to the Members of the Legislature of Maryland, Concerning the Establishment of a Loan Office for the Benefit of the Landowners of the State,* (Annapolis, 1817), 5.

62 Tamara Thornton, "'A Great Machine' or a 'Beast of Prey': A Boston Corporation and Its Rural Debtors in an Age of Capitalist Transformation," *Journal of the Early Republic* 27, no. 4 (2007): 567–97; Mark Stickle, "The Ohio Life Insurance and Trust Company: Eastern Capital and Mortgage Credit in Ohio, 1834–1845." Unpublished ms., 2011. John Denis Haeger, *The Investment Frontier: New York Businessmen and the Economic Development of the Old Northwest,* (Albany: State University of New York Press, 1981), 18–58. David Mason, *From Building and Loans to Bailouts: A History of the American Savings and Loan Industry, 1831–1995,* (New York: Cambridge University Press, 2004). Davis, "Investment Market," 358; Calder, *Financing,* 68. Robert E. Wright and George David Smith, *Mutually Beneficial: The Guardian and Life Insurance in America,* (New York: New York University Press, 2004), 326. J. B. C. Murray, *The History of Usury from the Earliest Period to the Present Time … And an Examination into the Policy of Laws on Usury and Their Effect Upon Commerce,* (Philadelphia: J. B. Lippincott & Co., 1866), 132–33; Calder, *Financing,* 64–69; Mechele Dickerson, *Homeownership and America's Financial Underclass: Flawed Premises, Broken Promises, New Prescriptions,* (New York: Cambridge University Press, 2014), 39.

A detailed study of all loans collateralized by real property in Champaign County, Illinois, from 1836 to 1895 is revealing. The population of the county in the former year was 1,045 and in the latter about 47,000, split almost evenly between rural and urban inhabitants throughout the period. Over the course of the century, the total dollar volume of mortgage borrowing trended upward while the average interest rate dropped from 12 percent in 1836 to 8 in 1846 and 1847. It increased to 9 and even 10 percent after that through 1876, when it trended downward to just above 6 percent in 1881, a level that held through 1895. Before 1854, average loan lengths varied from six months to three and a half years but thereafter tended to lengthen to as long as five years by the early 1890s for farm mortgages and up to 16.67 years for urban mortgages made by local building and loan associations, which were then the only major source of long-term amortized loans. In many years, more than half of the mortgages in the county were funded by lenders located outside of Illinois. Lenders outside of the county but domiciled elsewhere in Illinois (e.g., Chicago), however, rarely provided more than 20 percent of the total sum lent on mortgage in the county, especially after 1846. In the 1840s, most mortgage funds came from government units, primarily school boards and drainage commissions that sold government land on installment plans. Between 1850 and 1883, most mortgage funds came from private persons. Thereafter, however, financial intermediaries provided more than half, and usually more than two thirds, of the total lent.[63]

A national mortgage census taken in the 1890s showed that mortgage interest rates varied greatly from region to region, from 5.5 percent in the settled parts of the east to over 10 percent in the mountain and arid states of the West. (Short term interest rates also varied greatly, from an average of 4.85 percent in New England over the period 1893-97, to 8.58 percent in the Pacific States.) The average maturity was six years in the

---

63 Dan Immergluck, *Credit to the Community: Community Reinvestment and Fair Lending Policy in the United States*, (New York: M. E. Sharpe, 2004), 19. Robert F. Severson, James F. Niss, and Richard D. Winkelman, "Mortgage Borrowing as a Frontier Developed: A Study of Mortgages in Champaign County, Illinois, 1836–1895," *Journal of Economic History* 26, no. 2 (1966): 147–68.

East but only three in the South and not quite four in the West. Only about half of the nation's real estate was encumbered and that to about 35 or 40 percent of its market value. Most mortgagors borrowed out of strength to finance purchase or the construction of improvements, not debt consolidation.[64]

Occasionally, home developers sold new houses on the installment plan. City and Suburban Homes Company, for example, sold in 1898 modest single-family homes in New York City with 10 percent down and credit life insurance support for 20 years at five percent. Few companies, however, could tie up their capital that long. Nineteenth-century observers noted that mortgagees tended to hold mortgages until maturity rather than resell them, as was common in Europe. To make it easier for lenders to sell mortgages that they did not wish to hold to maturity (i.e., to make the market for mortgages more liquid and hence more attractive to lenders), various attempts to securitize them were made. Securitization lumped numerous mortgages together into one financial instrument, called an asset-backed (ABS) or mortgage-backed security (MBS), that was inherently less risky than a single mortgage. Lumping mortgages together diversified default risk and simultaneously made them more subject to the law of large numbers and hence more predictable. Nobody knew if Joe Farmer would go bankrupt before he repaid his loan, but if he did his mortgagee suffered the whole loss, while the mortgagee of his neighbor, Joe Rancher, would be just fine. But if the mortgages of Joe Farmer, Joe Rancher, Joe Artisan, and a thousand other Joes were lumped into one security, the mortgagee (now a security holder) could count on a certain number defaulting and build it into the price he, she, or it was willing to pay for the security. The ability to resell mortgages also allowed some companies to specialize in making new mortgage loans, called mortgage origination, while others specialized in holding mortgages for long periods.[65]

---

64 Davis, "Investment Market," 359, 375; Frederiksen, "Mortgage Banking," 206–7.

65 Richard Plunz, A History of Housing in New York City: Dwelling Type and Social Change in the American Metropolis, (New York: Columbia University Press, 1990), 116; Frederiksen,

All six securitization schemes attempted in the United States between 1870 and 1940, however, failed miserably after a few years of rapid growth and apparent success. In each case, default rates spiked unexpectedly, leaving MBS holders to suffer large losses. Sometimes, real estate prices tanked, setting off a wave of defaults. Other times, adverse selection reared its ugly head as originators sold off or securitized their riskiest loans without recourse or equity, retaining the cream of the crop for their own portfolios. Sometimes, securitizers like U.S. Mortgage and Mercantile Trust realized that they were receiving risky mortgages from their originators and withdrew from the market before heavy defaults hit.[66]

The private mortgages underlying those early MBSs remained short-term (an average of 3 years), with little or no amortization and large "balloon payments" of principal at the end. Such mortgages, like their colonial forebears, exposed borrowers to interest rate and real estate price risks. This caused several major blowups, including one following the mid-1920s real estate bubble and one during the Great Depression of the 1930s. Just as in the 1760s, real estate prices sank dramatically during the 1930s. Even people who kept their jobs and kept making interest payments got hit when the value of their houses dropped below the principal owed. Few could make the balloon payments at the end of the loans out of their savings. In normal times, most borrowers financed all or most of their balloon payments by taking out a new short-term mortgage. During the Depression, however, few could obtain new financing because the funds were unavailable or their homes had depreciated too much. So they defaulted, which only served to cause more mortgage funding to dry up.[67]

"Mortgage Banking," 210; Kenneth Snowden, "Mortgage Securitization in the United States: Twentieth Century Developments in Historical Perspective," in *Anglo-American Financial Systems: Institutions and Markets in the Twentieth Century*, ed. Michael Bordo and Richard Sylla (New York: Irwin Professional Publishing, 1995), 262.

66 Snowden, "Mortgage Securitization," 275–81.

67 Dickerson, *Homeownership*, 39; Eugene White, "Lessons from the Great American Real Estate Boom and Bust of the 1920s," National Bureau of Economic Research Working Paper 15573 (December 2009), 25–27.

The mortgage crisis during the Great Depression was so large, encompassing 2 out of every 5 mortgagors in the country, that numerous reforms were made. The first was the Federal Home Loan Bank (FHLB) system of 1932, which somehow managed to lend to only 3 of its first 41,000 applicants. The second, the Homeowners' Loan Corporation (HOLC), followed in 1933 as an agent of the FHLB. By 1936, the owners of one in every ten residences in the country had borrowed from HOLC, which was essentially an emergency government mortgage bank authorized to lend on much more liberal terms than private lenders could. Instead of 50 percent of the current market value of the home, HOLC refinanced loans for up to 80 percent of the home's "normal market value," i.e. its price *before* the Depression. In addition to replacing bad loans with cash on lenders' balance sheets, HOLC charged lower interest rates, extended maturities, and directly amortized, thus making mortgages easier for borrowers to service. To fund its activities, HOLC issued bonds guaranteed by the federal government. The guarantee was necessary given that HOLC foreclosed on one in every five loans it made, even though it allowed delinquent borrowers 18 to 24 months to catch up. It was inexperienced, of course, and a government lender (and hence, as described in Chapter 7, of dubious quality), and it attracted the riskiest borrowers, those who could not obtain mortgages in the private market. Rising home prices during World War II, though, allowed it to sell foreclosed homes at a profit and to wind up its affairs in 1951 with only about a 2 percent loss, a small price to pay, many argue, for the benefits it provided hard-strapped homeowners.[68]

HOLC was phased out but the FHLB became a sort of lender of second-to-last resort for mortgage lenders. In essence a co-op owned by its member-lenders, the FHLB remains in existence today and, in fact, its 11 regional banks played a quiet but important role in the stabilization of the

---

[68] Calder, *Financing*, 278–79; Snowden, "Mortgage Securitization," 290–92; Price Fishback, Jonathan Rose, and Kenneth Snowden, *Well Worth Saving: How the New Deal Safeguarded Home Ownership* (Chicago: University of Chicago Press, 2013), 120–31; Price Fishback, "How Successful Was the New Deal?: The Microeconomic Impact of New Deal Spending and Lending Policies in the 1930s," *Journal of Economic Literature* 55, 4 (2017), 1,476–77.

mortgage market after the Panic of 2008, a financial catastrophe brought on, in part, by yet other New Deal mortgage initiatives. Although not technically an obligation of the federal government, FHLB debt is considered a safer investment than the debt of its individual members.[69]

In 1934, the National Housing Act created the Federal Housing Administration (FHA) to provide government insurance on long-term, fully amortized mortgages that met its underwriting standards. That stimulated some lending but more was desired so in 1938 the government created the Federal National Mortgage Association (FNMA, later Fannie Mae or just plain Fannie) to purchase FHA mortgages and, later, Veterans Administration (VA) loans, and thereby provide liquidity for the mortgage market. The HOLC, FHA, and VA programs presumably taught private mortgagees that they could make long-term (15 to 30 year) fixed payment amortizing mortgages, i.e., mortgages with uniform monthly payments that ended in full repayment of the loan and ownership of the property, instead of IO mortgages requiring a balloon payment. (After World War I, Federal Land Banks had also lent on farm mortgages that amortized over several decades.)[70]

After World War II, thrifts and commercial banks made mortgage loans locally, while life insurers and mutual savings banks lent in large regions by purchasing mortgages originated by loan correspondents, some of which were commercial banks that simply did not have the resources to hold mortgages on their own balance sheets for long. By the late 1940s, for example, Rapid City National Bank of South Dakota made "loans in the ordinary course of business ... and when we have a sufficiently large bank of mortgages, we sell them. We receive one-half of one percent of the interest collected for our service."[71] Caution was

69 Katy Burne, "Windfall for Federal Home Loan Banks," *Wall Street Journal*, 24 January 2017.

70 Snowden, "Mortgage Securitization," 293; Calder, *Financing*, 282–83; B. M. Gile, *The Farm Credit Situation in Southwestern Arkansas*, (Fayetteville: University of Arkansas Agricultural Experiment Station, 1929), 36–37.

71 A. E. Dahl, *Banker Dahl of South Dakota: An Autobiography*, (Rapid City: Fenske Book Company, 1965), 134.

the watchword at most lenders because their own reputation and capital were at stake. "The intelligent and aggressive activities of the mortgage salesman should be continued and ... every effort should be made to get mortgages," one mutual savings bank concluded soon after World War II, "but ... the Loan Committee should review each and every loan ... a very conservative policy [should] be followed in the granting of mortgage loans."[72]

The largest of the national lenders, like Guardian Life Insurance Company of America, entered into so-called warehousing agreements with commercial banks whereby they promised to purchase so many dollars worth of mortgages over pre-specified periods of time. Such arrangements allowed cash poor insurers to close loans when borrowers needed by committing banks to front the cash for as long as a year in advance.[73]

In 1970, Fannie Mae began to securitize mortgages by pooling them together into mortgage backed securities that were easier for institutional investors like pension funds to hold than standalone mortgages were. It was joined the next year by the Federal Home Loan Mortgage Corporation (Freddie Mac or just plain Freddie). Securitization worked, at first, because Fannie and Freddie were government-sponsored enterprises (GSEs). In other words, they were owned by private investors but highly (though ultimately ineffectively) regulated and backed by implicit government guarantees that allowed them to borrow almost as cheaply as the federal government itself could. Moreover, the GSEs initially could only buy, guarantee, or securitize mortgages that were originated by approved originators and that conformed to strict underwriting standards.[74]

---

72 Recommendations of the Examining Committee, 1945, Recommendations, Exam. Com., East Side/Community, Rush Rhees Library.

73 Snowden, "Mortgage Securitization," 261; Wright and Smith, *Mutually Beneficial*, 321–31, 344–45.

74 Snowden, "Mortgage Securitization," 267–68.

Consumer Finance Then and Now

A river of red ink runs through American history. — *Lendol Calder,*
    Financing the American Dream: A Cultural History of Consumer
    Credit (Princeton: Princeton University Press, 1999), 26.

S mall or shaky businesses sometimes had to pay high rates of interest
or offer physical collateral in order to obtain loans but generally businesses borrowed out of strength when owners had good business projects
to pursue or financial assets, like accounts receivable, that could be sold
or used as collateral. Consumers sometimes borrowed out of strength,
too, as when they borrowed against certain future income, like a government bond set to mature, or a blue chip stock, or when they borrowed to
fund an education that promised to raise their annual earnings, or when
they borrowed to fund the purchase of a consumer durable (three or
more years of expected use) that could save them time (e.g., an automobile instead of public transportation) or money (e.g., a washing machine
instead of a laundress). Such borrowing contemporaries called "credit."[75]

Often, however, consumers borrowed out of weakness, when their
wants or needs exceeded their income, or what contemporaries called
"debt" and equated with "dirt, and the devil."[76] If an unpaid loan was not
collateralized, it went to a collection agency and possibly to court for a
wage garnishment.[77] If it was collateralized by some chattel, like a piano,
automobile, or boat, men like the father of historian Scott Reynolds Nelson, "repo men," would appear and take the property back.[78] Bankers
were not keen on repossession, which was costly and unseemly, and they
were slow "to realize that many people with moderate and low incomes
are capable of providing for a living and making payments on a loan at the

---

75 Black, *Buy Now*, 108, 213–15; Olney, *Buy Now*, 6.

76 As quoted in Calder, *Financing*, 92–93.

77 Black, *Buy Now*, 51–60.

78 Scott Reynolds Nelson, *A Nation of Deadbeats: An Uncommon History of America's Financial Disasters*, (New York: Alfred A. Knopf, 2012), vii-viii; Black, *Buy Now*, 56, 61.

same time."[79] They also disliked non-callable loans. So bankers would not lend to consumers in significant numbers until the 1920s and then only at high rates of interest. As late as 1929, only 14 percent of Americans qualified for traditional bank loans. Only after World War II did commercial bankers lend significant amounts to consumers.[80]

Minus the banks at first, consumer finance roughly paralleled small business finance. Loans from friends and family were obtained when possible but otherwise consumers, instead of trade credit, received personal credit from retailers, much as they had for thousands of years. In the colonial and early national periods, an estimated nine-tenths of all retail transactions (dry goods, groceries, artisanal goods, professional services, etc.) were done on credit. Surviving records show that from the urban northeast to the southern backcountry, most colonists and denizens of the early republic bought on open account. In other words, retailers noted in books what goods customers took away from their shops and stores and their prices. Days, weeks, or months later, the customers made payments, in cash, in kind, and/or in services, for part, all, or more than the balance due. So long as a balance did not grow too large, and the customer remained creditworthy, retailers were content to keep the account open in order to retain the individual's "custom." When balances grew too large or too old, creditors insisted on more formal evidence of debt, like promissory notes, bonds, or mortgages. In some rural areas, a fair facsimile of the colonial bookkeeping barter system lasted well into the twentieth century.[81]

Almost 12,000 probate records from colonial and early national Massachusetts show that credit networks typically included about 20 people

79 Dahl, *Banker Dahl*, 178.

80 Arnett G. Lindsay, "The Negro in Banking," *Journal of Negro History* 14, no. 2 (1929), 196; Herman E. Krooss and Martin R. Blyn, *A History of Financial Intermediaries*, (New York: Random House, 1971), 154.

81 Calder, *Financing*, 60–64, 76–77; Black, *Buy Now*, 3, 151; Plummer, "Consumer Credit," 385–409; Daniel B. Thorp, "Doing Business in the Backcountry: Retail Trade in Colonial Rowan County, North Carolina," *William and Mary Quarterly* 48, no. 3 (1991): 387–408; William Baxter, *The House of Hancock*, (New York: Russell and Russell, Inc., 1965).

and sometimes involved more than 100. In the colonial and Revolutionary period, about a third of creditors lived in the same town as their
customer-debtors, while over half lived no more than two towns apart.
In the early national period, by contrast, creditors were more likely to
live further away, even outside of the county of their debtors' residence,
no doubt due to improved transportation and communication infrastructure.[82] In the antebellum period, more retail transactions were done with
cash, especially in urban areas, but credit remained important. In 1858,
Edward Everett estimated that the indebtedness of U.S. households averaged $300 due to a "natural proclivity to anticipate income to buy on
credit, to live a little beyond our means."[83]

For larger purchases, like for stocks (equities) and bonds, horses,
wagons, agricultural equipment, furniture, pianos, or sewing machines,
sellers and buyers negotiated down payments and installment agreements.[84] Later, buyers could finance larger purchases elsewhere, using the
furniture or other durable good as collateral. The Provident Loan Society
of Rochester, New York, for example, formed in 1913 to lend "money to
wage-earners on household furniture at a just rate of interest." The organization thrived as "wage earners from every trade in the city ... made
application ... from the widow needing the very necessities of life to the
spendthrift desiring some wasteful luxury." The society "relieved sickness
and helped many over seemingly impassable obstacles"[85] for decades.
Most of the tens of thousands of loans it made were for between $25 and
$100, all funded by its capital, surplus, and undivided profits.[86]

---

82 Winifred Barr Rothenberg, *From Market-Places to a Market Economy: The Transformation
of Rural Massachusetts, 1750–1850,* (Chicago: University of Chicago Press, 1992), 126–30.

83 As quoted in Rowena Olegario, *The Engine of Enterprise: Credit in America,* (Cambridge:
Harvard University Press, 2016), 69 and Calder, *Financing,* 39.

84 Plummer, "Consumer Credit," 391; Black, *Buy Now,* 109; Calder, *Financing,* 56–57, 157–
66, 205; Olney, *Buy Now,* 105–6.

85 Anon., *First Annual Report of the Provident Loan Society of Rochester, New York* (1914), 1.

86 A run of the loan society's annual reports can be viewed in the Special Collections, Rush
Rhees Library.

Credit ultimately came from banks and wealthy individuals and cascaded through the economy following the flow of trade channels. Big seaport banks lent to international traders and big wholesale merchants who, in turn, extended credit to their customers, often smaller, regional wholesalers. The second and third tier wholesalers then sold to retailers on credit. Because they did not have to pay up immediately, the retailers could extend credit to consumers. All along the channel, companies competed on the price of their wares and their credit terms, which often led to easier terms (more credit for longer periods). That put tremendous pressure on traders to ascertain the creditworthiness of distant business clients, which led to the creation and refinement of third party credit reporting systems. Retailers, though, were at first left to screen and monitor their customers using more informal methods. Typically, they offered consumer durables on installment plans with fixed repayment schedules, interest charges, and late penalties. Smaller, softer purchases were made on open account with indefinite repayment terms but with interest charges embedded in prices.[87]

Extending credit to consumers became more difficult as retailers increased in size, complexity, and geographical pull. By the late nineteenth century, larger retailers were seeking ways to reduce their credit risks. One way was to accept only cash or layaway (collateralized) credit, but that could cut into sales. Another method was to factor (outright sell) receivables. Yet another was to establish captive finance companies that lent to consumers via so-called company-specific credit accounts. Yet another was to move from open accounts to installment selling because creditors of the latter type were in a much better legal position in case of default.[88]

Outside lenders, including consumer finance companies, credit unions, industrial banks, remedial loan societies, and consumer loan

---

87 Olegario, *Culture of Credit*, 26–29, 36–79, 98–99; Baskin and Miranti, *History of Corporate Finance*; Calder, *Financing*, 17, 165–75; Lewis Mandell, *The Credit Card Industry: A History*, (Boston: Twayne Publishers, 1990), 23–24.

88 Calder, *Financing*, 71–73, 276; Black, *Buy Now*, 112.

departments in commercial banks, also arose in the early twentieth century to lend cash to consumers. Some, like the remedial loan societies
and credit unions, sought to help the working poor but others sensed a
lucrative market. Before banks, personal finance companies, and other
institutional lenders lent widely to consumers, poorer individuals in need
of cash (as opposed to groceries, dry goods, or other products) had to
pawn valuables. Pawnshops numbered about 2,000 in 1911, spread over
300 of the nation's largest cities. Most borrowers redeemed their chattels
within a year, suggesting that they had borrowed rationally by anticipating future familial income and not out of desperation. Those without
possessions to pawn had to pay high interest rates to note shavers, payday
lenders, or loan sharks.[89]

Farmers and small town dwellers tended not to need emergency
consumption loans, beyond extension of their usual seasonal credits,
because in a pinch they often could live off the land and/or extemporize
("make due"), as many did during the Great Depression. Urban dwellers,
however, often found themselves entirely dependent on their wages. A
layoff or strike could quickly devastate familial finances and cause retail
credit to dry up, forcing the unemployed first to pawnshops and then into
the jaws of sharks who charged high rates and onerous terms. According
to a 1911 study conducted by Arthur Ham, director of the Russell Sage
Foundation's Division of Remedial Loans, every U.S. city with a population greater than 25,000 was "infested with loan sharks" who victimized at
least one in every five adult males. By trolling the gray edges of the law,
the sharks were able to openly advertise and even form extensive chains
of offices while traditional lenders remained lawfully unable or unwilling
to lend to the working poor. Sharks did not lend to the most downtrod-

---

89 Elyce Rotella and George Alter, "Working Class Debt in the Late Nineteenth Century
United States," *Journal of Family History* 18, 2 (1993): 111–134; Elisabeth Anderson, "Experts,
Ideas, and Policy Change: The Russell Sage Foundation and Small Loan Reform, 1909–1941,"
Theory and Society 37, no. 3 (2008): 287; Calder, *Financing*, 19, 42–55, 111–46; Wendy A.
Woloson, *In Hock: Pawning in America from Independence through the Great Depression*, (Chi-
cago: University of Chicago Press, 2009), 133; Teackle, *Address*, 8.

den, preferring the richer waters of people with substantial collateral and/ or a job, or at least serious prospects of one.[90]

After the Great War, consumer credit blossomed as financial innovators founded new institutions and found new ways of lending increasingly large sums to an ever larger number of borrowers. In the 1920s, automobile finance became an important business with Commercial Credit Company (later called C.I.T.) and GMAC (Ally Bank today) leading the way. Personal finance companies also sprang up to meet the credit needs of purchasers of other consumer durables, like appliances, radios, and furniture. By the mid-1930s, from two of three to nine of ten consumer durables (radios, automobiles, refrigerators, washing machines, and vacuum cleaners) were sold via installment plans, most offered by finance companies through retailers.[91]

Also in the 1920s, some large urban banks, including National City Bank of New York, finally opened consumer banking departments. By 1929, the number of personal loan departments in banks numbered 208, up from half a dozen in 1923. When during the Depression wage-earning borrowers proved themselves excellent risks who rarely defaulted, and the government's insurance scheme (the FDIC) decreased bankers' aversion to non-callable loans, bankers became even more interested in consumer lending.[92] Personal loan departments began to spring up even in conservative banking states like South Dakota, where Art Dahl opened one in his Rapid City National Bank so that "the man on monthly income could pay" for automobiles and other "personal needs ... by making monthly installments."[93] By 1939, a quarter of consumer lending was done by banks and 30 percent by finance companies. The wartime return to prosperity and postwar macroeconomic stability eventually drew all

---

90 Black, *Buy Now*, 153–54; Robert Mayer, *Quick Cash: The Story of the Loan Shark,* (DeKalb: Northern Illinois University Press, 2010).

91 Black, *Buy Now*, 192–93; Calder, *Financing*, 41–42, 184–201; Olney, *Buy Now*, 106; John Hamm, Frances M. Jones, and Rolf Nugent, *Wage Executions for Debt: Bulletin of the United States Bureau of Labor Statistics,* (1936), vii.

92 Calder, *Financing*, 270–71, 284–85.

93 Dahl, *Banker Dahl*, 77.

the banks into the consumer loan market. Subject to usury laws, banks skimmed the cream, leaving the poor for higher cost lenders.[94]

As historian Lendol Calder, following the pioneering work of economist E.R.A. Seligman, has shown, the 1920s marked more of a cultural shift than an economic one. For the first time, consumer "debt" (as distinguished from consumer "credit" as explained above) became a badge of aspiration rather than something unspoken and almost shameful, a source of prestige to be flaunted rather than secreted away. By one estimate, household non-mortgage debt as a percentage of income doubled from about 5 to 10 percent over the 1920s, so it appeared as though everyone started borrowing heavily for the first time. In fact, automobile credit was responsible for much of the growth, as was a statistical illusion created when credit shifted from the untabulated books of hundreds of thousands of retail establishments and wealthy individuals to those of regulated financial institutions.[95]

Americans did not suddenly jettison prudence for profligacy; they simply came to see consumer debt in a more favorable light. The notion that Americans lost their previous economic virtue in the booming 1920s, Calder called a myth created without fear or research. Like "community," thriftiness purportedly died several times (e.g., the 1860s, 1920s, 1950s) but each time its funeral was eventually forgotten and observers, pundits, and journalists resurrected it only so its demise could be lamented once again. And of course it did not help matters that some observers naively discussed historical credit statistics in absolute terms. Some divided by the number of households or individuals but few thought to adjust for inflation or, most importantly of all, economic growth. Once adjusted for prosperity and the continuously falling value of the dollar, consumer credit no longer looks like an "explosion."[96]

---

94 Olney, *Buy Now*, 109; Black, *Buy Now*, 168; Calder, *Financing*, 286.

95 Calder, *Financing*, 20–22; Black, *Buy Now*, 18–19; Olney, *Buy Now*, 86–95, 95–104.

96 Calder, *Financing*, 23–26; Thomas Bender, *Community and Social Change in America* (Baltimore: Johns Hopkins University Press, 1982); Paul H. Douglas, "Introduction," in Black, *Buy Now*, xiii; Black, *Buy Now*, 6–7.

The transition of credit to formal financial institutions, however, did spur technological changes with far reaching implications. The most important of those innovations were charga-plates, embossed metal plates issued to identify account holders. They began to appear in the 1920s, issued by oil companies, hotels, airlines, restaurants, food and dry goods retailers, and, eventually, by the citywide cooperative credit plans that cropped up in some cities, like Seattle, in the 1930s and 1940s. Out of this milieu emerged the modern credit card.[97]

Credit cards were in some ways a big improvement over pawn-shops and sharks. Interest rates on credit cards were generally lower, as were the penalties for default. The first "universal" card, i.e., the first card that could be used at multiple, unrelated businesses, was Diners' Club. Established in 1950 by Frank McNamara, Ralph Schneider, and Matty Simmons, Diners' Club offered a "charge card," the balance of which had to be paid off monthly. Like American Express, a universal charge card established in 1958, Diners' Club made money from an annual cardholder fee and merchant transaction fees rather than from interest. So, too, did the third member of the "Big Three" of charge cards, Carte Blanche.[98]

The modern "credit card" was universal and also offered cardholders "revolving credit," or the privilege of paying off balances over multiple months pretty much as they saw fit, though usually subject to a minimum payment. Revolving credit accounts had been pioneered by large retailers like Wanamaker's, Gimbel Brothers, and L. Bamberger in the late 1930s and early 1940s but were limited to the store of the issuer. Modern credit cards, by contrast, could be used at any participating vendor and soon came to dominate the market after Bank of America, Chase Manhattan, and a host of smaller rivals launched into the credit card business in the late 1950s. Bank of America went national with its BankAmericard in 1966 and invited other issuers to join its network, which came to be known as Visa. A rival network, Interbank Card Association (later Master Charge then MasterCard), soon appeared. By 1978, over 11,000 banks had joined

97 Mandell, *Credit Card Industry*, 72.
98 Mandell, *Credit Card Industry*, 11–13, 20.

one or both of the networks and 52 million Americans had at least two credit card accounts. By 1986, 55 percent of American families possessed at least one credit card.[99]

Charge cards did not die out entirely, however, as millions of Americans also came to hold American Express charge cards for travel or business purposes. They also held the charge cards of their favorite retailers, airlines, railroads, and oil companies (gasoline retailers). Even the giant telephone monopoly, American Telephone and Telegraph, issued over a million charge cards so its customers could charge some 50 million calls a year. Retailers got back into the credit game because it was lucrative, often more profitable than the merchandize or services they sold, and easier to do thanks to the rise of consumer credit reporting agencies. By 1960, 57 million credit and charge cards were active, almost one per U.S. household. Some charge cards were wildly popular. In 1981, for example, Sears issued more cards than either MasterCard or Visa! In 1985 its subsidiary, Dean Witter, leveraged that success by launching its own universal credit card and network, Discover.[100]

To increase their market share yet further, credit card issuers began offering "affinity" cards that offered bonuses for use, charitable donations, or branding links to celebrities. Prestige cards like the American Express gold card were designed to attract high income individuals because they were generally good credit risks who racked up large volumes, and hence merchant fees, each month.[101]

Of course credit cards were not the only way that consumers could borrow in postwar America. Loan sharks and pawnshops persisted, as did consumer finance companies and depository institutions like credit unions and commercial banks, some of which still issued charga-plates when Jack Kennedy sat in the Oval Office. Others allowed consumers

---

99 Louis Hyman, *Debtor Nation: The History of America in Red Ink*, (Princeton: Princeton University Press, 2011), 98–99, 118–31; Mandell, *Credit Card Industry*, xiv, xxi, 24; Black, *Buy Now*, 113–14.

100 Mandell, *Credit Card Industry*, xvi-xvii, xxii, 153; Black, *Buy Now*, 15–16, 111–12, 194–95, 205; Wright and Sylla, *Genealogy*, 16–23, 118–20.

101 Mandell, *Credit Card Industry*, xxi.

to write "Instant Money checks" that drew against a credit line rather than a traditional deposit.[102] "Today," one observer noted in 1961, "the average banker seeks the wage-earning customer with all the verve of a girdle salesman during a fire sale,"[103] i.e. heartily. Still, many consumers preferred friendlier but more costly personal loan companies. "Never supercilious," a banker explained, finance company personnel "are trained to be courteous and sympathetic without being condescending."[104] The two largest, Household Finance and Beneficial Finance, operated a combined 2,200 offices spread throughout the United States and Canada. By all accounts, they were extremely efficient operations run on a shoestring of cash and a decentralized decision-making model that allowed credit decisions to be made and cash paid out within a half hour. They were also less averse to advertising than banks were, at least prior to the 1970s.[105]

In the 1970s, a new twist on the credit card, the secured credit card, appeared. Although never a significant part of the market, the secured credit card, which required holders to deposit a sum with the lender equivalent to the credit line, was important to people with no or damaged credit. Although not really an extension of credit, such cards allowed their holders the convenience of using plastic at the point of sale in the era before debit cards came into widespread use. In terms of overall costs (fees, loss of interest on the deposit, interest charged on purchases, etc.), the cards were relatively expensive but they did help borrowers, most of whom were young or poor, to increase their credit scores if they paid their bills in a timely manner.[106]

In the postwar period, lenders extended credit based on information provided on credit applications and also information from credit reporting agencies. In 1960, the king of the consumer credit reporting industry was

---

102 Black, *Buy Now*, 4–5, 118–22.

103 Black, *Buy Now*, 168.

104 Black, *Buy Now*, 170.

105 Black, *Buy Now*, 170–75.

106 Larry Santucci, "The Secured Credit Card Market," Philadelphia Federal Reserve Discussion Paper (November 2016).

the Associated Credit Bureaus of America (ACB of A, now Consumer Data Industry Association), which was composed of 1,950 credit bureaus and 1,270 collection bureaus, each of which counted most major credit providers in their respective markets among its members. By sharing information on their customers with their local bureaus, which shared them with ACB of A, the system covered all fifty of the United States plus Australia, Canada, and Great Britain. For individuals without extensive credit or employment history, bureaus conducted in-person and tele-phone interviews. To escape the gaze of the ACB of A, one contemporary claimed, you had to be "under twenty-one or dead." Even the police, F.B.I. agents, and Treasury men consulted its files, which contained infor-mation including "name, age, residence, marriage, divorce, inheritance, earnings, criminal record, bank account, date debts assumed and paid, slow pay, fast pay, no pay."[107]

By 1960, consumer credit was as "scientific" as business credit had been half a century earlier. Loan officers were to look out for warning signs, "like people who make a living on fees earned at home, such as music teachers, tutors, masseurs, fortune tellers" as well as "salesmen who work on a commission basis only" and prostituted persons. But the credit bureaus noted that "danger signals" like those "suggest caution or careful investigation but are not all definite reasons for refusing credit."[108] Nevertheless, much of the information was still anecdotal, collected by Welcome Wagon women during personal visits as well as barkeeps, employers, and public utilities. Only in the 1970s and 1980s did credit bureaus collect financial data alone, via computers, and start to calculate credit "scores."[109]

By 1960, half of all consumer debt outstanding was covered by credit life insurance policies that repaid balances owing when a borrower died. Called "peace of mind" insurance, the policies were supposed to ensure that widows, widowers, and orphans were not burdened by debt as well

---

107 Black, *Buy Now*, 36–37, 41, 43–46.

108 Black, *Buy Now*, 47–48.

109 Hyman, *Debtor Nation*, 206–12.

as the death of a loved one. It protected creditors from default and the embarrassment of collecting from the bereaved but it was paid for by the borrower, sometimes at premiums three times higher than those of comparable term life policies. By contrast, GMAC and most credit unions offered credit life more cheaply than most people could buy an individual life policy. They could do so by purchasing large scale group insurance or by adding reasonable mortality risk directly into the interest charge.[110]

Many postwar lenders hid their actual charges from consumers by using nonstandard equations for calculating interest. By the late 1950s, the problems became so palpable that they created a political backlash that eventually led to the 1968 passage of the Truth in Lending Act, which mandated use of a uniform Annual Percentage Rate (APR) interest rate formula. Long under the purview of the Federal Reserve, enforcement of the Truth in Lending Act passed to the new Consumer Financial Protection Bureau (CFPB) in 2011 (The CFPB has such broad, arbitrary authority to combat financial discrimination that it has reduced competition and increased costs for borrowers according to Jeb Hensarling, chairman of the House Financial Services Committee. In my view, it is still too early to judge the CFPB's overall effectiveness, let alone its cost effectiveness, but early reviews are not encouraging.[111]).

Backers of the Truth in Lending Act hoped that uniform disclosure of interest rates and finance charges would enhance competition and even reduce borrowing and encourage savings by allowing consumers to easily compare borrowing and savings rates. The law helped at some margins but American consumers continued to borrow large sums, often on terms that appear onerous to people who are not parties to the transaction.[112]

110 Black, *Buy Now*, 180–89.

111 Douglas, "Introduction," xiv; Jeb Hensarling, "How We'll Stop a Rogue Federal Agency," *Wall Street Journal*, 9 February 2017; Lauren E. Willis, "The Consumer Financial Protection Bureau and the Quest for Consumer Comprehension," Loyola Law School, Legal Studies Research Paper Series No. 2016–02 (August 2016); Kevin M. McDonald, "Who's Policing the Financial Cop on the Beat?: A Call for Judicial Review of the Consumer Financial Protection Bureau's Non-Legislative Rules," *Review of Banking and Financial Law* 35, no. 1 (2015–16): 224–71.

112 Douglas, "Introduction," xiv-xv.

Investing in America from the Revolution to the Present

Unless money can be borrowed, trade cannot be carried on. — J. B.
C. Murray, The History of Usury from the Earliest Period to the
Present Time ... And an Examination into the Policy of Laws on
Usury and Their Effect Upon Commerce (Philadelphia: J. B. Lip-
pincott & Co., 1866), 127.

Of course not all Americans were spenders all the time. Most saved at appropriate times over the business cycle and their life cycles, knowing full well that unexpected bouts of unemployment were inevitable and superannuation a possibility.[113] A few of them, however, refused to invest and paid the appropriate price, which ranged from loss of interest to loss of principal, as in the case of Widow Zulinksy, who refused to open a savings bank account and had her life savings of $600 stolen out of her mattress circa 1900. Most savers, however, invested in American governments or business enterprises via financial markets and/ or intermediaries. Already by the early nineteenth century they bought U.S. government bonds, the bonds of state and municipal governments, and corporate bonds and equities (shares) in prodigious numbers. Over 20,000 corporations received special acts of incorporation before the Civil War and thousands of others chartered under general incorporation acts. During and after the Civil War, incorporation became even more widespread.[114] Not all corporations sold stock, but most did, allowing

113 Howard Bodenhorn, "Were Nineteenth Century Industrial Workers Permanent Income Savers?" NBER Working Paper 23948 (October 2017).

114 Calder, *Financing*, 43; Rothenberg, *From Market-Places*; John Majewski, "Toward a Social History of the Corporation: Shareholding in Pennsylvania, 1800–1840," in *The Economy of Early America: Historical Perspectives and New Directions*, ed. Cathy Matson (University Park: Pennsylvania State University Press, 2006), 294–316; Robert E. Wright, *The Wealth of Nations Rediscovered: Integration and Expansion in American Financial Markets, 1780–1850*, (New York: Cambridge University Press, 2002), 99–118; Sean Patrick Adams, "Soulless Monsters and Iron Horses: The Civil War, Institutional Change, and American Capitalism," in *Capitalism Takes Command: The Social Transformation of Nineteenth-Century America*, ed. Michael

surprisingly large numbers of Americans to own shares. While not many poor people could afford to buy stocks or bonds, even the "poorest persons," according to political economist Henry C. Carey, sometimes bought shares, especially of corporations that issued shares at low par values like $10.[115] His claim is verified by the available data. Between 1814 and 1859, almost 73,000 different individuals invested in the shares of joint stock corporations in Pennsylvania when they were first offered for sale.[116]

Those stockholders, and untold others of them in other states (including even peripheries like Maine), traded their shares frequently enough to create plenty of business for brokers.[117] As one of them explained in 1848:

Of the Capital Stock of all the Incorporated Companies, which are at one time or another offered for sale in this city and in all other parts of the Union, we can scarcely convey any definite idea; but when we reflect upon the almost innumerable number of rail road, canal, manufacturing, naviga-tion, and banking corporations, each perhaps with a capital of several mil-lions divided into a number of shares, varying in number from one to more than fifty thousand, together with the vast amount of Government and State Securities, we can only estimate the amount of investments which they repre-sent by hundreds and thousands of millions![118]

Some brokers at times certainly fleeced "outsiders ... those people of all ranks and classes who dabble in Stocks to a greater or lesser extent."[119] Outside investors who purchased "fancy" stocks, usually shares in beaten down or even bankrupt land companies and railroads, were most easily

Zakim and Gary J. Kornblith (Chicago: University of Chicago Press, 2012), 249–76; Earling, *Whom to Trust*, 142.

115 As quoted in Wright, *Wealth*, 69–70.

116 Records of the Department of State, Corporation Bureau, Letters Patent, 1814–1874, Boxes 1–13, RG-26, Pennsylvania State Archives.

117 Wright, *Wealth*, 99–121.

118 A Reformed Stock Gambler, *Stocks and Stock-Jobbing in Wall-Street, with Sketches of the Brokers, and Fancy Stocks*, (New York: New-York Publishing Company, 1848), 7.

119 A Reformed Stock Gambler, *Stocks*, 7.

enticed into trading too often, buying high, and/or selling low.[120] Those who bought and held safe investments, like government bonds and the stocks of established banks, however, did not fall so easily into the clutches of unscrupulous brokers because they sought a stream of interest payments or dividends, not mere speculative capital gains. But as one broker noted, "The number and variety of people who hazard their money upon anticipated fluctuations in prices would seem incredible" and included "merchants and milliners, confectioners and printers."[121]

By the 1920s, up to 12 percent of the population directly owned corporate stocks. Most corporations were closely held but more than a few were widely traded. By the Great Crash in 1929, over 70 U.S. corporations had more than 20,000 stockholders apiece and 3 had over 200,000. Shareholders as a percentage of the population decreased during the Depression and World War II, bottoming out at 3.7 in 1948. Thereafter, stock ownership increased from 5.5 percent in 1956 to exactly 15 percent in 1970 to approximately 21 percent twenty years later. Fifteen years after that, in 2005, almost 63 million U.S. households, about 2 in every five, owned corporate equities. About 1 in 3 individual Americans directly owned shares.[122]

Those who could not afford to buy stocks and bonds directly could do so through intermediaries, especially savings banks, which grew quickly in number and size after their introduction in the late 1810s. By the 1870s, savings banks, most organized as mutuals but some as joint

---

120 A Reformed Stock Gambler, Stocks, 13–20, 28–32.

121 A Reformed Stock Gambler, Stocks, 8.

122 David Hochfelder, "'Where the Common People Could Speculate': The Ticker, Bucket Shops, and the Origin of Popular Participation in Financial Markets, 1880–1920," Journal of American History 93, no. 2 (2006): 336; Adolf A. Berle and Gardiner C. Means, The Modern Corporation and Private Property, (New Brunswick, N.J.: Transaction Publishers, 1991), 48–49; Leslie White, Modern Capitalist Culture, (Walnut Creek, CA: Left Coast Press, 2008), 370; Nicholas Gianaris, Modern Capitalism: Privatization, Employee Ownership, and Industrial Democracy, (Westport, Conn.: Praeger, 1996), 161. "Household Ownership of Equities: 2002 and 2005," The 2006 Statistical Abstract of the United States (Washington, D.C.: U.S. Census Bureau, 2006), Table 1198; Paul Grout, William Megginson, and Anna Zalewska, "One Half-Billion Shareholders and Counting: Determinants of Individual Share Ownership Around the World," (September 2009), 21.

stock companies, controlled a full third of the assets of all financial inter-mediaries in the nation. In 1910, almost 9.2 million Americans (10 per-cent) owned over $4 billion in savings deposits.[123]

At first, savings bank deposits were fairly safe and remunerative because they had to be invested in government securities, good mort-gages, and other relatively safe investments that tended to yield in the five to seven percent range, which minus operating costs left three to five percent for dividends/interest and reserve accumulation.[124] Savings bank deposits were illiquid, however, because they could not be withdrawn at will. Later, deposits became more easily withdrawn but at the cost of lower returns as the savings banks had to hold higher cash balances to meet withdrawals. Safety, however, remained their mantra. "Since the bulk of our deposits are the hard-earned savings of thrifty working people who are unable or unwilling to invest for themselves," the leaders of the East Side Savings Bank argued in 1940, "the bank should, in the interests of safety, be content with the return on high quality bonds."[125] Thanks to their strong safety record, especially during the Great Depression, mutual savings banks continued to be a major vehicle for savings well into the postwar period, aided by innovations like payroll savings, which allowed wage earners to save conveniently by having predetermined sums deducted from their pay and credited directly to their savings accounts.[126]

Mutual savings banks essentially were mutual funds. As one mutual savings bank executive explained in 1951, mutual savings banks "are not properly banks at all, but simply mutual institutions or societies for the

123 United States, Office of the Comptroller of the Currency, *Annual Report*, 1910.

124 R. Daniel Wadhwani, "Protecting Small Savers: The Political Economy of Economic Security," *Journal of Policy History* 18, no. 1 (2006): 126–27.

125 "Bond Investment Policy for the East Side Savings Bank," November 25, 1940, Stocks, Bonds, Securities, East Side/Community, Agendas/Minutes: Exec. Committee Community, Rush Rhees Library.

126 Charles W. Carson to Arthur A. Barry, March 11, 1952, Business Correspondence, Community Savings; Printed Ephemera, East Side and Community Savings, Rush Rhees Library.

encouragement of thrift among low income people."[127] The rates of interest they could pay to depositors, however, were capped by law while the returns of mutual funds remained unregulated. So when inflation struck in the 1970s, depositors rationally took their money out of mutual savings banks and invested them in mutual and other investment funds. Mutual funds grew in number and value from 68 funds totaling $450 million in assets in 1940 to 98 funds totaling $2.5 billion in 1950 to 161 funds totaling $17 billion in 1960. They really took off in the 1970s, 1980s, and 1990s, hitting almost $135 billion in 564 funds in 1980 and over $1 trillion in over 3,000 funds in 1990. By 2000, over 8,000 different funds worth almost $7 trillion in net assets were in operation. Assets in the industry dropped from $12 trillion to $9.6 trillion in 2008 due to the financial crisis but had rebounded to almost $16 trillion by 2014. The number of funds, after a slight dip following the financial crisis, remains at about 8,000. The percentage of U.S. households owning mutual funds increased from about 6 in 1980 to about 45 in 2000, a figure that has held remarkably constant ever since.[128]

Americans have also invested large sums in exchange traded funds (ETFs) and hedge funds, either directly or via their pension funds, 401Ks, 403Bs, Roth IRAs, and other retirement funds. Formal and informal ESOPs (employee stock ownership plans, where employees regularly buy shares in the companies that employ them) also have a long history. American National Bank and Trust Company, for example, was 7.6 percent owned by its non-officer employees by 1964. By the mid-1990s, ESOPs had become an important vehicle for savings. By the end of 2015,

---

127 The Question of Imposing the Federal Corporate Income Tax Upon the Undistributed Earnings of Mutual Savings Banks, July 27, 1951, Misc. Bank Documents, N.Y. State Banking Dept., Rush Rhees Library.

128 George J. Benston, "Savings Banking and the Public Interest," *Journal of Money, Credit and Banking* 4, 1 (Feb. 1972), 133–226; Sheri J. Caplan, *Petticoats and Pinstripes: Portraits of Women in Wall Street's History*, (Denver: Praeger, 2013), 108; *2015 Investment Company Fact Book: A Review of Trends and Activities in the U.S. Investment Company Industry* (New York: Investment Company Institute, 2015), 173; "Ownership of Mutual Funds, Shareholder Sentiment, and Use of the Internet, 2013," *ICI Research Perspective* 19, 9 (October 2013), 3, 26–27.

almost 10,000 ESOPs and ESOP-like plans were in place nationwide, boasting 15 million participants and approximately $1.3 trillion invested.[129]

While savings banks accepted the deposits of the poor, they did not lend to those without significant capital. Building and loan associations, by contrast, were mutual intermediaries that lent to the very working poor and members of middling income groups whose deposits they agglomerated. By the 1920s, it was said that "everyone" built their houses with help from the local building and loan, i.e., their neighbors, much as portrayed in the fictional town of Bedford Falls, New York in the movie *It's a Wonderful Life*.[130]

As we will see, even married women could be avid investors when they were able to save. In the role of investors in financial markets, minority Americans faced relatively little exclusion and discrimination as most borrowers either did not know who they were borrowing from and/ or were happy to get all the help they could. Brokers could be biased but they typically worked on commission or other volume-based forms of remuneration so an accommodating one, typically a newbie without a large clientele to lose, could usually be found no matter one's gender, religion, class, or skin hue.

Saving via commercial banks was a little trickier for African-Americans, American Indians, poor whites, women, and other minorities because commercial bankers did not want to be burdened by small accounts that imposed net costs on their institutions. They also had to worry about check kiting and other scams. Commercial banks also usually provided spaces where all customers mixed, so bankers were keen to keep "the wrong sort" out of doors. To this day, banks can deny applications for checking accounts. The attitude of commercial banks towards

---

129 Dahl, *Banker Dahl*, 248; Gianaris, *Modern Capitalism*, 162. https://www.nceo.org/articles/statistical-profile-employee-ownership. Accessed 16 May 2016.

130 Calder, *Financing*, 294.

poorer folks, we will see, was a major reason for the establishment of savings banks and credit unions.[131]

Evolving Mechanisms of Insurance and Risk Management

I t was even more difficult for minorities to save by purchasing insurance policies because insurers were extremely interested in who their policyholders were.[132] Insurers can be relatively easily defrauded and even honest policyholders can inflict large losses. Discrimination in insurance might not seem like a major problem because everyone, in a sense, is insured against everything, if only via "self-insurance," i.e., bearing losses themselves. But self-insurance is rarely optimal, *especially* for poor people and small businesses because they are more vulnerable to shocks. A single fire is not going to wipe out Walmart but one easily could destroy a family's home or a mom and pop shop.[133]

In many areas of life and business, self-insurance has slowly given way to risks managed by markets and intermediaries. Insurers, however, long engaged in exclusionary discrimination as well as more subtle dis-

---

131 The best description of check kiting I have seen is Dahl, *Banker Dahl*, 149–50. For other check-related scams, see 179–82.

132 For the sake of space and expositional clarity, the focus here is on domestic insurers and their domestic business. For an introduction to international insurance, both U.S. insurers conducting business abroad, and foreign insurers operating in the United States, see Mira Wilkins, "Multinational Enterprise in Insurance, an Historical Overview," In *Internationalisation and Globalisation of the Insurance Industry in the 19th and 20th Centuries*, ed. Peter Borscheid and Robin Pearson (Zurich: Phillipps-University, Marburg, 2007).

133 This section is based on Robert E. Wright, "Insuring America: Market, Intermediated, and Government Risk Management Since 1790," in *Encuentro Internacional Sobre la Historia del Seguro*, ed. Leonardo Caruana (Madrid: Fundacion MAPFRE, 2010), 239–298. Peter L. Bernstein, *Against the Gods: The Remarkable Story of Risk*, (New York: John Wiley & Sons, 1996); Joseph M. Conder and Gilbert Hopkins, *The Self-Insurance Decision*, (New York: National Association of Accountants, 1981); Marquis James, *The Metropolitan Life: A Study in Business Growth*, (New York: Viking, 1947); Peter M. Lencsis, *Insurance Regulation in the United States: An Overview for Business and Government*, (Westport, Conn.: Quorum Books, 1997); David Moss, *When All Else Fails: Government as the Ultimate Risk Manager*, (Cambridge: Harvard University Press, 2002).

criminatory practices. Some so-called wild cat insurers, unincorporated fly-by-night companies with impressive-sounding names, engaged in predation. They accepted anyone who applied, took their premiums, but disappeared whenever a substantial claim was made. Some 185 such companies operated in Chicago alone in 1900, but concerted efforts by the insurance industry, the U.S. Postal Service, and the Chicago police department had stamped out such practices by 1905.[134]

Individuals and small businesses did not have much to do, directly, with America's first major insurance sector, marine insurance, or even its domestic cousin, inland transportation insurance, because only large international and domestic wholesalers needed such coverage. By the 1860s, European marine insurers had made major inroads into the U.S. market; by the Great War, foreign companies had won about two-thirds of it. The demise of the domestic marine insurance industry was tied to the long, slow decline of the American merchant marine, which is another story entirely.[135]

Between the world wars, marine insurers increasingly engaged in multiple line underwriting, including marine, fire, and casualty and dry inland risks on rail and truck freight. The transformation continued in the postwar period so that by 1970 many old line "marine" insurers obtained less than 10 percent of their premium revenue from marine policies. Companies underwriting the other traditional type of property insurance,

---

134 H. Roger Grant, *Insurance Reform: Consumer Action in the Progressive Era*, (Ames, Iowa: Iowa State University Press, 1979); Clifton R. Wooldridge, *The Grafters of America*, (Chicago: Monarch Book Company, 1906), 38.

135 Christopher Kingston, "Marine Insurance in Philadelphia during the Quasi-War with France, 1795–1801," *Journal of Economic History* 71, no. 1 (2011): 162–84; Robin Pearson, "Insurance: Historical Overview." In *The Oxford Encyclopedia of Economic History*, ed. Joel Mokyr (2003), 3:83–86; Robert E. Wright, *The First Wall Street: Chestnut Street, Philadelphia, and the Birth of American Finance*, (Chicago: University of Chicago Press, 2005); Robert E. Wright and David J. Cowen, *Financial Founding Fathers: The Men Who Made America Rich*, (Chicago: University of Chicago Press, 2006); Solomon Huebner, "The Development and Present Status of Marine Insurance in the United States," *Annals of the American Academy of Political and Social Science* 26 (1905): 241–72; C. Bradford Mitchell, *A Premium on Progress: An Outline History of the American Marine Insurance Market, 1820–1870*, (New York: Newcomen Society, 1970); Wilkins, "Multinational Enterprise."

fire, experienced a broadly similar transformation and of course faced more direct demand for policies from small businesses and individuals.[136]

Mutual fire insurance began after the Great London Fire of 1666 and spread to Britain's mainland North American colonies in the mid-eighteenth century. The first fire insurance mutual in America closed in 1741, after just six years of operation, following a major fire in its home city, Charleston, South Carolina. A decade later, however, Benjamin Franklin helped to establish another mutual fire insurer, The Philadelphia Contributionship for the Insurance of Houses from Loss by Fire, which is still in operation today with assets of about $500 million.[137]

In the 1790s, several joint-stock fire insurers formed. To spread their risks, most underwrote both urban and rural structures. They also quickly developed elaborate premium scales based on the location, use, construction, and roof characteristics of insured buildings. Manhattan's great fire in 1835, however, showed that many fire insurers had not diversified sufficiently or charged premiums commensurate to the risks incurred. In response, fire insurers began to solicit business through geographically dispersed networks of agents. In prosperous years, scores of new fire insurers formed each year. That kept premiums low but bankruptcies high, especially after the enormous conflagrations that frequently struck American urban areas throughout the nineteenth century.[138]

Mutual mill insurers responded by cajoling businesses into adopting modern fire safety standards and technologies by charging higher premiums, or refusing to insure at all, those that represented the greatest risks.

---

136 Kenneth J. Meier, *The Political Economy of Regulation: The Case of Insurance*, (Albany: State University of New York Press, 1988); Mitchell, *American Marine Insurance*.

137 Dalit Baranoff, "Shaped by Risk: The American Fire Insurance Industry, 1790–1920," (Ph.D. diss., Johns Hopkins University, 2003); F. C. Oviatt, "Historical Study of Fire Insurance in the United States," *Annals of the Academy of Political and Social Science* 26 (1905):155–78; Nicholas Wainwright, *A Philadelphia Story: The Philadelphia Contributionship for the Insurance of House from Loss by Fire*, (Philadelphia, 1952).

138 *Delaware Gazette and State Journal*, 8 August 1826. Edwin Perkins, *American Public Finance and Financial Services, 1700–1815*, (Columbus: Ohio State University Press, 1994); Baranoff, "American Fire Insurance"; Grant, *Insurance Reform*; Oviatt, "Historical Study of Fire Insurance"; Wilkins, "Multinational Enterprise."

That pressure allowed managers to justify to owners and stockholders the cost of safety improvements. Scientific rating of risks promised to ensure that everyone paid actuarially fair premiums and economic entities seemed to believe they were getting a fair shake as they demanded more insurance than ever. In 1875, half of the property that burned in the United States was insured. By the start of the Great War, that figure had increased to 75 percent.[139]

In the late 1940s and early 1950s, insurance regulators finally allowed multi-line insurers to coalesce from "groups" or "fleets" of loosely affiliated companies.[140] Both businesses and households appreciated the change, which allowed them to purchase comprehensive coverage from a single company rather than "obtaining numerous policies and endorsements" only to end up with what one contemporary called "a disjointed patchwork of complexities riddled with omissions and exclusions."[141] So, like marine insurers, fire insurers over the course of the twentieth century became increasingly generalized or "multi-line," offering automobile and other vehicular coverage, as well as insurance against theft and lawsuits, in addition to underwriting fire-related hazards. Fire insurance per se is now a minor player, accounting for less than 7 percent of total property and liability premiums since the early 1970s. Automobile insurance assumed the top spot after World War II, accounting for 40 to 50 percent of all property and liability insurance premiums since the 1970s. Liability insurance also increased in importance after the war, largely because

---

139 Pierre-Andre Chiappori and Christian Gollier, "Introduction," in *Competitive Failures in Insurance Markets: Theory and Policy Implications,* ed. Pierre-Andrew Chiappori and Christian Gollier (Cambridge: MIT Press, 2006); Grant, *Insurance Reform*; Meier, *Political Economy of Regulation*; Oviatt, "Historical Study of Fire Insurance"; William Wandel, *The Control of Competition in Fire Insurance,* (Lancaster, Pa.: Art Printing Co., 1935); Loftin Graham and Xiaoying Xie, "The United States Insurance Market: Characteristics and Trends," in *Handbook of International Insurance: Between Global Dynamics and Local Contingencies,* ed. J. David Cummins and Bertrand Venard (New York: Springer, 2007); Baranoff, "American Fire Insurance"; Wermiel, *The Fireproof Building.*

140 Lencsis, *Insurance Regulation*; Meier, *The Political Economy of Regulation*; Valgren 1941.

141 John E. Pierce, *Development of Comprehensive Insurance for the Household,* (Homewood, Ill.: Richard D. Irwin, 1958), 3.

courts supplanted the doctrine of contributory negligence with the much
more liberal doctrine of comparative negligence. That change induced
the U.S. tort system to grow from 0.6 percent of GDP in 1950 to 2.2 percent in 2003.[142]

Beginning in the late 1960s, failure rates increased and kept growing
due the Great Inflation (which raised claims above expectations) and regulatory caps on premium growth. By the early 1990s, some feared that a
Savings and Loan-style crisis loomed in property insurance. Cooler heads
knew that was highly unlikely but warned that about one in five property-
liability insurers were severely undercapitalized and three in five were
exposed extensively to interest rate risk.[143] Public and political dissatisfac-
tion with the industry was, according to two contemporary observers,
"widespread and ... growing" and the reasons are not difficult to detect.[144]

Property-liability insurance underwriting tends to cycle between
"soft" and "hard" every six years or so. In soft periods, ample insurance
is available and prices decline, hurting profits. Eventually that leads to
exit, less insurance availability, higher premiums, and more robust profits. The swings can be wild. In 1985 and 1986, for example, the market
became extremely hard as premiums more than doubled industry-wide
and numerous applicants could not obtain coverage at any price. In 1987,
Mission Insurance Group, one of the nation's top fifty property-liability
insurers, failed, becoming a $500 million charge against its guaranty fund.

142 Graham and Xie, "United States Insurance Market"; Baranoff, "American Fire Insurance";
Meier, *The Political Economy of Regulation*; Lencsis, *Insurance Regulation*.

143 Scott E. Harrington, "Public Policy and Property-Liability Insurance," in *The Financial
Condition and Regulation of Insurance Companies*, ed. Richard E. Randall and Richard W.
Kopcke (Boston: Federal Reserve Bank of Boston, 1991); Richard E. Randall and Richard W.
Kopcke, "The Financial Condition and Regulation of Insurance Companies: An Overview,"
in *The Financial Condition and Regulation of Insurance Companies*, ed. Richard E. Randall and
Richard W. Kopcke (Boston: Federal Reserve Bank of Boston, 1991).

144 J. David Cummins and Mary A. Weiss, "The Structure, Conduct, and Regulation of the
Property-Liability Insurance Industry," in *The Financial Condition and Regulation of Insurance
Companies*, ed. Richard E. Randall and Richard W. Kopcke (Boston: Federal Reserve Bank of
Boston, 1991), 117.

Tort liability reforms helped the industry return to profitability but other reforms, including tougher rate regulations, hurt.[145]

For the most part, property-liability insurers steered clear of health insurance as well as income insurance, i.e., disability and life insurance and annuities. Such products protect policyholders and beneficiaries from the loss of income associated with life events, like dying too soon (while the insured remains employed) or too late (after the insured stops working). They also help people to save for final expenses like medical and funeral bills.

The earliest forms of life insurance, Roman burial societies and medieval European and Japanese fraternal and guild insurance, provided just burial expenses. Modern life insurance began in Italy in the fourteenth century as credit life insurance that paid off creditors if a borrower died before making repayment. In addition to facing resistance from religious authorities, life insurers long based their premiums on mortality tables of dubious accuracy.[146]

---

145 Patricia Born and W. Kip Viscusi, "Insurance Market Responses to the 1980s Liability Reforms: An Analysis of Firm-Level Data," *Journal of Risk and Insurance* 61 (1994):192–218; Cummins and Weiss, "Structure, Conduct, and Regulation"; Anne Gron, "Capacity Constraints and Cycles in Property-Casualty Insurance Markets," *RAND Journal of Economics* 25 (1994):110–27; Harrington, "Public Policy"; Scott E. Harrington, "The History of Federal Involvement in Insurance Regulation," in *Optional Federal Chartering and Regulation of Insurance Companies*, ed. Peter J. Wallison (Washington: AEI Press, 2000); Scott E. Harrington and Patricia M. Danzon, "Price Cutting in Liability Markets," *Journal of Business* 67 (1994):511–38; J. Robert Hunter, "Discussion," in *The Financial Condition and Regulation of Insurance Companies*, ed. Richard E. Randall and Richard W. Kopcke (Boston: Federal Reserve Bank of Boston, 1991); Meier, *The Political Economy of Regulation*; Henry G. Parker, "Discussion," in *The Financial Condition and Regulation of Insurance Companies*, ed. Richard E. Randall and Richard W. Kopcke (Boston: Federal Reserve Bank of Boston, 1991); Ralph Winter, "The Liability Insurance Market," *Journal of Economic Perspectives* 5 (1991): 115–36.

146 Dora Costa, *The Evolution of Retirement: An American Economic History, 1880–1990*, (Chicago: University of Chicago Press, 1998); Carole Haber and Brian Gratton, *Old Age and the Search for Security: An American Social History*, (Bloomington: Indiana University Press, 1994); James, *Metropolitan Life*; Paul Johnson, "Insurance: Life Insurance," in *The Oxford Encyclopedia of Economic History*, ed. Joel Mokyr (New York: Oxford University Press, 2003); Robin Pearson, "Insurance: Fire Insurance," in *The Oxford Encyclopedia of Economic History*, ed. Joel Mokyr. (New York: Oxford University Press, 2003).

The first American life insurance policies were issued for the benefit of the families of clergymen by several small non-profit corporations formed in the colonial period. In the 1790s, marine insurers issued term life policies to captains, sailors, and supercargoes but demand was weak at the premiums sought. In the 1810s, the Pennsylvania Company for Insurance on Lives and Granting Annuities formed but found it difficult to sell life policies because pessimistic mortality assumptions rendered them too expensive. Annuities based on those tables, on the other hand, were relatively cheap and unsurprisingly their sales were brisk. Few life insurance companies were established prior to 1844 and some ceased operations not long after commencing business.[147]

Total life insurance in force grew rapidly in percentage terms in the 1830s but remained at low absolute levels. In the 1840s, technological improvements led to more accurate pricing, new laws shielded benefits from husbands' creditors, several important mutual insurers began operations, and new marketing and distribution techniques increased demand. Combined, those forces drove sales upward but soon after overly-litigious insurers and the bankruptcies of many of the new mutual insurers decreased demand. New York and some other states responded by requiring life insurers to maintain more equity capital, which led to the creation of mixed companies that were partly mutual and partly joint-stock. Though ingenious, mixing the mutual and joint-stock forms exacerbated agency problems within insurers. In other words, policyholders and stockholders fought over profits.

For those reasons, the growth of insurance in force slowed in the first half of the 1850s. Growth accelerated, however, in the second half of the decade.[148] Before mid-century, most life insurers were unprofessional,

---

147 Gerard M. Brannon, "Public Policy and Life Insurance,"in *The Financial Condition and Regulation of Insurance Companies*, ed. Richard E. Randall and Richard W. Kopcke (Boston: Federal Reserve Bank of Boston, 1991); James, *Metropolitan Life*; Perkins, *American Public Finance*.

148 James, *Metropolitan Life*; Sharon Ann Murphy, "Life Insurance in the United States through World War I," in *EH.Net Encyclopedia*, ed. Robert Whaples (2002); Harvey G. Tuckett, *Practical Remarks on the Present State of Life Insurance in the United States, Showing the Evils Which Exist, and Rule for Improvement*, (Philadelphia: Smith and Peters, 1850); Robert

staffed, as one contemporary noted, by "any idler – any broken-down individual."[149] By the Civil War, however, the industry had begun to attract and retain talent at both the home office and in sales, whether field offices were staffed by brokers, general agents, or company employees.

Life insurance in force increased dramatically from less than $200 million in 1860 to about $2 billion in 1870. Improved government regulation in Massachusetts and New York helped to reduce policyholders' fears of policy surrender and nonpayment by insurers. The decision of several large companies to insure soldiers during the war also improved the industry's public image. Despite improvements, the 1870s and 1880s were difficult for the life insurance industry because panics and recessions took their toll on smaller, weaker companies, the bankruptcies of which again decreased public confidence in the industry. Insurance in force shrank from its 1870 high, recovering in nominal terms only in 1888, largely due to tontine or deferred dividend policies that promised high returns to policyholders who lived long and did not lapse (give up their policies due to non-payment of premiums).[150]

By the early twentieth century, life insurers were perhaps the most important investors in the nation's burgeoning capital markets. But with power came abuse. The Armstrong and other legislative investigations revealed that the largest insurers engaged in a number of shady business and investment practices. In 1907, New York, the most important insurance regulator, retaliated with a series of strict regulations on tontines, investments, lobbying practices, agent activities, proxy voting, and policy forms. Other states soon followed suit. The new regulations eventually aided the industry by increasing public confidence in its fairness and soundness.[151]

E. Wright and George David Smith, *Mutually Beneficial: The Guardian and Life Insurance in America,* (New York: New York University Press, 2004).

149 Tuckett, *Practical Remarks,* 25.

150 Meier, *The Political Economy of Regulation*; Wright and Smith, *Mutually Beneficial*; Murphy, "Life Insurance in the United States."

151 Davis, "Investment Market," 380–81; Miles Dawson, "Fraternal Life Insurance," *Annals of the American Academy of Political and Social Science* 26 (1905):128–36; Graham and Xie,

In the 1950s, 1960s, and 1970s, life insurers faced disintermediation pressure on two fronts, reduced sales and increased policy loans. Instead of buying individual whole life insurance, postwar workers increasingly obtained term coverage through inexpensive group policies negotiated by their employers. Although coverage was lost when a worker left a job, group quickly supplanted industrial insurance, burial insurance sold to large numbers of the poor in the late nineteenth and early twentieth centuries. Others bought cheaper individual term policies instead of traditional whole life and invested the difference in high yielding mutual funds.

Life insurers, the equity holdings of which were by limited by law, found it difficult to compete with such funds in an era of unprecedented and persistent inflation. Regulations and traditional investment habits left insurers with huge portfolios of long-term fixed income assets that lost value in the inflationary environment. In addition, many whole life insurance policyholders took out policy loans, the interest rates on which were contractually capped at 5 or 6 percent, invested their borrowings in higher yielding money market money funds, and pocketed the difference. Still others lapsed or surrendered their policies for cash.[152]

Life insurers responded to disintermediation by transforming themselves into financial services firms. They introduced their own mutual funds, created interest-sensitive life insurance products, including universal, variable, and flexible premium variable life and variable annuities, changed their investment strategies to increase liquidity, and cut expenses. Some also increased their risk profile, on both the asset and

---

"United States Insurance Market"; William G. Lehrman, "Diversity in Decline: Institutional Environment and Organizational Failure in the American Life Insurance Industry," *Social Forces* 73 (1994):605–35; Murphy, "Life Insurance in the United States"; George Zanjani, "The Rise and Fall of the Fraternal Life Insurer: Law and Finance in U.S. Life Insurance, 1870–1920," Working paper, 2003.

152 Conder and Hopkins, *Self-Insurance Decision*; Graham and Xie, "United States Insurance Market"; Davis Gregg, *Group Life Insurance: An Analysis of Concepts, Contracts, Costs, and Company Practices*, (Homewoood, Ill.: Richard D. Irwin, 1957); Randall and Kopcke, "Financial Condition and Regulation"; Francis Schott, "Disintermediation Through Policy Loans at Life Insurance Companies," *Journal of Finance* 26 (1971):719–29; Kenneth Walker, *Guaranteed Investment Contracts: Risk Analysis and Portfolio Strategies*, (Homewood, Ill.: Dow Jones-Irwin, 1989).

liability sides of their balance sheets, hoping that increased returns would keep investors interested in their shares, policies, and guaranteed investment contracts (GICs) or other short-term borrowings. Two new life insurers that grew aggressively in the 1980s, only to fail in the early 1990s, First Capital and Executive Life, invested heavily in junk bonds financed from the sale of GICs. Others, including Monarch, overextended themselves in commercial real estate mortgages and suffered the same fate.[153]

The response of surviving life insurers to disintermediation was successful, but only in part. Industry assets and insurance in force grew in nominal terms but life insurers' relative share of total savings eroded. Several high-profile scandals (vanishing premium policies; policy twisting; investment churning) injured the industry's prospects further.[154]

Income risks loomed in areas other than life and death and increasingly were mitigated by specialized companies. In the late nineteenth century, companies that specialized in accident policies sprouted up to offer income protection to those injured or killed while traveling, a common occurrence on the rails and seas.[155]

Superannuation also emerged as an increasingly difficult problem. Before the twentieth century, few Americans ceased all gainful employment due to advanced age, instead moving into positions requiring less strenuous physical labor. Those too old to do any work relied on children, private charity, public poor houses, and/or personal savings and real estate. Government pensions helped servicemen and their families who lived into old age and widows increasingly received government payments, but stingy ones. Some labor unions also aided aged members with pensions and some employers offered explicit or implicit pension plans,

---

153 Graham and Xie, "United States Insurance Market"; Lennon 1991; Moloney 1991; Randall and Kopcke, "Financial Condition and Regulation"; Walker, *Guaranteed Investment Contracts*; Kenneth Wright, "The Structure, Conduct, and Regulation of the Life Insurance Industry," in *The Financial Condition and Regulation of Insurance Companies*, ed. Richard E. Randall and Richard W. Kopcke (Boston: Federal Reserve Bank of Boston, 1991).

154 Lencsis, *Insurance Regulation*; Pearson, "Insurance: Fire Insurance"; Randall and Kopcke 1991a; Wright, "Structure, Conduct, and Regulation"; Wright and Smith, *Mutually Beneficial*.

155 Anon., *The Present Status of Mutual Benefit Associations*, (New York: National Industrial Conference Board, 1931), 1.

but neither were a significant source of retirement income. Life insurers also tried to help people to insure against superannuation, which increasingly became more of a social phenomenon than a physiological one. They continued to sell annuities and by 1900 had begun offering pensions as well. After World War II, life insurers expanded further into the pension business but regulations that prevented them from investing more than a few percent of their assets in common stocks slowed their growth. In the late 1950s and early 1960s, however, state regulators began to allow insurers to set up separate accounts in which investment gains and losses accrued to the policyholder rather than the insurance company itself. By that time, Social Security was also important in individual retirement planning.[156]

Sickness insurance that replaced some of the wages that workers lost when they were too ill to work became important in the late nineteenth century. While commercial insurers offered expensive policies for the well-to-do, various non-profit organizations, including benevolent associations, fraternal orders, and labor unions, as well as employers, offered lower cost, lower benefit alternatives. Sickness insurance began to lose out to health insurance beginning in the 1920s, when the cost of healthcare began to replace lost wages as the bigger risk to income.[157]

---

156 Beatrix Hoffman, *The Wages of Sickness: The Politics of Health Insurance in Progressive America*, (Chapel Hill: University of North Carolina Press, 2001); Lott 1938; Moss, *When All Else Fails*; I. M. Rubinow, *The Quest for Security*, (New York: Henry Holt and Co., 1934); Robert Whaples and David Buffum, "Fraternalism, Paternalism, the Family, and the Market: Insurance a Century Ago," *Social Science History* 15, no. 1 (1991): 97–122; Blanche Coll, *Safety Net: Welfare and Social Security, 1929–1979*, (New Brunswick, N.J.: Rutgers University Press, 1995); Costa, *Evolution of Retirement*; Haber and Gratton, *Old Age*; Lencsis, *Insurance Regulation*; Quadagno 1988; Walker, *Guaranteed Investment Contracts*; Wright, "Structure, Conduct, and Regulation."

157 Robert Cunningham III and Robert M. Cunningham, Jr., *The Blues: A History of the Blue Cross and Blue Shield System*, (Dekalb, Ill.: Northern Illinois University, 1997); Graham and Xie, "United States Insurance Market"; Hoffman, *Wages of Sickness*; Harry A. Millis, *Sickness and Insurance: A Study of the Sickness Problem and Health Insurance*, (Chicago: University of Chicago Press, 1937); Melissa Thomasson, "Health Insurance in the United States," in *EH.Net Encyclopedia*, ed. Robert Whaples (2003); John E. Murray, *Origins of American Health Insurance: A History of Industrial Sickness Funds*, (New Haven: Yale University Press, 2007).

At first limited to specific hospitals, prepaid hospitalization plans were eventually rationalized to a degree by the American Hospital Association under the auspices of non-profit Blue Cross plans. Enabling legislation allowed such plans to form without meeting the capital minimums required of joint-stock insurers or the assessment liabilities or reserve requirements of mutual insurers. Freed from taxation and insurance laws and their attendant costs, the plans offered insurance at rates low enough to grow the market considerably in the 1930s and 1940s, a period when commercial health insurers suffered from extremely high lapse rates. At the same time, physicians began to offer prepaid plans under the Blue Shield brand. Aided by enabling legislation similar to that encouraging the growth of Blue Cross plans, tax- and insurance regulation-exempt Blue Shield plans thrived in the 1930s. Commercial insurers countered, but their experiments with low premium, low benefit industrial-style policies that combined life, health, and accident insurance found little acceptance in the marketplace.[158]

Blue Cross and Blue Shield plans, however, showed commercial insurers that adverse selection and moral hazard could be mitigated enough to allow the health insurance market to function relatively efficiently. Commercial insurers entered the health insurance market tentatively in the late 1930s but after the war, with the help of improved actuarial tables and tax breaks, they entered in force. Because they charged the same premium to everyone within a given community, Blue Cross and Blue Shield plans faced significant adverse selection after commercial insurers began to offer lower premiums to healthier individuals. By the early 1950s, greatly aided by tax breaks for employers that provided health insurance to employees, commercial insurers outstripped the Blues in terms of the total number of persons insured. In 1958, 75 percent of Americans had some form of private health insurance, up from just 25

---

158 Cunningham and Cunningham, *The Blues*; Malvin E. Davis, *Industrial Life Insurance in the United States*, (New York: McGraw-Hill Book Company, 1944); Millis, *Sickness and Insurance*; Thomasson, "Health Insurance."

percent in 1945. Many of the uninsured were elderly or poor, leading to the passage of Medicare and Medicaid legislation in the 1960s.[159]

Commercial life companies also helped millions to mitigate the risk of significant long-term illness or disability. In 1917, an Illinois Health Insurance Commission study showed that serious sickness afflicted about one in five wage earners annually. Some 35 percent of those missed a month or more of work and almost 10 percent lost over 3 months. Average wages lost from disability exceeded over $100 at a time when the annual income of many workers was around $800 per year. The first disability clauses in life insurance contracts, which began to appear in earnest circa 1910, merely waived the premiums of disabled policyholders. Demand for cash payments, however, drove many insurers to add disability benefit riders to their policies.[160]

Income riders worked well at first but the Depression dealt disability insurance a major blow by increasing moral hazard and precipitating losses estimated at half a billion dollars. Some companies responded by making contractual changes, improving screening, and expanding group disability coverage. Many others withdrew, but some returned to the market after World War II. The addition of disability coverage to Social Security in the 1950s, however, decimated the low end of the market, so-called "any occ" policies, which pay out only if the insured can no longer work at all. In contrast, high-end "own occ" policies, which pay out if the worker cannot return to his or her specific occupation, continue to thrive to this day.[161]

---

159 Cunningham and Cunningham, *The Blues*; Millis, *Sickness and Insurance*; David M. Cutler and Jonathan Gruber, "Does Public Insurance Crowd Out Private Insurance?" *Quarterly Journal of Economics* 111, no. 2 (1996): 391–430; Thomasson, "Health Insurance"; Melissa A. Thomasson, "The Importance of Group Coverage: How Tax Policy Shaped U.S. Health Insurance," *American Economic Review* 93, 4 (2003): 1,373; Christy Ford Chapin, *Ensuring America's Health: The Public Creation of the Corporate Health Care System* (New York: Cambridge University Press, 2015), 40–41.

160 Millis, *Sickness and Insurance*, 23.

161 Coll, *Safety Net*; Kenneth Herrick, *Total Disability Provisions in Life Insurance Contracts*, (Homewood, Ill.: Richard D. Irwin, 1956); Hoffman, *Wages of Sickness*; Lencsis, *Insurance Regulation*; Millis, *Sickness and Insurance*; Gerald Morgan, *Public Relief of Sickness*, (New York:

Employer liability and accident insurance and modern workers compensation arose in the late nineteenth and early twentieth centuries as highly specialized and highly regulated products sold directly to employers. The same was the case with unemployment insurance, which began in earnest only during the Great Depression. So, like marine insurance, those types of insurance play little direct role in the history of financial exclusion, discrimination, and predation.[162]

Finally, as part of their goal to protect lives and property, governments have long acted as insurers of last resort for catastrophic events and when private insurance is not available at any price or at a price so high most entities opt for self-insurance. As discussed elsewhere in this book, various state governments and the federal government have often engaged in financial exclusion, discrimination, and predation, so it is not surprising to find that government insurance programs have sometimes been implicated in such behaviors. FEMA's response to Hurricane Katrina in New Orleans in 2005 appalled many and it was not by coincidence that wealthier neighborhoods were on higher, drier ground. In other places, however, especially ocean coastlines, the rich and the white live in the danger zone (at least during the summer) and receive substantial support

---

Macmillan Company, 1922); Dominick Pratico, *Eisenhower and Social Security: The Origins of the Disability Program*, (New York: Writers Club Press, 2001); Wright and Smith, *Mutually Beneficial*.

162 Ralph Blanchard, *Liability and Compensation Insurance*, (New York: D. Appleton and Co., 1917); Cummins and Weiss, "Structure, Conduct, and Regulation"; Hoffman, *Wages of Sickness*; Shawn Kantor and Price Fishback, "Coalition Formation and the Adoption of Workers' Compensation: The Case of Missouri, 1911 to 1926," in *The Regulated Economy: A Historical Approach to Political Economy*, ed. Claudia Goldin and Gary Libecap (Chicago: University of Chicago Press, 1994); Price Fishback and Shawn Kantor, *Prelude to the Welfare State: The Origins of Workers' Compensation* (Chicago: University of Chicago Press, 2000); Lencsis, *Insurance Regulation*; Meier, *The Political Economy of Regulation*; W. F. Moore, "Liability Insurance," *Annals of the American Academy of Political and Social Science* 26 (1905): 319–39; Moss, *When All Else Fails*; Barbara Armstrong, *Insuring the Essentials: Minimum Wage Plus Social Insurance – A Living Wage Program*, (New York: Macmillan Company, 1932); James J. Hughes and Richard Perlman, *The Economics of Unemployment: A Comparative Analysis of Britain and the United States*, (New York: Cambridge University Press, 1984).

when Mother Nature destroys their homes.[163] Neither of those outcomes bodes well for the efficacy of government insurance, further discussion of which I leave for Chapter 7.

The Panic of 2008: A Failed Attempt to Create Equal Access to the Financial System

If people can't get mortgages or they can't get home insurance which enables them to get mortgages, the whole system starts to just malfunction and die right on the spot. We can't have that. That's not what America is about. — Committee on Banking, Housing, and Urban Affairs, U.S. Senate, 103rd Congress, 2nd Sess., "Homeowners' Insurance Discrimination," May 11, 1994, (Washington: GPO, 1994), 3.

The hoary mantra of liberal reformers, "equal access," was not designed to mean equal outcomes. Legislation passed during the Civil Rights movement, historian Enrico Beltramini insists, was "never intended to provide equality as a result, or to grant credit to all applicants."[164] Equal access, in other words, does not mean that everyone should be able to obtain loans or insurance on exactly the same terms; it means equal outcomes *holding objective variables constant*. If A and B have nearly identical incomes, credit histories, down payments, and so forth, they should be able to borrow on nearly identical terms. If B has to pay a palpably higher interest rate or cannot obtain a loan at all, s/he is being discriminated against for some reason, probably because of

163 Chiappori and Gollier, "Introduction"; Michael Faure and Ton Hartlief, *Insurance and Expanding Systemic Risks*, (OECD Policy Issues in Insurance No. 5, 2003); Ernest Fisher and Chester Rapkin, *The Mutual Mortgage Insurance Fund: A Study of the Adequacy of Its Reserves and Resources*, (New York: Columbia University Press, 1956); Moss, *When All Else Fails*; Stiglitz 1993; Michael Eric Dyson, *Come Hell or High Water: Hurricane Katrina and the Color of Disaster*, (New York: Basic Civitas, 2007).

164 Enrico Beltramini, "Consumer Credit as a Civil Right in the United States, 1968–1976," in *The Cultural History of Money and Credit: A Global Perspective*, ed. Chia Yin Jus, Thomas Luckett, and Erika Vause (New York: Lexington Books, 2016), 81.

her race, ethnicity, socioeconomic status, or gender. That outcome is immoral, and illegal, but difficult to establish statistically.

U.S. regulators traditionally did not respond to financial discrimination by punishing the putative discriminator. Rather, they encouraged groups that felt they did not have equal access to credit, insurance, and other financial services to form and operate their own financial institutions. Most of the time, that entailed lowering barriers to entry for companies that will not discriminate against specific groups because they are owned and run by members of said group. With such a policy, Big Bank will still discriminate against B in favor of A, but that does not matter, to B or the economy, if B can secure a loan like A's from Little Bank because B can then pursue an education or buy a car, home, or business on the same terms as A.

Encouraging entry was a shrewd move because it was the lowest cost method of providing equal access to the most people possible. Beginning in the 1990s, however, policymakers took a different tack. In an effort to ensure that everyone could achieve the "American Dream" without attempting politically fraught reforms to reduce unemployment, underemployment, and the other root causes of income disparities, policymakers opened up access to credit for people who traditionally, and for rational reasons, could only borrow small sums for short periods, if they could borrow at all. To get the banks on board, regulators threatened sanctions while simultaneously helping lenders to relax their credit standards. The result was dystopian: financial predation on a scale so massive that it almost brought down the global economy. Many financial firms failed and many reforms were undertaken in the wake of the crisis but predatory practices survived. A recent NBER study, for example, shows that female and low-income borrowers are more likely to be "steered" to mortgages with higher interest rates or more onerous terms like negative amortization or prepayment penalties.[165]

---

165 Robert Wagmiller, "Debt and Assets Among Low-Income Families," (National Center for Children in Poverty, October 2003); Hyman, *Debtor Nation*, 283–85; Sumit Agarwal, Gene Amromin, Itzhak Ben-David, "Loan Product Steering in Mortgage Markets," NBER Working Paper No. w22696 (September 2016).

The details of discrimination varied over time and place as well as the specific attributes of the loan or insurance applicant. (Wealthy, single white women, for example, enjoyed access to the financial system almost on a par with white men while poor, married women of color sometimes found it difficult even to pawn personal items because pawn shop operators presumed the items had been stolen.) Both law and custom commanded those proscriptions, which changed only slowly until the 1960s and 1970s, when various pieces of legislation removed the legal basis for outright discrimination and basically made access to credit a civil right in the United States.[166] Financial institutions, however, remained the final arbiters of with whom they would, or would not, do business.

Perhaps the biggest challenge to the right of financial institutions to choose their own customers was the Community Reinvestment Act of 1977 (CRA), which mandated that government-insured banks (i.e., nearly all depository institutions) take affirmative steps to provide mortgage loans throughout their respective areas of operation, even poor ones.[167] Most economists, including Andrew Brimmer, disliked the act. An African-American governor on the board of the Federal Reserve, Brimmer thought that a "one-to-one ratio" between savings and investment "applied across the board" would "greatly" damage "if not" destroy "the efficiency of our machinery for mobilizing and channeling funds."[168]

Pragmatic bankers, however, suffered CRA's passage because it was, initially, toothless. When William Jefferson Clinton assumed the presidency in early 1993, however, most policymakers, undoubtedly influenced by journalist stories like the "Color of Money" series in the *Atlanta Journal/Constitution* and a *Boston Globe* exposé (both from 1988), were convinced that African-Americans and other "minorities," including women and the poor, still faced discrimination in the nation's financial

---

166 Beltramini, "Consumer Credit," 81–94.

167 Stephen Ross and John Yinger, *The Color of Credit: Mortgage Discrimination, Research Methodology, and Fair-Lending Enforcement* (Cambridge: The MIT Press, 2002), 34.

168 Andrew F. Brimmer, "Financial Institutions and Urban Rehabilitation," Speech by Member of the Federal Reserve System's Board of Governors, September 22, 1967, 17.

markets and intermediaries. Some academics were not so sure because discrimination was difficult to detect as it had evolved to be much more subtle than outright Jim Crow-style exclusion. Moreover, direct tests of lender and insurer conduct towards legally protected groups proved costly to conduct and difficult to interpret.[169]

Perhaps, skeptics argued, financial intermediaries turned away members of X not out of bigotry but because the rejected applicants were, objectively speaking, not good risks. Teasing valid results from statistical tests of datasets is difficult due to problems like omitted variables, sample bias, endogeneity, and other niceties best left to others to explain in detail. Early studies, for example, failed to consider applicants' credit history, i.e., how their credit scores changed over time, and even the revised Boston Fed Study of 1996 may have missed important variables like the verifiability of information provided on loan applications[170] and individual financial fragility created, as one careful *ProPublica* study put it, by "generations of discrimination [that] have left black families with grossly fewer resources to draw on when they come under financial pressure."[171]

For decades, uncertainty about the extent of financial discrimination handcuffed policymakers not eager to tamper with "market forces" or arouse the ire of Wall Street. The Clinton administration, which wanted to increase the homeownership rate out of a genuine (but largely mistaken) notion that homeowners are better for communities and society in general than renters. The homeownership rate, though, had fallen a few points from its 1980 high of almost 66 percent, so the administration hit upon a compromise with devastating unintended consequences. It gave the CRA some teeth by preventing banks with low CRA compliance scores from merging. That was a major penalty by 1993 because deregulation of branching restrictions had set off a major merger wave.[172] The

---

169 Immergluck, *Credit to the Community*, 168–69.

170 Ross and Yinger, *Color of Credit*, 44, 80–99, 108–122.

171 Paul Kiel and Annie Waldman, "The Color of Debt: How Collection Suits Squeeze Black Neighborhoods," *ProPublica*, 8 October 2015.

172 Immergluck, *Credit to the Community*, 4, 21; Robert Hetzel, *The Great Recession: Market Failure or Policy Failure?* (New York: Cambridge University Press, 2012), 170–71; John Spiegel,

change allowed community interest groups like ACORN (Association of
Community Organizations for Reform Now) to "work with" (or "black-
mail" depending on one's ideological perspective) banks infected with
the "urge to merge" to increase lending in poorer areas.[173] The power of
such groups was so pervasive that CRA has been called a leading example
of "regulation from below."[174] Starting in 1999, good CRA ratings were
also necessary for banks that desired to form financial holding companies
under the Gramm-Leach-Bliley Act, which many did in order to par-
ticipate in a wider variety of financial markets. That, perversely, allowed
banks to reduce mortgage lending, opening the door to a large influx of
non-depository mortgage lenders not subject to the CRA.[175]

At the same time, the government undertook several policy reforms
that made it easier for banks to lend to higher risk borrowers. First, it
pushed its government sponsored enterprises (GSEs) — Fannie Mae and
Freddie Mac — to make housing more affordable. In March 1994, the
GSEs responded by promising $1 trillion to enable 10 million low income
earners and minorities to purchase their own homes. The GSEs borrowed the money for the risky endeavor under an implicit government
guarantee of their debt. In 1995, HUD (the department of Housing and
Urban Development) mandated that 42 percent of all mortgages traded
by Fannie and Freddie had to go to households with "low and moderate income" and 14 percent to families with "very low income." With
the government footing the risk, Fannie and Freddie actually exceeded
their quotas, which the government increased to 50 and 20 percent,
respectively, in 1999. The following year, Fannie pledged $2 trillion to
support low income borrowers. At the same time, the FHA also lowered

Alan Gart, and Steven Gart, *Banking Redefined: How Superregional Powerhouses Are Reshaping Financial Services*, (Chicago: Irwin Professional Publishing, 1996).

173 Alexandra Lajoux and Dennis J. Roberts, *The Art of Bank M&A: Buying, Selling, Merg-ing, and Investing in Regulated Depository Institutions in the New Environment*, (New York: McGraw Hill, 2014), 34.

174 Immergluck, *Credit to the Community*, 14, 167.

175 Lajoux and Roberts, *The Art of Bank M&A*, 48–49, 54; Ross and Yinger, *Color of Credit*, 19, 24, 34; Immergluck, *Credit to the Community*, 32, 247.

its standards by reducing the minimum down payment to just 3 percent while raising the maximum loan to $235,000.[176]

To originate such loans, however, mortgage companies like Countrywide had to "stretch the rules a bit." Many good bankers did not like the new order of things and had always questioned government-led lending liberalization. In the 1960s, for example, South Dakota banker Art Dahl complained about the liberalization of FHA and GI loan terms: "We feel perhaps they are too liberal. Loans have been made for as long as thirty-five years with a small down payment."[177] But Dahl also noted significant competitive pressures to conform, as bankers always did whenever rules were relaxed. The directors of the Community Savings Bank in Rochester, New York, for example, noted in a 1951 meeting that it had to start making 20-year loans (up from 15) under the new, less stringent Regulation X mortgage rules or "a number of our builders, who have been supplying us with a substantial volume of new mortgages, would take their business to other institutions."[178]

When regulators like the Boston Fed signaled that lending guidelines should be loosened, originators became increasingly bold and competitive pressures forced others to follow. Personal interviews of borrowers went the way of the dinosaurs, as did checks on property appraisals. Poor credit histories were just that, history, under new regulatory guidelines that demanded "flexibility." Starting in the mid-1990s, subprime mortgages, as mortgage loans to high-risk borrowers came to be known, became increasingly easy to obtain. By the first decade of the new millennium, NINJA (no income, no job or assets) and liar's (no documentation) loans became commonplace. In the end, the definition of financial discrimination devolved from *unwarranted* unequal access to loans into banks refus-

---

176 Johan Norberg, *Financial Fiasco: How America's Infatuation with Homeownership and Easy Money Created the Economic Crisis,* (Washington, DC: Cato Institute, 2009), 26–35.

177 Dahl, *Banker Dahl,* 243.

178 Regular Board Meeting, September 12, 1951, Agendas/Minutes: Board Meetings, Rush Rhees Library.

ing "loans to people they considered poor credit risks," the very definition of prudent banking![179]

Under the new policies promulgated by the Clinton and Bush II administrations, an unknown amount of mortgage lending discrimination had essentially morphed into financial predation on a scale that could not be precisely measured but was certainly massive. (The best that can be said is that not all subprime mortgages are predatory, but almost all predatory loans are subprime.) Redlining was reversed as people who traditionally could not obtain credit because of where they lived were suddenly bombarded with loan offers, very expensive offers that threatened the equity stakes they had already built in their homes.[180]

A similar process took place in consumer debt, with new computerized risk assessment technologies and less stringent regulations combining to render the issuance of credit cards to the working poor increasingly attractive. In 1989, 18 percent of families in the bottom quintile and 35 percent of families in the second lowest quintile of the national income distribution held at least one credit card. By finding ways to lend to those with thin or bad, but likely to improve, credit histories, card issuers by 2001 extended credit to 31 and 45 percent of families in the bottom two income quintiles, respectively.[181]

Predatory lending is not new, but pressures to lend to minorities and changes in regulations and in the ownership structure of important financial intermediaries (especially investment banks, which took on more risks after changing from partnerships to publicly owned joint stock corporations) created new incentives for engaging in it. Community activists and scholars saw the rise of predatory lending but moved against it

---

179 Norberg, *Financial Fiasco*, 29–32; Immergluck, *Credit to the Community*, 110–11; Jacqueline Jones, *A Dreadful Deceit: The Myth of Race from the Colonial Era to Obama's America*, (New York: Basic Books, 2013), 286.

180 Ross and Yinger, *Color of Credit*, 21; Gregory Squires, "The New Redlining," in *Why the Poor Pay More: How to Stop Predatory Lending*, ed. Gregory D. Squires (Westport, Conn.: Praeger, 2004), 2.

181 Hyman, *Debtor Nation*, 270–75; Christian E. Weller, "Pushing the Limit: Credit Card Debt Burdens American Families," (Washington, D.C.: Center for American Progress, 2006), 2–3.

laconically, as many at first saw the rise of subprime lending as a way of increasing access to mortgages. Meanwhile, regulators essentially taught bankers that fines for predatory lending would be less than the profits they could make. Along with the stick represented by the CRA, bankers also saw the carrot of more business and, eventually, the carrot cake of massive bonuses.[182]

Bankers know that more reward means more risk but they convinced themselves that "this time is different;" that they could make many lucrative loans to shaky borrowers safely. The key was "securitization," the bundling of many risky mortgages into one ostensibly safe one. Some predictable, relatively low percentage of subprime mortgages would default but no one could predict which specific ones. By putting them all together (into mortgage-backed securities, or MBS, and collateralized debt obligations, or CDOs, and similar instruments), the idiosyncratic risk inherent in each mortgage was essentially rubbed out by the law of large numbers and "diversification." For a fee, rating agencies happily applied AAA ratings to such issues, allowing them to be sold to even the most conservative institutional investors. When one of the rating agencies, Fitch, essentially declared "shenanigans" on an unusually risky type of security called a CPDO (constant proportion debt obligation), the issuers simply shopped it to Moody's and S&P instead.[183]

The new mortgage system functioned well as long as housing prices stayed buoyant, as many assumed they would. Some people, however, both inside and outside of the industry, were not so sure. A few in academe knew that six previous mortgage securitization schemes had blown up and many others were skeptical of the GSEs. One member of the Bush administration, Armando Falcon, Jr., raised alarms about the GSEs in

---

182 Charles R. Geisst, *The Last Partnerships: Insider the Great Wall Street Money Dynasties*, (New York: McGraw Hill, 2001); Keith Ernst, Deborah N. Goldstein, and Christopher A. Richardson, "Legal and Economic Inducements to Predatory Practices," in *Why the Poor Pay More: How to Stop Predatory Lending*, ed. Gregory D. Squires (Westport, Conn.: Praeger, 2004), 103–32; Ross and Yinger, *Color of Credit*, 26; Squires, "The New Redlining," 10–12.

183 Alexandre Linden, Stefan Bund, John Schiavetta, Jill Zelter, and Rachel Hardee, "First Generation CDPO: Case Study on Performance and Ratings," (April 28, 2007). http://www. defaultrisk.com/pp_crdrv141.htm. Accessed 17 May 2016; Norberg, *Financial Fiasco*, 60.

2003 but was immediately sacked by the new president, who wanted to
create an "ownership society." Falcon was brought back after accounting
scandals rocked the GSEs but the mortgage giants used a small portion
of their massive profits to successfully lobby against substantive reforms.
The ensuing battle, however, left them beholden to Democratic congress-
men who wanted even more loans for the poor, especially the poorest
of the poor. Eager to make up for profits lost during their accounting
scandals and with their implicit government subsidy fully intact, the GSEs
were happy to comply. Fannie CEO Daniel Mudd told his employees to
"get aggressive on risk-taking or get out of the company." Meanwhile,
Freddie CEO Richard Syron in effect told his company's chief risk officer
that Freddie "could no longer afford to say no to anybody."[184]

What Bush and other acolytes of the "ownership society" did not
grasp was that government policies, particularly the mortgage interest
deduction (without deductibility of interest paid on other types of debt
after 1986) and low interest rates, encouraged Americans to borrow to the
hilt rather than to accumulate equity in their homes. So consumers had a
big incentive to seek loans with minimal, or even negative, equity. Instead
of having to plop down 10 or 20 percent of the purchase price of a house,
homeowners were allowed to borrow 10 or 20 percent more than the
purchase price because, you know, "Murica."[185]

Some players in the financial system were not so taken by that
impeccable logic after they realized that subprime adjustable rate mortgages, low-rate mortgages designed for people who wanted to rapidly
"flip" homes in a rising market, were ticking time bombs once the bubble
in house prices stopped expanding. Those critics, however, had incentives
to keep their conclusions quiet so they could successfully short the market
(profit from the impending bust). And of course nobody listened to egg-
head professors, like New York University's Nouriel Roubini, who made

184 As quoted in Norberg, *Financial Fiasco*, 38–41.
185 Dickerson, *Homeownership*, 28, 51; Norberg, *Financial Fiasco*, 36–37.

it clear in a 2006 speech at the IMF (International Monetary Fund) that the sky was about to fall.[186]

Big banks and the GSEs ignored all the warnings because of their implicit government guarantees and their inadequate corporate governance. The former was called "Too Big to Fail" policy and it was basically a license to print money because it encouraged the biggest banks to take big gambles. The latter was due to the erosion of almost all the checks against arbitrary CEO power created by Thomas Willing, Robert Morris, and Alexander Hamilton when they designed America's first business corporations in the late eighteenth century. Most recently, CEOs had developed "poison pills" that prevented corporate raiders like KKR (Kohlberg Kravis Roberts & Co.) from taking over poorly run companies. Again all-powerful, CEOs and other top bank executives wrote themselves "heads I win, tails I win" contracts. If their banks performed well financially, according to their own books, for as little a period of time as 3 months, the executives took home enormous bonuses. If their banks were headed for a crash, they could jump out wearing a "golden parachute" that gave them more money than most Americans make over their entire lifetimes. Basically, if bankers took big risks that paid off, even for a short period of time, they became fabulously wealthy. If they took big risks that eventually turned sour, they became wealthy too. Few could avoid such temptation. Merrill Lynch CEO Stanley O'Neal, for example, walked away from the company that he helped to bankrupt with $161 million in his pocket.[187]

The doomsayers were proven right in 2007–9 as the housing market stalled, recession hit, unemployment increased, defaults soared, and the stock market lost about half its value. Scholars are pretty certain that the main causes of the subprime crisis and subsequent global recession were the federal government's aggressive homeownership policies, its TBTF policy, and weak corporate governance because other factors, including

---

186 Stephen Mihm, "Dr. Doom," *New York Times Magazine*, 15 August 2008.

187 Hetzel, *Great Recession*, 22, 150–57, 296, 300, 309; Robert E. Wright, *Corporation Nation*, (Philadelphia: University of Pennsylvania Press, 2014); George Baker and George D. Smith, *The New Financial Capitalists: Kohlberg Kravis Roberts and the Creation of Corporate Value*, (New York: Cambridge University Press, 1998); Norberg, *Financial Fiasco*, 76.

low interest rates, securitization, and weak regulatory supervision were present in earlier real estate bubbles of similar magnitude, including one in the 1920s, that did not lead to financial or economic meltdown. Moreover, scholars like Charles Calomiris and Edward J. Pinto have shown that federal policies greatly distorted housing and mortgage markets without increasing the homeownership rate.[188]

Due to such meddling, millions of Americans lost their homes and savings while a few thousand bank executives received taxpayer-funded bonuses. Subsequent reforms, including Dodd-Frank, initially did little to change the basic system of easy loans. Soon, however, bankers discovered the jumbo mortgage, the name for mortgages for more than $417,000. By 2016, jumbos had emerged as a gilt-edged (ultra-safe) type of mortgage and, unsurprisingly, very few went to African-Americans or members of other minority groups. Property-assessed clean energy (PACE) home improvement loans also surged to the fore because the courts consider them taxes (even though they are just loans securitized much like subprime mortgages were) and hence prior to mortgages in cases of default, delinquency, and bankruptcy. Untrained construction contractors often push the loans on old or unsuspecting customers, positioning them as a "government program" designed to make homes more energy efficient when in reality Wall Street investors own $3 billion in PACE-backed securities.[189]

At the same time, some middling banks, like Hudson City Savings Bank of New Jersey, even returned to practices reminiscent of redlining

---

188 Eugene White, "Lessons from the Great American Real Estate Boom and Bust of the 1920s," in *Housing and Mortgage Markets in Historical Perspective*, Eugene White, Kenneth Snowden, and Price Fishback, eds. (Chicago: University of Chicago Press, 2014), 115–160; Charles Calomiris, "An Economist's Case for GSE Reform," in *Serving Two Masters, Yet Out of Control*, Peter J. Wallison, ed. (Washington: AEI Press, 2001), 85–106; Edward J. Pinto, "Why the 20-Year Mortgage Is the Answer to the Housing Finance Mess," *American Banker* (5 Feb. 2016).

189 Viral Acharya and Thomas Cooley, *Regulating Wall Street: The Dodd-Frank Act and the New Architecture of Global Finance*, (New York: John Wiley & Sons, 2010); "Jumbo Loans Benefit Few Blacks, Hispanics," *Wall Street Journal*, 2 June 2016, A1, A10; Kirsten Grind, "New Loans, Same Old Dangers," *Wall Street Journal*, 11 January 2017.

while big banks drastically reduced their participation in the regular mortgage market, leaving more than half the field to smaller, less regulated, specialized mortgage lenders. But the latter have not taken up all the slack in large measure due to increased federal regulation of mortgage lenders, regulations so costly that they have dissuaded entry into the middle part of the market. Growing regulatory hurdles, for example, forced Sean Dobson, CEO of Amherst Holdings, out of the mortgage market and into the landlord game, where he rents property to middling folks with lower credit scores rather than lending to them. In other words, it appears that America currently has three financial systems, a predatory one for the poor and politically powerless, a stingy one for middle income folks with stellar credit, and a healthy one for the wealthy and (mostly) white.[190]

The saddest thing about the subprime fiasco is that, instead of endangering the world economy by lowering lending standards, policymakers could have followed the more difficult but more responsible path of self-help. Throughout American history, as we will see in the final chapter, groups that have been unable to obtain financing through existing institutions and markets have established their own, often with great success. Because laws cannot mandate outcomes, additional top-down attempts to control the financial system are unlikely, as explained in Chapter 7, to provide much in the way of benefits and could lead to another financial crisis like that experienced in 2008. No path will be perfect but some policies are clearly less fraught than others. It is time to put partisan views aside and support self-help. Americans did so for generations and their economy was the larger and stronger for it.

---

190 Rachel L. Swarns, "Biased Lending Evolves, and Blacks Face Trouble Getting Mortgages," *New York Times*, 30 October 2015; AnnaMaria Andriotis, "Banks Fall Back in Mortgage Lending," *Wall Street Journal*, 3 November 2016; Nick Timiraos, "Home Buyers Miss Out on Low-Cost Loans: Postcrisis Tightening Curbs Economy as it Hurts Those with Poor Credit," *Wall Street Journal*, 5 December 2016; Squires, "The New Redlining," 5–7.

CHAPTER THREE

Yet Enslaved: African-Americans Fight Jim Crow Finance

The legacy of racial discrimination and segregation is real, and the scars it has inflicted on all our citizens are deep and enduring. ... I am unalterably opposed to any kind of racial discrimination or segregation in whatever form it may appear. — Andrew F. Brimmer, "The Black Revolution and the Economic Future of Negroes in the United States," Speech by Member of the Federal Reserve System's Board of Governors, June 8, 1969, 3.

At a general level, the history of African-American interaction with the U.S. financial system follows the arc described in the introduction. First, they were excluded as slaves, largely excluded as quasi-slaves, and blatantly discriminated against as second-class citizens. After cultural, economic, legal, and political changes, discrimination became more subtle and difficult to measure. Finally, just when it appeared that government watchdogs were finally going to crack down, loans for African-Americans became easy to procure, far too easy. As a result, many blacks were caught up in the subprime mortgage debacle of 2007–9 and lost their

85

homes (and later their jobs) as a result. Since the end of the crisis in 2009, interest rates have been so low, and other problems so salient, that few have paid attention to questions of financial system access for African-Americans, or any other group for that matter, though discrimination and predation persist.

Like all surveys, however, the general story just related hides many important details about how slaves, free blacks, freedpersons, and African-Americans responded to financial exclusion and discrimination, gaining access here and there via sundry means. Detailed discussion of the most important of those mechanisms of resistance, the formation of black-owned financial institutions, will come in the final chapter, 8.

Slaves, Free Blacks, and Unfree Finance

There's discrimination, all right. There'll be discrimination as long as we live. — Audrey Olsen Faulkner, Marsel A. Heisel, Wendell Holbrook, and Shirley Geismar, When I Was Comin' Up: An Oral History of Aged Blacks (Hamden, Conn.: Archon Books, 1982), 59.

Since at least Roman times, slaves owned nothing in the eyes of the law. In 1812 in *Bynum v. Bostwick*, a South Carolina judge held that "by the civil law, slaves could not take property, by descent or purchase, and I apprehend this to be the law of this country."[191] In another case, a man took banknotes from a slave owned by another man and the court held that the taker had to make restitution, *to the slaveholder*. Plantation owners could and did grant slaves privileges, like access to garden plots, as they saw fit but the land, the slaves themselves, and anything the slaves possessed were, in the final analysis, the property of their respective masters. In most U.S. jurisdictions, slaves were forbidden to possess money

191 Jacob D. Wheeler, *A Practical Treatise on the Law of Slavery, Being a Compilation of all that Decisions Made on That Subject, in the Several Courts of the United States, and State Courts*, (Allan Pollock, Jr., 1837), 191.

or to exchange goods with anyone but their masters. Such rules were designed to keep slaves completely in thrall to their masters (and are still used by enslavers today).[192]

Some plantation owners paid their slaves bonuses in the form of book credit good only in the master's storehouse. This provided slaves with incentives to work harder without granting them access to the market economy. Many felt that was a necessary precaution because almost all slaves displayed some "hustle," some penchant for buying and selling, making and taking. Slave enterprise was so ubiquitous that numerous state and municipal laws were passed in an effort to suppress it. Some slave dealings undoubtedly were based in dire physical necessity but much of it was culturally ingrained. Stereotypes of African "savages" barely subsisting in their homeland to the contrary notwithstanding, most African slaves prior to their capture had lived in sophisticated market economies, replete with large flows of trade and a considerable division of labor.[193] They all knew how to barter and most easily came to the use of Euroamerican forms of cash, as evidenced by numerous court cases that unequivocally stated that such and such slave "went into his house, purchased liquor, drank it," and so forth.[194] Some slave narratives mention slaves buying consumer durables, like Bibles. Historical archeologists have also established that slaves stashed their earnings in walls, trunks,

---

192 William Goodell, *The American Slave Code in Theory and Practice*, (London: Clarke, Beeton, and Co., 1853), 74–89; Juliet E. K. Walker, *The History of Black Business in America: Capitalism, Race, Enterpreneurship*, Vol. 1, 2nd ed. (Chapel Hill: University of North Carolina Press, 2009), 36–38, 68; Wheeler, *A Practical Treatise on the Law of Slavery*, 438; Robert E. Wright, *The Poverty of Slavery: How Unfree Labor Pollutes the Economy*, (New York: Palgrave Macmillan, 2017).

193 Wheeler, *A Practical Treatise on the Law of Slavery*, 441; John Sibley Butler, *Entrepreneurship and Self-Help Among Black Americans: A Reconsideration of Race and Economics*, (Albany: State University of New York Press, 1991), 38–39; Rowena Olegario, *A Culture of Credit: Embedding Trust and Transparency in American Business*, (Cambridge: Harvard University Press, 2006), 112; Walker, *History of Black Business*, 1–21, 89–106.

194 Wheeler, *A Practical Treatise on the Law of Slavery*, 439.

and other caches. A few slaves amassed enough coins to become money-lenders, on a small scale of course.[195]

Despite tremendous obstacles, a tiny minority of slaves managed to become successful entrepreneurs but of course they were credit-constrained because technically they owned nothing and could not enter into contracts. Still, a few managed to establish savings bank accounts, as slave ironworker Sam Williams did. Maroons and other slaves living as free men were not considered good credit risks either as their *de facto* freedom was tenuous. Even *de jure* free blacks, we will see, had difficulty obtaining credit in most circumstances.[196]

Most slaves were included in the financial system only as objects, not as customers. Most notoriously, slaves could be mortgaged, or otherwise collateralized to secure loans, and also insured, not like people, but like livestock. "Oppression," Alexis de Tocqueville rightly lamented, "has with one blow taken from the descendants of the Africans almost all the privileges of humanity!"[197]

Richard Kilbourne was the first scholar to clearly elucidate the crucial role that slaves played as collateral in the planter economy, and his work, though supplemented with new details, has yet to be superseded. Basically, plantation owners purchased inputs (seeds, slaves) and consumer goods on credit from factors who, in turn, marketed the planters' crops (typically cotton but also other cash crops like tobacco). If yields or prices were below expectations, as one of them often was, planters ended up in debt to the factors because their purchases, at inflated credit prices, exceeded their revenues. If yields or prices exceeded expectations for a number of years, as sometimes happened, planters also often went into debt to finance expansion (more land and/or slaves). Crop liens were

---

195 J. P. Clark, ed., *Interesting Account of Thomas Anderson, A Slave, Taken from His Own Lips*, (1854?), 6; Jonathan Levy, *Freaks of Fortune: The Emerging World of Capitalism and Risk in America*, (Cambridge: Harvard University Press, 2012), 121; Walker, *History of Black Business*, 113, 115.

196 Walker, *History of Black Business*, 67–69.

197 Alexis De Tocqueville, *Democracy in America*, trans. Harvey C. Mansfield and Delba Winthrop. (Chicago: University of Chicago Press, 2000), 304.

insufficient collateral for larger, longer-term debts so planters often had to post collateral. Land was often in the mix but slaves offered the ultimate collateral security because they were liquid assets; i.e., they could be quickly moved to the highest market and sold for cash. Factors often sold such collateralized debts to banks, which in turn financed their operations in part by selling bonds to foreign investors. In that way, slaves became part of a trans-Atlantic asset-backed securities (ABS) market.[198]

Historians have long known about the existence of insurance on slaves but only recently has Sharon Murphy delved into the business in sufficient detail to show that, although typically written by life insurance companies, slave insurance was more akin to livestock insurance than the life insurance policies bought by Euroamericans. Most importantly, any proceeds went to the slaveholder rather than to the deceased slave's family. In addition, payouts were tied to a percentage of the market price of slaves rather than the slave's individual economic value because moral hazard, the threat of the master killing a slave for the insurance payout, was thought to be very high. Numerous companies entered the business but those that did not specialize in underwriting slave risks typically suffered losses, probably due to adverse selection, although they insisted on medical screenings, monitored slaveholder treatment of slaves, risk-rated, required significant co-insurance, and took other precautions. The companies that profited from the business specialized in writing insurance on slaves. Had the Civil War not ended slavery, slave insurance likely would have grown as quickly as other forms of property insurance.[199]

The financial system's objectification of African-Americans was a function of their status as assets rather than their African-ness or color per

---

198 Richard Kilbourne, *Debt, Investment, Slaves: Credit Relations in East Feliciana Parish, Louisiana, 1825–1885*, (Tuscaloosa: University of Alabama Press, 1995); Richard Kilbourne, *Slave Agriculture and Financial Markets in Antebellum America: The Bank of the United States in Mississippi, 1831–1852*, (London: Routledge, 2006).

199 Cheryl Chen and Gary Simon, "Actuarial Issues in Insurance on Slaves in the United States South," *The Journal of African American History* 89, no. 4 (2004): 348–57; Kenneth J. Meier, *The Political Economy of Regulation: The Case of Insurance*, (Albany: State University of New York Press, 1988); Sharon Ann Murphy, *Investing in Life: Insurance in Antebellum America*, (Baltimore: Johns Hopkins University Press, 2010).

se. Slaves who were American Indian could also be mortgaged, for example, while free blacks could not be. Similarly, the lives of free blacks could be insured by whites with an economic interest in them (as in what is today called "key person" insurance) but free blacks could not be insured like livestock. Free blacks could also insure themselves, though usually at a higher premium than Euroamericans, *ceteris paribus*.[200]

Free blacks with little or no collateral found it difficult to raise money to start or extend their businesses but that was, and pretty much remains, true of all poor persons.[201] In 1788, however, race was a factor according to J. P. Brissot de Warville, who argued that "those Negroes who keep shops live moderately, and never augment their business beyond a certain point. The reason is obvious: the whites ... like not to give them credit to enable them to undertake any extensive commerce."[202]

How many requests for money were rejected solely because of race is, however, impossible to know as lender records from the period, even bank records, generally do not discuss the rationale for loan decisions in much detail. Some early bankers expressed very liberal or enlightened views against discrimination. The "Philosophical Banker" Alexander Bryan Johnson, for example, told John Adams, his father-in-law and second president of the United States, that he disdained prejudices based on race, class, religion, or even nativity. But what really mattered, of course, was actions, not words.[203]

It is clear that many blacks were trusted for small sums. We know that because imprisonment for debt did not disappear entirely until the 1850s and poor people, a disproportionate number of them black, were thrown into debtors' prison in Baltimore in the 1820s and 1830s. In 1831,

---

200 Alan Gallay, *The Indian Slave Trade: The Rise of English Empire in the American South, 1670–1717*, (New Haven: Yale University Press, 2002), 247.

201 Butler, *Entrepreneurship and Self-Help*, 40.

202 As quoted in Walker, *History of Black Business*, 41. For a similar sentiment employing somewhat different language, see Dan Immergluck, *Credit to the Community: Community Reinvestment and Fair Lending Policy in the United States*, (New York: M. E. Sharpe, 2004), 52.

203 Charles L. Todd and Robert Sonkin, *Alexander Bryan Johnson: Philosophical Banker*, (Syracuse: Syracuse University Press, 1977), 120.

almost 1,000 were incarcerated there, 53 of them for owing less than $1. Half owed less than $10. The proportion of free blacks imprisoned for debt in Baltimore and Washington was about 1.5 times their proportion of the entire population. That may have been because they had a more difficult time repaying but that raises the question of why creditors lent them money or goods in the first place. The discrepancy may also have arisen because creditors were less hesitant to throw black debtors into prison.[204]

In any event, at some point on the income scale early banks (and insurers) ceased excluding African-Americans. We know from tax records that some free blacks owned real and personal property. In 1779, for example, John of Lancaster, Pennsylvania, "a negro," owned 8 acres of land and a horse. Over time, free blacks came to own considerable amounts of property in aggregate. In New Orleans in 1836, for example, 855 free blacks owned property (including slaves) assessed at $2.5 million. In 1853, they owned real estate in the New York City area worth over $1.1 million.[205] Presumably, such people may have come to own such assets through gift or savings rather than borrowing, but good collateral was almost certainly colorblind.[206]

Another key determinant of access was the ownership of deposit accounts and (especially bank) stock as owners of both classes of assets tended to have more access to bank loans. In many southern states, free blacks were prohibited from owning corporate shares but where they were not, as in Pennsylvania, some of them, like Robert Purvis of Byberry (near Philadelphia), owned shares in financial and non-financial

---

204 Hillel Black, *Buy Now, Pay Later,* (New York: William Morrow and Company, 1961), 60; Seth Rockman, *Scraping By: Wage Labor, Slavery, and Survival in Early Baltimore,* (Baltimore: Johns Hopkins University Press, 2009), 185–86; Leonard P. Curry, *The Free Black in Urban America, 1800–1850: The Shadow of the Dream,* (Chicago: University of Chicago Press, 1981), 116–17.

205 Harris, *Negro as Capitalist,* 6–8.

206 Abram L. Harris, *The Negro as Capitalist: A Study of Banking and Business Among American Negroes,* (New York: American Academy of Political and Social Science, 1936), 5. Walker, *History of Black Business,* 46–56, 62–65.

corporations.[207] Samuel Wilcox of Cincinnati owned so many shares in
the Kentucky Trust Company that he was "often invited over to meet
the Directors."[208] And of course many blacks were depositors, especially
in savings banks. By the late 1850s, free blacks had over $60,000 deposited
with banks in New York City and almost $30,000 in Philadelphia banks. In
Maryland, by contrast, an 1852 law made it illegal for blacks to own bank
deposits.[209]

A few free blacks had commercial bank accounts. Moses Johnson
of Philadelphia, for example, had an account with the Bank of North
America as early as 1790. Free blacks even established a few business corporations of their own, including the Iron Chest Company of Cincinnati,
which built three brick business buildings that it rented to white tenants.
African-Americans first discovered the strengths of the corporate form by
chartering non-profits, especially churches, beginning with St. Thomas
Church and Bethel Church in Pennsylvania in 1796.[210]

Most free black businesses, however, were modest affairs that took
the form of proprietorships and partnerships. Most businesses owned by
free blacks, including leased farms and ranches, retail groceries and dry
goods stores, restaurants, and personal services providers (barbers, cater-
ers, tailors, washers, etc.) required little start-up capital. About 5,000 free
blacks ran businesses by 1860 but a dearth of capital, legal restrictions, low
wages, and mob violence prevented most of them from gaining much
traction economically.[211]

---

207 Walker, *History of Black Business*, 113, 117; Immergluck, *Credit to the Community*, 54;
Harris, *Negro as Capitalist*, 8.

208 Walker, *History of Black Business*, 112–13.

209 Harris, *Negro as Capitalist*, 23; Arnett G. Lindsay, "The Negro in Banking," *Journal of
Negro History* 14, 2 (April 1929), 158–59; Immergluck, *Credit to the Community*, 53.

210 Walker, *History of Black Business*, 112–13; Robert E. Wright, "Banking and Politics in
New York, 1784–1829," (Ph.D. Diss., SUNY Buffalo, 1997), 696; Harris, *Negro as Capitalist*,
14; Sarah Barringer Gordon, "The African Supplement: Religion, Race, and Corporate Law in
Early National America," *William and Mary Quarterly* 72, 3 (July 2015), 399, 403.

211 Walker, *History of Black Business*, 42, 109; Harris, *Negro as Capitalist*, 10–13, 24; Olegario,
Culture of Credit, 113.

A few free blacks, however, managed to become rich despite the obstacles. After they became rich, the handful of wealthy free blacks sprinkled across antebellum America found so little difficulty raising cash that they often became lenders themselves. Such men included James Forten, a wealthy sailmaker based in Philadelphia, and lumber merchant Stephen Smith, who was worth $500,000 in 1864 when $100,000 was enough to qualify somebody as wealthy. Smith, the wealthiest free black in the North, even sat on the board of directors of the Columbia Bank in the 1830s. He owned more stock in the company than anyone else but he was not allowed to become its president.[212]

Obtaining fire insurance was also possible for antebellum black businessmen. Ex-slave Henry Boyd insured the Cincinnati factory in which he, and the 25 to 50 workers in his employ, manufactured his famous Boyd Bedstead and other products, until, that is, the fourth fire set by jealous white arsonists made it impossible for any insurer to underwrite his property.[213]

Jeremiah G. Hamilton, the so-called Prince of Darkness, made a good living as a broker-dealer on Wall Street in the 1830s, partly, perhaps, because he was able to pass himself off as a dark-skinned Latino. Although he went bankrupt and likely was never a millionaire, as some claimed, Hamilton was able to live out his life in some comfort. In the 1850s, another African-American broker applied for, but was denied, a seat on the New York Stock Exchange. By the time the Civil War erupted, several black capitalists were in business, a few with rave credit remarks in their R. G. Dun files.[214]

In 1830, some 3,777 African-Americans in the United States owned slaves. Many of those owners were, however, merely nominal as they were spouses and parents who bought loved ones to free them from

---

212 Walker, *History of Black Business*, 41, 113; Lindsay, "The Negro in Banking," 157; Butler, *Entrepreneurship and Self-Help*, 39.

213 Butler, *Entrepreneurship and Self-Help*, 43.

214 Shane White, *Prince of Darkness: The Untold Story of Jeremiah G. Hamilton, Wall Street's First Black Millionaire*, (New York: St. Martin's Press, 2015); Butler, *Entrepreneurship and Self-Help*, 126; Walker, *History of Black Business*, 108–63.

white masters. Some, however, were free people of color who amassed considerable fortunes, including slaves who they worked on plantations and used to finance their operations, just as Euroamerican slaveholders did. Jean Baptiste Meullion, for example, secured bank loans collateralized by his slaves.[215]

Unlike Euroamerican planters, free black slaveholders in many southern states were forbidden from diversifying into bank or other corporate stock so they often acted as private bankers themselves, taking deposits from the poor and lending to middling businessmen. Thomy Lafon, a dry goods merchant in New Orleans, for example, loaned money and died worth over $400,000. Cyprian Ricaud, another wealthy black in Louisiana, was said to have done a profitable real estate and brokerage business. By 1850, at least 8 mulattoes were in the brokerage business in the Big Easy. Another black slaveholder, John C. Stanley of Berne, North Carolina, made a small fortune discounting notes, as did Joseph Cassey of Philadelphia.[216]

Overall, though, it was difficult for free blacks to get past the intense racism of the antebellum period, which was often quite violent. In 1824, for example, fifty-plus white Rhode Islanders burned and dismantled the most important buildings in the Hard Scrabble section of Providence. Far from suffering for their crimes, the perpetrators were lauded by local elites who saw to it that the ringleaders were slapped on the wrist or not even brought to trial at all.[217]

More subtle forms of racism were also pervasive. In cities throughout America, free blacks were, in the words of antebellum journalist George G. Foster, "crammed into lofts, garrets and cellars, in blind alleys and narrow courts."[218] Blacks who made large bank deposits were often assumed to be criminals and, with rare exceptions, banks only hired

---

215 Harris, *Negro as Capitalist*, 4; Walker, *History of Black Business*, 56–62, 117.

216 Butler, *Entrepreneurship and Self-Help*, 41; Walker, *History of Black Business*, 113; Lindsay, "The Negro in Banking," 156–57.

217 Jacqueline Jones, *A Dreadful Deceit: The Myth of Race from the Colonial Era to Obama's America*, (New York: Basic Books, 2013), 98–99.

218 As quoted in Curry, *The Free Black*, 49.

African-Americans to clean offices, move around heavy boxes of coins, or complete other menial chores.[219] John Malvin, a free black shipper on the Great Lakes, "found every door was closed against the colored man in a free state, excepting the jails and penitentiaries."[220] One joke, though, suggested that free blacks could be at least as financially sophisticated as "white trash." In it, a free black took a hog on credit by leaving half the hog with the rube of a seller "as security."[221]

The Jim Crow Experience

White folks don't give you but something they don't want themselves.
— *Audrey Olsen Faulkner, Marsel A. Heisel, Wendell Holbrook, and Shirley Geismar, When I was Comin' Up: An Oral History of Aged Blacks (Hamden, Conn.: Archon Books, 1982), 23.*

Whites justified the Jim Crow regime of racial segregation and oppression in much the same way that they had justified slavery, with supposed lessons from history, religion, and pseudo-science. By the early twentieth century, pseudo-scientific "evidence" for African-American racial inferiority abounded. It was all bunk, of course, but it was more convincing bunk than antebellum pseudo-scientific concepts like "Drapetomania," a fictional disease that induced African-Americans to run away from their masters, or "Dysaethesia Aethiopica," a malady that allegedly induced free blacks and slaves allowed too much freedom to behave in a listless, thoughtless, and destructive manner. Particularly damaging were the claims of Social Darwinists and racist anthropometrists. The latter claimed that Africans' brains were smaller and smoother (i.e., less surface area and hence less processing power) than the brains of Euroamericans while the former justified oppressive policies on the grounds that African-Americans were doomed to extinction in the Darwinian struggle for

219 Lindsay, "The Negro in Banking," 158; Wright, "Banking and Politics," 697–98.

220 As quoted in Walker, *History of Black Business*, 109.

221 Wright, "Banking and Politics," 697.

existence. If any doubt remained, early IQ tests demonstrated the mental (and hence cultural, economic, and moral) superiority of northern Europeans over the allegedly lesser races, with Africans and aboriginals at the bottom of the rankings.[222]

Considered infants or even members of an inferior species by many white Southerners, many freedpersons after the Civil War fell victim to new systems of bondage and exploitation, some arguably worse than slavery itself because they did not include the same inherent incentives to protect African-Americans that slavery had. The convict labor system was arguably the worst of these new systems. Some who fell into its maw were violent criminals but many victims simply did not have a job or were insufficiently respectful towards whites. Although technically full citizens, unlike the chattel slaves they replaced, almost all were excluded from the financial system by virtue of being convict laborers. Carrie Massie, who went into prison as an adolescent and was impregnated by white guards at least four times before she died at age 26, from complications during childbirth, was obviously not an applicant for a bank loan. Most of the convicts were imprisoned, in fact, because they could not borrow enough money to cover fines and court costs.[223]

Even newfound freedoms turned into curses for many freedpersons. Jane Simpson, for example, managed to amass "$4,000 in de bank at Mound Bayou, Mississippi. De bank went down," though, and Simpson had "been a beggar ever since. Never did get one penny of dat money."[224] Similarly, Abe Whitess of Alabama lost $658.05 that he had stashed in a bank that went bust. Other African-Americans did not lose their life

---

222 I. A. Newby, *Jim Crow's Defense: Anti-Negro Thought in America, 1900–1930*, (Baton Rouge: Louisiana State University Press, 1965).

223 Talitha LeFlouria, *Chained in Silence: Black Women and Convict Labor in the New South*, (Chapel Hill: University of North Carolina Press, 2015), 47, 103; Emmett J. Scott, *Negro Migration During the War* (New York: Oxford University Press, 1920), 19–22; Douglas A. Blackmon, *Slavery by Another Name: The Re-Enslavement of Black Americans from the Civil War to World War II*, (New York: Anchor Books, 2008); Wright, *Poverty of Slavery*.

224 Federal Writers' Project, *Slave Narratives: A Folk History of Slavery in the United States From Interviews with Former Slaves, Vol. X Missouri Narratives*, (Washington: Work Projects Administration, 1941), 245.

savings in bank failures but discovered that white-owned savings banks, like one in Massingford, Virginia, violated their privacy by providing information on their financial status to nosey, and potentially violently jealous, white neighbors.[225]

As in the antebellum period, postbellum African-Americans rarely found employment in white banks, except as menial laborers. Charlie Richardson, for example, fired the boiler for the First National Bank of Webb City, Missouri, in the winter.[226]

But the postbellum period was not all negative. Black homeowner-ship rates trebled from just 8 percent in 1870 (up slightly from 7.5% of free blacks in 1850) to 24 percent by 1910. Most of those purchases, apparently, were of modest farmsteads from accumulated cash savings. Of course the national average hid pockets where African-Americans found it more dif-ficult to save, borrow, or buy. In the Delta, for example, only 6 percent of African-American farmers owned land in 1900.[227]

African-Americans responded to Jim Crow segregation laws, lynch-ings, voting restrictions, and other indignities by migrating north as soon as the Great War and immigration restrictions raised relative wages and living standards in the north's major industrial centers. In just three years, 1916–1919, some 400,000 African-Americans moved north, spurring stud-ies by the federal government and the Carnegie Endowment for Inter-national Peace, a major think tank. The diaspora, which had begun in a small way after the Civil War, continued until the 1960s and was spurred, at the margin, by adverse credit conditions in the South.[228]

225 Federal Writers' Project, *Slave Narratives: A Folk History of Slavery in the United States From Interviews with Former Slaves, Vol. I Alabama Narratives,* (Washington: Work Projects Administration, 1941), 291; Lindsay, "The Negro in Banking," 173.

226 Federal Writers' Project, *Slave Narratives, Vol. X Missouri,* 227.

227 Curry, *The Free Black,* 37–48, 245–71; William J. Collins and Robert A. Margo, "Race and Home Ownership from the End of the Civil War to the Present," *American Economic Review* 101, no. 3 (May 2011), 356–57; Jones, *Dreadful Deceit,* 215.

228 Scott, *Negro Migration,* 3, 6, 13–14; R. H. Leavell, T. R. Snavely, T. J. Woofter, Jr., W. T. B. Williams, and Francis D. Tyson, *Negro Migration in 1916–17,* (Washington: U.S. Depart-ment of Labor, 1917), 11–12, 101.

After the government emancipated their slaves, landowners needed laborers and preferred cheap, docile ones. The convict labor system could meet only a portion of the overall demand. After significant experimentation and adjustment, a system of seasonal debt peonage arose to fill the gap. Under that system, landowners controlled mostly black sharecroppers by systematically keeping them in debt through the manipulation or outright monopoly or monopsony control of provisions, credit, and cash crop prices. Through subtle adjustments in the cost of credit (like charging interest on the entire credit line instead of just that actually used), the prices of goods at their stores, and the prices paid for cotton and other produce, some landowners were able to keep croppers in their debt year after year and hence subject to stringent debtor laws. Many sharecroppers were able to avoid perpetual entrapment to the same landowner, as evidenced by their high rate of geographical mobility and the fact that trends in their indebtedness clearly correlated to the agricultural business cycle. In Georgia in the 1880s, for example, tenant indebtedness decreased in good years (good prices and harvests). Yet few were able to escape cropping and tenancy altogether and simply shuffled between landowners until they died or emigrated.[229]

Even if outright debt peonage was not prevalent, the crop mortgage system left croppers of all skin hues extremely vulnerable to bad weather, boll weevil infestations, weak demand, and other misfortunes. After just a bad season or two, the landowner's credit ran out, making it impossible for him or her to borrow enough to buy provisions or seed. Left without productive work, money, or credit, croppers first moved west, where wages and opportunities were initially greater, and then flooded into southern cities, where they also depressed wages. At that point, migration to the North was the only viable option unless employment could be found at large corporations, like the Newport News Shipbuilding & Dry Dock Company of Virginia. In the first decades of the twentieth century,

229 Leavell, et al, *Negro Migration*, 21, 37, 105; Matthew Jaremski and Price Fishback, "Did Inequality in Farm Sizes Lead to Suppression of Banking and Credit in the Late Nineteenth Century?" *Journal of Economic History* 78, 1 (2018): 165; Price Fishback, "Debt Peonage in Postbellum Georgia," *Explorations in Economic History* 26, 2 (April 1989): 220–28.

large numbers of the South's rural underclass, white and black, left to take up jobs in the urban North.[230]

Clearly, many of the migrants remained outside the financial system of the North. The poorest of the poor lamented needing money for clothes, school, and even food and shelter but never about borrowing to get by. Some mentioned keeping small caches of cash, as slaves had done. Others were clearly part of networks of kin and friends who lent small sums to each other for short periods (much as in white trash communities discussed in Chapter 4). One later bragged that her illiterate mother was nonetheless so numerate that she couldn't get cheated out of a penny. "She could get on the ground and make marks. She could count down to the last cent that anybody *owed her*, but she didn't know to write her name when she died."[231]

Other migrants, however, established savings accounts in their new communities to make it easier to save up and send remittances to loved ones still in the South. When remittances poured into the South from family members who had first ventured North, they often took the form of special-delivery letters (cash but also checks) and money orders, many issued by Western Union. Others financed their move North using the proceeds of life insurance policies stashed in the bank for safekeeping and to earn interest.[232]

As the use of financial instruments to make long distance remittances suggests, Jim Crow was never able to entirely exclude African-Americans from the financial system. Some freedmen were even able to obtain credit at white banks. Dave Harper recalled buying a team of horses on credit. He was down with typhoid when his promissory note came due but Dr. Sharp gave Harper a check for $90 to cover it. After Harper recovered he "sold a span of mules to Joe McCleary and put de check in de bank for Dr.

---

230 Scott, *Negro Migration*, 14–15; Leavell, et al, *Negro Migration*, 94.

231 Audrey Olsen Faulkner, Marsel A. Heisel, Wendell Holbrook, and Shirley Geismar, *When I was Comin' Up: An Oral History of Aged Blacks*, (Hamden, Conn.: Archon Books, 1982), 23–24, 35, 45.

232 Leavell, et al, *Negro Migration*, 101; Scott, *Negro Migration*, 124–25; Faulkner, Heisel, Holbrook, and Geismar, *Oral History of Aged Blacks*, 120, 165.

Sharp. Dat was to pay him for de note and taking care of me dat summer and fall."[233]

A black farmer in Chamberlain, North Carolina, was able to borrow on the installment plan in the early twentieth century. "Seymore Daniels was sellin' old furniture right there in town," he later related, "so I got me some old furniture and paid for it in a year's time." The local loan shark, however, would not lend him seed money even though "the white people there knowed we had land, knowed I had property," presumably because he was getting too big for his britches. Neighbor Bud Andrews, however, lent him $150 worth of fertilizer and seed and it proved sufficient to get "that crop out." Later, the black farmer was able to borrow $500 from a bank in the next county on the collateral of his "'bacca crop." A lady who owned a service station near his house would also lend him gasoline when necessary. That was important when the farmer was offered only 40 cents per pound for his best tobacco in Chamberlain but $1.02 in Seeman, with 35 cents for his junk tobacco.[234]

The farmer ended up losing his farm, however, when he stopped paying on a mortgage when the lender, a one Daniel Hopkins, died. He did not realize that he had to keep paying Hopkins's daughter and his lawyer, who was also the lawyer of the daughter, did not correct him or attempt to collect until it was too late. "White people," he lamented, "don't care for us, only our work. Some of them do like you enough, long as you stay in your place and don't try to get up there with them."[235]

Most pawnshops also opened their doors to freedpersons. An illustration from *Harper's Weekly* in 1867 showed women, black and white, as well as a poor white man waiting for the pawn shop to open.[236] "It made good business sense," historian Wendy Woloson noted, "to serve as many legitimate pawners as possible, regardless of gender, race, or

---

233 Federal Writers' Project, *Slave Narratives, Vol. X Missouri*, 138.

234 Faulkner, Heisel, Holbrook, and Geismar, *Oral History of Aged Blacks*, 90–95.

235 Faulkner, Heisel, Holbrook, and Geismar, *Oral History of Aged Blacks*, 94, 98, 101.

236 Wendy A. Woloson, *In Hock: Pawning in America from Independence through the Great Depression*, (Chicago: University of Chicago Press, 2009), 95.

ethnicity." Some African- American pawners were highly sought after because they repaid promptly. I. C. Bell, for example, was considered "the best pay on the book" of Steel City pawnshop. Similarly, African- American Frederick Hendrix was considered "good for $500."[237]

In 1903, the *Birmingham Ledger* claimed that "Alabama has negroes who own land and cattle ... and who can go to the bank and borrow money without security."[238] There is no reason to doubt that statement, which of course only meant that a few Alabama African-Americans had accumulated sufficient wealth and credit history to allow bankers to ignore the color of their skin. The rest could only borrow under unusual circumstances, as when William H. Holtzclaw, a Booker T. Washington acolyte and founder of the Utica Normal and Industrial Institute of Colored Young Men and Women, managed to borrow from Mississippi's Bank of Utica on the collateral of donor pledges.[239] If African-Americans could obtain loans at banks in the Deep South, they could also obtain them in the North where Jim Crow was supported mostly by custom rather than force of law. Many Northerners were racist and often made life "highly unpleasant" for blacks but they were less discriminatory in employment and lending than most Southerners.[240] In fact, some migrants to the North recalled so little difficulty obtaining credit that they considered getting "more than you can pay for" a potential problem.[241]

A very large, very detailed U.S. Bureau of Labor study completed in 1918 and 1919 revealed that 22 percent of African-American families and 25 percent of white families used merchant or store credit. African-Americans actually used the installment plan to buy durable goods more frequently than white families did, presumably because they were more cash constrained (i.e., needy) but equally as creditworthy because the

237 As quoted in Woloson, *In Hock*, 80.
238 As quoted in Blackmon, *Slavery by Another Name*, 168.
239 Jones, *Dreadful Deceit*, 222–223.
240 John Gunther, *Inside U.S.A.*, (New York: Harper Brothers, 1947), 283.
241 Faulkner, Heisel, Holbrook, and Geismar, *Oral History of Aged Blacks*, 199.

durable good served as collateral.[242] "Contract maturities were generally short and down payments were generally substantial," economist Martha Olney explained, "so repossession of the collateral in the event of default typically more than compensated the lender for the remaining installment payments."[243]

In 1915, a credit bureau handbook included "color" among creditworthiness characteristics.[244] Later "scientific" credit books, however, were more careful to stick to objective measures and stressed that every loan with a positive expected present value was a good loan. Unsurprisingly, then, a 1953 study found that blacks were not "shut out of the credit market" but had access to loans in both the north and south and at all the income levels at which credit was also available to whites. Any significant difference in loan application acceptance rates at lower incomes, some scholars suggested, was entirely rational, due to the simple fact "that low income Negroes are permanently low while Whites may often be low for temporary reasons."[245] In other words, lenders were not the problem, they just reflected reality because their continued profitability, nay their very existence, depended upon their rationality.[246]

Euroamerican life insurers, however, largely ignored the African-American market or tried to overcharge blacks by using the Glover Life Tables, which deliberately and grossly overstated the mortality rates of African-Americans by using cherry-picked data. In the 1960s, as black incomes finally rose to high enough levels to excite their interest, several major life insurers made a concerted effort to win the business of African-Americans. By 1965, blacks were more likely to be interviewed by life

---

242 Martha Olney, "When Your Word Is Not Enough: Race, Collateral, and Household Credit," *Journal of Economic History* 58, no. 2 (1998): 408–31.

243 Olney, "Race, Collateral, and Credit," 409.

244 Rowena Olegario, *The Engine of Enterprise: Credit in America*, (Cambridge: Harvard University Press, 2016), 119.

245 L. R. Klein and H. W. Mooney, "Negro-White Savings Differentials and the Consumption Function Problem," *Econometrica* 21, no. 3 (July 1953): 426, 453–55.

246 Davis McEntire, *Residence and Race: Final and Comprehensive Report to the Commission on Race and Housing*, (Berkeley: University of California Press, 1960), 225.

insurance agents than whites were and the length and quality of the conversations were not significantly different on average.[247]

A big problem, however, remained in the interlinked housing and mortgage markets. As the number of African-Americans moving north increased, whites began to resent them and their dampening effect on wages. Truth be told, many white Americans had never felt comfortable living near blacks. In the 1830s, neighborhood whites threatened to demolish a house rather than allow the landlord to rent it to a free black family. Where blacks were few, and shared some of the cultural traits of New Englanders, problems like that could be worked out. But as southern, more redneck-like African-Americans flooded into northern cities, invisible barriers soon prevented blacks from buying houses in some neighborhoods or even at all.[248] According to some members of the diaspora, Newark, New Jersey was at first a pleasant place to relocate to. Circa 1895, several later reported, "being black never affected us. We never noticed it. We never had any trouble with our neighbors. Most of them were white."[249] By 1920, Newark was home to over 300 black-owned restaurants, hairdressers, and professional service providers (doctors, lawyers, etc.)[250] and still, according to one of the residents there, "you could get a whole house for $12 a month. Two-family house. … You used to find a house anywhere you wanted up here on this hill without any trouble. The landlord see you standin' up, lookin' up there, he'd come down and they'd be fightin' over you."[251] After World War II, however,

---

247 Shennette Garrett-Scott, "To Do a Work that Would Be Very Far Reaching: Minnie Geddings Cox, the Mississippi Life Insurance Company, and the Challenges of Black Women's Business Leadership in the Early Twentieth-Century United States," *Enterprise & Society* 17, no. 3 (2016), 481; Andrew F. Brimmer, "Financial Institutions and Urban Rehabilitation," Speech by Member of the Federal Reserve System's Board of Governors, September 22, 1967, 1–2, 17; Starr Roxanne Hiltz, "Why Black Families Own Less Life Insurance," *Journal of Risk and Insurance* 38, no. 2 (1971): 228–30.

248 Curry, *The Free Black*, 49; Thomas Sowell, *Black Rednecks and White Liberals*, (San Francisco: Encounter Books, 2005), 47–48.

249 Faulkner, Heisel, Holbrook, and Geismar, *Oral History of Aged Blacks*, 185.

250 Faulkner, Heisel, Holbrook, and Geismar, *Oral History of Aged Blacks*, 215.

251 Faulkner, Heisel, Holbrook, and Geismar, *Oral History of Aged Blacks*, 164.

the market for houses seemed to disappear and "colored folks couldn't get no house to live in," only rooms to rent.[252]

Many African-Americans found themselves mired in a Catch-22 and self-fulfilling prophecy that limited their ability to profit from the owner-ship of real estate. In the decades before World War II, everyone, even Guardian Life Insurance Company of America, a mid-sized mutual life insurance corporation with a sterling reputation for probity and fairness, believed that blacks caused property values to decrease.[253] As Frederick H. Ecker, Chairman of Metropolitan Life Insurance Company, put it, "Negroes and whites don't mix."[254] According to Charles Abrams, "mort-gage-lenders were conditioned by the same attitudes on the racial issue as were the realtors and home-builders. Their mortgage officers read the same texts, swallowed the same myths."[255] So when in 1946 a small bank in Rochester, New York told its employees that "on appraisals of existing property the following factors will be taken into account – the neighbor-hood, the property itself, the borrower, and the mortgage pattern," "the neighborhood" meant not just the quality of the neighborhood and its location (vicinity to parks, schools, public transportation, etc.), it was code for its racial homogeneity.[256]

Convinced that their property values would plummet if many African-Americans moved in nearby, whites sold as quickly as they could as soon as the number of blacks reached a tipping point, econometrically estimated at about 30 to 40 percent in New York City in the 1930s.[257] Pan-

---

252 Faulkner, Heisel, Holbrook, and Geismar, *Oral History of Aged Blacks*, 31.

253 Robert E. Wright and George David Smith, *Mutually Beneficial: The Guardian and Life Insurance in America*, (New York: New York University Press, 2004), 320; Charles Abrams, *Forbidden Neighbors: A Study of Prejudice in Housing*, (New York: Harper & Brothers, 1955), 174; Immergluck, *Credit to the Community*, 91.

254 Abrams, *Forbidden Neighbors*, 174.

255 Abrams, *Forbidden Neighbors*, 174.

256 Executive Committee Meeting, March 4, 1946, Agendas/Minutes: Exec. Committee Community, Rush Rhees Library.

257 Price Fishback, "Panel Discussion on Saving the Neighborhood, Part III," *Arizona Law Review* 56, 3 (2014): 39–49; Trevor Kollmann, "Housing Markets, Government Programs, and Race During the Great Depression," (Ph.D. Diss., University of Arizona, 2011), 64.

icked selling of course drove property values downward, thus reinforcing the notion that once a neighborhood went black, it never went back.[258] "The panic area suffers desertion the moment one or a few minority members move into it," a 1955 study noted. "Offerings glut the market, vacancies appear, maintenance and upkeep are put off, and blight sets in." The relatively easy "availability of alternative housing for the whites speeds the exodus."[259] What frightened lenders, be they sellers "holding the mortgage," insurers, or building and loan associations, were not African-American borrowers but so-called "twilight zones" transitioning between all-white and all non-white occupancy. "It is impossible to predict what change in value will occur before the racial shift is complete," one lender frankly told investigators in 1960.[260]

To combat this nightmare scenario, which of course ultimately hurt everyone, many homeowners began writing restrictive covenants and deed restrictions wherein they promised never to sell the property to an African-American (and often to a Jew or Catholic as well). Blacks and other groups discriminated against fought the covenants in the courts but without much success until the U.S. Supreme Court finally struck down restrictive covenants in *Shelley v. Kraemer* in 1948 by removing the authority of state courts to enforce them. Covenants had come in a variety of flavors. One, the Aesopian, put a floor on occupant income and a ceiling on density. The Van Sweringen covenant required that sales be approved by the owner of the entire housing tract. In other jurisdictions, that was replaced by an option agreement whereby the tract owner could repurchase the property. The most infamous covenants, reversion clauses, outright invalidated transfers to minority groups.[261]

---

258 McEntire, *Residence and Race*, 212; Richard Sterner, Lenoir Epstein, and Ellen Winston, *The Negro's Share: A Study of Income, Consumption, Housing and Public Assistance*, (New York: Harper & Brothers, 1943), 202; Wright and Smith, *Mutually Beneficial*, 320, 365–66.

259 Abrams, *Forbidden Neighbors*, 277.

260 Eunice Grier and George Grier, *Privately Developed Interracial Housing: An Analysis of Experience*, (Berkeley: University of California Press, 1960), 117.

261 Karen Brodkin, "How Jews Became White," in *Race, Class and Gender in the United States* 5th ed., ed. Paula S. Rothenberg (New York: Worth, 2001), 40; Gunther, *Inside U.S.A.*,

By 1948, white homeowners, lenders, real estate agents, and the government itself had already developed other bulwarks against minority incursion, including steering blacks into segregated neighborhoods, restrictive zoning ordinances (e.g., large minimum lot sizes or house square footage requirements), redlining (refusing to lend to people due to where they lived), social pressure against selling to blacks, and even violence, including race riots and home bombings. Eager to avoid such self-defeating extremes, some neighborhoods formed associations and restricted residency to association members. Associations were also used to enforce covenants by suing anyone who violated them.[262]

New housing near established tracts also met obstacles. "The moment the community hears that a Negro community is intended," Charles Abrams complained in 1955, "the land is either not for sale or becomes impossible to build on because of threatened sanctions."[263] If the property were somehow acquired, fire insurance would suddenly become impossible to obtain. If fire insurance was available, the African-American's "house may be burned before it is even enclosed" so that insurance would become impossible to obtain on "objective" grounds.[264]

As long as the color barrier held, whites believed their property would appreciate and African-Americans were locked into low-quality, high-cost rental housing in segregated neighborhoods. But all those obstacles, even restrictive covenants when they were enforceable, generally came to naught if enough black (or Hispanic, especially Mexican) families managed to buy houses in a formerly all-white neighborhood. It was not that hundreds of whites backed by the police and courts feared losing a physical confrontation with a few African-Americans; it was the dual fear of miscegenation (forced or consensual) and the loss of equity in their

285; Mechele Dickerson, *Homeownership and America's Financial Underclass: Flawed Promises, Broken Promises, New Prescriptions,* (New York: Cambridge University Press, 2014), 55; Immergluck, *Credit to the Community,* 96; Abrams, *Forbidden Neighbors,* 182–83, 224–25.

262 Abrams, *Forbidden Neighbors,* 174–75, 179, 182–83, 226; Dickerson, *Homeownership,* 13; Sterner, Epstein, and Winston, *The Negro's Share,* 206.

263 Abrams, *Forbidden Neighbors,* 178.

264 Abrams, *Forbidden Neighbors,* 178–9.

homes that induced them to sell out quickly to the highest bidder, regardless of race or creed.[265]

Many white neighborhoods were racially transformed by white speculators who engaged in a process called "blockbusting." The speculator knowingly broke the National Association of Real Estate Board's code of ethics, which from 1924 to 1950 matched public sentiment by specifically forbidding realtors from "introducing into a neighborhood ... any individual whose presence will clearly be detrimental to property values in the neighborhood."[266] The speculator began by buying a house from an unsuspecting white seller, then flipping the house to an African-American eager to move out of a high rent ghetto or slum. The speculator then gave low ball but quick cash offers to the most panicked whites, which he subsequently sold to yet more African-Americans at a hefty markup. After a round or two, most whites gave up, sold out, and fled to the suburbs. Occasionally, though, as on East 95th Street in Manhattan and a certain neighborhood upstate, in Schenectady, whites refused to panic, accepted their new neighbors, and lived happily (though one doubts ever after).[267]

When blacks could find housing, perhaps thanks to the efforts of a blockbusting speculator, they often found obtaining financing difficult. According to a 1934 study, blacks had smaller mortgages, as a percentage of given property's value, than whites did. While that indicated that blacks owned more equity in their homes than comparable whites did, the lower loan-to-value also suggested that blacks were not considered as good a credit risk as whites, that they were, in a sense, being forced to invest more in their homes than whites were.[268]

---

265 Gregory D. Squires, "Community Reinvestment: An Emerging Social Movement," in *From Redlining to Reinvestment: Community Responses to Urban Disinvestment*, ed. Gregory D. Squires (Philadelphia: Temple University Press, 1992), 5; Arnold Rose, *The Negro in America: The Condensed Version of Gunnar Myrdal's* An American Dilemma, (New York: Harper & Row, 1948), 24; McEntire, *Residence and Race*, 205–7; Grier and Grier, *Privately Developed*, 116–17; Sterner, Epstein, and Winston, *The Negro's Share*, 209.

266 Squires, "Community Reinvestment," 4.

267 Abrams, *Forbidden Neighbors*, 277–78.

268 Sterner, Epstein, and Winston, *The Negro's Share*, 195.

According to a 1943 study, life insurers lent "to only a small extent" to blacks "and it seems that Negroes more often than whites were forced to obtain a large part of their mortgage credit from individuals. Interest rates on mortgage credit were often high, particularly for Negroes. ... The situation has improved in recent years, but those income groups in which most Negroes are concentrated have received less than their proportionate share of the benefits of the reforms in home financing."[269] That was problematic because individual lenders faced higher costs than larger lenders did. Individual lenders did not enjoy economies of scale and often made smaller loans so they had higher fixed costs.[270]

Individual lenders were able to pass those higher costs, sometimes called the "Black Tax," on to their borrowers because institutional lenders, like life insurers, largely avoided the African-American market. In late-Depression Atlanta, Georgia, for example, life insurers funded only 8 percent of mortgages to blacks, compared to 32.6 percent of the mortgages of whites. Individual blacks in that city were much more likely to resort to loans from individuals, 31.3 vs. 18.9 percent for whites. Percentages in Birmingham were even worse. There, only 0.3 percent of mortgages to blacks came from life insurers while one in three whites received their mortgages from life insurers. Blacks were much more reliant on individual lenders (34.1%) than whites (16.8%).

African-Americans also paid more on average. In Atlanta, more than half of all mortgages made to blacks ran at 8 percent or higher interest versus only 14.5 percent of mortgages to whites. In Birmingham, over three quarters of mortgages to blacks ran at higher than 8 percent, versus only one in three mortgages to white borrowers. Even in the mid-1950s, African-Americans borrowed mostly from individuals at relatively high rates

269 Sterner, Epstein, and Winston, *The Negro's Share*, 196.

270 Gale Cincotta and Arthur J. Naparstek, *Urban Disinvestment: New Implications for Community Organization, Research and Public Policy*, (Washington, DC: National Center for Urban Ethnic Affairs, 1976), 13, 17–18.

of interest. Savings and loans would lend to them but even they often exacted a point or two more and would only lend in approved areas.[271]

Due to the huge disruption in mortgage markets caused by the Great Depression, the federal government shifted much of the risk of mortgage lending from private lenders to itself through the emergency Homeowners Loan Corporation, the loan guarantee programs of the Federal Housing Administration (FHA) and the Veterans Administration (VA), and the establishment of a secondary market in mortgages by the Federal National Mortgage Administration (FNMA) and, later, government-sponsored (implicitly guaranteed) enterprises (GSEs) known as Fannie Mae (formerly the FNMA) and Freddie Mac.[272]

Ironically, however, the federal government at first encouraged segregation because of its ideological commitment to "ordinary business principles" and a strong desire to limit subsidies.[273] "One of their main interests," Richard Sterner and his coauthors argued in 1943, "must be to protect real-property values. Rightly or wrongly the Negro has always been regarded as a menace to real-estate values."[274] The FHA, therefore, "is careful not to refer to Negroes as an adverse influence" but its manual did refer to "lower class occupancy, and inharmonious racial groups"[275] and prohibited loans to members of any other race than "the race for which they [the properties] are intended."[276] As late as 1940, the FHA still asked potential borrowers if "the neighborhood [was] homogeneous in population?" "These were no slips of the pen nor the irresponsible utterances of a senseless clerk," Charles Abrams complained. "They were part and parcel of FHA policy from its inception to 1948."[277]

271 Sterner, Epstein, and Winston, The Negro's Share, 408–9; Abrams, Forbidden Neighbors, 175–76.

272 Sterner, Epstein, and Winston, The Negro's Share, 310–14.

273 Rose, The Negro in America, 119.

274 Sterner, Epstein, and Winston, The Negro's Share, 314–15.

275 Rose, The Negro in America, 120.

276 Sterner, Epstein, and Winston, The Negro's Share, 315.

277 Abrams, Forbidden Neighbors, 232.

FHA documents lauded restrictive covenants as "the surest protection against undesirable encroachment and inharmonious use"[278] but after covenants were finally struck down, the FHA pushed zoning restrictions to bar minorities, in part by placing African-Americans in the same category as nuisances like "stables, pig pens" according to a 1955 study.[279] The FHA changed its forms to render "the language vague enough to take the heat off while still affirming the anti-racial policy."[280] Playing segregationist was the FHA's path of least resistance but its policies obviously injured blacks who wished to be homeowners by providing the federal government's imprimatur to racist stereotypes whenever its policies pandered to entrenched prejudices. In recompense, the government gave African-Americans access to subsidized government housing, which may have seemed like a good deal until the unpleasant nature of most federal housing projects came to light.[281]

The Economic Paradox of Segregation

Yet the very fact that ... blacks appeared at all in the Dun ledgers, and in great numbers, deserves some comment. Had these individuals been dismissed as undeserving of credit by the fact of their ... race alone, the credit-reporting agencies would not have wasted the resources to report on them. — Rowena Olegario, A Culture of Credit: Embedding Trust and Transparency in American Business (Cambridge: Harvard University Press, 2006), 115.

While there was much truth in Bernard Shaw's claim that "the haughty American nation ... makes the negro clean its boots and then

278 Abrams, *Forbidden Neighbors*, 232.

279 Abrams, *Forbidden Neighbors*, 231.

280 Abrams, *Forbidden Neighbors*, 232.

281 Immergluck, *Credit to the Community*, 94; Sterner, Epstein, and Winston, *The Negro's Share*, 316; Kollmann, "Housing Markets," 20–21, 140.

proves the ... inferiority of the negro by the fact that he's a shoeblack,"[282] many African-Americans were not content to become, or remain, shoe shine "boys." They did what they could to create their own businesses and Jim Crow segregation laws actually helped them to achieve their goals, though on a smaller scale than many would have preferred.[283]

For African-American consumers, segregation posed major costs because it "drastically" limited their choices in banking, healthcare, housing, insurance, and legal services, not to mention bathrooms and water fountains.[284] Limited choices meant less competition, which meant higher prices for consumer durables and real estate, which meant more risk for lenders, which meant higher financing costs for blacks.[285]

African-American workers were also somewhat hurt by segregation, which largely kept them out of the employ of the highest paying companies, which were almost invariably white-owned. At the same time, however, black workers found similar positions in companies owned by African-American entrepreneurs who found that segregation created market power, i.e., the ability to charge higher prices for their goods than they could have in a more competitive market. From auto-repair to hair care and hotels to restaurants, black-owned service and public accommodation businesses sat behind what African-American economist Andrew Brimmer called the equivalent of a tariff wall in an economy all their own.[286]

---

282 Bernard Shaw, *Man and Superman: A Comedy and a Philosophy*, (Cambridge, Mass.: University Press, 1903), 17. For a slightly different version of this quotation, see Gunther, *Inside U.S.A.*, 703.

283 Walker, *History of Black Business*, xiii.

284 United States Department of Labor, *The Negroes in the United States: Their Economic and Social Situation*, (Washington: GPO, June 1966), 3.

285 Alan Batchelder, "Poverty: The Special Case of the Negro," in Burton Weisbrod, ed., *The Economics of Poverty: An American Paradox*, (Englewood Cliffs, N.J.: Prentice-Hall, 1965), 101.

286 United States Department of Labor, *The Negroes in the United States*, 31; Andrew F. Brimmer, "Small Business and Economic Development in the Negro Community," Speech by Member of the Federal Reserve System's Board of Governors, July 25, 1969, 2–3; Brimmer, "Financial Institutions and Urban Rehabilitation," 5.

By 1930, African-Americans owned some 70,000 business enterprises, the bulk of which were small but cloistered by segregation laws or
social customs. By 1960, 46,000 blacks were self-employed, most, as was
traditional, in the provision of services, mostly for African-American clientele. Only ten percent were engaged in manufacturing or construction.[287]

Unsurprisingly, blacks starting their own businesses found it difficult to obtain credit. After World War II, only about 3 percent of them
received bank credit and in the South most of them needed a white co-
signer as well. Competent, established black businessmen (and the occa-
sional woman), however, found it possible to finance their segregated,
economically protected businesses. Credit records, the mere existence of
which is revealing in and of itself as pointed out in the head quote to this
section, also reveal that some black businessmen were able to discount
their notes at banks as well as obtain trade credit. They paid more for
credit on average than white-owned businesses, however, because their
businesses were smaller and inherently more fragile as they had access
only to the relatively small, segmented, lower income African-American
market.[288]

As soon as African-Americans tried to expand beyond the confines of
the black economy, however, they usually could no longer raise sufficient
funds. While that might appear like an overt racist conspiracy it really
reflected the increased risk associated with more competition, i.e., the loss
of Brimmer's tariff wall. Most African-American enterprises were simply
too small and loosely managed to compete directly against larger, more
professionally managed white-owned businesses. While black workers
could generally be hired more cheaply than white ones, they were also

---

287 Harris, *Negro as Capitalist*, xi, 172; Andrew F. Brimmer, "The Negro in the American
Economy in 1975," Speech by Member of the Federal Reserve System's Board of Governors,
April 1, 1966, 12.

288 Immergluck, *Credit to the Community*, 60; Olegario, *Culture of Credit*, 113; Butler, *Entrepreneurship and Self-Help*, 73–75, 143–64.

not as productive on average due to lower levels of education and experience (due to longer periods of unemployment).[289]

Starting in the 1920s, scientists, historians, and religious leaders began to question the empirical and theoretical underpinnings of Jim Crow. Racism remained rampant as indicated by the response of an African-American girl queried about the best way to punish Hitler: "Paint him black and bring him over here." Or a poem current in the Midwest in the 1940s: "Eenie, meenie, minie, moe / Catch a nigger by the toe / If he hollers make him pay / Fifty dollars every day." Even sympathetic white authors referred to the "Negro problem" as if African-Americans were causal agents instead of victims struggling to make the best of a bad situation.[290]

World War II, however, helped in several ways. First, the war created millions of new jobs and opened up millions of others vacated by men heading off to war. Second, the Fair Employment Practice Committee (FEPC) established by FDR tried to place all workers, including African-Americans, into the most highly skilled jobs they could successfully perform. Employment gave black workers valuable work experience, raised confidence in their own abilities (which some whites perceived as "aggressive" behavior), and also served to defeat racist stereotypes. The valor of black servicemen and women of course did likewise, as did a jump in African-American literacy, education, and longevity. In addition, the volatile postwar geopolitical environment, especially the threat posed by authoritarian enemies both east and west, provided the federal government with incentives to aid African-Americans lest they become communist subversives. So when the leaders of the Civil Rights movement began to call for reforms, the federal government was generally responsive and

---

289 Rose, *The Negro in America*, 108–9; Andrew F. Brimmer, "Education, Income, and Wealth Accumulation in the Negro Community," Speech by Member of the Federal Reserve System's Board of Governors, May 28, 1970, 13–14; Edwin Embree, *Brown Americans: The Story of a Tenth of the Nation*, (New York: Viking Press, 1943), 132; Andrew F. Brimmer and Henry S. Terrell, "The Economic Potential of Black Capitalism," American Economic Association Annual Meeting, December 29, 1969, 3–4, 9; Theodore L. Cross, *Black Capitalism: Strategy for Business in the Ghetto*, (New York: Atheneum, 1969).

290 Gunther, *Inside U.S.A.*, 60, 283, 683.

with its help Jim Crow crumbled. Progress was slow but cumulative until
only the ignorant and misinformed could justify racist public policies.[291]

By the 1940s, the economic costs of segregation, made poignantly
clear by African-American reporters like Alice Allison Dunnigan and Ethel
L. Payne, were also becoming apparent.[292] "The economic cost of segregation," wrote John Gunther in 1947, "is of course preposterous and stag-
gering. It is a cardinal reason why the South is so poor."[293] Almost twenty
years later, a study that showed that segregation cost Americans billions
of dollars through a variety of conduits, including higher unemployment,
less tourism, and less investment.[294]

Just as important as the change in public sentiment and the lost GDP,
though, may have been the increase in the purchasing power of African-
Americans, which even before World War II had grown large enough, in
aggregate, to cause a shift in social mores in some places. Traditionally,
Southerners refused to refer to black men as Mister or Doctor "even in
correspondence."[295] But starting in the 1930s, white businessmen eager
for any business began to call cherished African-American customers
Mister and their wives Mrs. That social recognition, though seemingly
minor, was the beginning of a sea change in race relations in the South.
Soon, newspapers began to call African-American women "Miss" and
even fancy department stores allowed them to shop if they had money, or
credit, in pocket.[296]

After World War II, African-Americans' average incomes grew faster
than those of whites (though a substantial gap remained) and reached into

291 Embree, *Brown Americans*, 230–31; Gunther, *Inside U.S.A.*, 355; Malcolm Ross, *All Manner of Men*, (Harcourt, Brace & World, 1948), 71; Blackmon, *Slavery by Another Name*; Newby, *Jim Crow's Defense*.

292 Rodger Streitmatter, *Raising Her Voice: African-American Women Journalists Who Changed History*, (Lexington: University Press of Kentucky), 107–28.

293 Gunther, *Inside U.S.A.*, 682.

294 Barbara Patterson, *The Price We Pay for Discrimination* (Atlanta: Southern Regional Council, 1964).

295 Gunther, *Inside U.S.A.*, 680–81.

296 Arthur Raper and Ira De A. Reid, *Sharecroppers All*, (Chapel Hill: University of North Carolina Press, 1941), 83–84; Gunther, *Inside U.S.A.*, 682.

the billions of dollars by the mid-1960s. Between 1955 and 1965 alone, the share of all income earned by African-Americans increased from 5.6 to 6.9 percent.[297] "With that amount of purchasing power," Eli Ginzberg opined in 1964, "Negroes can get banks to treat them civilly; they can get sales-people in department stores to want to sell to them."[298] As the number of white-owned businesses that would cater to blacks increased, demand declined for *The Negro Motorist Green Book*, an annual travel guide begun in 1936 by Victor Hugo Green that listed safe businesses (hotels, restaurants and taverns, garages and service stations, barber shops, and even sometimes banks) for African-American tourists to patronize. The last edition appeared in 1966.

Basically, some white business owners wanted to end segregation so they could seize African-Americans' money for themselves and in this they were largely successful. By 1997, African-Americans owned only about 2 percent of the nation's businesses although they composed 12.3 percent of the nation's population as many of the mom and pop shops that had thrived under Jim Crow succumbed to competition or the eventual death of their proprietors.[299]

In many inner cities, however, *de jure* segregation simply morphed into *de facto* segregation as African-Americans were cajoled or corralled into remaining in minority enclaves popularly termed "slums" or "ghettos." Federal housing projects, highways, and redlining were the major culprits and the economic effect was similar to that under *de jure* segregation as many African-Americans would not, or conveniently could not, shop outside of their own neighborhoods, where installment credit persisted well after revolving credit (i.e., credit cards) had taken over the

---

297 United States Department of Labor, *Negroes in the United States: Their Employment and Economic Status,* (December 1952); Brimmer, "The Negro in the American Economy in 1975," 4.

298 Eli Ginzberg, ed. *The Negro Challenge to the Business Community,* (New York: McGraw-Hill Book Company, 1964).

299 Juliet E.K. Walker, "White Corporate America: The New Arbiter of Race?" in Kenneth Lipartito and David B. Sicilia, eds. *Constructing Corporate America: History, Politics, Culture,* (New York: Oxford University Press, 2004), 246–93.

suburbs. Local retailers used their market power to extract higher prices from blacks and, by refusing to turn over their credit records to credit bureaus, they kept black credit customers in their power. The urban uprisings of the late 1960s were so ubiquitous because the uprisings promised to exact revenge against high cost retailers (only some of whom were themselves African-American) through physical looting of their stores as well as the destruction of their credit records. It was not quite Jubilee but it afforded relief from debt repayments as well as the stigma of having goods repossessed, a fear that credit card holders in the suburbs had forgotten.[300]

The slow death of *de jure* segregation pretty much spelled the end of financial exclusion, but not discrimination, for African-Americans. According to a study published in 1960, mortgage lenders "in increasing number, feel that they have had enough experience with Negroes as creditors to lend to them if they meet the usual credit qualifications."[301] In 1965, 2 in 3 blacks with an income less than $5,000 owned life insurance, a bank account, and/or a stock or mutual fund investment. That same year, 9 in 10 whites could say the same. Over all income ranges, 3 in 4 blacks were included in some aspect of the financial system, compared to 19 in 20 whites. At all income levels, whites were also more likely to have hospital insurance and surgical insurance than African-Americans were, but nonwhites with high incomes had health insurances at a much higher rate (4 out of 5) than poor whites did (about half). In short, although racial parity was still far from achieved, the age of exclusion was clearly long gone.[302]

Overt discrimination also waned after passage of the Civil Rights Act of 1968, the Fair Housing Act of 1968, and the Equal Credit Opportunity Act of 1974. The former two were direct responses to the urban uprisings

---

300 Louis Hyman, *Debtor Nation: The History of America in Red Ink,* (Princeton: Princeton University Press, 2011), 175–80.

301 Grier and Grier, *Privately Developed,* 116–17.

302 Hiltz, "Why Black Families Own Less Life Insurance," 227–28; United States Department of Labor, *The Negroes in the United States,* 226.

that racked dozens of the nation's urban centers between 1964 and 1968; the latter two prohibited discrimination on the basis of race, color, religion, sex, or national origin (and, after a 1988 amendment, on the basis of age, disability, and presence of children in the household) for real estate sales and mortgages.[303] By the end of the 1960s, "discrimination against minority, female, or unmarried applicants" was considered to run counter "to accepted notions of social justice and is now illegal."[304] Nevertheless, troubling disparities persisted, as indicated by a reference to easy credit ripoffs in the song that opened every episode of *Good Times*, a CBS network television program that ran in the second half of the 1970s about a poor black family's quotidian struggles while living in a Chicago public housing project. Disparities in the mortgage market loomed even larger.

Housing and Mortgage Discrimination in the Second Half of the Twentieth Century

The origins of the redlining controversy should provide a fascinating set of puzzles for future historians of political and economic thought.
—Jack M. Guttentag and Susan M. Wachter, Redlining and Public Policy Monograph 1980–1 (New York: Salomon Brothers Center, 1980), 49.

In the 1960s, African-Americans were as likely to own life insurance as Euro-Americans of the same level of income and occupation were, though at much lower dollar levels due to the higher cost associated with their higher mortality rate and their heavier reliance on higher cost industrial (weekly debit) insurance. The equal degree of market penetration

303 Robert Schafer and Helen F. Ladd, *Discrimination in Mortgage Lending* (Cambridge: MIT Press, 1981), 8; Immergluck, *Credit to the Community*, 3–4; George C. Galster, "Use of Testers in Investigating Discrimination in Mortgage Lending and Insurance," in *Clear and Convincing Evidence: Measurement of Discrimination in America*, ed. Michael Fix and Raymond J. Struyk (Washington, DC: Urban Institute Press, 1993), 287; Collins and Margo, "Race and Home Ownership," 358–59.

304 Schafer and Ladd, *Discrimination*, 5.

may have been due to the competitive national market for life insurance or, more likely given the only relatively recent interest in the African-American market by white-owned insurers, the existence of numerous black-owned industrial life insurance companies, of which more in the final chapter. At the same time, however, African-Americans owned significantly fewer automobiles and houses than whites with comparable incomes did. The question was why.[305]

Interestingly, most researchers, policymakers, and other observers focused on the gap between white and black homeownership levels rather than changes in the absolute level. Between 1940 and 1980, homeownership among African-American households increased by a whopping 37 percentage points off their Depression-era lows. While some blacks simply self-financed the construction of their homes, some substantial but others "mere shacks," or bought mobile homes or "much older" existing housing, about half already by 1956 were obtaining mortgages. The biggest problem was that those mortgages were only available in black neighborhoods.[306]

One possible reason for the discrepancy was that African-Americans were getting less help from the government. "Of the homeowners with mortgages in 1960," one study showed, "nonwhites were much less likely to have received FHA or VA assistance than the whites or to have bought a new house."[307] But that masked the fact that newer mortgages, especially those made after 1950 or so, showed much more equitable treatment of minority applicants by the FHA.[308]

African-Americans, however, were much more likely to pay more than 6 percent interest on a first mortgage and African-American

---

305 United States Department of Labor, *The Negroes in the United States*, 39; U.S. Department of Labor, *Black Americans: A Chartbook* (Washington: GPO, 1971), 76–77; Hiltz, "Why Black Families Own Less Life Insurance," 230–31.

306 McEntire, *Residence and Race*, 218–20; Collins and Margo, "Race and Home Ownership," 356–57; Kate Porter Young, "Rural South Carolina: An Ethnographic Study of Homeownership, Home Financing, and Credit," *Cityscape* 3, no. 1 (1997): 16–22.

307 United States Department of Labor, *The Negroes in the United States*, 39.

308 McEntire, *Residence and Race*, 221.

homeowners were more likely, holding income constant, to have to pay private mortgage insurance (PMI), which was basically a higher interest rate, ostensibly paid to a third-party insurer against borrower default, that was *not* tax deductible. They were also much less likely to own their homes outright, presumably because they could not get cheap government loans as readily as their white counterparts. Even after the FHA began making loans to minorities with more alacrity, the process remained slow, expensive, and laden with restrictions.[309]

Another possibility was that African-Americans were poorer credit risks than whites because their net asset positions were not as good due to society-wide discrimination. While in 1966 African-Americans had the same level of debt as whites with the same income, they owned fewer assets, including less corporate stock. (That year the appearance of African-Americans at AT&T's and GE's stockholder meetings actually made *The New Yorker*!) They carried higher levels of installment debt than whites, as they had since at least the 1910s, but had less equity in their homes despite similar levels of mortgage debt. In short, the average market price of African-Americans' houses did not increase as rapidly (or decreased more rapidly) than the average market price of white-owned houses. This was due to the smaller, more segmented market for homes in black neighborhoods as well as the generally lower quality housing stock that blacks were steered into buying.[310]

Anyone tempted to suggest that African-Americans simply were worse real estate investors than whites does not understand the context in which houses were sold in the United States up to at least the 1960s. Real estate agents steered buyers into neighborhoods that matched their economic class but also their race. While people ultimately chose the

---

309 McEntire, *Residence and Race*, 222; United States Department of Labor, *The Negroes in the United States*, 39; Dickerson, *Homeownership*, 23; Brimmer, "Small Business and Economic Development," 7; David Listokin and Stephen Casey, *Mortgage Lending and Race: Conceptual and Analytical Perspectives of the Urban Financing Problem*, (New Brunswick: Center for Urban Policy Research, 1980), 5.

310 Brimmer and Terrell, "The Economic Potential of Black Capitalism," 7–8, 13; John Brooks, "Stockholder Season," *New Yorker*, 8 October 1966; Brimmer, "Small Business and Economic Development," 6–7; McEntire, *Residence and Race*, 230–35.

particular house they would buy, they were largely constrained to the neighborhoods into which they were steered by real estate agents.

The tendency of appraisers to make conservative appraisals on houses in minority or transitional (from white to minority) neighborhoods was often taken as a means of "discriminating against minority homeseekers" by making it more difficult for them to obtain mortgage financing.[311] Given the decline (or slower appreciation) of houses owned by African-Americans due to steering, however, it now appears that appraisers were not conservative enough on average. In fact, African-Americans in Chicago, and likely elsewhere as well, paid 25 percent more for their homes than whites did for comparable properties. Had appraisers been tougher, fewer African-Americans would have received loans but fewer would have overpaid or lost equity in their homes.[312]

Another possibility was that institutional lenders discriminated against African-American borrowers, who were much more likely to borrow from savings and loans or individual lenders than whites were, and much less likely to borrow from a commercial bank, mutual savings bank, or a life insurance company. In fact, technically speaking many African-Americans (half in Chicago according to one study but about 1 in 7 overall according to another, compared to 1 in 14 for whites) did not finance their homes with mortgages at all but rather with land contracts, essentially installment plans wherein the seller maintained title to the property until the buyer met the terms of the credit agreement, which often included large down payments and relatively high rates of interest. If the borrower defaulted, ejection was more akin to eviction than foreclosure in terms of the time and costs involved. Little wonder that African-

311 U.S. Commission on Civil Rights, *Mortgage Money: Who Gets It? A Case Study in Mortgage Lending Discrimination in Hartford, Connecticut* (Washington: U.S. Government Printing Office, 1974), 16.

312 U.S. Commission on Civil Rights, *Mortgage Money*, 17; Thomas Pettigrew, "White-Negro Confrontations," in *The Negro Challenge to the Business Community*, ed. Eli Ginzberg, (New York: McGraw-Hill Book Company, 1964), 47; Batchelder, "Poverty," 102–3.

Americans did not own homes at the same frequencies whites did, even holding income constant.[313]

In 1964, it seemed obvious to Kenneth C. Clark that discrimination was to blame for that discrepancy. A decade later, the U.S. Commission on Civil Rights concurred, placing the blame for the continued large disparity between white homeownership rates (65%) and black (42%) and Hispanic (44%) homeownership rates squarely on "discrimination by real estate brokers and mortgage lenders." The latter, it claimed, used "imprecise, subjective criteria in granting mortgages" but the authors of the report later admitted that "data are unavailable, inadequate, or difficult to obtain." Moreover, they claimed that most discrimination occurred before applications were even made so it "never bec[a]me part of a written record." "At each stage opportunities exist for denying mortgage loans to qualified minority families on the basis of nothing more than the personal prejudice of individuals in positions to decide," the authors lamented, without explaining why for-profit institutions would allow good prospects to be steered away.[314]

The authors of the Civil Rights study claimed that most rejections were informal and not based on "objective credit factors" but they could present nothing but anecdotes in support, and even then their stories were subject to multiple interpretations. For example, an African-American homeseeker with good income and credit was steered to a minority neighborhood but he "subsequently changed brokers, found a suburban house, and obtained a mortgage," which suggested that the steering he was subjected to was idiosyncratic and not systemic. Likewise, "a black couple" was turned "down ... on the grounds that they could not meet a newly imposed higher ratio. Subsequently, [however], they obtained a loan from a different institution and were the first blacks to move into the development." "To the extent discrimination does occur," the authors

---

313 McEntire, *Residence and Race*, 222–23; United States Department of Labor, *The Negroes in the United States*, 220; Karen Orren, *Corporate Power and Social Change: The Politics of the Life Insurance Industry*, (Baltimore: Johns Hopkins University Press, 1974), 140–42; Immergluck, *Credit to the Community*, 5.

314 U.S. Commission on Civil Rights, *Mortgage Money*, 3–4, 9.

concluded, "it is subtle, often unconsciously practiced, and difficult to detect." So, the authors of the Civil Rights study ultimately conceded that they did not have the data to support their brash conclusions.[315]

To his credit, Kenneth Clark admitted that he did not know what to do about mortgage discrimination or other "difficult and stubborn areas."[316] Everyone agreed, however, that more data was necessary, so that soon became the mantra and data collection focused on redlining, or arbitrary refusal of lenders to make loans to applicants from certain neighborhoods or districts (The practice was usually associated with mortgage loans but credit card issuers and fire insurers were also accused of redlining.[317]).

In the early 1970s, redlining became the central focus of community activists concerned about urban blight and the plight of the urban poor, especially members of minority groups. The irony was that mortgage redlining may have been functionally obsolete by the time that it became a major public issue but the catchy name and basic idea became catchwords or code words, much like in the aftermath of the Panic of 2008 the phrase "repeal of Glass-Steagall" came to stand in for a panoply of complex policies more aptly called deregulation. The original practice of redlining can be traced to a few private lenders but the practice, like many forms of discrimination, took hold in part due to federal government policies. Specifically, redlining proliferated with help from the Home Owners Loan Corporation (HOLC), an emergency New Deal vehicle designed to stop the downward spiral of home prices during the Great Depression. HOLC developed an elaborate neighborhood rating system and outlined safe (white, middle-class) areas on its maps in green for new and blue for good and white. Transitional or crumbling neighborhoods it colored yellow, and beat down, usually nonwhite neighborhoods in red. Although

---

315 U.S. Commission on Civil Rights, *Mortgage Money*, 9–10, 15, 18.

316 Kenneth C. Clark, "The Negro in Turmoil," in *The Negro Challenge to the Business Community*, ed. Eli Ginzberg (New York: McGraw-Hill Book Company, 1964), 67.

317 Immergluck, *Credit to the Community*, 87; Lewis Mandell, *The Credit Card Industry: A History*, (Boston: Twayne Publishers, 1990), 57.

the short- and long-term effects of HOLC's maps are still being debated, many HOLC neighborhood descriptions were blatantly racist as they gave higher grades, *ceteris paribus*, to neighborhoods with residents of the right ancestry, i.e., British and German, lower grades to ones with Irish, Italian, or Jewish residents, and of course the lowest of all for neighborhoods with many African-American residents.[318]

According to historian Craig Wilder, it was the legacy of HOLC's maps that enabled bankers, insurers, and municipal governments to financially starve large portions of inner cities, including his beloved Brooklyn, by depriving them of reinvestment capital. The Mortgage Conference of New York (MCNY), a consortium of several score large mortgage lenders in New York City, formed in 1932 but did not start producing detailed maps of the blocks where African-Americans lived until 1937 by building on HOLC's work and precedent. Unlike HOLC, however, the private lenders were uninterested in Catholics or Jews, concentrating their wrath on brown-skinned peoples. The federal government sued MCNY in 1946 on the grounds that it engaged in price fixing as well as that it violated the civil rights of African-Americans and Hispanics.[319]

As described above, by the 1950s and 60s many lenders did not hesitate to lend to African-Americans per se, just to blacks who might start a dreaded neighborhood racial transition. Of course, there was also reticence to lend to anyone, regardless of race, without sufficient collateral looking to buy property in a slum, ghetto, or other type of dysfunctional neighborhood. The net effect certainly looked racist. Into the 1960s, for

---

318 Cincotta and Naparstek, *Urban Disinvestment,* 5; Squires, "Community Reinvestment," 2–4; Jack M. Guttentag and Susan M. Wachter, *Redlining and Public Policy,* (New York: Salomon Brothers Center, 1980), 49; Immergluck, *Credit to the Community,* 13, 93; Lendol Calder, *Financing the American Dream: A Cultural History of Consumer Credit,* (Princeton: Princeton University Press, 1999), 280–81; Brodkin, "How Jews Became White," 41; Craig Wilder, *A Covenant with Color: Race and Social Power in Brooklyn,* (New York: Columbia University Press, 2000), 187–94; Richard Rothstein, *The Color of Law: A Forgotten History of How Our Government Segregated America,* (New York: W. W. Norton, 2017); Price Fishback, "Panel Discussion on Saving the Neighborhood, Part III," *Arizona Law Review* 56, 3 (2014): 45; Daniel Aaronson, Daniel Hartley, and Bhashkar Mazumder, "The Effect of the 1930s HOLC 'Redlining' Maps," Federal Reserve Bank of Chicago Working Paper WP 2017–2 (August 3, 2017).

319 Wilder, *Covenant with Color,* 185–86, 201–204.

example, banks in San Francisco lent to blacks but only on properties "within an established Negro neighborhood," unless, of course, that neighborhood was a "slum." In effect, then, they would lend only to middle and upper class blacks. In their defense, the banks noted that they did not want to be blamed for destroying white neighborhoods and that they certainly did not want to destroy the value of the collateral for their existing loan portfolios.[320]

By May 1975 the issue was before the Senate Banking Committee, which was inundated with studies, mostly by left-leaning community groups that failed to measure loan demand, purporting to show the pervasiveness of redlining.[321] Testimony placed the blame for urban squalor squarely on the shoulders of lenders. One community group study, for example, boldly asserted that due to "discrimination" lenders conspired to deliberately limit lending to certain areas and justified their decisions "by claiming to perceive the risk of deterioration." The bankers' analyses, of course, soon became self-fulfilling prophecies:

Loans cut off from the neighborhood insure that the housing stock will decline. Home repairs and improvements are left unattended. General confidence in the neighborhood is undermined. Potential buyers go elsewhere for loans, and find themselves steered to other, 'safer' neighborhoods.[322]

Although the reasons why for-profit lenders ("well-connected developers," it was argued, profited from urban blight, which rendered real estate cheap) would want to destroy perfectly "healthy communities" through redlining were never made clear, key legislators like Senator William Proxmire (D-Wisconsin) found the community groups' narratives "compelling," so Congress several months later enacted the Home Mortgage Disclosure Act (HMDA), which required savings and loans, mutual

---

320 McEntire, *Residence and Race*, 224–25.

321 Guttentag and Wachter, *Redlining*, 15; Cincotta and Naparstek, *Urban Disinvestment*, 5.

322 Cincotta and Naparstek, *Urban Disinvestment*, 9.

savings banks, and commercial banks to report their annual lending volumes by census tract.[323]

As hoped, availability of data spurred the research efforts of a variety of social scientists. Sociologists and more left-leaning scholars tended to find aggregate evidence of redlining or other forms of discrimination but also "wide variation in lenders' treatment of racial minorities both across regions and among lenders within a given region."[324] Economists and more right-leaning scholars, by contrast, tended not to find compelling evidence for redlining. (In the parlance of statistics, they could not reject the hypothesis that lending was based on objective economic characteristics alone.) Others argued that a high level of correlation between race, ethnicity, gender, and other easily observed variables and negative credit indicators justified discrimination on efficiency grounds. "Although only some people of a particular identifiable group may be irresponsible debtors," George Benston explained, "it might be less costly for a lender to deny loans to all members of that group than to ignore this relationship. In this situation, the lender saves the costs of monitoring, collecting, and writing off bad loans which, the lender believes, are greater than the net profits that would have been made on 'good' members of the discriminated-against group."[325]

A 1978 study conducted by three economists at the University of Rochester, including Benston, concluded that there was "no adequate evidence for [the] assertion [that] redlining is ... a major problem." At issue, they argued, was the failure to consider demand for mortgages "in the presumed redlined areas" and the lack of data on collateral and creditworthiness of borrowers. Their own study of mortgage lending in Rochester, New York, overcame those shortcomings but did not find conclusive evidence of redlining even in central Rochester, where com-

323 Cincotta and Naparstek, *Urban Disinvestment*, 5, 10; George J. Benston, Dan Horky, and H. Marting Weingartner, *An Empirical Study of Mortgage Redlining*, (New York: Salomon Brothers Center, 1978), 1–34.

324 Schafer and Ladd, *Discrimination*, 8.

325 George J. Benston, *Regulating Financial Markets: A Critique and Some Proposals*, (Washington, D.C.: AEI Press, 1999), 51.

munity activists were certain redlining must have been practiced. Even
in periods of "tight money," lenders made loans in the allegedly redlined
zones. Borrowers with the same objective characteristics (collateral, loan
to value, income, creditworthiness) were charged the same rates of interest. Borrowers from the central city district, however, did receive shorter-
term mortgages *ceteris paribus*. The economists also conducted telephone
surveys to judge mortgage demand and again found nothing suggesting
that Rochester-area financial institutions redlined the central city.[326]

HMDA data at first was devoid of several important variables,
including loan demand and detailed data on individual borrowers. The
former was important because blacks, especially older ones, might have
been more conservative about borrowing, i.e., less likely to seek a loan
in the first place. Many blacks who might have qualified for mortgages,
one study showed, did not bother to apply because they believed their
credit was worse than it actually was. Loan demand for specific areas
was a function of a large number of factors, including the ratio of home
ownership to renting, the volume of new construction, turnover rates,
and property values, all of which were related to tax, insurance, and crime
rates, public transportation routes, perceptions of public school quality,
and employment availability, to name just a few of the more important
variables. In other words, loan volumes in a neighborhood might be low
because nobody wanted to buy a home there, not because banks would
not lend. Detailed data on individual borrowers was important because
borrowers who might look identical in HDMA data might have posed
very different risks to potential lenders due to differences in job security,
prospects for income growth, family size and age structure, and a host of
other considerations.[327]

To circumvent the HDMA's data inadequacy, the Federal Home
Loan Bank Board authorized a special, detailed survey of savings and

326 Benston, Horky, and Weingartner, *Mortgage Redlining*, ix-xi, 4–5, 45–50, 70–73.

327 Listokin and Casey, *Mortgage Lending*, 258; Young, "Rural South Carolina," 22; Sheila D.
Ards and Samuel L. Myers, Jr., "The Color of Money: Bad Credit, Wealth, and Race," *Ameri-
can Behavioral Scientist* 45, no. 2 (2001): 229–30; Immergluck, *Credit to the Community*, 65–66;
Guttentag and Wachter, *Redlining*, 2, 16, 19.

loans mortgage lending in three cities, Miami, San Antonio, and Toledo, for one fiscal quarter in 1978. The study considered accusations of "under-appraisal,"[328] i.e., that lenders deliberately reduced appraisals on properties sought by blacks and other unwanted borrowers to justify, on paper, the rejection of their applications. It also examined mortgage terms to try to discern if lenders systematically charged blacks or other groups higher interest rates or offered them shorter term mortgages. It found that many appraisals strayed from the best estimate of value in both directions (too high and too low) regardless of the characteristics of the borrower. (So appraisers were just inaccurate, not bigots.) Likewise, mortgage terms were not clearly affected by the race, gender, age, or marital status of the borrower.[329]

The study did uncover 11 cases of individual black and Hispanic applicants who should have received loans based on the information in their application files but in every case further investigation revealed extenuating circumstances. In one instance, for example, a mortgage was technically denied only because another lender offered the applicant a lower cost loan that the applicant accepted instead. Another was simply miscoded as rejected when, in fact, the mortgage had been approved. In several other cases, applicants claimed far higher incomes than they could verify. Another applicant lost her job after applying and had no compa-rable job prospects.[330]

By 1980 or so, it was clear to many researchers that "the disclosure of lending activity required by the Home Mortgage Disclosure Act of 1975 provides data wholly inadequate to analyze discrimination." Redlining would lead to disinvestment as community activists argued, researchers noted, but disinvestment could also occur "in the absence of any redlining

---

328 Cincotta and Naparstek, *Urban Disinvestment*, 13.

329 A. Thomas King, *Discrimination in Mortgage Lending: A Study of Three Cities*, (New York: Salomon Brothers Center), 27–28, 65.

330 King, *Discrimination in Mortgage Lending*, 71–74.

by banks."[331] So disinvestment in urban neighbors, palpable as it was in the 1960 and 70s, did not constitute *prima facie* evidence of redlining.

New York, however, mandated more stringent data reporting requirements than HDMA, including each borrower's marital status, net wealth, and years at present occupation. And California reported house price and borrower income in exact dollars, rather than ranges. Using the more detailed data, Robert Schafer and Helen Ladd concluded "that, as expected, objective factors such as the ratios of requested loan amount to income and to appraised value explain the vast majority of lending decisions." While some blighted neighborhoods appeared to have been redlined, others did not.[332]

Moreover, in 1980, David Listokin and Stephen Casey were able to use new data to show that mortgage lending in Chicago was affected by the racial composition of neighborhoods, all else constant. They also concluded, however, that while the effect was statically significant, it was not economically important. The main drivers of mortgage lending, in other words, were objective economic variables. Racial discrimination was difficult to detect because it was marginal, meaning that it took place on the last dollar lent, and the fact that there was a last dollar lent (as opposed to banks lending whenever a positive net present value application was presented) was due to government regulations, especially usury caps, not to bankers. In practice, that meant that African-Americans just outside certain objective limits were encouraged not to apply, while marginal Euroamerican applicants were coached through the application process.[333]

The real world, however, looked much more sinister than that. So when African-Americans lost their farms at a rate ten times faster than Euroamerican farmers did, leaving only 33,000 black-owned farms in operation by the end of 1982, the obvious culprits were racist bankers and USDA officials, not the fact that most black farms tended to be

---

331 Schafer and Ladd, *Discrimination*, 9–10, 315.

332 Schafer and Ladd, *Discrimination*, 10–11, 280–81, 300.

333 Listokin and Casey, *Mortgage Lending*, 90–93; Guttentag and Wachter, *Redlining*, 1; Benston, *Regulating Financial Markets*, 57; Squires, "Community Reinvestment," 13.

smaller and in marginal geographical regions.[334] And of course politicians believed they had to act, whether there was a real solution to marginal discrimination or not. "Well, I'm not a statistician," Senator Alan J. Dixon admitted in 1990, "but when blacks are getting their loan applications rejected twice as often as whites … I conclude that discrimination is part of the problem."[335]

But matters were not so simple. After it became clear that HDMA data was insufficient to prove redlining, community groups started pointing to "several indirect tactics such as unfavorable terms and systematic under appraisal of property that could have the same effect" as a blanket refusal to lend within a certain area. They were part of a larger group of "angry residents" who joined with "local public officials, sympathetic academics, reporters" and others "to fight back" against institutions they felt must lay at the root of urban blight.[336] Some activists alleged that banks engaged in all sorts of dastardly tricks, including simply delaying the appraisal until the purchase-and-sale contract had expired, in order to avoid leaving direct evidence of redlining.[337] While such accusations were damning, they were not credible enough to prompt policy changes.

Finding it difficult to prove the existence of redlining statistically, some researchers also argued that "a finding that banks do not appear to discriminate against minorities in making mortgage loans might be due to advance screening by real estate brokers who tell their minority clients that they should not even apply for a bank loan," or steer them into, or away from, certain neighborhoods, or even from "insurance companies who [sic] may refuse to sell fire insurance in certain geographic areas or to some categories of home owners."[338] The real culprits in the insurance situation, though, were a higher risk environment combined with gov-

---

334 Osha Gray Davidson, *Broken Heartland: The Rise of America's Rural Ghetto* (New York: Free Press, 1990), 36–37.

335 Squires, "Community Reinvestment," 1.

336 Squires, "Community Reinvestment," 1.

337 Schafer and Ladd, *Discrimination*, 2, 8–9.

338 Schafer and Ladd, *Discrimination*, 2.

ernment rate regulations. Due to premium caps and higher claim rates, in other words, fire insurers could not profitably write business in many blighted areas, including the Bronx, much of which was intentionally burned in the 1970s.[339]

By the late 1980s, the discussion moved away from strict redlining to more general forms of discrimination. HMDA data made it clear to researchers that blacks were less likely to receive mortgage loans than non-blacks across a wide swath of loan products and markets/MSAs. Lacking access to detailed individual loan applications, however, researchers found it difficult to parse racism (skin color of the applicant) from other, economically legitimate variables including precise property location, credit and employment histories, additional wealth/collateral, ability of applicants to obtain the signatures of acceptable co-signers, loan-to-value ratios, or other factors.[340]

Interestingly, researchers were able to discern that rejection rates did not vary much between different lenders; those that lent the most (least) money to blacks were those that received the most (fewest) applications, not those with the highest (lowest) loan approval rates. Mortgage lenders, in other words, were all about equally racist or were responding to

---

339 Jeffrey Cohen, "Discussion," in *The Financial Condition and Regulation of Insurance Companies*, ed. Richard E. Randall and Richard W. Kopcke (Boston: Federal Reserve Bank of Boston, 1991); J. David Cummins, ed., *Deregulating Property-Liability Insurance: Restoring Competition and Increasing Market Efficiency*, (Washington, DC: AEI-Brookings Joint Center for Regulatory Studies, 2002); Scott E. Harrington, "Public Policy and Property-Liability Insurance," in *The Financial Condition and Regulation of Insurance Companies*, ed. Richard E. Randall and Richard W. Kopcke (Boston: Federal Reserve Bank of Boston, 1991); Richard Syron, "Administered Prices and the Market Reaction: The Case of Urban Core Property Insurance," *Journal of Finance* 28, no. 1 (1973): 147–56; Richard Plunz, *A History of Housing in New York City: Dwelling Type and Social Change in the American Metropolis*, (New York: Columbia University Press, 1990), 323.

340 See Robert B. Avery, Patricia E. Beeson, and Mark S. Sniderman, "Underserved Mortgage Markets: Evidence from HMDA Data," Federal Reserve Bank of Cleveland Working Paper 9421 (December 1994); Robert B. Avery, Patricia E. Beeson, and Mark S. Sniderman, "Accounting for Racial Differences in Housing Credit Markets," Federal Reserve Bank of Cleveland Working Paper 9310 (December 1993) and Robert B. Avery, Patricia E. Beeson, and Mark S. Sniderman, "Cross-Lender Variation in Home Mortgage Lending," Federal Reserve Bank of Cleveland Working Paper 9219 (December 1992).

the same objective applicant characteristics. So while African-American mortgage applicants were clearly less likely to obtain a loan, it remained unclear whether they were denied at a higher rate (2.5 times higher!) because they were objectively less creditworthy or because lenders were discriminating against them on the basis of their race.[341]

In 1989, troubled by the vast difference in loan acceptance rates, Joseph P. Kennedy II (Robert Kennedy's son) urged the expansion of HDMA, which was added to FIRREA (Financial Institutions Reform, Recovery, and Enforcement Act) and went into effect starting in 1990. In 1992, after their initial findings had been leaked in the press, several researchers associated with the Boston Federal Reserve made public the draft of a paper that used the newly expanded HDMA data.[342] They argued that their analysis proved beyond a doubt that after controlling for important variables associated with creditworthiness, blacks were less likely to obtain a mortgage than whites. The study was soon attacked along several fronts, including shoddy data collection (GIGO). Others argued that even the expanded HMDA did not require the reporting of enough information to parse racial discrimination from the complex maelstrom of lending variables. (Similar problems hounded examination of the homeowners' insurance industry where state regulators mandated the disclosure of HMDA-like data.)[343]

The authors responded to the criticism and in 1996 published their findings in the *American Economic Review*, arguably the most important

---

341 Avery, Beeson, and Sniderman, "Cross-Lender Variation"; Stephen Ross and John Yinger, *The Color of Credit: Mortgage Discrimination, Research Methodology, and Fair-Lending Enforcement* (Cambridge: The MIT Press, 2002), 3–4.

342 Stan J. Liebowitz, "Anatomy of a Train Wreck: Causes of the Mortgage Meltdown," in *Housing America: Building Out of a Crisis*, ed. Randall Holcombe and Benjamin Powell (New Brunswick: Transaction Publishers), 292.

343 Anon., "Mortgage Lending Discrimination," Field Hearing Before the Committee on Financial Services, U.S. House of Representatives, One Hundred Tenth Congress, 1st Sess., 15 October 2007, 2; Ross and Yinger, *Color of Credit*, 3; Avery, Beeson, and Sniderman, "Cross-Lender Variation"; James Campen, "The Struggle for Community Investment in Boston, 1989–1991," in *From Redlining to Reinvestment: Community Responses to Urban Disinvestment*, ed. Gregory D. Squires (Philadelphia: Temple University Press, 1992), 41; Liebowitz, "Anatomy of a Train Wreck," 291–92. Galster, "Use of Testers," 290, 295–98.

peer-reviewed journal in economics. The study concluded that blacks (and Hispanics) were 80 percent more likely to be turned down for a mortgage than comparable whites were. The Boston Fed study continued, however, to be widely criticized. In addition to never being replicated or improved upon, the study contained some findings that went against accepted wisdom. Most importantly, perhaps, was the claim that wealthy blacks faced twice as much discrimination as poor blacks did.[344]

Scholarly discussion of the Boston Fed Study culminated in 2002, when Stephen Ross and John Yinger argued in *The Color of Credit* that the study was correct. Lenders did discriminate against black mortgage applicants, but the study itself had not definitively proven that point, an achievement Ross and Yinger claimed for themselves thanks to a series of methodological improvements.[345]

From Subtle Discrimination to Voracious Predation

As a general, and almost an invariable rule, you had better not place any dependence upon any body's honor or honesty. — A Reformed Stock Gambler, Stocks and Stock-Jobbing in Wall-Street, with Sketches of the Brokers, and Fancy Stocks (New York: New-York Publishing Company, 1848), 24.

While econometricians battled over the quality of the Boston Fed study and other statistical examinations of lending data, most of which turned up indefinite results, other researchers tried a different, more direct, but much more costly approach; the "audit," "test," or, more specifically, the "matched paired field test." In those studies, a trained member of a minority group and a Euroamerican are given false credit profiles (always slightly in favor of the minority) sent to actual lenders a few days apart to feign interest in obtaining a mortgage. To remain

344 Ross and Yinger, *Color of Credit*, 4, 8–9.
345 Ross and Yinger, *Color of Credit*, 8–12.

ethical and legal, the parties never actually apply for a mortgage but they do take detailed notes on how they are treated during the information gathering process to see if lenders signaled not to bother applying for a mortgage, thus keeping them out of HMDA, steered them into higher cost products, and so forth. Overall, the studies find that some lenders do sometimes treat putative minority applicants differently than white ones by giving them less information or follow up. Some even steer minorities into cheaper housing or quote them higher interest rates. The good news is that such subtle forms of discrimination, while definitely extant, do not appear to be pervasive, although some studies have shown higher levels of differential treatment than others.[346]

From October 2005 to January 2006, for example, Ginny Hamilton of the Fair Housing Center of Greater Boston sent "racially matched pairs of trained volunteers to visit 10 banks and 10 mortgage lenders, and to report in detail on their experiences" trying to obtain a $475,000 mortgage on a $500,000 property. Ten had credit scores around 750 and ten had scores of about 650. In each matched pair, the testers of color (African-American, Latino, and Asian) had slightly better credit scores and lower debt loads than their white counterparts but in 9 of the 20 cases, the white applicant received more product information, better initial interview follow-up, and offers of lower closing costs than their darker-skinned matched pair. Although Hamilton admitted the discrimination was "subtle," she insisted the results were "disturbing" and would have had a major impact on real applicants.[347]

---

346 Michael Fix, George C. Galster, and Raymond J. Struyk, "An Overview of Auditing for Discrimination," in *Clear and Convincing Evidence: Measurement of Discrimination in America*, ed. Michael Fix and Raymond J. Struyk (Washington, DC: Urban Institute Press, 1993), 1, 2, 10; Shanna L. Smith, "The Fair-Housing Movement's Alternative Standard for Measuring Housing Discrimination: Comments," in *Clear and Convincing Evidence: Measurement of Discrimination in America*, ed. Michael Fix and Raymond J. Struyk (Washington, DC: Urban Institute Press, 1993), 335–36; Schafer and Ladd, *Discrimination*, 316; King, *Discrimination in Mortgage Lending*, 3; Galster, "Use of Testers," 300, 304–14; Margery Turner, Fred Freiberg, Erin Godfrey, Carla Herbig, Diane K. Levy, and Robin R. Smith, *All Other Things Being Equal: A Paired Testing Study of Mortgage Lending Institutions*, (Washington, D.C.: Urban Institute, April 2002).

347 Anon., "Mortgage Lending Discrimination," 26–27, 96.

Unsurprisingly, the methodology of matched pair testing has come under increased scrutiny, especially when the principal investigators, like Hamilton, are already on record regarding the prevalence of financial discrimination. Some critics claim "that it is virtually impossible to match auditors on all characteristics that are perceived by the agent as relevant."[348] Others note that the testers are not particularly motivated to act as they really would because they get paid the same regardless of the outcome of the interview. Moreover, assigning an actor a certain income, education, and so forth does not mean that they can ad lib the appropriate dialogue, attitude, clothes, and so forth. Loan officers may sense something amiss and not put much effort into what might prove to be a difficult application to deny. Other tests must be dismissed due to idiosyncratic errors committed by the investigators.[349]

In rare cases, undercover "sting" operations have revealed wrongdoing and are difficult to dispute. In the 1990s, for example, a Milwaukee district sales manager was caught on tape criticizing agents for writing too many homeowners policies for African-Americans and providing tips on how to avoid writing policies for black homeowners, a clear violation of the 1968 Fair Housing Act. Taping and reviewing everything that financiers say, however, is clearly not cost effective.[350]

None of the anti-discrimination laws passed in the 1960s, 1970s, and 1980s helped to close the gap between white and black homeownership rates. The least helpful may have been the Community Reinvestment Act (CRA) passed in 1977. The approach taken by CRA was to force lenders accused of redlining to prove that they were not discriminating on the basis of race or other protected characteristics. By the late 1980s, that put tremendous power into the hands of community groups, like Boston's Community Investment Coalition (CIC), that could impose heavy costs

---

348 Fix, George C. Galster, and Raymond J. Struyk, "An Overview of Auditing, 29.

349 Fix, Galster, and Struyk, "An Overview of Auditing," 30–32; Galster, "Use of Testers," 314–20.

350 Committee on Banking, Housing, and Urban Affairs, U.S. Senate, 103rd Congress, 2nd Sess., "Homeowners' Insurance Discrimination," 11 May 1994, (Washington: GPO, 1994), 2.

on lenders that wanted to merge, establish new branches, form holding companies, engage in a broader array of financial services, and so forth. There were also potential fines and lawsuit and settlement costs, like the $1 million Decatur Federal of Atlanta was forced to pay to 48 black mortgage applicants in 1992. Those higher costs, of course, induced lenders to withdraw from, or avoid entering, the very areas the CRA was supposed to help. It also caused mortgage origination to shift from banks, which were covered by the Act, to other, non-covered financial institutions. To this day, CRA has enough bite to induce big banks to take big steps to improve their ratings, including establishing extraneous branches in high traffic areas, like various business districts, considered low income areas by government bean counters.[351]

Starting in earnest in the 1960s, community activists and certain politicians appealed to banks to lend to inner city residents and businesses as a sort of social crusade. They were supposed to set aside the notion of profit and loss on specific loans and simply invest in failing neighborhoods either as part of the 'white man's burden' to 'civilize' the brown peoples of the world or, more selfishly, to save their own institutions in the long run. Edward McDonald, Community Relations Officer for Norwest Bank (now Wells Fargo), argued the latter when he noted that "a growing and significant number of lenders today see both the future of their cities and the self-interest of their institutions as inseparable from increased community reinvestment."[352] So did Guardian and other life insurers who concluded in the late 1960s that it was in the best interest of their policyholders (and shareholders in the case of joint-stock insurers) to invest one percent of their assets in low-income housing and new job-producing enterprises in the "hard core" areas of American cities. By one count, by

---

351 Collins and Margo, "Race and Home Ownership," 356–58; Campen, "The Struggle for Community Investment in Boston," 42–46; Squires, "Community Reinvestment," 11; Ross and Yinger, *Color of Credit*, 4; Hyman, *Debtor Nation*, 185; Guttentag and Wachter, *Redlining*, 3, 40–44; Anon., "Mortgage Lending Discrimination," 6; Rachel Louise Ensign and AnnaMaria Andriotis, "Banks See Low Income Where the Rich Shop," *Wall Street Journal*, 19 May 2017.

352 Edward McDonald, "Community Reinvestment Is Good for Cities, Good for Lenders," in *From Redlining to Reinvestment: Community Responses to Urban Disinvestment*, ed. Gregory D. Squires (Philadelphia: Temple University Press, 1992), vii.

1992 $18 billion in urban reinvestment commitments had been negotiated with lenders in more than seventy cities throughout the nation, but especially in Boston due to the media's sensationalization of the Boston Fed Study. Although seemingly impressive at first, $18 billion was but a drop in the ocean and not even all of it was employed to battle blight.[353]

With all else a dismal failure (either because of bad regulations or insufficient enforcement depending on one's ideological views), the final solution for financial discrimination, if you will forgive the expression, was simply to lower credit standards. The first move came in 1992, with passage of the Housing and Community Development Act (HCDA), which directed the two government-sponsored mortgage behemoths Fannie Mae and Freddie Mac to satisfy "unmet housing needs" by increasing their lending activities/mortgage purchases in "underserved areas" like central cities and rural areas. Like CRA, HCDA presumed, without clear evidence, that a market failure (racial discrimination) prevented well-qualified borrowers from securing mortgages at market rates.[354]

Lowering credit quality would have sounded crazy to generations of bankers who believed that the strength of a bank lay not in its size but in the soundness of its assets and the size of its equity base vis-à-vis its liabilities. There, however, were claims, plausible on their face if history was ignored (as it too often is in policy debates), that mortgage securitization, the packaging of many risky mortgages into a single security, could make the risks that individual mortgages represented more predictable and hence manageable. Fintech (financial technology) would save the day and render traditional, conservative bank management obsolete.[355]

Were it so! What actually happened was that products rooted in lower credit standards, like subprime mortgages, tended to become predatory, i.e., designed to cause foreclosure and loss of homeowner equity.

---

353 Wright and Smith, *Mutually Beneficial*, 320, 365–66; Squires, "Community Reinvestment," 2; Campen, "The Struggle for Community Investment in Boston," 38.

354 Immergluck, *Credit to the Community*, 4; Liebowitz, "Anatomy of a Train Wreck," 292–97; Avery, Beeson, and Sniderman, "Underserved Mortgage Markets."

355 Should We permit a Large Increase in Deposits?, Misc. Bank Documents East Side/Community, Rush Rhees Library.

African-Americans had long suffered at the hands of financial predators. But prior to the 1990s, most predatory exploitation was either illegal or at least partially economically justified. One woman in 1950s Texas who borrowed $50 from three different loan sharks, for example, ended up paying $10,000 to 39 different sharks over 4 years but still owed $2,884 in interest plus the original $150 debt! Those transactions, though, were illegal. By contrast, the "Black Tax," the higher mortgage rates paid by most African-American homeowners, and the "Ghetto Tax," the higher rates and possibility of repossession suffered by African-Americans living in urban enclaves, were legal but at least ostensibly justified by the higher costs associated with making smaller, riskier loans in a market that was far from its competitive equilibrium.[356]

For decades, lenders sloughed off the risk associated with shakier borrowers by encouraging them to purchase PMI, or private mortgage insurance. Though it raised the costs of borrowing, PMI was not, and is not, tax deductible. It essentially rendered redlining unnecessary by protecting lenders against default. Due to regulatory changes, however, lenders increasingly wanted to keep that risk, and the higher rates associated with it, for themselves. Starting in the mid-1990s and culminating in the early 2000s, mortgage lending to all but the wealthiest African-Americans became systematically predatory in that subprime mortgages, many of which were made in the hopes of inducing default (to extract fees) or foreclosure (to gain title to collateral), came into widespread, legal, and even government-condoned use. Between 1993 and 1998, subprime mortgages to blacks exploded almost 3,000 percent, compared to just a 270 percent increase for all subprime mortgages. By the latter year, subprime mortgage lending dominated black neighborhoods throughout the nation. Already by 1999, observers were warning that high rates and onerous terms were leading to foreclosures and, in the heady market, significant losses of equity for black borrowers. And matters deteriorated further from there. By 2002, default rates on subprime mortgages in some African-American neighborhoods, like "Back of the Yards" in Chicago, were

---

356 Black, *Buy Now*, 161; McEntire, *Residence and Race*, 222; Hyman, *Debtor Nation*, 178–79.

already above 10 percent, with more defaults expected as abandoned housing drove down property values and hence increased the incentive of remaining homeowners to default.[357]

Beginning in 2004, the HMDA finally began to include interest rates and clearly showed that blacks paid more. The data also revealed a sort of reverse redlining, with mortgage companies making predatory loans in the same downtrodden neighborhoods where banks had traditionally feared to tread.[358]

The new "liars' loans" (no income verification but a credit check thought to be a sufficient substitute), "no doc" loans (no verification of any claims made on loan applications), "IO" loans (interest-only loans with giant balloon payments due at the end of the term), "120" loans (loans deliberately made with a 20 percent *negative* down payment), "ARMs" (mortgages with low initial rates that adjusted upward after a few years), "negative am" loans (mortgages with payments so low that the borrower actually owed more at the end of each month), and similar exotic products made sense only for flippers and speculators in a bull housing market. Most such loans, however, went to minority borrowers: women, American Indians, white trash, Latinos, and, of course, African Americans. But what else would one expect from lenders, like Wells Fargo, that regularly referred to African-Americans in internal correspondence, *in the 1990s and 2000s*, as "mud people"?[359]

According to Mechele Dickerson, "more than 50 percent of all loans blacks used to purchase homes ... were subprime loan products. These

---

357 Stephen M. Miller and Geoffrey M. B. Tootell, "Redlining, the Community Reinvestment Act, and Private Mortgage Insurance," Economics Working Papers, DigitalCommons@ UConn (2000); Anon., "Mortgage Lending Discrimination"; National Community Reinvestment Coalition, "The 2005 Fair Lending Disparities: Stubborn and Persistent II," (Washington: National Community Reinvestment Coalition, 2006); Immergluck, *Credit to the Community*, 6, 112–13; Bill Dedham, "Study Discerns Disadvantage for Blacks in Home Mortgages," in *Race, Class and Gender in the United States* 5th ed., ed. Paula S. Rothenberg (New York: Worth, 2001), 228–30; Ross and Yinger, *Color of Credit*, 24–26.

358 Anon., "Mortgage Lending Discrimination," 18, 23–25, 49.

359 Dickerson, *Homeownership*, 12.

subprime loans had higher fees and riskier payment options."[360] When the bubble burst, many of those borrowers lost their homes (and their jobs). While median net worth for whites fell 16 percent between 2005 and 2009, over those same awful years it fell 53 percent for blacks (and a whopping 66 percent for Latinos).[361]

What began as the government's attempt to bring homeowner-ship rates closer to racial parity ended as one of the most heinous cases of financial expropriation in American history. And nobody has done anything about it, though IO mortgages continue to mature with bor-rowers deeply underwater (owing more than the current market value of the home). That slow motion train wreck derailed economic recovery for almost a decade by pinching consumption, the modern American economy's steam engine.

Most damning of all, even lowering credit standards did not end discrimination, at least not in the estimation of Massachusetts Congress-man Barney Frank, who in 2007 called a hearing to discuss what he called "the sad record of discrimination in the granting of mortgages. ... The data shows," he claimed, "that racial and ethnic discrimination persists ... if you are African- American or Hispanic in this country ... you are less likely to get a mortgage, and more likely, if you do get a mortgage, to have to pay more for it than you should."[362]

Tellingly, where subprime mortgages did not reach, much evi-dence of discrimination remains. Black businesses remained starved of capital throughout the final decades of the twentieth century and into the twenty-first (though apparently partly out of business location rather than race per se). According to a 2014 study conducted by the U.S. Census Bureau, African-American entrepreneurs (47%) were much less likely than whites (76%) to obtain the full amount of business loans requested. According to Alicia Robb, a senior fellow at the Ewing Marion Kauff-

---

360 Dickerson, *Homeownership*, 14.

361 Dickerson, *Homeownership*, 15.

362 Field Hearing Before the Committee on Financial Services, "Mortgage Lending Discrimi-nation," 2.

man Foundation (EMKF), a think tank dedicated to the study of new businesses, "across the board, blacks have higher denial rates, even after controlling for credit and wealth." According to research conducted by EMKF, black entrepreneurs were almost three times more likely than whites to cite access to capital as a constraint on their profitability.[363]

Only those who had deluded themselves into thinking progress had been made were surprised by those findings. Even more damning, African-Americans are not the only group still subject to discrimination and even, in the case of American Indians, outright exclusion.

---

363 Immergluck, *Credit to the Community*, 6, 64–69; Ruth Simon and Paul Overberg, "Credit Gap for Black-Owned Firms," *Wall Street Journal*, 10 November 2016.

CHAPTER FOUR

The First Peoples:
The Last to be Banked

To be unbanked is to be under an economic disadvantage. It means
that many people have to rely on fringe banking services, such as
check-cashing outlets with high fees. But what is worse is the savings
deficit that it creates for many ... citizens, who have a much harder
time acquiring and building assets. —*Joseph Lieberman, as quoted*
in Ebonya Washington, "The Impact of Banking and Fringe Banking
Regulation on the Number of Unbanked Americans," Journal of
Human Resources 41, 1 (Winter 2006): 106.

Some people prefer not to use banks. The brother of South Dakota
banker Art Dahl, for example, would not use the banks in Minneapolis, where he lived in 1954, because he did not like the way they did
business, which was typically very slowly. So he cashed his checks at the
local hardware store and bought money orders to pay his bills. That was
Dahl's choice, and the choice of many other people who prefer to feel
respected by a finance company rather than disrespected by banks. Many
poor Americans, however, are unbanked against their will. In the 1980s
and 1990s, 35 to 45 percent of the poorest households in the country did

not have access to a traditional bank, a far higher unbanked rate than the rest of the population. As indicated in the head quote, the involuntarily unbanked pay high fees, as high as 10 percent of face value, to cash checks and very high rates to borrow, when they can borrow at all.

As the poorest of the poor, Indians living off the reservation are among the least likely to be banked and face the same sort of discrimination faced by African-Americans and Hispanics. This chapter isn't about those largely urban Indians, who have made some strides in recent decades, it is about Indians enrolled in specific tribes and living on reservations. Their access to the financial system is even more highly restricted and costly.[364]

Call them what you will — First Peoples, Native Americans, Amerindians, "feather" Indians, or, as most of them prefer, American Indians or just plain Indians – indigenous peoples are subjected to racial stereotypes so destructive that they greatly inhibit social justice and racial harmony. In Winner, South Dakota, for example, Indians mostly live on the north side and Euroamericans on the south side of the highway, while in nearby Wagner, Indians and whites dine at different restaurants and attend different churches and sociocultural activities. Indians in the West were long subjected to a type of Jim Crow system of segregation, partly legal and partly normative, that led to the establishment of Indian-only schools, bars and so forth.[365]

---

364 A. E. Dahl, *Banker Dahl of South Dakota: An Autobiography* (Rapid City: Fenske Book Company, 1965), 168–69; Kate Porter Young, "Rural South Carolina: An Ethnographic Study of Homeownership, Home Financing, and Credit," *Cityscape* 3, no. 1 (1997): 33; Ebonya Washington, "The Impact of Banking and Fringe Banking Regulation on the Number of Unbanked Americans," *Journal of Human Resources* 41, no. 1 (2006): 106–7; Duane Champagne, "Tribal Capitalism and Native Capitalists: Multiple Pathways of Native Economy," in *Native Pathways: American Indian Culture and Economic Development*, ed. Brian Hosmer and Colleen O'Neill (Boulder: University Press of Colorado, 2004), 317–20; Robert Miller, "Indian Entrepreneurship," in *Unlocking the Wealth of Indian Nations*, ed. Terry Anderson (New York: Lexington Books, 2016), 255.

365 Stephen L. Pevar, *The Rights of Indians and Tribes*, 4th ed. (New York: Oxford University Press, 2012), 1, 236–38; Colin G. Calloway, *Pen and Ink Witchcraft: Treaties and Treaty Making in American Indian History*, (New York: Oxford University Press, 2013), xii; Stuart Banner, *How the Indians Lost Their Land: Law and Power on the Frontier*, (Cambridge: Belknap Press, 2005), 8; Jeff Corntassel and Richard C. Witmer, *Forced Federalism: Contemporary Challenges to*

Considered "noble savages" after first contact, people who simply needed time to "catch up" to "civilization," Indians became increasingly reviled by Euroamerican elites as native peoples countered violence with violence and deception with deception in a complicated game of tit-for-tat that lasted centuries. While the roots of the ideology of Indian biological inferiority can be traced to nineteenth-century pseudo-sciences like phrenology and Social Darwinism, the tree of racism flourishes still. Derogatory team mascots and ridiculous Hollywood characters are only the most visible branches of a very large and ugly root system of hatred lurking just below the surface. In 1999, just twenty years ago, someone actually posted a "license" to hunt and trap Indians allegedly issued by the South Dakota Department of Game, Fish, and Parks that included gruesome details like bag and possession limits, as well as racist tips on how to bait and track Indians by following "trails of empty wine bottles."[366]

Where such stereotypes make no sense, new stereotypes have arisen or been resuscitated. One stereotype is of the "idle savage" or lazy Indian. According to this myth, Indians, all Indians, both before and after contact with the West, worked just enough to live and no more. Even their agricultural practices were denigrated as lazy even though they were as efficient as possible given the technology available. A related and equally pernicious stereotype is of the "rich Indian," the notion that indigenous peoples are no longer "authentic" and do not have to work for what they consume or own because it comes from unfair casinos,

---

Indigenous Nationhood, (Norman: University of Oklahoma Press, 2008), xiv, 27; Terry Anderson, *Sovereign Nations or Reservations? An Economic History of American Indians*, (San Francisco: Pacific Research Institute for Public Policy, 1995), xvi; Harry F. Thompson, ed. *A New South Dakota History*, 2nd ed. (Sioux Falls: Center for Western Studies, 2009), 511–12; David Murray, *Indian Giving: Economies of Power in Indian-White Exchanges*, (Amherst: University of Massachusetts Press, 2000), 2, 22–23, 31, 86–88.

366 H. Craig Miner, *The Corporation and the Indian: Tribal Sovereignty and Industrial Civilization in Indian Territory, 1865–1907*, (Norman: University of Oklahoma Press, 1976), 134; Naomi Schaefer Riley, *The New Trail of Tears: How Washington Is Destroying American Indians*, (New York: Encounter Books, 2016), 9; Banner, *How the Indians Lost Their Land*, 248; Alexandra Harmon, *Rich Indians: Native People and the Problem of Wealth in American History*, (Chapel Hill: University of North Carolina Press, 2010), 233; Dean Chavers, *Racism in Indian Country*, (New York: Peter Lang, 2009), 67–69.

natural resource endowments "given" to them, or government handouts, including exemptions from taxation and other "special rights." Although more widespread than ever, the rich Indian stereotype is not new, despite claims to the contrary. Actually, for over a century wealthy Indian ranchers and oil magnates have spawned negative commentary from jealous Indians and Euroamericans alike.[367]

Most of the time, though, most Euroamericans simply ignore native peoples, perhaps hoping that they will somehow go away. A few even believe they are already 'extinct.' With precious few exceptions, economic historians have long ignored Indians. Even historians of America's underclass often forget about them! Native peoples, for example, are explicitly mentioned only *once* in Jacqueline Jones's otherwise excellent book *Dispossessed*, which also referenced South Dakota as the home of the nation's poorest counties without mentioning their status as reservations.[368] Many historians, it seems, think of Indians as somehow special or different. "We have a long way to go to come around to the belief that Indians are full human beings, as capable in their pursuits as other people," notes Dean Chavers, an Indian and a scholar. "Indians can love, work hard, get an education, raise families, write books, build businesses, and do all the other things other people can do; however, barriers are built to prevent Indians from doing almost all these things."[369] Chavers also points out that while Indians are far from an homogenous group, that does not mean that they do not share much in common, with each other and with the rest of humanity.[370]

367 David Arnold, "Work and Culture in Southeastern Alaska: Tlingits and the Salmon Fisheries," in *Native Pathways: American Indian Culture and Economic Development*, ed. Brian Hosmer and Colleen O'Neill (Boulder: University Press of Colorado, 2004), 156–57; Corntassel and Witmer, *Forced Federalism*, 24–26, 30–46, 135; Harmon, *Rich Indians*.

368 Riley, *New Trail of Tears*, x; Harmon, *Rich Indians*, 11; Linda Barrington, "Native Americans and U.S. Economic History," in *The Other Side of the Frontier: Economic Explorations into Native American History*, ed. Linda Barrington (New York: Westview Press, 1999), ix-x; Jacqueline Jones, *The Dispossessed: America's Underclasses from the Civil War to the Present* (New York: Basic Books, 1992), 269, 284.

369 Chavers, *Racism*, 5.

370 Riley, *New Trail of Tears*, xii.

The peoples who lived in North America when Christopher Columbus first bumbled into the continent in 1492 were simply human beings trying to make a living, and for the most part doing a darn good job of it. For all the rich diversity in detail, their cultures were, in essence, fundamentally similar to those of peoples throughout the globe employing similar subsistence strategies, which ranged from simple hunting and gathering to mixed horticulture to full blown ranching. Like African-Americans (and poor whites and women as we will see), Indians were stereotyped by those who sought to control them. Ultimately, though, their intelligence, temperament, capabilities, beliefs, and values varied not just from individual to individual but within individuals over time, place, and context.

So, as historian Alexandra Harmon has shown, history reveals not "clearly demarcated bands of people, with greedy Whites at one edge of a limited spectrum, and poor but generous Indians at the other." Instead, history reveals "a broader, fuzzier spectrum of skin colors and behaviors that includes Euro-Americans who championed Indian property rights and Indians who sought additional wealth for selfish ends."[371] What most Indians have wanted is simply freedom to do as they please. As Chief Joseph put it in 1879, "Let me be a free man, free to travel, free to stop, free to work, free to trade where I choose, free to follow the religion of my fathers, free to talk, think, and act for myself."[372]

Due to war, massacre, enslavement, disease, and economic disruption, the population of Indians in North America plummeted from as many as 12 million in 1492 to a rock bottom of about 250,000 in 1900. By 1991, however, their numbers had rebounded to about 2 million and have since grown to about 2.1 million. About one in five now reside on reservations and hence live under the ultimate control of the Bureau of Indian Affairs (BIA, formerly the Office of Indian Affairs or OIA), a brutal bureaucracy composed, ironically, of wonderful, compassionate individuals too

---

371 Harmon, *Rich Indians*, 15.

372 As quoted in Terry Anderson, ed., *Unlocking the Wealth of Indian Nations*, (New York: Lexington Books, 2016), v.

dull to see that, like their bureaucratic forebears, they daily crush Indians' native initiative. Unemployment rates on reservations run as high as 80 percent while average incomes generally lurk well below the federal poverty line. Unsurprisingly, sundry social and health problems, like criminal gangs and diabetes, associated with poverty abound even though Indians on reservations have access to free government healthcare.[373]

Contrary to myth, Indians were not/are not all and always natural environmentalists, primitive communists, or lazy savages; they were and are people who respond rationally (well, semi-rationally like the rest of us) to the circumstances they face at any given time. They did not/do not live outside of (some would say above) the laws of supply and demand any more than they live outside the laws of physics or chemistry. They were and are economic actors who respond(ed) to incentives, just like everyone else. If you believe otherwise, you probably have imbibed too much of the Leftist anthropological literature of the 1960s-1980s, almost all of which has since been reinterpreted or outright debunked. What were once called "gifts" are increasingly likened to "bribes," "kinship obligations" are now seen as a form of "nepotism," "reciprocity" is only a form of "exploitation," "sharing" is now understood as "insurance," and even "potlatches" have become "credit markets."[374]

---

373 The best recent overview of the enslavement of Indians is Andrés Reséndez, *The Other Slavery: The Uncovered Story of Indian Enslavement in America*, (New York: Houghton Mifflin Harcourt, 2016) but see also Alan Gallay, *The Indian Slave Trade: The Rise of English Empire in the American South, 1670–1717*, (New Haven: Yale University Press, 2002) and Margaret Newell, *Brethren by Nature: New England Indians, Colonists, and the Origins of American Slavery* (Ithaca: Cornell University Press 2015). On the population, see Barrington, "Native Americans," 1 or Robert J. Miller, *Reservation "Capitalism": Economic Development in Indian Country*, (Denver: ABC-CLIO, 2012), 1–2, 29. On warfare, see Anderson, *Sovereign Nations*, 70, 76–85; Beth B. Hess, Elizabeth W. Markson, and Peter J. Stein, "Racial and Ethnic Minorities: An Overview," in *Race, Class and Gender in the United States* 5th ed., ed. Paula S. Rothenberg (New York: Worth, 2001), 324–25; David Benson, Aaron Lies, Albert Okunade, Phanindra Wunnava, "Economic Impact of a Private Sector Micro-Financing Scheme in South Dakota," *Small Business Economics* 36 (2011): 158; Ian Frazier, *On the Rez* (New York: Farrar, Straus and Giroux, 2000), 258.

374 Riley, *New Trail of Tears*, 14, 25–27; Banner, *How the Indians Lost Their Land*, 261, 264–65; Harmon, *Rich Indians*, 11–12, 22, 43, 63–66; Miller, *Reservation "Capitalism"*; Craig Galbraith, Carlos Rodriguez, and Curt Stiles, "False Myths and Indigenous Entrepreneurial

Establishing the reality of the economic, human Indian is essential because many non-Indians believe that native peoples (with the exception of "mostly white casino" Indians) *want* to be poor because it is in their "nature" or part of their "culture."[375] That despite the fact that Indians regularly assert that "traditional … values do not include poverty" and that "we had tried poverty for 200 years, so we decided to try something else."[376]

This chapter shows that Indians are not culturally or genetically bound to poverty. Before Columbus unleashed a chain of events that forever changed the continent, Indians were entrepreneurs seeking to improve the conditions of their material existence. They successfully adapted to Euroamerican colonization and would have thrived economically and spiritually had not government policies rendered them mere infants in the eyes of the law, their liberty, property, and very lives under the absolute control of others.[377] In 1934, Rides at Door, a member of the Blackfeet tribe, put the matter in the starkest terms. Oil had been discovered on his reservation and oil wells were pumping it out. All the tribe needed now was "some law or protection whereby I can always hold that property intact so that no white man can take it away."[378] To this day,

---

Strategies," in *Self Determination: The Other Path for Native Americans*, ed. Terry Anderson, Bruce Benson, and Thomas Flanagan (Stanford: Stanford University Press, 2006), 4–5; Lance Greene and Mark R. Plane, "Introduction," in *American Indians and the Market Economy, 1775–1850*, ed. Lance Greene and Mark R. Plane (Tuscaloosa: University of Alabama Press, 2010), 10–13; Kathleen Ann Pickering, *Lakota Culture, World Economy*, (Lincoln: University of Nebraska Press, 2000), 28; Paul C. Rosier, "Searching for Salvation and Sovereignty: Blackfeet Oil Leasing and the Reconstruction of the Tribe," in *Native Pathways: American Indian Culture and Economic Development*, ed. Brian Hosmer and Colleen O'Neill (Boulder: University Press of Colorado, 2004), 41; Ann Carlos and Frank D. Lewis, "Native American Property Rights in the Hudson Bay Region: A Case Study of the Eighteenth-Century Cree," in *Self Determination: The Other Path for Native Americans*, ed. Terry Anderson, Bruce Benson, and Thomas Flanagan (Stanford: Stanford University Press, 2006; Ann Carlos and Frank Lewis, "Native Americans, Exchange, and the Role of Gift-Giving," in *Unlocking the Wealth of Indian Nations*, ed. Terry Anderson (New York: Lexington Books, 2016), 39–40, 47–51, 84.

375 Galbraith, Rodriguez, and Stiles, "False Myths," 25–27.

376 As quoted in Miller, *Reservation "Capitalism,"* 4–5.

377 Riley, *New Trail of Tears*, 8.

378 Rosier, "Searching for Salvation," 28.

Indian entrepreneurs, be they individual businesspeople or entire tribes, find themselves stymied at every turn, including a lack of property rights and the attendant dearth of access to external financing.[379]

Except for members of the lucky few tribes that were geographically positioned to tap the casino boom of the 1990s, most Indians today remain poor, even by Appalachian or inner city standards. America's poorest counties all contain Indian reservations. Very few Indians have easy or inexpensive access to any sort of financial institution, rendering attempts at self-help, like entrepreneurial ventures, doomed to remain nano-sized.[380]

Precontact Indian Enterprise, Money, and Finance

S cholars are no longer as certain as they once were about precisely when and how the first humans arrived in the New World. It remains clear, however, that Indians dominated the Western hemisphere for at least ten millennia and they did not do so sitting around like Hollywood stereotypes stoically sucking on peace pipes and making sweet love to Mother Nature.[381] Their cultures *must* have provided incentives for productive activity or Indians would have starved, frozen, and/or been overtaken by predators, human or animal. And those incentives, those set of cultural beliefs and practices, must have adapted, and rather quickly at that, to a rapidly changing climate and landscape. Although they may have not directly caused the extinction of the megafauna (woolly mammoths and other gigantic critters), Indians were prodigious hunters who used fire to both funnel game into kill boxes and to create habitat more conducive to their favorite prey animals. They also used

---

379 Jennifer Malkin and Johnnie Aseron, *Native Entrepreneurship in South Dakota: A Deeper Look*, (CFED, December 2006), 12; Champagne, "Tribal Capitalism," 320–26.

380 Pickering, *Lakota Culture*, xi.

381 Neil Diamond, *Reel Injun* documentary. Barrington, "Native Americans," 5; Miller, *Reservation "Capitalism,"* 9.

fire to clear land to create travel lanes and for agriculture. Contrary to a myth that grew up in the early nineteenth century to justify the expropriation of Indian lands without compensation, many pre-contact Indians were skillful farmers. Even tribes not typically considered agricultural specialists, like those of New England, received some two-thirds of their calories from cultivated plots, with the balance coming from foraging, fishing, and hunting.[382]

Indians also built and ran manufacturing sites that created large quantities of goods like obsidian arrowheads, textiles, pottery, salt, shells, and pemmican, a highly nutritious mixture of fat, meat, and fruit that remained edible for long periods. Those goods were then traded, often over long distances, with help from rivers, chain trade (where durables like arrow points move long distances by being traded from neighbor to neighbor), peripatetic tribes, and periodic trade fairs later called "rendezvous" though they long predated the arrival of the French. After contact, some tribes, like the Caddo, leveraged their manufacturing traditions to add value to European trade goods for resale to other tribes.

Pre-contact Indians also built canals, dams, huge earthen temple mounds, paved road systems, and irrigation systems for business and public purposes. Several great cities arose and prospered before fading for reasons unknown. One of those cities, Cahokia, near present-day St. Louis and not coincidentally the confluence of the mighty Mississippi and Missouri Rivers, was home to tens of thousands of people and for half a millennia served as the economic, political, and spiritual center of a civilization that extended for hundreds of miles. In addition to being

---

382 Anderson, *Sovereign Nations*, xiv-xv; Riley, *New Trail of Tears*, 26; Vernon Smith, "Economy, Ecology, and Institutions in the Emergence of Humankind," in *The Other Side of the Frontier: Economic Explorations into Native American History*, ed. Linda Barrington (New York: Westview Press, 1999), 64–66, 72; William Cronon, *Changes in the Land: Indians, Colonists, and the Ecology of New England*, (New York: Hill and Wang, 1983), 13, 28, 47–51, 57–8, 108, 118–19; Richard White, *The Roots of Dependency: Subsistence, Environment, and Social Change Among the Choctaws, Pawnees, and Navajos*, (Lincoln: University of Nebraska Press, 1983), 10–11, 184–86, 195–96, 316–17; Galbraith, Rodriguez, and Stiles, "False Myths," 15; Banner, *How the Indians Lost Their Land*, 152–57; Miller, *Reservation "Capitalism,"* 9–10.

the major trade center, Cahokia also supported numerous artisanal
workshops.[383]

Like other human groups, Indians marshaled resources when they
were scarce (expensive) but were profligate when resources were ample
(cheap). For example, when beaver prices were high, they trapped more
beaver. And while they sometimes used every part of the bison, much
like modern agriculturalists use every part of the cow, at other times they
ate only the tongue or the unborn calf (the equivalent of veal). Indeed,
ancient mass kill sites suggest many bison killed by human hands were
never butchered or otherwise exploited. In the historical period, the
stench from rotting, unbutchered bison corpses lingered for months.
Indians also killed more jackrabbits and other herdable animals than they
could readily consume or trade. Several Indian civilizations, including that
of the Anasazi, may have collapsed due to the overexploitation of water
or timber resources.[384]

---

383 Smith, "Economy, Ecology, and Institutions," 64–65; Linda Barrington, "The Mississippians and Economic Development Before European Colonization," in *The Other Side of the
Frontier: Economic Explorations into Native American History*, ed. Linda Barrington (New
York: Westview Press, 1999), 86–102; Carlos and Lewis, "Native Americans," 42, 45–47; Pickering, *Lakota Culture*, 3–4; Miller, *Reservation "Capitalism,"* 19–23; Tressa Berman, "'All We
Needed Was Our Gardens': Women's Work and Welfare Reform in the Reservation Economy," in *Native Pathways: American Indian Culture and Economic Development*, ed. Brian Hosmer and Colleen O'Neill (Boulder: University Press of Colorado, 2004), 144; Terry Anderson
and Bryan Leonard, "Institutions and the Wealth of Indian Nations," in *Unlocking the Wealth
of Indian Nations*, ed. Terry Anderson (New York: Lexington Books, 2016), 3, 8; Miller, "Indian
Entrepreneurship," 248; Colin G. Calloway, *First Peoples: A Documentary Survey of American
Indian History*, 5th ed. (New York: Bedford/St. Martin's 2016), 34; Cody Newton, "Business
in the Hinterlands: The Impact of the Market Economy on the West-Central Great Plains at
the Turn of the 19th Century," in *American Indians and the Market Economy, 1775–1850*, ed.
Lance Greene and Mark R. Plane (Tuscaloosa: University of Alabama Press, 2010), 67–79; P.
Shawn Marceaux and Timothy K. Perttula, "Negotiating Borders: The Southern Caddo and
Their Relationships with Colonial Governments in East Texas," in *American Indians and the
Market Economy, 1775–1850*, ed. Lance Greene and Mark R. Plane (Tuscaloosa: University of
Alabama Press, 2010), 89, 92; Barrington, "Native Americans," 5–6; Miller, *Reservation "Capi-
talism,"* 19.

384 Riley, *New Trail of Tears*, 26–27; Carlos and Lewis, "Native American Property Rights,"
70, 76; Barrington, "Native Americans," 5; Terry Anderson and Steven LaCombe, "Institutional Change in the Indian Horse Culture," in *The Other Side of the Frontier: Economic
Explorations into Native American History*, ed. Linda Barrington (New York: Westview Press,

Large-scale manufacturing operations appear to have been owned by tribes, the Indian equivalent of corporations. Dwellings, agricultural land, livestock, weapons, and personal items, however, were generally owned by individuals.[385] As Manny Jules put it, the pit houses his people (the Kamloops in present-day British Columbia) built were substantial buildings "nice and toasty warm in the winter. In the summer we went out and gathered salmon, berries, wild vegetables, and hunted game. In the winter we came back to settled villages. There is no way we would have left and come back to allow some other family to live in our pit house."[386]

Substantial archeological and historical evidence compiled by Robert J. Miller, a member of the Eastern Shawnee Tribe, and others suggests that Jules was right and the Kamloops were the rule rather than the exception. Other tribes, like the Nootka, extended property rights beyond land and homes to clam beds, beaches, and even oceanic rocks and fishing holes.[387]

Truly communal property was rare among Indians. Fee simple ownership was also rare, but even in the Anglo-American legal tradition many other rights in land, like tenancy in common, were recognized and even extolled. Importantly, pre-contact Indians also had sundry cultural and political mechanisms for enforcing property rights and these were strongest where agriculture or ranching, like the ranching of salmon in the Northwest, was practiced. (Indians ranched salmon by controlling access to the streams leading from their pasturage in the ocean to their spawning beds.)[388]

1999), 115; Smith, "Economy, Ecology, and Institutions," 64; Anderson, *Sovereign Nations*, 58; Galbraith, Rodriguez, and Stiles, "False Myths," 16–18.

385 Pevar, *Rights of Indians*, 104–6, 262–64; Banner, *How the Indians Lost Their Land*, 264, 276; Harmon, *Rich Indians*, 137; Anderson and Leonard, "Institutions," 7.

386 As quoted in Riley, *New Trail of Tears*, 25–26.

387 Galbraith, Rodriguez, and Stiles, "False Myths," 6–12; Miller, "Indian Entrepreneurship," 247.

388 Miller, *Reservation "Capitalism,"* 11–18; Anderson, *Sovereign Nations*, 26–43; D. Bruce Johnsen, "A Culturally Correct Proposal to Privatize the British Columbia Salmon Fishery," in *Self Determination: The Other Path for Native Americans*, ed. Terry Anderson, Bruce Benson, and Thomas Flanagan (Stanford: Stanford University Press, 2006), 94–121; D. Bruce Johnsen,

Contrary to a modern myth *au courant* in certain circles, humans did indeed sometimes engage in barter, or the exchange of one good or service directly for another, without the use of money. Long-distance trade almost certainly involved barter at times while local transactions were usually handled informally, as amongst friends, family, and neighbors today. Intratribal exchange, by contrast, was conducted more formally but did not require monetary exchange either, as within a modern corporation where departments or plants share some resources and exchange others on a non-cash basis.[389]

Barter was so inefficient, however, that where trading became regularized and relatively large in volume, as it did throughout much of North America, commodity monies like wampum and copper came into use. Wampum was manufactured from seashells, then sometimes strung into necklaces or woven into belts for ceremonial or diplomatic purposes, but also often used to make payments. (California Indians also used a shell money.) Copper was shaped into small ingots from naturally occurring float copper by native peoples in Wisconsin and Michigan as early as 7500 BC. Use of copper as a medium of exchange was noted in historical sources and can also be inferred from caches discovered at archeological sites that contained ingots of two distinct sizes worked so they were flat and smooth for easy handling. Copper plates also served monetary purposes in the Northwest. Turquoise may have served as a currency in the Chaco Canyon region of what is today called New Mexico.[390]

"The Potlatch as Fractional Reserve Banking," in *Unlocking the Wealth of Indian Nations*, ed. Terry Anderson (New York: Lexington Books, 2016), 65–67, 71.

389 L. Randall Wray, "Introduction to an Alternative History of Money," Working Paper No. 717 (May 2012); Michael J. Francisconi, *Kinship, Capitalism, Change: The Informal Economy of the Navajo, 1868–1995* (New York: Routledge, 1998), 5, 43–44.

390 Barrington, "Native Americans," 6; Miller, *Reservation "Capitalism,"* 11–12; Robert E. Wright, "Banking and Politics in New York, 1784–1829," (Ph.D. Diss., SUNY Buffalo, 1997), 685–88; Murray, *Indian Giving*, 116–40; Cronon, *Changes in the Land*, 95–97; Calloway, *Pen and Ink Witchcraft*, 3, 30; Carlos and Lewis, "Native Americans," 41; E. J. Neiburger and Don Spohn, "Prehistoric Money," *Central States Archaeological Journal* 54, no. 4 (2007): 188–94;

Some Indians even developed credit markets and a form of banking. Miller, an Indian and a scholar, claims that some Indians specialized in lending native currencies to other Indians. Although not a native, D. Bruce Johnsen has an insightful interpretation of potlatching not just as a credit market but as a form of fractional reserve banking. So when American and Canadian authorities cracked down on potlatching in the early twentieth century they effectively undermined the monetary and credit systems of the Northwest Coast Indians and hence their entire economies.[391]

We should be careful, however, not to exaggerate the sophistication of Indian financial arrangements. The word "interest," in the sense of rent paid on the use of money or physical capital, was not to be found in many Indian languages, including Creek.[392] Of course that does not mean that interest did not exist in pre-contact America any more than that gravity did not exist before Newton; it simply means that finding evidence of interest is difficult.

Indian and Euroamerican Economic Interaction

In weakening sentiment for one's native country among the Indians of North America, in dispersing their families, in obscuring their traditions, in interrupting the chain of their memories, in changing all their habits, and in increasing their needs beyond measure, European tyranny has rendered them more disordered and less civilized than they already were. — Alexis De Tocqueville, Democracy in America. Trans. Harvey C. Mansfield and Delba Winthrop. (Chicago: University of Chicago Press, 2000), 305.

Indians did not need to be taught how to trade when Euroamericans arrived on the scene. They knew that market power and price discrimi-

---

Harmon, *Rich Indians*, 43; Johnsen, "The Potlatch," 75–76; Miller, *Reservation "Capitalism,"* 19.

391 Miller, *Reservation "Capitalism,"* 24; Johnsen, "The Potlatch," 61–83.

392 Daniel H. Usner, Jr., *American Indians in the Lower Mississippi Valley: Social and Economic Histories* (Lincoln: University of Nebraska Press, 1998), 89.

nation created economic rents (profits in excess of those in competitive markets) and used various cultural devices, like gifting and haggling, to their advantage when playing different traders or nations off of each other.[393] No wonder Lewis and Clark described the Indians they encountered on their legendary sojourn across the western states as an "independent, business-like lot – sharp entrepreneurs and shrewd dealers."[394] Indians were not duped out of property rights in their land as often claimed. Rather, they lost their land in a variety of ways ranging from market contract to armed conquest. Generally speaking, as legal historian Stuart Banner has carefully shown, early land cessions to Euroamericans were outright sales, the exchange of land for guns, ammunition, knives, and other manufactured goods. Later, as the balance of power on the continent shifted, sales increasingly became shams supported by alcohol, chicanery, and, in the end, the U.S. Cavalry. Note that Banner's generalizations hold for *property* rights (to own, use, alienate, etc.), not *sovereignty* (right to rule over a geographical area), which from the start was simply asserted and always backed by force. By one estimate, Indians all told received $800 million (in current or nominal dollars) for their lands.[395]

At first contact, Indians were so accustomed to trade that it was through Indian trading networks that Euroamerican goods penetrated the continent long before white men's faces were seen beyond a few miles of the coast. In exchange for manufactured goods like alcohol, blankets, guns, gunpowder, kettles, knives, mirrors, traps, and whistles, Indians bartered hides, pelts, foodstuffs, and slaves (mostly other Indians but African-Americans and Euroamericans too, when available). Soon, Indians and Europeans established commodity trade monies, like standardized beaver pelts called "made beaver" or "castor," to facilitate trade between members of the two groups.[396] One Montagnais chief even said that "the

---

393 Carlos and Lewis, "Native American Property Rights," 72; Miller, *Reservation "Capitalism,"* 21, 23; Carlos and Lewis, "Native Americans," 51–56.

394 As quoted in Anderson and Leonard, "Institutions," 4.

395 Banner, *How the Indians Lost Their Land,* 4–9; Anderson, *Sovereign Nations,* 74.

396 Wilbur C. Plummer, "Consumer Credit in Colonial Philadelphia," *Pennsylvania Magazine of History and Biography* 46, 4 (October 1942): 392; Arnold, "Work and Culture," 160; Nancy

beaver does everything perfectly well, it makes kettles, hatchets, swords, knives, bread; and in short it makes everything" because it could be traded for anything.[397] "Made beaver" even became a unit of account and standard of deferred payment and spawned several token currencies made of wood. In the Southeast, rotgut rum became a medium of exchange. According to some, buck became slang for dollar because deerskins served as currency in the eighteenth-century Mississippi Valley. Hudson Bay blankets also served as money over a wide area. In Mexico, by contrast, silver was mined extensively and whether by the ounce or minted into pesos became the major medium of exchange for Indians, mestizos, and Euroamericans alike throughout what would become the American Southwest.[398]

In early eighteenth-century New York, Indians obtained credit from Euroamerican merchants and repaid their debts in furs and other commodities but also in cash money. Numerous primary sources, like the Bucks County Pennsylvania Treasurers' Records, show that by the mid-eighteenth century Indians also accepted coins and paper money in payment for services, like killing wolves, crows, squirrels, and Frenchmen. Archeological sources reveal the presence of lost or cached coins in Indian settlements. By the end of the century, in long settled places like New York, treaty annuities and gifts often came in the form of money, usually silver dollars or French Crowns, as well as clothing and food. By 1830, Iroquois chiefs accepted annuity payments in the form of bills of exchange! West of the Appalachians, though, Indians sometimes rejected Western monies because they did not understand their value and had no trading partners who would accept the stuff. The tokens issued by some

Isenberg, *White Trash: The 400-Year Untold History of Class in America* (New York: Viking, 2016), 144; Reséndez, *The Other Slavery*, 110–11; Gallay, *Indian Slave Trade*, 347–49; White, *Roots of Dependency*, 132–35, 152; Harmon, *Rich Indians*, 61, 100–1; Galbraith, Rodriguez, and Stiles, "False Myths," 9–10; Carlos and Lewis, "Native American Property Rights," 77.

397 As quoted in Murray, *Indian Giving*, 44–45.

398 Usner, *American Indians*, 66; Miller, *Reservation "Capitalism,"* 12; Johnsen, "The Potlatch," 74; Reséndez, *The Other Slavery*, 112–13.

trading posts were deliberately designed to be of limited currency in order to capture monopoly rents.[399]

Eventually, Indians used Euroamerican monies like coins and banknotes in both their domestic and intertribal trade. During the American Revolution, for example, American troops found 14 silver dollars under the bark floor of an Indian dwelling in Canandaigua in western New York and Indians were documented selling goods to each other for Euroamerican money. Members of the most remote tribes, like the Navajo and Metlakatla, began using coins and banknotes only after large numbers of them began to work for wages. The Sioux first used banknotes, legend has it, after taking the cash off dead soldiers following their victory over Custer. Later, they sold logs, furs, wild fruit, and game animals to raise the needful. By the late nineteenth century, the Tlingit of Alaska preferred silver dollars, which they were famous for hoarding for potlatches and other uses.[400]

When it came to money matters, Indians learned from Euroamericans and vice versa. Euroamericans sometimes used beaver pelts, wam-

---

399 Kees-Jan Warren and Jan Noel, "Not Confined to the Village Clearings: Indian Women in the Fur Trade in Colonial New York, 1695–1732," *New York History* 94, 1–2 (2013): 40–58; Tyler Boulware, *Deconstructing the Cherokee Nation: Town, Region, and Nation Among Eighteenth-Century Cherokees* (Gainesville: University Press of Florida, 2011), 99; Mark R. Plane, "'Remarkable Elasticity of Character': Colonial Discourse, the Market Economy, and Catawba Itinerancy, 1770–1820," in *American Indians and the Market Economy, 1775–1850*, ed. Lance Greene and Mark R. Plane (Tuscaloosa: University of Alabama Press, 2010), 42; Max M. Mintz, *Seeds of Empire: The American Revolutionary Conquest of the Iroquois* (New York: New York University Press, 1999), 138; Bruce E. Johansen, ed. *The Encyclopedia of Native American Economic History* (Westport, Conn.: Greenwood Press, 1999), 17–18; Brian Gettler, "Money and the Changing Nature of Colonial Space in Northern Quebec: Fur Trade Monopolies, the State, and Aboriginal Peoples During the Nineteenth Century," *Social History* 46, 92 (2013): 271–93; Francisconi, *Kinship*, 5–6.

400 David Wishart, "Could the Cherokee Have Survived in the Southeast?," in *The Other Side of the Frontier: Economic Explorations into Native American History*, ed. Linda Barrington (New York: Westview Press, 1999), 166; James W. Oberly, "Land, Population, Prices, and the Regulation of Natural Resources: The Lake Superior Ojibwa, 1790–1820," in *The Other Side of the Frontier: Economic Explorations into Native American History*, ed. Linda Barrington (New York: Westview Press, 1999), 192; Mintz, *Seeds of Empire*, 138, 161; Francisconi, *Kinship*, 47; Brian C. Hosmer, *American Indians in the Marketplace: Persistence and Innovation Among the Menominees and Metlakatlans, 1870–1920* (Lawrence: University Press of Kansas, 1999), 173–75; Pickering, *Lakota Culture*, 63; Arnold, "Work and Culture," 166.

pum shells, and Indian coppers amongst themselves. During his uprising after the French and Indian War, Pontiac created his own bills of credit out of bark stamped with his totem. Lesser known Indians also marked dried skins and circulated them like promissory notes.[401]

By the late nineteenth century, several tribes tried to create corporations so they could own and control their own railroads and mines. Tellingly, the U.S. government, including BIA commissioner and mixed-blood Seneca Indian Ely S. Parker, refused to recognize Indian corporations. At the time, officials claimed that opposition from within the tribes themselves scuttled the formation of the native companies but it is now clear that Washington policymakers did not want to encourage Indians to form corporations as that might liberate them from the control of the BIA and hurt Euroamerican business interests.[402]

Indians involved in commercial exchange with Euroamerican traders often received lines of credit, a natural outgrowth of simultaneous barter. Some of the advances, however, were evidently predatory in nature, designed to get an Indian mark drunk so that he could be robbed or conned. Or the credit was used to try to entrap Indians in the "market economy" generally or into a debt peon-like subservience to the trader or some fur, mining, or ranching company. Sometimes, debts were used to induce Indians, who were no strangers to price discovery ('shopping around'), to sell their wares at below market prices. Or the advances were designed to extract resources from relatively wealthy chiefs who owed socio-political obligations to save members of their tribes from penury. Or debts were used to obtain title to Indian land as chiefs ceded territory in order to extinguish traders' claims against members of their tribes stretched too thin by economic reality and the travails of the market, hunt, and harvest to repay old debts. Numerous treaties involving land cession stipulated repayment of the debts individual Indians owed

---

401 John Hickcox, *History of the Bills of Credit or Paper Money Issued by New York, from 1709 to 1789*, (New York: Burt Franklin, 1866), 1; Wright, "Banking and Politics," 685, 689–95; Murray, *Indian Giving*, 121–23; Miller, *Reservation "Capitalism*," 24.

402 Miner, *The Corporation and the Indian*, 24–29, 64–65.

to Euroamerican traders but how often that was the actual intent of extending credit is unclear as the traders were merely repaid and did not come to own the land, the federal government did. Little wonder that President Thomas Jefferson pushed trade credit as a means of bringing tribes to the bargaining table.[403]

It is important to note that such tactics only worked to the extent that Indians believed it important to repay debts or they would have found it exceedingly easy to expropriate resources from traders willing to extend credit. The Pennacook Indians, for example, were said to have absconded to Canada after taking large advances from Euroamerican traders in the 1720s. Yet at the same time the Yamasee were able to run up a debt of 100,000 deerskins, 250 per man, to Indian traders in South Carolina without absconding, though they did successfully lobby for debts contracted for rum, the sale of which to Indians was illegal by colonial law, to be set aside.[404] The Cherokee hesitated to go to war in the 1760s because they had to "hunt very strong" lest the traders "never trust us again" with credit.[405] By 1803, members of the Creeks owned John Forbes and Company (JFC) $113,000, a princely sum for the time. They and other southeastern tribes gave up their lands to make restitution and even made payments beyond those stipulated in treaties. JFC ended up collecting all but $7,000 of the $192,526 it had lent to the Choctaws, Chickasaws, Cherokees, and Upper Creeks. Northeastern Indians could be punctilious too: the Iroquois long used the expression to "cheat like a white man" to differentiate

---

403 Plummer, "Consumer Credit," 389, 393; Karen Clay, "Intertwining Economies," in *The Other Side of the Frontier: Economic Explorations into Native American History*, ed. Linda Barrington (New York: Westview Press, 1999), 12; Harmon, *Rich Indians*, 112, 204–5; White, *Roots of Dependency*, 58–59, 96; Gettler, "Money," 284–86; Reséndez, *The Other Slavery*, 113, 309; Hosmer, *American Indians in the Marketplace*, 44, 171; Usner, *American Indians*, 66, 73, 77, 103–4; Miller, *Reservation "Capitalism,"* 33, 35; Calloway, *Pen and Ink Witchcraft*, 114–15, 119.

404 E. M. Ruttenbur, *History of the Indian Tribers of Hudson's River: Their Origin, Manners and Customs*, (1872), 194; Gallay, *Indian Slave Trade*, 249–50.

405 As quoted in Boulware, *Deconstructing the Cherokee Nation*, 138.

their own view of the sanctity of contracts from that of many of the Euroamericans with whom they interacted.[406]

Clearly, some traders extended credit to Indians to win their patronage, not to steal their land. In 1770, British traders extended credit to war-ravished Indians reduced "to nakedness and extreme poverty" in the hopes that they would eventually regain their strength and bring in many furs.[407] Early merchants in Buffalo, New York extended credit to Indians, over $1,000 to one chief and lesser sums to lesser men, and according to an early historian "this confidence in their word of honor, was seldom misplaced."[408] At the same time, Mushulatubbee of the Choctaw owed traders over $1,000 and Tisho Hollatlak and Mingo Pushmataha, also Choctaw, owed hundreds of dollars each.[409]

An Eastern European Jew who moved to the heartland of North America in search of a better life, Bertha Martinsky encountered nothing but drought and divorce. When she moved to Interior, South Dakota before the Great War, she befriended the local Lakota by selling them beads, bread, and doughnuts out of a rickety wagon. When in 1917 she moved to Kadoka, 25 miles northeast of Interior along the main rail line, many of those same Indians helped to make her general store a success. By being one of the few merchants to extend them credit, hire them as peak time helpers, and extend good prices to them, Martinsky won their business, which in aggregate was considerable enough to allow her to venture into several other businesses in the 1920s.[410]

In the Southwest, traders extended credit to Diné (individuals of the Navajo Nation) until, under pressure from the draconian "conservation" stock reduction policies imposed by BIA Commissioner John Collier

406 Calloway, *Pen and Ink Witchcraft*, 102, 114–15; White, *Roots of Dependency*, 95–96; Usner, *American Indians*, 78–80.

407 Boulware, *Deconstructing the Cherokee Nation*, 145.

408 Samuel Welch, *Recollections of Buffalo: During the Decade from 1830 to 1840, or Fifty Years Since*, (Buffalo: Peter Paul and Bro., 1891), 115.

409 Usner, *American Indians*, 76.

410 Orlando J. Goering and Violet Miller Goering, "Keeping the Faith: Bertha Martinsky in West River South Dakota," *South Dakota History* 25, no. 1 (1995), 37–48.

during the New Deal, they lost their goats and began to eat their sheep, the wool of which had been their main cash crop for decades. Collier also allowed the Euroamerican creditors to recoup debts by seizing the live-stock of Diné at below market prices.[411]

Except for "civilized" Christian Indians living amongst Euroameri-cans, native peoples in the Early Republic could not own bank deposits or insurance policies and could not obtain bank loans. In mixed race couples, Euroamerican wives sometimes held title to real estate despite the restrictions of coverture. (Women, even married ones, enjoyed some property rights before the Civil War. See Chapter 6 for details.) Indians were considered "savages" until forcibly removed from the East, resettled on very different lands in the West, and ultimately safely locked away on reservations, at which point they became wards of the Office of Indian Affairs (now the BIA), the only part of the Department of the Interior charged with overseeing human beings. By then, rich Indians, like Osage men in the early twentieth century who received $8,000 per year from the tribe's oil trust fund, found it easy to borrow huge gobs of money from banks even though most of them spent their annual windfalls on items of conspicuous consumption that would have made Jay Gatsby blush, at least according to Euroamerican observers shocked to find Indians driving luxury automobiles and enjoying fine wines.[412]

As Alexis de Tocqueville once observed, "oppression has not exerted less influence on the Indian races, but the effects are different."[413] From

411 White, *Roots of Dependency*, 265–66; Francisconi, *Kinship*, 52–56; Kathleen P. Chamber-lain, *Under Sacred Ground: A History of Navajo Oil, 1922–1982* (Albuquerque: University of New Mexico Press, 2000), 72–77.

412 Wright, "Banking and Politics," 694; Lance Greene, "Identity in a Post-Removal Chero-kee Household, 1838–50," in *American Indians and the Market Economy, 1775–1850*, ed. Lance Greene and Mark R. Plane (Tuscaloosa: University of Alabama Press, 2010), 55–59; Chavers, *Racism*, 9, 16; C. Joseph Genetin-Pilawa, *Crooked Paths to Allotment: The Fight over Federal Indian Policy After the Civil War* (Chapel Hill: University of North Carolina Press, 2012), 94–95, 112–13; Calloway, *Pen and Ink Witchcraft*, 114, 138, 181–82; Miller, *Reservation "Capi-talism,"* 35–36; Harmon, *Rich Indians*, 193, 197, 206.

413 Alexis de Tocqueville, *Democracy in America*, (Chicago: University of Chicago Press, 2000), 304.

its inception, the BIA engaged in paternalism, treating Indians as if they were mere children who desperately needed the assistance of bureaucrats, most of whom resided many hundreds of miles away. As part of its program of coercive assimilation, which included forcing Indians into Christian nuclear families headed by good Victorian wives and mothers, the BIA forced Indian children into horrific boarding schools, the staff members of which attempted to strip the youths of their native identities while putting them to hard labor and, in some instances, sexually abusing them. When those same children grew up and could not find work, drank too much, or became abusive themselves, the BIA blamed Indian culture and doubled down on its attempt to turn Indians into brown-complexioned "white people."[414]

In the economic realm, the BIA's paternalism was an experiment in state socialism that, like all the other experiments in state socialism, led to nothing but poverty and despair.[415] "We are the highest regulated race in the world," Conrad Stewart, a member of the Crow tribe, recently asserted.[416] That might be an exaggeration but laws applicable only to Indians are so numerous that they have their own volume in the U.S. Code, Title 25. Congress and its hatchet man, the BIA, could not have done more to stymie the economic development of Indian Country (the collective name for Indian reservations) if it tried. (Some think it consciously kept Indians impoverished, while others chalk up its failures to general government incompetence and still others think the BIA the most inefficient of all federal bureaucracies.)[417]

---

414 Jane E. Simonsen, *Making Home Work: Domesticity and Native American Assimilation in the American West, 1860–1919* (Chapel Hill: University of North Carolina Press, 2006), 78–87; Chavers, *Racism*, 5, 11; Riley, *New Trail of Tears*, viii, 150–56.

415 Riley, *New Trail of Tears*, 63; Wilcomb E. Washburn, "Foreword," in *Sovereign Nations or Reservations? An Economic History of American Indians*, by Terry Anderson (San Francisco: Pacific Research Institute for Public Policy, 1995), ix.

416 As quoted in Riley, *New Trail of Tears*, 19.

417 Pevar, *Rights of Indians*, 59; Miller, *Reservation "Capitalism,"* 39–40; Chavers, *Racism*, 13. Like those in Peter H. Schuck, *Why Government Fails So Often and How It Can Do Better*, (Princeton: Princeton University Press, 2014); Riley, *New Trail of Tears*, 8.

After learning that they could not count on the U.S. government to fulfill its treaty obligations to pay and/or feed them, many Indians, virtually imprisoned on Reservations, began to engage in farming and/or ranching depending on the prevailing climate and their past experience. Although often relegated to marginal land, they made a go of it, especially the younger ones, and, had they been supported with financial services (intermediation and risk management), most tribes would have thrived, or at least become self-sufficient. Evidence that from the mid-nineteenth to the early twentieth centuries most Indians were quite willing and capable of running farms, ranches, canneries, mines, logging operations, mills, and other businesses now abounds. Instead of allowing Indians to create their own economic destinies, Washington, facing political pressure from Euroamerican constituents who wanted cheap land, interceded and passed one of the most disastrous laws of all time, the General Allotment or Dawes Act of 1887.[418]

Senator Henry L. Dawes of Massachusetts mistakenly believed that Indians were being held back economically because tribes, not individual Indians, owned reservation lands. Like many others in this period, he confused holding land in common tenure (like stockholders in a corporation) with working the land in common (as in a Soviet farming collective). Moreover, he attributed the economic rise of Britain to the enclosure movement, which privatized common pastures. Although frequently contested by Indians and policymakers who knew that Indian agriculture was thriving, his legislation, which allotted reservation land to individual Indians and put the rest up for sale to Euroamerican settlers, ultimately prevailed. Hailed by some as the Indian equivalent of the Emancipation Proclamation and others as a "mill" that would "grind out" assimilated American citizens, allotment proved disastrous as it destroyed established property rights and functioning agricultural systems on reservations and led to a land grab by whites. By the time it was all over, in 1934, Indians

---

418 Anderson, *Sovereign Nations*, 113–16; Hosmer, *American Indians in the Marketplace*, 221–24; Leonard Carlson, *Indians, Bureaucrats, and Land: The Dawes Act and the Decline of Indian Farming* (New York: Greenwood Publishing, 1981), 115–32.

had lost 86 million acres of the 138 million acres they owned before allotment began.[419]

The devil, as always, was in the details. Indians could not own the
land allotted to them outright for at least 25 years and then only with
permission of the BIA, which claimed, like any good paterfamilias, that
it had to protect Indians from their own improvidence. Some plots
were so badly surveyed that the boundaries were disputed for years and
Euroamerican courts and law enforcement officials hesitated to evict
white squatters and trespassers. Much of the best land, typically the river
bottoms, ended up in the hands of Euroamericans, who either came to
own it outright or on long term lease.[420]

By the Great War, Indian reservations that were thriving economically, like South Dakota's Pine Ridge, where private cattle ownership
combined with open range grazing and great roundups led by Indian
cowboys (an oxymoron only to those steeped in the mythology of the
American West), or the Menominee Reservation's extensive timber and
milling complex, were subverted by the BIA or the policies of its individual agents, some of whom favored the interests of young, "mixed bloods"
over those of older, "real" Indians. Even the profits from tribal enterprises
had to be "invested" with the BIA, which allowed five percent interest
per annum. Unfortunately, when it came to the safeguarding of Indians'
funds, the federal government repeatedly proved itself an untrustworthy
steward. It took almost a million bucks out of the Navajo oil fund, for
example, to help pay for projects, including distant bridges, that the Diné
did not support and would not benefit from. More than once, it invested
in the securities of the very corporations that were getting sweet lease
deals on reservation resources through the BIA. When left with tribal

---

419 Banner, *How the Indians Lost Their Land*, 257–59, 266–68; Genetin-Pilawa, *Crooked Paths to Allotment*, 2–3, 12, 133–35, 142–47, 151–54, 160; Harmon, *Rich Indians*, 137, 162–64.

420 The best book length overview of the Dawes Act is still Carlson, *Indians, Bureaucrats* but see also Banner, *How the Indians Lost Their Land*, 257–90 and Terry Anderson, Bryan Leon-ard, Dominic Parker, and Shawn Regan, "Natural Resources on American Indian Reserva-tions," in *Unlocking the Wealth of Indian Nations*, ed. Terry Anderson (New York: Lexington Books, 2016), 22–29.

governments, trust monies also disappeared, often in the form of "loans" that were never repaid. Placing money with private Euroamerican asset managers, including big trust companies in New York and Chicago, was stymied by the fact that BIA men charged with negotiating the deals were stockholders in the trusts. "The great dance of greed" surrounding the BIA, explained one historian, was the root problem.[421]

To stop the transfer of Indian land to Euroamericans, and in recognition of the fact that Indian agriculture was less productive in 1930 than it had been in 1880, the Indian Reorganization Act (IRA) of 1934 placed land in trust for individual Indians and ensconced the BIA into the federal bureaucratic complex by giving it virtually complete control over land transactions on reservations, even those from individual Indian to individual Indian or his tribal government.[422] When Ivan Small, a member of the Crow tribe, tried to sell some of his land to another Crow, the BIA blocked the deal because it considered the purchase price agreed to by the seller and the buyer to be too low. The BIA deliberately appraised Indian owned-land too high, ostensibly so Indians do not get expropriated. Of course all the policy does is make it impossible to sell land because, as Small so eloquently put it, "land is worth what someone will pay for it," not what the BIA says it is worth.[423] Small could not borrow the value of the land either. Because lenders cannot own reservation land, putative borrowers cannot use the land as collateral.[424]

Not all tribes opted into the IRA. Econometric evidence shows that the tribes that stayed out had higher but more volatile growth rates than IRA tribes, all else equal. The IRA, in effect, put a floor, a very low one, on Indian poverty but at the cost of squelching almost all private enterprise

---

421 Carlson, *Indians, Bureaucrats*, 124–25; Hosmer, *American Indians in the Marketplace*, 44, 48, 59, 61, 67; Pickering, *Lakota Culture*, 65; Rosier, "Searching for Salvation," 39, 41; Banner, *How the Indians Lost Their Land*, 277; Chamberlain, *Under Sacred Ground*, 38–40, 43; Miner, *The Corporation and the Indian*, 9–10, 192–97.

422 Banner, *How the Indians Lost Their Land*, 285; Riley, *New Trail of Tears*, 10–12, 17; Anderson, *Sovereign Nations*, 139–40.

423 As quoted in Riley, *New Trail of Tears*, 7.

424 Riley, *New Trail of Tears*, 5, 12.

and risk. Little wonder that most male Indians, if employed at all, worked at low-paid agricultural jobs.[425] "Of all minorities," wrote one researcher in 1960, "the most disadvantaged occupationally are the Indians."[426]

The IRA also did not reverse allotment which, combined with the fact that most Indians die intestate (without a will), left many tracts of Indian lands fractionated, or owned by multiple persons, and hence unavailable for use as collateral. In one documented case, a tract in South Dakota worth about $8,000 was, by the late twentieth century, owned by 439 different Indians, a third of whom received nothing more than one bright, shiny nickel in rent every year. But even that was better than the Indian who owned the smallest share, who was entitled to one cent every 177 years! Because the use of fractionated land requires a consensus among owners, even division among a dozen different owners causes logistical nightmares that are usually insurmountable. The number of highly fractionated lands has been doubling every generation with no end in sight because dividing tracts and assigning them to individual owners, as has been suggested, would leave many Indians with lots smaller than a postage stamp.[427]

Allotment and the IRA also have left most reservations checker-boarded, or a confusing hodge-podge of different types of land that renders development almost impossible.[428] As Dean Chavers put it: "Indian property is next to non-Indian property, which lies next to tribal property, which lies next to Forest Service lands, and so on." A Navajo reservation called Ramah located southeast of Gallup, Chavers noted, "has seven different

---

425 Dustin Frye and Dominic Parker, "Paternalism versus Sovereignty: The Long-Run Economic Effects of the Indian Reorganization Act," in Unlocking the Wealth of Indian Nations, ed. Terry Anderson (New York: Lexington Books, 2016), 224–41; Miller, "Indian Entrepreneurship," 245.

426 Davis McEntire, Residence and Race: Final and Comprehensive Report to the Commission on Race and Housing (Berkeley: University of California Press, 1960), 110.

427 Banner, How the Indians Lost Their Land, 285; Jacob Russ and Thomas Stratmann, "Divided Interests: The Increasing Detrimental Fractionation of Indian Land Ownership," in Unlocking the Wealth of Indian Nations, ed. Terry Anderson (New York: Lexington Books, 2016), 129–59.

428 Chavers, Racism, 12; Banner, How the Indians Lost Their Land, 289–90.

kinds of land on it."[429] In a 1987 survey of 39 large reservations, 77 percent of Indian land was in tribal trust, 20 percent in individual trust, and 2 percent was owned by the federal government. But almost half of the land within the boundaries of reservations was not under tribal or BIA jurisdiction and owned in fee simple, some of it by Indians but much of it by non-Indians.[430]

Of course all that variation is an economist's dream. One team, Terry Anderson and Dean Lueck, has shown, holding other variables constant, that lands owned in fee simple (i.e., outright, as Dawes intended) were much more productive than trust lands owned by individuals or tribal governments. But it is still, in the words of development economist Hernando de Soto, dead capital because it is nary impossible to use it as collateral for a loan. Valuable personal property, like cattle, was always much better collateral than land in Indian Country.[431]

Financial Institutions and Indian Reservations

Are there 'patterns and practices' of discrimination against Indians in these areas? How serious are they? Is there anyone out there with the legal knowledge, the skilled and trained people, and the sense of outrage necessary to investigate these questions? Does anyone care, except Indians? — Dean Chavers, Racism in Indian Country (New York: Peter Lang, 2009), 72.

Banks and other lenders rightfully want nothing to do with fractionated land, a checkerboarded landscape, or tribal governments that do not have balance sheets because everything they own is subject to

---

429 Chavers, *Racism*, 62.

430 Anderson, *Sovereign Nations*, 116–17.

431 Riley, *New Trail of Tears*, 13; Anderson, *Sovereign Nations*, 121–34; Galbraith, Rodriguez, and Stiles, "False Myths," 6; Shawn Regan and Terry Anderson, "Unlocking the Energy Wealth of Indian Nations," in *Unlocking the Wealth of Indian Nations*, ed. Terry Anderson (New York: Lexington Books, 2016), 123; Jessica Cattelino, "Casino Roots: The Cultural Production of Twentieth-Century Seminole Economic Development," in *Native Pathways: American Indian Culture and Economic Development*, ed. Brian Hosmer and Colleen O'Neill (Boulder: University Press of Colorado, 2004), 70–71.

the BIA's control. Even successful Indian businesses with solid financials, including popular ecotours and golf courses, find it difficult if not impossible to borrow. The costs and risks are just too high, even with tribal or BIA guarantees. The latter require down payments of 20 percent that few Indians can meet and come laden with "red tape." Only about $400 million worth were made throughout Indian Country between 1936 and 1984. The former require tribes to find Indian buyers in the case of foreclosure or risk bankrupting tribes. Lending to Indians was so complicated that in 1996 the government itself created a guide to its own lending on restricted Indian lands (via the BIA, the Veterans Administration, HUD, and the USDA), which it updated and expanded to 189 pages in 2006. Small business lending programs operated by the BIA and SBA also require hefty down payments and approval can take up to a year, which is simply too long for most businesses. Also, their minimum loan sizes tend to be too large for modest reservation-scale businesses.[432]

Moreover, Indian Country has a bad reputation amongst investors who have heard horror stories about venal tribal governments, mountains of red tape, and so forth. Pork processor Sun Prairie, for example, lost a $20 million plant on the Rosebud Reservation after a tribal referendum ruled that the plant could not open and the BIA backed voters instead of investors. Although such stories are often exaggerated and were never generalizable to all tribes, the negative reputation has remained. New research, however, may help investors to identify tribes with a higher chance of achieving governance success, which, unsurprisingly, are those that were traditionally centralized, not those that were traditionally decentralized yet glommed together by bureaucrats into a single Reservation and hence a single tribal government.[433]

---

432 Riley, *New Trail of Tears*, 17–18, 24, 37, 40–41; Malkin and Aseron, *Native Entrepreneurship*, 89; Anderson, *Sovereign Nations*, 15–16; Susan Peck and David Saffert, *Lending on Native American Lands: A Guide for Rural Development Staff*, (Washington, DC: Housing Assistance Council, June 2006); Pickering, *Lakota Culture*, 74–75.

433 David Haddock and Robert Miller, "Sovereignty Can be a Liability: How Tribes Can Mitigate the Sovereign's Paradox," in *Self Determination: The Other Path for Native Americans*, eds. Terry Anderson, Bruce Benson, and Thomas Flanagan (Stanford: Stanford University Press, 2006), 207; Miller, *Reservation "Capitalism,"* 95; Christian Dippel, "Forced Coexistence

But even tribes with a higher chance of successful governance suffer from what has been called the sovereign's paradox. The stronger the government, the more investors have to fear being expropriated by it; the weaker the government, the more investors have to fear being expropriated by rogue officials. So rather than assume that a given tribal government will protect their rights, investors assume the opposite and invest next door, in the good old USA, until the tribe creates a good reputation or otherwise makes a credible commitment to investor rights.[434]

Physical risks are also higher on reservations because criminal jurisdiction is confused and confusing, gangs are rampant, and law enforcement officials, tribal, state, and federal, are few and far between.[435] Binge *Longmire* on Netflix for some of the details.

Risk- and cost-averse banks had no incentive to master such intricacies in order to make a few, small loans so they avoided reservations like the plague. GMAC, for example, "redlined" reservations until a 1984 consent decree. In 1992, the Justice Department went after the Decatur Federal Savings and Loan, Barnett Banks of Jacksonville, Florida, and Shawmut National Corp. of Hartford, Connecticut for redlining Indian reservations. All settled and Shawmut agreed to beef up its compliance programs. In 1994, Blackpipe State Bank of Martin, South Dakota settled for $125,000 a lawsuit filed by the U.S. Justice Department under the Equal Credit Opportunity Act and the Fair Housing Act complaining that the tiny bank ($18 million in assets) refused to make loans secured by reservation real estate or subject to tribal court jurisdiction. It also required native borrowers to have higher credit scores and to post more collateral than non-Natives seeking equivalent loans. The First National Bank of Gordon, Nebraska simply charged Indians higher interest rates. It rebated $275,000 to them in a May 1997 settlement initiated by the U.S. Justice Department under the Equal Credit Opportunity and Fair Housing acts.

and Economic Development," in *Unlocking the Wealth of Indian Nations*, ed. Terry Anderson (New York: Lexington Books, 2016), 160–94.

434 Haddock and Miller, "Sovereignty Can be a Liability," 194–213.

435 Frazier, *On the Rez*, 258.

A decade later, Aegis Mortgage Corp. of Houston settled a lawsuit for $475,000 after allegations that it had redlined Indian reservations and Ameriquest Mortgage gave up $325 million for the same reason at about the same time.[436]

The vacuum left by banks was filled by pawn shops, payday or title loan shops, and specialized individual mortgage lenders. Although many Navajo traders exchanged goods with Diné strictly on a cash basis, for example, others lent on the collateral of pawned items when their hard-up customers could not obtain credit elsewhere. As Bill Malone of Gallup, New Mexico noted, small loans are "what the Navajo [sic] needs" and banks "won't mess with loans that small."[437] Pawn shops also safeguarded the most treasured assets of the Diné, which often took the form of jewelry.[438]

Of course to pawn something one must own something of value to put up as collateral, something not all Indians have. Title loan lenders cannot help those who get around with their thumbs or in an illegal "Rez car." To get a payday loan, one must have a regular job. And owning a house means little when it is cemented to tribal or trust land. For decades, dealers of used automobiles, trailers, and mobile homes had deliberately lent to impoverished Lakota on the expectation that they would soon be able to repossess the collateral and still profit from the deal. All were moveable and hence were better collateral than land or homes with foundations.[439]

Unsurprisingly, subprime lenders, many with predatory intent, were quick to reverse redline Indian reservations. In one instance, a Creek

---

436 Chavers, *Racism*, 71–74; Steve Cocheo, "Justice Department Sues Tiny South Dakota Bank for Loan Bias," *ABA Banking Journal* (January 1994), 6, 13.

437 As quoted in William S. Kiser, "Navajo Pawn: A Misunderstood Traditional Trading Practice," *American Indian Quarterly* 36, no. 2 (2012), 151, 153.

438 Mechele Dickerson, *Homeownership and America's Financial Underclass: Flawed Premises, Broken Promises, New Prescriptions* (New York: Cambridge University Press, 2014), 46; Malkin and Aseron, *Native Entrepreneurship*, 64; White, *Roots of Dependency*, 266.

439 Pickering, *Lakota Culture*, xi–xiv, 69–70, 72; Frazier, *On the Rez*, 63; *Reel Injun*; Miller, *Reservation "Capitalism,"* 94.

couple struggled to repay $62 a month for a tribal loan when a preda-
tory lender swept in and somehow convinced them that they were better off repaying the tribal loan and paying the predatory lender $380 per
month! The couple soon defaulted and lost their home to the predator. A
double amputee lost his home, which he owned outright after paying off
a 30-year mortgage, when an unscrupulous home improvement lender
foreclosed.[440]

By 2003, Indians were almost 200 percent more likely than whites to
receive a subprime mortgage. That meant that on average throughout
the nation over one in four Indian borrowers received a subprime mortgage. In New Mexico, where automobile dealers had a long history of
making predatory loans to needy Indians, the number was an astonishing
four out of five. The average mortgage rate paid by Indians was 15.3 percent when the national average was 5.21 percent. In New Mexico, six out
of ten Indians, but only one out of ten whites, got high-cost housing loans.
In South Dakota, a third of Indians paid the highest loan rate, a rate paid
by only one in ten whites. No wonder almost 7 out of 10 respondents to a
survey by the National American Indian Housing Council perceived subprime mortgages as problematic. Those steered into subprime mortgages
usually had some equity to seize. Most Indians did not own anything of
value, however, so rejection rates even for subprime mortgages were
as high as three out of four, driving some Indians to pay as much as 25
percent annual interest to individual lenders. Government programs that
may have reduced predation, like HUD's Mutual Help Home program,
were thwarted by the BIA's inability, or unwillingness, to process approv-
als in a timely manner.[441]

---

440 Kyle Smith, *Predatory Lending in Native American Communities* (Fredericksburg, Va.:
First Nations Development Institute, 2003), 4, 18; Peck and Saffert, *Lending on Native American Lands*, 2, 36, 44, 57.

441 Chavers, *Racism*, 74–75, 164–65; Smith, *Predatory Lending*, 10, 15–16; Kiser, "Navajo
Pawn," 164–65; Tex G. Hall, "Requesting the BIA to Streamline the Title Status Reports and
Mutual Help Home Conveyance Process for Indian Housing Programs." National Congress
of American Indians Resolution #ABQ-03–012 (21 November 2003).

Like African-Americans and white trash, Indians are often steered into housing thought suitable for them, typically cheap mobile homes or trailers. It is not necessarily the case that real estate agents hate members of X; it is that they feel they cannot afford to spend considerable amounts of time with relatively uneducated clients who will in the end only be able to buy an inexpensive house and hence generate only an insignificant commission for the agent.[442]

Lacking Internet access or reliable transportation, many Indians find that they have to shop for essentials in so-called "border towns" like Gallup, New Mexico, and White Clay, Nebraska where merchants charge them monopoly prices but serve up racial epithets for free. In addition to such insufferable treatment, consistently paying high prices prevents Indians from saving up for a down payment, which of course stymies the financial and economic development of reservations because money simply passes right through them instead of being put to multiple uses as in more economically developed communities.[443]

Not that most Indians would have convenient access to a bank to deposit savings in anyway. While a few big banks, like Wells Fargo, have crept into some Indian reservations in recent years, most Indians still do not enjoy a nearby branch. As the new millennium dawned, 15 percent of Indians had to travel more than 100 miles to reach the nearest bank or ATM and 30 percent had to travel at least 30 miles. Only 14 percent of Indian communities had at least one financial institution. Little wonder that most Indians have never had a bank account and that hardly any Indian entrepreneurs receive any help from banks. Most also cannot borrow significant sums from the other major source of entrepreneurial

---

442 Chavers, *Racism*, 163; Young, "Rural South Carolina," 34.

443 Chavers, *Racism*, 57; Philip Belangie and Sue Woodrow, "Turning Equity Into Opportunity: Montana Fund Helps Native Entrepreneurs Enter the Financial Mainstream," *Federal Reserve Bank of Minneapolis Community Dividend* (2008), 1; Pickering, *Lakota Culture*, 99, 106; Miller, *Reservation "Capitalism,"* 4.

startup funds, friends and relatives, because so few Indians have significant savings from which to draw.[444]

The lack of lenders, however, is merely symptomatic of the key
problem with Indian Country, the federal government. A succession of
businesses on Pine Ridge, including a golf course, a drug store, a bowling
alley, and moccasin, fishhook, and shirt factories, all bit the dust thanks to
the accumulated weight of the federal bureaucracy and the tyranny of distance. Whenever Indians somehow manage to get ahead a little, the government violates their property rights and takes away most of their gains,
leaving them wondering why they should bother at all. Econometric
evidence clearly shows that improving property rights and disentangling
the legal red tape surrounding most business dealings on Reservations
would work wonders for economic growth, and hence the well-being of
Indians.[445]

Indian reservations look bleak on the surface (in part because people
have little incentive to look after houses they do not own or to improve
land that can be seized by tribal, state, or federal governments virtually
at will), but underneath many teem with natural resources. Unsurprisingly, Indian reservations were gerrymandered around known resources
but new discoveries and technologies have revealed hitherto unknown
deposits of valuable minerals, metals, and fossil fuels. Today, reservations
contain about a third of the nation's coal reserves west of the Mississippi
River, about half of its uranium, and about 20 percent of its oil and natural
gas. The goodies underneath Montana's Crow Reservation, for example,
have been valued at $27 billion, or over $3 million per tribal member.

---

444 Smith, *Predatory Lending*, 25; Miller, *Reservation "Capitalism,"* 2, 94, 118–19, 148; Pickering, *Lakota Culture*, 73.

445 Frazier, *On the Rez*, 169–70; Pickering, *Lakota Culture*, 17–18; Terry Anderson and Dominic Parker, "The Wealth of Indian Nations: Economic Performance and Institutions on Reservations," in *Self Determination: The Other Path for Native Americans*, ed. Terry Anderson,
Bruce Benson, and Thomas Flanagan (Stanford: Stanford University Press, 2006), 159–93.

Yet the tribe's unemployment rate is almost four in five and its wealth is nearly nil.[446]

Rather than just seize the subsurface rights, Washington used its trust duties to strip Indians of most of the windfalls from natural resources found under their reservations. To tap into reserves themselves, Indians must follow a 49-step process that involves the Department of Justice, the Commerce Department, and the Bureau of Land Management in addition to the Department of the Interior. To lease access to outside companies, tribes must gain BIA approval and most leases, unsurprisingly, greatly aid Euroamerican corporate interests but barely help the Indians, whom federal bureaucrats still consider wards of the state.[447]

In addition, Indians continued to lose tribal lands throughout the twentieth century. Land-hungry pioneers, though, gave way to water and energy-hungry urbanites who in the postwar period pressed for dam projects, like the Pick Sloan dams along the upper Missouri River, which flooded the most fertile parts of several Indian reservations, and the Kinzua Dam in Pennsylvania and Southern New York, which cost the Seneca Nation 10,000 acres, a third of its fertile farmland. Various irrigation projects also cost Indians some of their land. Ironically, many western tribes also lost significant water rights over the years. Memories of such losses run strong in part because to this very day Indians are threatened with the loss of land to pipeline projects and national parks. Every twenty years or so, the federal government changes Indian policy and the results tend to be more shocking than salubrious. And there is nothing that Indians, or would-be investors in Indian Country, can do about it.[448]

---

446 Anderson and Leonard, "Institutions," 5; Anderson, Leonard, Parker, and Regan, "Natural Resources," 21–23, 29–32; Regan and Anderson, "Unlocking the Energy Wealth," 108.

447 Anderson, Leonard, Parker, and Regan, "Natural Resources," 29; Riley, *New Trail of Tears*, 19; Regan and Anderson, "Unlocking the Energy Wealth," 114, 118; Miller, *Reservation "Capitalism,"* 38–9, 110–13: Miner, *The Corporation and the Indian*, 184–206.

448 Riley, *New Trail of Tears*, 61; Leonard Carlson, "The Economics and Politics of Irrigation Projects on Indian Reservations, 1900–1940," in *The Other Side of the Frontier: Economic Explorations into Native American History*, ed. Linda Barrington (New York: Westview Press, 1999), 235–58; James Huffman and Robert Miller, "Indian Property Rights and American Federalism," in *Self Determination: The Other Path for Native Americans*, ed. Terry Anderson, Bruce

In a process that went by the macabre appellation "termination," between 1953 and 1968 109 tribes lost the federal government's recognition of their sovereign status and hence their reservations, 1.3 million acres of land, as well as access to federal services and monies. A related program, called "relocation," displaced 100,000 Indians from their reservations in exchange for promises of job training and housing assistance in major urban areas. About a third later returned to their reservations when the promised jobs and apartments did not materialize.[449]

Some Indian tribes located near major metropolitan centers, like the Seneca of western New York and the Seminole of central Florida, used to generate considerable revenue from selling tax-free gasoline, alcohol, and tobacco but that privilege was recently restricted. Indians rightly feel expropriated, again, every time they lose land, natural resources, or so-called "sovereign advantages" like preferential taxes or regulations.[450] As one Indian from Kyle, South Dakota, put it, "I think the people around here really had their trust abused, with the BIA."[451]

The simple, ugly fact is that the federal government does not have to heed its own treaties. In the last few decades of the nineteenth century, SCOTUS repeatedly upheld federal laws that abrogated Indian treaties, which themselves were banned in 1871. In 1921, the Snyder Act allowed the federal government to treat all tribes identically, regardless of specific treaty obligations.[452] As legal scholar Stephen Pevar notes, "Indian tribes can only hope that Congress has the integrity to honor the promises it made decades ago ... an integrity that in many instances has fallen

---

Benson, and Thomas Flanagan (Stanford: Stanford University Press, 2006), 289; *Waterbuster* documentary; Corntassel and Witmer, *Forced Federalism*, 16; Haddock and Miller, "Sovereignty Can be a Liability," 198.

449 Pevar, *Rights of Indians*, 11–12; Frazier, *On the Rez*, 121–22; Corntassel and Witmer, *Forced Federalism*, 18; Miller, *Reservation "Capitalism,"* 46–47.

450 Riley, *New Trail of Tears*, 50, 56–57, 61; Cattelino, "Casino Roots," 81–82.

451 Pickering, *Lakota Culture*, 42.

452 Banner, *How the Indians Lost Their Land*, 244–47; Riley, *New Trail of Tears*, 21.

short."[453] No wonder many Indians wonder why they should bother to try to improve their lot at all.

Even if Indians could come to trust Washington, they would still hesitate to partner with Euroamericans for fear that they would be too easily expropriated with little hope of winning in white-controlled courts. Even seeming wins for Indians, like the salmon and shellfish fishing rights won by Indians in Washington State in the 1970s, turned out to be less lucrative than originally imagined because of changing market conditions, fishery yields, and competition.[454]

On the rare occasions when Washington grants Indians something, they suffer for it. When bureaucrats beefed up tribal sovereignty, for example, they often simply subjected individual Indians to local tyrannies, in the form of corrupt or inept tribal governments that put nepotism or patronage ahead of merit. Because most Northern Cheyenne lands are held in tribal trust, for example, almost every economic activity needs to be approved by a plebiscite in addition to the BIA. As a result, almost all of the jobs on the reservation are government ones, not private ones. Talented Indians therefore tend to leave.[455]

Even Indian casinos are under threat. In 1987, SCOTUS ruled 6–3 in *California v. Cabazon Band of Mission Indians* that states that allowed gambling for any purpose had to allow Indians to run gambling operations. Soon Indian bingo parlors began running card games and slot machines. Nevada gambling interests and various state governments battled back, leading to the passage of the Indian Game Regulatory Act (IGRA) in 1988. Despite giving states some control over Indians' natural right to games, IGRA sparked a casino boom on Indian reservations. By 2012, 230 or so tribes in 28 states operated more than 400 casinos. By 1996,

---

453 Pevar, *Rights of Indians*, 59.

454 Riley, *New Trail of Tears*, 40; Dominic Parker, Randal Rucker, and Peter Nickerson, "The Legacy of *United States v. Washington*: Economic Effects of the Boldt and Rafeedie Decisions," in *Unlocking the Wealth of Indian Nations*, ed. Terry Anderson (New York: Lexington Books, 2016), 195–223.

455 Riley, *New Trail of Tears*, 20–21, 64–67, 89; Pickering, *Lakota Culture*, 6–7, 14–16.

Indian gaming generated revenue of $6.3 billion, by 2006 $25.1 billion, and by 2009 $26.5 billion.[456]

Those revenues were not evenly spread across all tribes but largely accrued to 20 or so tribes located near major metropolitan centers. Many non-Indians were immediately jealous of their success, which led to deregulation of state gaming laws designed to increase competition for native casinos. South Dakota's response was particularly rapid and vehement, as it responded to IGRA by easing regulations on both video lottery machines throughout the state and person-to-person gambling in Deadwood, its historic tourist trap in the Black Hills. Although tribal casinos in South Dakota turned profits (it is difficult for the house not to win), they were not nearly as large as they would have been in the absence of such competition. The state also denied Indians the right to establish casinos off reservation land, which severely reduces the revenue potential of the state's remote western tribes, especially the Cheyenne River Tribe, and has in several instances refused to increase the number of slot machines allotted to eastern tribes. Meanwhile, the original limits placed on gaming in Deadwood, including the number of slots and the maximum size of bets, have been continuously liberalized.[457]

As the immense but ultimately finite size of the gambling market became clear, more states began to allow non-Indians to operate casinos, each of which cuts into the revenue of rivals more than it expands the overall market. New York, for example, first allowed racetracks to run slots and now have allowed large non-Indian companies to set up in direct competition with the Indian casinos in the state. Now the big thing for some tribes is federal contracting. But that advantage, too, can be taken away if it gets too lucrative.[458]

---

456 Pevar, *Rights of Indians*, 275–76; William V. Ackerman, "Indian Gaming in South Dakota: Conflict in Public Policy," *American Indian Quarterly* 33, no. 2 (2009): 253–79; Miller, *Reservation "Capitalism,"* 71.

457 Riley, *New Trail of Tears*, 6; Pevar, *Rights of Indians*, 275; Miller, *Reservation "Capitalism"*, 71; Ackerman, "Indian Gaming," 253–79.

458 Riley, *New Trail of Tears*, 53, 58–60.

Interestingly, at least one Indian group, located on the Cheyenne
River Sioux Reservation in South Dakota, tried to make big money by
lending small sums for short terms to hard up Euroamericans across the
nation. The company, Western Sky, closed down in 2013, however, after
getting entangled in litigation in New York, which did not appreciate
having its usury laws broken by an out-of-state company, from South
Dakota no less. (South Dakota had lured away Citibank's credit card
business from New York in the early 1980s in part by doing away with
interest rate caps.)[459]

Natural resource development and gambling were large-scale efforts
and hence for the most part were undertaken by tribal governments
rather than individual Indian entrepreneurs. As a result, many Indians
who are well-off today are entirely dependent on the success of tribal
enterprises. Many members of the Seneca tribe, for example, are happy
to live off casino annuities instead of investing in small businesses. If the
tribal enterprises shrink or fail, as some are bound to do, tribal members
will be thrown back into poverty unless they are lucky enough to be
members of one of the relatively few tribes to invest some of their windfall into education, infrastructure, and small business development.[460]

Individual entrepreneurship in Indian Country is much weaker
than in the rest of the U.S. because Indians have difficulty financing their
businesses, have few role models to follow, fewer family resources to
draw upon, and little entrepreneur-specific education to help them. Most
importantly, perhaps, they cannot rationally expect that the BIA will
respond to their needs in a timely way. One coffee shop in Pine Ridge,
for example, went under after the BIA failed to give it permission to post
a sign advertising the business. Even obvious business opportunities, like
establishing a laundromat in an isolated town without one, are forgone

459 Anne Fleming, "City of Debtors, Law, Loan Sharks, and the Shadow Economy of Urban
Poverty, 1900–1970," *Enterprise & Society* 17, no. 4 (2016): 734–35; Wright, *Little Business.*

460 Philip Belangie and Sue Woodrow, "Turning Equity Into Opportunity: Montana Fund
Helps Native Entrepreneurs Enter the Financial Mainstream," *Federal Reserve Bank of Minneapolis Community Dividend* (2008), 1, 4; Riley, *New Trail of Tears*, 48–49.

because the chance of successfully navigating the BIA's regulatory laby-
rinth is so low.[461]

Of course some Indians, about one in twenty of working age in
South Dakota, have found business ownership and innovation too allur-
ing to forgo and forge ahead regardless of the barriers. Tellingly, up to
four out of five Indians engage in nano-entrepreneurship, basically self-
employment, to try to make the two ends meet without endangering
their access to government income streams like SSI and TANF. In the
Navajo Nation, for example, most individual Diné work in the informal
economy making and selling blankets and rugs because of limited opportunities in the formal economy and the sense of freedom that self-employ-
ment creates.[462]

But more individual initiative leading to larger scale enterprises is
needed to drive economic development on reservations similar to that
which animates the rest of the American economy. And that means
accessing lenders, investors, and insurers.[463] Yet to this day few in Indian
Country look to banks or other formal financial institutions for assistance
because of the widespread belief that banks "are not for us ... they are too
exclusive."[464]

---

461 Malkin and Aseron, *Native Entrepreneurship*, 57–58; Pickering, *Lakota Culture*, 36–42;
Miller, "Indian Entrepreneurship," 254; Riley, *New Trail of Tears*, 81, 84.

462 Malkin and Aseron, *Native Entrepreneurship*, 41–42; Pickering, *Lakota Culture*, 44–45; Galbraith, Rodriguez, and Stiles, "False Myths," 25; Francisconi, *Kinship*, 83–86.

463 Malkin and Aseron, *Native Entrepreneurship*, 61.

464 As quoted in Malkin and Aseron, *Native Entrepreneurship*, 63.

CHAPTER FIVE

Tales from the Trailer Park: Preying on Assorted "White Trash"

I had a good buddy from New York City, he never called me by my name, just "Hillbilly" – Hank Williams, Jr.

"These people," complained a Euroamerican denizen of Indianapolis in 1956, "are creating terrible problems in our cities. They can't or won't hold a job, they flout the law constantly and neglect their children, they drink too much and their moral standards would shame an alley cat."[465] That might sound like just another racist attack on African-Americans, Hispanics, or some other despised group and it was. In this case, however, the people with alley cat morals were a group of Euroamericans with white complexions. Moreover, such sentiments were common then and have continued largely unabated to this day. In a survey conducted in Detroit in 1951, one in five respondents ranked poor, rural whites as the least desirable members of the community. Only one in nine ranked African-Americans that low. The only group less desirable than white trash in their minds were "gangsters," a term then largely associated with Euroamerican criminals active in organized rackets like Cosa

---

465 As quoted in Thomas Sowell, *Black Rednecks and White Liberals* (San Francisco: Encounter Books, 2005), 1.　　　179

Nostra. White flight from Detroit and other cities in the postwar period was as much about escaping white Southerners as black ones.[466] With the term "white privilege" now *au courant* in some circles, and the recognition of "colorism," a subtle form of racism among people of color favoring those with lighter skins, growing, it may seem odd to suggest that some people of Euroamerican descent and white skin were, and remain, decidedly underprivileged. Like other racial and ethnic labels, "white trash" is ultimately a fiction, a means of lumping people, who may share certain characteristics but who are ultimately unique individuals, into a single category, often for the purpose of denigrating or exploiting them. Socially, however, "white trash" is as authentic as Santa Claus, Spiderman, and other legends. Whether they are objectively real or not, legends and other social constructs, like race, influence real people's real behaviors and that makes them forces that must be acknowledged and confronted if the world is to be understood in anything close to its actual complexity. If nothing else, the concept of white trash is "good to think with," because it helps to separate issues of class and race.[467]

Origins and Varieties of White Trash

The term white trash is difficult to define, much like the term the "underclass," of which white trash constitute a part. White trash come in many varieties, including, but not limited to: Arkies, blockheads, bogtrotters, briar hoppers, buckram, bumpkins, clay eaters, crackers, degenerates, feculum, fungus, hayseeds, hicks, hillbillies, hoboes,

---

466 Sowell, *Black Rednecks*, 1; Clyde B. McCoy and Virginia McCoy Watkins, "Stereotypes of Appalachian Migrants," in the *Invisible Minority: Urban Appalachians*, ed. William W. Philliber and Clyde B. McCoy (Frankfort: University Press of Kentucky, 1981), 24; John Hartigan, Jr., "Objectifying 'Poor Whites' and 'White Trash' in Detroit," in *White Trash: Race and Class in America*, ed. Matt Wray and Annalee Newitz (New York: Routledge 1997), 42.

467 Talitha LeFlouria, *Chained in Silence: Black Women and Convict Labor in the New South* (Chapel Hill: University of North Carolina Press, 2015), 40; Annalee Newitz and Matt Wray, "Introduction" in *White Trash: Race and Class in America*, ed. Matt Wray and Annalee Newitz (New York: Routledge 1997), 4.

hoosiers, lint heads, low-downers, lubbers, mudsills, offscourings, Okies, pineys, rascals, rednecks, ridge runners, rubbish, rubes, sand hillers, scalawags, scum, simple folk, squatters, swamp people, tackies, trailer park trash, tramps, vagabonds, vagrants, waste people, white niggers, white trash, and yokels.[468]

All such names were derogatory and sprang from specific historical contexts. Clay eaters, for example, refers to geophagy or pica practiced in parts of the rural South. Eating clay may have introduced minerals lacking in the regular diet of the poor and helped impoverished pregnant women to reduce nausea. It was not responsible for hookworm, which was prevalent due to the combination of bare feet and unsanitary disposal of fecal matter in the backwoods South. On net, clay eating probably did not appreciably help or hurt its practitioners, but it did help to set them apart from their fellow Euroamericans and make them seem more akin to African-Americans, some of whom also ate clay.[469]

Similarly, lint heads were the downtrodden white workers in the cotton mills of the New South. A journalist who grew up in towns like Talladega and Sylacauga recalled that retail clerks often asked lint heads "to wait while other customers were being attended to, and the cotton mill

468 John Sibley Butler, *Entrepreneurship and Self-Help Among Black Americans: A Reconsideration of Race and Economics* (Albany: State University of New York Press, 1991), 321–25; Jacqueline Jones, *The Dispossessed: America's Underclasses from the Civil War to the Present* (New York: Basic Books, 1992), 257; Nancy Isenberg, *White Trash: The 400-Year Untold History of Class in America* (New York: Viking, 2016), xv, 2, 320; Harry K. Schwarzweller, James S. Brown, and J. J. Mangalam, *Mountain Families in Transition: A Case Study of Appalachian Migration* (University Park: Pennsylvania State University Press, 1971), 155; Wayne Flynt, *Poor But Proud: Alabama's Poor Whites* (Tuscaloosa: University of Alabama Press, 1989), 33, 106–7; Hartigan, "Objectifying," 53; Phillip J. Obermiller, "The Question of Appalachian Ethnicity," in the *Invisible Minority: Urban Appalachians*, ed. William W. Philliber and Clyde B. McCoy (Frankfort: University Press of Kentucky, 1981), 21; Barbara Ching, "Acting Naturally: Cultural Distinction and Critiques of Pure Country" in *White Trash: Race and Class in America*, ed. Matt Wray and Annalee Newitz (New York: Routledge 1997), 233.

469 Dorothy Kunkin and Michael Byrne, *Appalachians in Cleveland*, (Cleveland: Institute of Urban Studies, 1973), 25; Susan Antilla, *Tales from the Boom-Boom Room: The Landmark Legal Battles that Exposed Wall Street's Shocking Culture of Sexual Harassment* (New York: HarperBusiness 2003), 88; Flynt, *Poor But Proud*, 27, 29, 32, 173, 177–79.

people never seemed to mind" because they knew their place, behind the real whites but ahead of the negroes.[470]

Traditionally, the ghetto, barrio, or reservation of white trash was the backcountry, marginal lands, often in the hills, accessible only via a few, bad roads. Since World War II, so many white trash have found refuge in suburban or exurban trailer "parks" that they came to be known as trailer park trash. Calling the assemblages of cheap, mobile houses "parks" was a cruel double entendre. Originally designed to elicit pastoral scenes, most trailer parks were sullen places where one literally parked one's quasi-mobile home. Like traditional white trash habitations, most trailer parks were located on marginal lands, even garbage dumps, near railroad tracks or other barriers, including fences built specifically to keep "those people" out of respectable neighborhoods. In my part of Sioux Falls, South Dakota, a swamp separates the trailer park from the "real" houses, and hence the trashy people from the respectable ones.[471]

The most widely used label for the poorest of poor whites, white trash, was first penned in the 1830s but popularized by slaveholder turned antislavery writer Hinton Helper in his 1857 book *The Impending Crisis of the South*. For Helper, white trash were the unwitting victims and tools of slaveholding elites, people who supported the slave regime on the slim hope that they would one day own a slave or two themselves.[472]

As the large number and wide variety of their labels suggest, white trash were not, and are not, homogenous. Some are zealous Protestants while others think of religion as hokum designed to separate them from what little cash they can command. Among the latter group, it was said that a Methodist was just a Baptist who wore shoes, while a Presbyterian was a Methodist with a bank account. Episcopalians were at the top, Presbyterians who lived off their investments rather than by working.[473]

---

470 As quoted in Flynt, *Poor But Proud*, 107.

471 Isenberg, *White Trash*, 236–47.

472 Lee Irby, "Taking Out the Trailer Trash: The Battle Over Mobile Homes in St. Petersburg, Florida," *Florida Historical Quarterly* 79, no. 2 (2000): 182.

473 Schwarzweller, Brown, and Mangalam, *Mountain Families*, 165; Matthew Pehl, *The Making of Working-Class Religion* (Chicago: University of Illinois Press, 2016), 106–14; Flynt,

The Census Bureau does not track white trash directly, nor do any other federal agencies. Generally speaking, however, white trash are socially, culturally, and even geographically isolated from mainstream society. They are not just poor but lacking in the skills, education, and experience necessary to improve their material lot in any significant way. And they *live* differently than other whites do. Their rates of dropping out of high school, welfare use, crime, unemployment, substance abuse, and births are much higher than those of the rest of the Euroamerican population.[474]

White trash, it is said, have literacy rates and vital statistics comparable to Indians or African-Americans and many of the stories and jokes told about them are analogous to those told of other minority groups. Most such stories portray members of those groups as alcoholic, violent, vindictive, and cunning but ultimately none too smart. A trashy boy named MacArthur Shelton, for example, was said to have shown up to his *first grade* class drunk. The trashy teacher paddled him and sent him home where his trashy parents waited until he sobered up before spanking him so that he would feel the punishment. A "Kentucky virgin" was said to be a sister who can outrun her brothers and, according to another joke, she must have been a rarity because Jesus was not born in Kentucky as God could not find a virgin, or three wise men, in the entire state.[475]

Other stories suggested that white trash are virtually immune to police beatings because they are more dumb brute than human being. Others portray white trash as fornicators who cannot or will not work due to some self-induced ailment like hookworm, diabetes, or syphilis. White trash will not clean themselves, watch their children, or remove the pet feces, dead critters, and junk cars littering their yards. They are

---

Poor But Proud, 29.

474 Sowell, *Black Rednecks*, 2; Erol R. Ricketts and Isabel V. Sawhill, "Defining and Measuring the Underclass," *Journal of Policy Analysis and Management* 7, no. 2 (1988): 316–25.

475 Naomi Schaefer Riley, *The New Trail of Tears: How Washington Is Destroying American Indians* (New York: Encounter Books, 2016), 83; Warren Moore, *Mountain Voices: A Legacy of the Blue Ridge and Great Smokies* (Chester, Conn.: Globe Pequot Press, 1988), 182; McCoy and Watkins, "Stereotypes of Appalachian Migrants," 20–31.

mean spirited and, if religious, more likely to follow some demonic-occult stuff or Pentecostal prosperity gospel than mainstream religious beliefs.[476]

Is any of this beginning to sound familiar? It has to researchers who noted that "both Appalachian and black migrants are frequently identified as welfare recipients, bearers of large families, unemployed, and poorly educated."[477] And it has to those who noted that redneck jokes were often just rehashed versions of jokes told about African-Americans, "Pollocks," and other despised minority groups. One rehashed oldie posited a Kentuckian and a West Virginian wasting time and nails while building a house because the Kentuckian insisted that some of the heads of the nails were on the wrong side while the West Virginian chided that "we always save those and use them on the other side of the house."[478]

Stereotypes about white trash are often as contradictory as they are for other groups, belying their real purpose as mechanisms of explanation that do not require extensive socio-economic reforms. Just as Hispanics are often assailed for being lazy loafers who (somehow) steal the jobs of real Americans, white trash are often castigated for moving to cities to take advantage of more generous welfare payments while simultaneously chastised for being too proud to go on welfare (and hence endangering the health of their children, the look of the neighborhood, etc.).

A positive stereotype of white trash as "practical, democratic, down-to-earth, hospitable, common people, outdoorsmen, independent, witty, fun-loving, not materialistic or hypocritical" also persists though it is usually swamped by more negative views. Like all stereotypes, white trash stereotypes, both negative and positive ones, are both true in individual cases and false as generalizations. Nevertheless, negative stereotypes of

---

476 McCoy and Watkins, "Stereotypes of Appalachian Migrants," 25; Newitz and Wray, "Introduction," 2; Hartigan, "Objectifying," 46; Constance Penley, "Crackers and Whackers: The White Trashing of Porn," in *White Trash: Race and Class in America*, eds. Matt Wray and Annalee Newitz (New York: Routledge 1997), 91; Allan Berube and Florence Berube, "Sunset Trailer Park," in *White Trash: Race and Class in America*, ed. Matt Wray and Annalee Newitz (New York: Routledge 1997), 19.

477 McCoy and Watkins, "Stereotypes of Appalachian Migrants," 26.

478 McCoy and Watkins, "Stereotypes of Appalachian Migrants," 20–31.

white trash remain widespread, deeply ingrained in popular culture, and often carelessly perpetuated by the media, the schools, and even social service agencies. Long after it became verboten to wear blackface or use the "n"-word, Euroamerican stand-up comedians wore "redneck" face on stage and sitcoms, like *The Simpsons*, made cruel jokes about white trash living in shacks, having sex with close relatives, giving their flotilla of hoodlum children outrageous names, eating roadkill, and so forth.[479] I recently saw the following on Facebook, posted without apology:

Two hillbillies walk into a restaurant. While having a bite to eat, they talk about their moonshine operation. Suddenly, a woman at a nearby table, who is eating a sandwich, begins to cough. After a minute or so, it becomes apparent that she is in real distress. One of the hillbillies looks at her and says, 'Kin ya swallar?' The woman shakes her head no. Then he asks, 'Kin ya breathe?' The woman begins to turn blue, and shakes her head no. The hillbilly walks over to the woman, lifts up her dress, yanks down her drawers, and quickly gives her right butt cheek a lick with his tongue. The woman is so shocked that she has a violent spasm, and the obstruction flies out of her mouth. As she begins to breathe again, the Hillbilly walks slowly back to his table. His partner says, 'Ya know, I'd heerd of that there 'Hind Lick Maneuver' but I never seed nobody done it.

While many employers favored white trash because they were seen as too unmotivated to look for better work, others wanted nothing to do with them in the first place.[480] In the late 1940s, for example, one Chicago employer "told the guard at the plant gate to tell the hillbillies that there were no openings."[481] "Unless your brother or your brother-in-law is working for them," one trashy jobseeker later recalled, "there is no use in trying to get on."[482] That was because many employers learned that it was

479 Flynt, *Poor But Proud*, 27; Kunkin and Byrne, *Appalachians in Cleveland*, 1, 18; Hartigan, "Objectifying," 49; Gael Sweeney, "The King of White Trash Culture: Elvis Presley and the Aesthetics of Excess," in *White Trash: Race and Class in America*, ed. Matt Wray and Annalee Newitz (New York: Routledge 1997), 251.

480 Kunkin and Byrne, *Appalachians in Cleveland*, 8.

481 Sowell, *Black Rednecks*, 1.

482 Schwarzweller, Brown, and Mangalam, *Mountain Families*, 154.

better to hire family members of current employers rather than random individuals because family work groups tended to be more stable.

Similarly, landlords did not like the reputation of white trash for violently abusing property, leaving garbage in their yards, favoring alcohol purchases over rent payments, and so forth. Any white trash holding a grudge was likely to resort to vandalism or violence rather than reason or the courts, or so most landlords believed.[483] Some housing advertisements baldly stated that "No Southerners need apply."[484] Some restaurants, hotels, and other service companies also banned hillbillies, ridge runners, and assorted other types of trash. Like African-Americans, Hispanics, Indians, and other minority groups, white trash were herded into their own low-rent neighborhoods, where they wallowed with inferior access to public goods like education, police protection, and clean air and water. In Bayonne, New Jersey, for example, one landlord sank barges in Newark Bay so that he could pave them over to squeeze in a few more trailer homes.[485]

In the past, many observers considered white trash members of a separate race, white in complexion but genetically inferior to proper Euroamericans. Alabama planter Daniel R. Hundley, for example, considered "crackers" a separate race born from paupers, convicts, and servants. They were the result of bad blood, Hundley asserted, not victims of a hostile environment. In the 1950s, bullies showed allegiance to this racialized view of white trash when they called Allan Berube (who later became a highly respected historian despite dropping out of college) a "nigger-boy" and a "monkey-boy" because he lived in a trailer park and sported a deep, dark tan from playing shirtless all day in the summer sun. Selected images reinforced the notion that white trash were a breed apart.[486]

---

483 Kunkin and Byrne, *Appalachians in Cleveland*, 9–10.

484 Jones, *The Dispossessed*, 257.

485 Gary L. Fowler, "The Residential Distribution of Urban Appalachians," in *The Invisible Minority: Urban Appalachians*, ed. William W. Philliber and Clyde B. McCoy, eds. (Frankfort: University Press of Kentucky, 1981), 80; Berube and Berube, "Sunset Trailer Park," 17.

486 Flynt, *Poor But Proud*, 33–34; Anon., "Allan Berube (1946–2007)," *History Workshop Journal* 69 (Spring 2010): 294–96; Berube and Berube, "Sunset Trailer Park," 33.

Clearly, however, white trash are not a distinct race as many traits stereotypical of white trash are linked directly to environmental factors. Hookworm infestation, for example, caused the "slow gait, sallow complexion, and lack of energy" often associated with "shiftless" and "lazy" white trash. Hookworm infected about one in three Alabamans into the twentieth century and could be found in a significant portion of the population in 63 of the state's 67 counties. It was also widespread in other parts of the South and Appalachia.[487]

Yet the notion that white trash are a genetically inferior race persisted for a long time because it helped to maintain the myth of a classless American society. White trash, according to this vein of thinking, were not poor whites, they were whites degraded by inbreeding and miscegenation, i.e., white on the outside but dark on the inside. Such a view had the added appeal of relieving others of any responsibility for their plight, of justifying white poverty with the notion that poor whites were poor because they were unworthy or inferior.[488]

Other observers considered white trash to be members of a distinct cultural, or rather countercultural, group almost akin to an ethnicity. White trash were racially Caucasian according to proponents of this view but members of a "primitive" or "uncivilized" tribe very unlike their middle and upper class cousins. Although white trash do not share all of the attributes of an ethnicity, like separate institutions or a consciousness of being a separate group, they certainly share some of the attributes of ethnicity, including shared customs, race, and language. And they might share others, including a common national origin and common ancestors. Some scholars trace white trash to the periphery of England, or the Celtic Fringe, i.e., Ulster County, Ireland; Wales; Highland Scotland; and even Northern England. People from those areas who emigrated to

---

487 Flynt, *Poor But Proud*, 177–78.

488 Gregory Mantsios, "Class in America: Myths and Realities," in *Race, Class and Gender in the United States*, 5th ed., ed. Paula S. Rothenberg (New York: Worth, 2001), 168–69; Newitz and Wray, "Introduction," 2; Laura Kipnis and Jennifer Reeder, "White Trash Girl: The Interview," in *White Trash: Race and Class in America*, ed. Matt Wray and Annalee Newitz (New York: Routledge 1997), 152.

British North America, often referred to as the Scots-Irish, tended to move directly to the mountainous frontier where they perpetuated a violent culture spawned by British imperial control of their homelands.[489] As economist Thomas Sowell put it, "in this world of impotent laws, daily dangers, and lives that could be snuffed out at any moment, the snatching at whatever fleeting pleasures presented themselves was at least understandable. Certainly prudence and long-range planning of one's life had no such payoff in this chaotic world."[490]

Part of trashiness is political and social apathy and confusion about one's confusing place in American society, native-born and white skinned yet relatively poor, uneducated, and unprivileged. When they fled rural Appalachia by the millions in the 1950s, 1960s, and 1970s to explore economic opportunities in the factories of Cleveland, Buffalo, Rochester, Detroit, and elsewhere, white trash tended to live near each other in ghettos like Goodrich and Collingwood in Cleveland, or the Cass Corridor in Detroit, but they did not see themselves as a distinct minority group and did not form social or self-help organizations the way immigrant groups did. Instead of focusing on their shared plight as white trash, they focused intensely on their traditional kin groups.[491] This made them what one pair of social scientists called an "invisible minority" that was "ignored, neglected, or ... forgotten."[492] They had no equivalent of the NAACP, Urban League, B'Nai B'rith, or Hibernian League to help them so they were rarely accorded the legal protections extended to other vulnerable groups.[493]

---

489 Obermiller, "Appalachian Ethnicity," 9–13; Annalee Newitz, "White Savagery and Humiliation, or a New Racial Consciousness in the Media," in White Trash: Race and Class in America, ed. Matt Wray and Annalee Newitz (New York: Routledge 1997), 134–35; Sowell, Black Rednecks, 3–4.

490 Sowell, Black Rednecks, 5.

491 Kunkin and Byrne, Appalachians in Cleveland, 1–6; Pehl, Making of Working-Class Religion, 107, 157.

492 Kunkin and Byrne, Appalachians in Cleveland, 1.

493 Obermiller, "Appalachian Ethnicity," 15.

Scholars and critics heap praise on the cultures of seemingly every single racial, ethnic, and tribal group except that of white trash, who are either denied a unique culture of their own or who find their culture denigrated as deeply dysfunctional, pornographic, or even feculent. Superhero White Trash Girl, a character created by trashy Jennifer Reeder, for example, was a child of incest, flushed down the toilet after birth, who grew strong on a steady diet of human feces. Even the closest thing that white trash have to music, bluegrass, country, and associated styles, has been attacked as dumb, primitive, hokey, and contrived. In short, white trash culture is itself trash or, like Elvis's music, stolen from other groups.[494] (Incidentally, trashiness should not be confused with camp. "Camp and White Trash may buy the same portrait of Elvis and hang it proudly in the living room," explains Gael Sweeney, "but Camp displays it as parody, to outrage the dominant taste, while White Trash displays it because it is so beautiful."[495])

According to Nancy Isenberg, poor whites have been treated little better than African-Americans and other minority groups throughout U.S. history. Perceived as extra or expendable people, they were kicked out of Britain and sent off to die in the colonies where some managed to scrape together enough of a living to successfully reproduce. A few rose into the burgeoning middle class or beyond but most lived generation after generation at the margins, their numbers replenished by fallen members of the middle class as well as their own legendary fecundity.[496]

None of this is to say, of course, that white trash had it as bad as African-Americans, Hispanics, or Indians did/do. But they just as clearly did not enjoy the full-blown privileges of whiteness. The unemployment rate among white trash in Cleveland in the 1960s and 70s, for example, was twice the national rate, which is to say only about half that of Cleveland's

---

494 Penley, "Crackers and Whackers," 89–112; Kipnis and Reeder, "White Trash Girl," 113–30; Ching, "Acting Naturally," 231; Sweeney, "The King of White Trash," 250.

495 Sweeney, "The King of White Trash," 251.

496 Isenberg, White Trash, 226, 308.

black population. When it comes to access to the financial system, white trash also inhabit the awkward space between.[497]

Perhaps, some have speculated, white trash are simply poor whites who suffer solely due to their low class standing. But such suggestions are belied by the often careful distinctions made between poor whites and white trash. The former work hard, send their well-groomed children to school, and maintain both the look and moral reputation of their households. White trash, by contrast, refuse to work, spend most of their time hunting, fishing, drinking, and carousing, pay little attention to their too numerous children or the condition of their yards, and never join groups, except maybe the local Protestant church.[498] They "act like blacks"[499] and have been known to call each other "niggers."[500] Poor whites were strivers who might move up and out while white trash were doomed to poverty, even if they won the lottery, a people who managed to make ends meet, if they did at all, through various combinations of irregular employment, hunting, fishing, gathering (including in dumpsters and junkyards), petty theft, handouts from relatives, and the public dole.[501]

The biggest advantage that white trash have over darker skinned members of the underclass is the relative ease with which they "pass" as white, sans the trash. Many do so by simply moving out of trailer parks and other white trash neighborhoods and holding down a job or getting a college degree. Passing, however, is never a sure tactic as many white trash possess an inferiority complex that undermines their confidence and betrays them at crucial moments.[502] Moreover, other "tells" abound. White trash often talk non-standard English, much akin to, and possibly the progenitor of, the African-American version of English known as

---

497 Kunkin and Byrne, *Appalachians in Cleveland*, 7.

498 Obermiller, "Appalachian Ethnicity," 12; Flynt, *Poor But Proud*, ix.

499 Sweeney, "The King of White Trash," 252.

500 Hartigan, "Objectifying," 44.

501 Newitz and Wray, "Introduction," 2; Hartigan, "Objectifying," 46; Penley, "Crackers and Whackers," 91; Berube and Berube, "Sunset Trailer Park," 19.

502 Obermiller, "Appalachian Ethnicity," 15; Fowler, "Residential Distribution," 91; Kunkin and Byrne, *Appalachians in Cleveland*, 13.

Ebonics. So, for example, white trash will "ax" a question or use the past participle of the verb to see instead of the past tense, as in "I seen him at the store this morning and axed him why he was dere."[503]

Other subtle signals, from accent to certain mannerisms to clothing choices, also threaten to expose the redneck roots of socially mobile white trash, like Clarice Starling in *Silence of the Lambs*.[504] Not everyone pays as much attention to details as Anthony Hopkins' character in that movie, but one study showed that "verbal, well-dressed people got better attention" at Cleveland clinics. And one need not be a linguist to note that white trash-speak can be "almost a foreign language" to the point that legal aid societies have often sought the help of "translators" to help translate information for their Appalachian clients.[505]

While you can take white trash out of the mountains or trailer park, you can never truly replace the early educational and social experiences they missed. I know because I grew up on the tenuous edge of trashdom. My mother was a coal miner's daughter and my paternal grandfather was a drunken gambler who literally died in a gutter. He was so bad that family lore long had it that he was half-Indian. A vial of my saliva, however, recently proved that he was just a drunken Irishman who loved gambling more than he loved his family. My inheritance was a prominent horny growth in the center of my forehead (which you can touch for a dollar but you can see for free) that resulted from the time my grandfather, in a drunken euphoria after learning that he had hit the trifecta, dropped my infant body down a flight of stairs.

My dead yellow front tooth, though, I have to blame on some long since forgotten episode in my rough and tumble childhood, first on a small horse farm outside Canandaigua, New York, then in a federal housing project in nearby Webster. But just as Roy Clark proudly never picked

503 Sowell, *Black Rednecks*, 27.

504 McCoy and Watkins, "Stereotypes of Appalachian Migrants," 24; Antilla, *Tales*, 19; Rita Chaudhry Sethi, "Smells Like Racism," in *Race, Class and Gender in the United States* 5th ed., ed. Paula S. Rothenberg (New York: Worth, 2001), 110; Sowell, *Black Rednecks*, 1–2.

505 Kunkin and Byrne, *Appalachians in Cleveland*, 15, 20.

cotton, I never lived in a trailer park (I would lord that fact over Allan
Berube had he not passed in 2007 so I will lord it over sociologist Margie
Edwards instead.[506]). My parents, both high school graduates but no more,
got their act together in time for me to attend sixth through twelfth grade
in affluent Fairport but they inadvertently screwed that up by registering
me for sixth grade after a particularly long, hot, successful (read smelly)
fishing trip. Due to some bureaucratic oversight, Webster had not sent
along my (of course stellar) academic records. The Fairport officials took
one look at my fish gut besotted family, assumed (reasonably) that we
were trash, and stuck me in a class with a group of academically-chal-
lenged degenerates. The teacher immediately surmised (after I carefully
explained that my last name meant "maker" not "correct") that I did not
belong but by the time official proof arrived from Webster it was thought
too late to change my "track" that year. I spent the year in the library
doing independent reading, which spurred my interest in history, but I
lost an entire year of mathematics that I was never able to recover.

It is not difficult, therefore, for elite academics to identify me as an
interloper, a "gate crasher at the citadels of Culture," a thief trying to steal
a tenured job from a truly deserving academic, with an eighth or less of
my publication record, but from the right sort of family.[507] I would be bit-
ter but I earn more than faculty at most elite universities and have a good
time doing it. Because of my high income, I have no trouble obtaining
loans or insurance. But I have cousins, descendants of the same damnable
drunk, who lost their father, my uncle, at a young age. They long had
difficulty staying out of jail much less getting a good deal on a mortgage.
And they are far from alone because sometimes luck is all that separates a
life of garbage from one of reasonable happiness and respectability. Berube reported that his family emerged from the trailer park because they
were able to get a decent loan from an acquaintance and Berube himself

---

506 Berube and Berube, "Sunset Trailer Park," 15–16; Anon., "Allan Berube (1946–2007),"
294–96; Margie L. Kiter Edwards, "'We're Decent People': Constructing and Managing Family Identity in Rural Working-Class Communities," *Journal of Marriage and Family* 66, no. 2
(2004): 517.

507 Kipnis and Reeder, "White Trash Girl," 115.

avoided the pitfalls that had ensnared his parents by taking the advice of a researcher who warned him away from a loan shark outfit.[508] There but by the Grace of God …

When Hunters Become the Prey

Some banks, merchants, and other finance organizations foreclose at the first legal opportunity; others foreclose only as a last resort. — Arthur Raper and Ira De A. Reid, Sharecroppers All (Chapel Hill: University of North Carolina Press, 1941), 34–35.

White trash are a difficult group to study because, as noted above, they go by many different monikers, none of which are systematically tracked by government bean counters. While not wholly neglected by scholars, white trash studies is a relatively new field, far behind African-American, Latino, and even Native American studies both empirically and theoretically. Little is known about how white trash responded to oppression, let alone exactly how much oppression they faced.[509]

White trash fell victim to many of the same abuses that plagued African-Americans, though rarely to the same degree. Many came to the New World as indentured servants rather than slaves so they soon had their freedom but their freedom dues, while greater than nothing, fell far short of the proverbial forty acres and a mule. Many moved to the frontier, where they eked out a subsistence mode of living that they passed on to their children and grandchildren. Others took up small lots near plantations, where they lived in material and cultural circumstances remarkably similar to those of the nearby slaves with whom they often traded and consorted.[510]

---

508 Berube and Berube, "Sunset Trailer Park," 33, 35.

509 Roxanne A. Dunbar, "Bloody Footprints: Reflections on Growing Up Poor White," in *White Trash: Race and Class in America*, eds. Matt Wray and Annalee Newitz (New York: Routledge 1997), 79.

510 Timothy J. Lockley, "Partners in Crime: African Americans and Nonslaveholding Whites in Antebellum Georgia," in *White Trash: Race and Class in America*, eds. Matt Wray and Annalee Newitz (New York: Routledge 1997), 57–72.

Due to sundry misfortunes, some self-induced and others the natural functioning of a game pitted against them, many trashy families lost their lands. Most moved further west, to the Ozarks or the sundry other hills that border the Great Plains (the Black Hills of South Dakota, the sandhills of Nebraska, the Arbuckle Mountains of south central Oklahoma, etc.), while land was still cheap. Others, however, became itinerants (hoboes, vagabonds) or the debt peons of labor-hungry mining companies or plantation owners. Where outright coercion became legally untenable, employers controlled workers by paying them in company scrip, called in some places clacker or goo-ga-loo, good only at the company store and for company-owned housing. While many African-Americans were enmeshed in this system of quasi-slavery, so too were many white trash, hence Tennessee Ernie Ford's song "Sixteen Tons," which describes the plight of white coal miners so indebted to their employers that they imagined they owed their very souls to the company store.[511]

During the Civil War, hyperinflation combined with the loss of property destroyed by the war and by government edict understandably decimated the South's financial sector. What is more difficult to fathom are the reasons behind the region's century-long postbellum financial underdevelopment. The South was not re-integrated into the nation's credit and capital markets before the Great War. Essentially, lenders discriminated against it, as evidenced by higher interest rates and lower levels of lending there. Deposits per person and banks per head lagged the rest of the country, arguably due to the exit of many banks in the South (as well as the Midwest) due to the National Banking Act and the tax on state bank notes. As late as 1895, 125 counties in Georgia had no banking facilities whatsoever. According to the late economist historian John James and economists Raghuram Rajan and Rodney Ramcharan, southern elites deliberately repressed the financial system in order to prevent potential rivals, including African-Americans and poor whites, from

---

511 Butler, *Entrepreneurship and Self-Help*, 197–98; Flynt, *Poor But Proud*, 101, 118–20, 151–55, 339, 348; James T. Laing, "The Negro Miner in West Virginia," *Social Forces* 14, no. 3 (1936), 418–19.

obtaining credit on good terms (or even at all). That repression, which took the form of fewer banks per capita and higher interest rates, reduced the likelihood of successful resistance of elite dominance of both business and politics. Here is a clear case where freer entry would have benefited both the middle class and the poor.[512]

Whether intentional or not, the South's financial backwardness certainly kept blacks, trashy whites, and even respectable poor whites down. (Similarly, poll taxes ostensibly aimed at African-Americans also prevented whites from voting, more whites than blacks according to journalist John Gunther.) Interest rates of 50 percent and higher drove many freeholders into tenancy, where they became subject to the crop lien system. Collateralizing loans with crops still in the ground was not a problem in and of itself but tying tenants to particular stores, gins, mills, and warehouses left them exposed to monopolists and monopsonists that naturally bilked them as much as possible.[513]

The share tenancy system of the South was largely based on seasonal credit, but to many observers it looked a lot like debt peonage, even for white croppers, especially on more marginal land. Generally speaking, croppers received credit from their landlords while share tenants obtained their own financing from merchants and banks. The former were much more likely to be trashy than the latter but occasionally they could borrow enough to buy a used automobile. Most of their credit, however, came from their landlords – farm owners in other words – who borrowed from banks at from 6 to 8 percent on average. Landlords were objectively

---

512 Richard Kilbourne, *Debt, Investment, Slaves: Credit Relations in East Feliciana Parish, Louisiana, 1825–1885*, (Tuscaloosa: University of Alabama Press, 1995); Lance E. Davis, "The Investment Market, 1870–1914: The Evolution of a National Market," *Journal of Economic History* 25, no. 3 (1965), 392; John A. James, "Financial Underdevelopment in the Postbellum South," *Journal of Interdisciplinary History* 11, no. 3 (1981): 445; Raghuram G. Rajan and Rodney Ramcharan, "Land and Credit: A Study of the Political Economy of Banking in the United States in the Early 20th Century," *Journal of Finance* 66, no. 6 (2011): 1,895–931; Jaremski and Fishback, "Did Inequality in Farm Sizes Lead to Suppression of Banking and Credit in the Late Nineteenth Century?"

513 Flynt, *Poor But Proud*, 65–67; John Gunther, *Inside U.S.A.* (New York: Harper Brothers, 1947), 701.

more creditworthy than croppers because, in the words of one contemporary researcher studying agricultural credit, "nearly always the farm owner has property which can be turned into cash in an emergency, either by mortgaging it or as a last resort by sale. Frequently the cropper has nothing to offer as security" aside from an uncertain crop.[514]

And landlords were in a better position than banks to monitor croppers and to discern honest, hardworking ones from dishonest, lazy ones. So the risks and rewards of lending to croppers naturally fell to farm owners, who over the years learned how safe or risky lending to croppers could be. In Edgecombe County, North Carolina in the late 1920s, only about 3 percent of credit extended to croppers was unpaid by the end of the year on average, while in nearby Pitt County almost 15 percent went unpaid. As theory predicts, interest rates and credit prices were higher in Pitt than in Edgecombe.[515]

Overall, contemporaries thought the rates charged to croppers quite reasonable given the trouble and expense of making many small advances of cash and goods for short terms.[516] "This service," explained one observer, "required that the farmer keep a stock of supplies on the farm all the time or else make frequent trips to town to buy goods for his croppers. The time and funds thus invested were due a reasonable reward." Moreover, "when the cropper moved away from a farm and still owed an account, the majority of owners said it was almost impossible to collect."[517]

That does not mean, however, that the system was an easy one for croppers. "If we come out even with all debts paid," one cropper's wife noted, "we don't complain and if we have enough money to last till about

---

514 Jaremski and Fishback, "Did Inequality in Farm Sizes Lead to Suppression of Banking and Credit in the Late Nineteenth Century?"; R. Y. Winters, *Credit Problems of North Carolina Cropper Farmers*, (Raleigh: Experiment Station Library, 1930), 6, 9, 18–19, 27–28; Margaret J. Hagood, *Mothers of the South: Portraiture of the White Tenant Farm Woman*, (Chapel Hill: University of North Carolina Press, 1939), 85.

515 Winters, *Credit Problems*, 19–20.

516 Winters, *Credit Problems*, 22–23, 27.

517 Winters, *Credit Problems*, 24.

March we say we done well." But that does not mean that the system was not exploitative, just that the level of exploitation decreased when crops were good and prices high. "Them that has can always fix it," another cropper's wife explained, "so the po' won't even have a chance to make anything."[518]

White tobacco croppers in Depression-era North Carolina lived in conditions reminiscent of slavery. Those were bad years for sure, but the croppers were hardly thriving before or after the unprecedented global downturn. In one case, 12 people shared a 2-room shack equipped with 4 beds. (Little wonder the incest stereotype is so pervasive!) The children were undernourished (one Thanksgiving dinner consisted of a possum) and hence they were much smaller than their ages would indicate, yet their countenances, beaten upon by years of hard labor, made them look older than they actually were. The father suffered from diabetes, high blood pressure, and rheumatism. The mother and father were illiterate and only two of the children completed the fourth grade. Because they bought on credit, the family overpaid for everything, like $120 for a stove that for cash went for $70 and $10 for curtains that were only $2–$3 for cash. (On average, time prices ranged from 10 to 40 percent higher than cash prices in interwar North Carolina but those less creditworthy, like the family discussed here, paid even higher prices.) After years of struggling to pay off their debts, they finally lost all credit and had to live off a dollar a week in return for which they gave up two-thirds of the crops they grew. They would have starved to death, as would many a trashy family throughout rural America, had they not supplemented their diets with wild fish, game, and other gathered or scavenged edibles.[519]

That said, some agricultural laborers were able over time to move up to cropping, cash tenancy, and even farm ownership.[520] Moreover,

---

518 Hagood, *Mothers of the South*, 2, 13.

519 Hagood, *Mothers of the South*, 15, 18–19, 53–54, 206–7; Winters, *Credit Problems*, 8, 15; Moore, *Mountain Voices*, 215–21.

520 Lee J. Alston and Joseph P. Ferrie, "Time on the Ladder: Career Mobility in Agriculture, 1890–1938," NBER Working Paper No. 11231 (March 2005).

the existence of a multiracial seasonal peonage system in the postbellum South does not mean that respectable poor whites were credit-
constrained throughout American history. (In fact, even the poor cropper
family described above managed to get store credit to buy a stove and a
truck.) Some early historians of the laboring classes, like Howard Rock,
assumed that artisans and other poor whites in the eighteenth and early
nineteenth centuries were unable to obtain bank loans with any fre-
quency but numerous scholars, including myself, have since shown that
creditworthy artisans and even mechanics and small retailers could borrow from banks most of the time. A careful study of bank failure-related
riots in Baltimore in the 1830s revealed that many people of relatively low
socioeconomic status had bank accounts and/or held banknotes. Rioters included Leon Dyer, a butcher who lost much of his savings due to a
bank failure. Most of the rioters were "mechanics," i.e., semi-skilled working men, and most were white.[521] Tellingly, the rioters also attacked the
homes of note shavers like John B. Morris, who they claimed, presumably
based on personal experience, was "a d—d shaver at 35 per cent."[522] Others borrowed from pawn shops instead but apparently no one rioted due
to a lack of access to credit.[523]

In the early 1960s, even poor white prison inmates could borrow
enough to buy a television set on the installment plan. The prisoners
had very low-paying prison jobs but their signatures were not binding
while they were incarcerated so the loans were all "based on character"![524]

---

521 Hagood, *Mothers of the South*, 16; Howard Rock, *Artisans of the New Republic: the Tradesmen of New York City in the Age of Jefferson* (New York: New York University Press, 1984), 4–5,
165; John Curl, *For All the People: Uncovering the Hidden History of Cooperation, Cooperative
Movements, and Communalism in America* (Oakland: PM Press, 2009), 35; Robert E.Wright,
Origins of Commercial Banking in America, 1750–1800, (Lanham, Md.: Rowman & Littlefield,
2001); Robert E. Wright, *The First Wall Street: Chestnut Street, Philadelphia, and the Birth
of American Finance*, (Chicago: University of Chicago Press, 2005); Robert E. Shalhope, *The
Baltimore Bank Riot: Political Upheaval in Antebellum Maryland* (Chicago: University of Illinois
Press, 2009), 62–63.

522 Shalhope, *Baltimore Bank Riot*, 62.

523 Seth Rockman, *Scraping By: Wage Labor, Slavery, and Survival in Early Baltimore* (Baltimore: Johns Hopkins University Press, 2009), 186.

524 Hillel Black, *Buy Now, Pay Later* (New York: William Morrow and Company, 1961), 35.

In California after World War II, "crude cardboard signs, CHECKS CASHED HERE" could "be seen almost everywhere," suggesting that credit was available, though for a price.[525] In many places, bars would cash checks too, with the understanding that they would get much of the money right back in exchange for overpriced libations.[526] So the problem for white trash was not so much exclusion as it was predation, i.e., loans extended with the intention of seizing collateral or imposing onerous fees.

"Desertion because of debt," was the name given in the postwar period to the phenomenon where men (of all types but especially white trash) left their families so their wives and children could qualify for public assistance because wage garnishments were so big they could no longer support their families. Chicago's Inland Steel struck back in 1960, when 3,000 garnishments were brought against the plant's poorest employees. All involved predatory court costs of $6, a sum that in some cases exceeded the amount of the debt plus interest. Instead of firing workers whose wages were garnished, as many employers traditionally did, or encouraging them to desert their families, Inland set up a program to help its employees get out of debt on reasonable terms.[527]

Predatory lending took other forms as well. In one instance, a single refrigerator was sold and repossessed six times, each time earning the lender the $50 down payment and any other payments made before the hapless borrower defaulted. "The gouger's potential prey," Hillel Black explained to readers, "usually those who earn less than $4,000 a year, is legion."[528] If borrowers somehow managed to stay up with their payments, the rate of interest charged was more than sufficient to ensure a profit anyway. It was not uncommon, Black claimed, for borrowers "to continue to pay for merchandise they have thrown away" to safeguard

---

525 Gunther, *Inside U.S.A.*, 63.

526 Kunkin and Byrne, *Appalachians in Cleveland*, 28.

527 Black, *Buy Now*, 57–59.

528 Black, *Buy Now*, 124, 127.

their reputations and credit scores. Similarly, croppers were known to repay debts even after crop liens expired.[529]

Preserving one's credit at all costs could backfire, however, because predatory lenders often sent fake negative information on borrowers to credit bureaus to ensure that they would be unable to borrow from lower cost lenders. Credit gougers, as they were sometimes called, also garnished wages simply to harass borrowers who had not the knowledge or cash sufficient to obtain adequate legal advice. "Such practices had dreadful consequences for the low-income family" noted Guy Sparks, executive assistant to the Alabama Commissioner of Revenue.[530] Unfortunately, the extent of such practices is unknown and will probably never be known with any degree of certainty.

Although predatory lenders enjoyed a veritable encyclopedia's worth of deceitful practices to employ, most relied on a few standard "tricks of the trade." Unfortunately for their victims, which included white trash but also members of other downtrodden groups, predatory lenders used literal tricks to get what they wanted, above market rates of interest and/or ownership of borrower collateral. A veteran of the Great War lost his modest home in Jacksonville, Florida, for example, when he fell for the old "blank contract" ruse, which worked because of the parol evidence rule, i.e., the fact that courts refused to take oral agreements into consideration in contract cases. That allowed unscrupulous lenders to come to an oral agreement with a borrower on reasonable terms, induce the borrower to sign a blank contract, and then fill up the blanks with onerous terms.[531]

"No Money Down" deals were a means of enticing borrowers to sign not one but two high interest promissory notes, one for the down payment and one for the balance. The seller then sold the notes to investors so they could hide behind "holder in due course" doctrine when the borrowers complained about the terms of the loan and/or the shoddiness

---

529 Black, *Buy Now*, 130; Hagood, *Mothers of the South*, 85.

530 Black, *Buy Now*, 144–46, 155.

531 Black, *Buy Now*, 137–40, 148.

of the merchandize financed. According to that doctrine, the borrower had to pay up regardless of the "unfairness" of the original deal out of "fairness" to the new, presumably innocent, holders of the notes. Used car dealers often hid behind holder in due course doctrine, as did unscrupulous mortgage lenders, like Wells Fargo, during the subprime mortgage debacle of the early Third Millennium.[532]

Debt poolers promised to consolidate the debts of people swamped by their obligations. Some just rolled their exorbitant fees into the consolidated debt while others took out new, high commission loans in the names of their impoverished clients but did not pay off their clients' old obligations. Lawyers sometimes pretended to help such borrowers but they really worked in the interests of the pooler. Occasionally such dastardly schemes were uncovered but the lawyers simply settled to avoid being disbarred and were at it again the next day.[533]

Prepayment penalties were ubiquitous because they protected the lender from competition by imposing a large penalty on borrowers who found better deals elsewhere and tried to repay their high cost loans early. They also protected lenders from any temporary windfalls that the borrower might receive from overtime pay, a small gambling victory, a minor inheritance, and so forth. The hope was that the borrower would spend the windfall before the end of the loan term, when often a large balloon payment fell due and had to be paid or refinanced.[534] This fit well with the stereotype of improvident white trash who spent any "extra money" that came their way as quickly as if it was on fire rather than saving it for the trouble that "always comes."[535]

Those and other predatory lending practices took its toll on the trashy parts of the nation. A 1964 presidential commission called

---

532 Black, *Buy Now*, 140, 147–48; Keith Ernst, Deborah N. Goldstein, and Christopher A. Richardson, "Legal and Economic Inducements to Predatory Practices," in *Why the Poor Pay More: How to Stop Predatory Lending*, ed. Gregory D. Squires (Westport, Conn.: Praeger, 2004), 117.

533 Black, *Buy Now*, 142–43, 146–47.

534 Black, *Buy Now*, 144–49.

535 Hagood, *Mothers of the South*, 216; Winters, *Credit Problems*, 18.

Appalachia "a region apart," palpably poorer than both the seaboard to its
east and the industrial Midwest to its west. Many reasons were adduced,
including the lack of locally controlled capital. "Much of the wealth produced by coal and timber was seldom seen locally," the commissioners
explained. "Even the wages of local miners returned to faraway stockholders via company houses and company stores."[536] After higher income
residents left the Ozarks in the 1950s and 1960s, waves of small business
failures reduced the number of banks serving the area, commercial real
estate prices, and employment opportunities as well as homestead values.
That, in turn, attracted white trash, the presence of whom made it difficult to lure back businesses, higher income residents, or non-predatory
lenders. Local capital was difficult to accumulate where distant intermediaries bilked locals left and right. With the local economy moribund and
family homesteads overcrowded,[537] many white trash left their traditional
enclaves in the mountains and backwoods South for factory jobs in burgeoning urban centers. They did not mix easily with the urbanites they
found there because "their clothes and values are different" as Reggie
Goldberg, director of Kansas City Jewish Family and Children Services
said.[538] Torn from hearth and kin, they were even more easily victimized
by predatory lenders.[539]

Readers of authentic white trash fiction, like *The Beans of Egypt,
Maine* by Carolyn Chute, will find very little about finance. When characters need cash, they obtain small loans from relatives, not banks or
even credit unions, pawnshops, or payday lenders. Or, more likely, they
sell assets (land, cars, firearms) rather than borrow against them. The

536 President's Appalachia Regional Commission and Committee on Education and Labor,
"Regional Poverty: Appalachia and the Upper Great Lakes Region," in *The Economics of Poverty: An American Paradox*, ed. Burton Weisbrod (Englewood Cliffs, N.J.: Prentice-Hall, 1965),
133.

537 Osha Gray Davidson, *Broken Heartland: The Rise of America's Rural Ghetto* (New York:
Free Press, 1990), 54, 133; Patricia Duane Beaver, *Rural Community in the Appalachian South*
(Lexington: University Press of Kentucky, 1986), 64–78.

538 Davidson, *Broken Heartland*, 82, 158.

539 Schwarzweller, Brown, and Mangalam, *Mountain Families*, 152.

characters live in squalor but they own their squalor outright, worrying only about taxes or lot rent. That gives them the freedom to quit jobs, as many characters do, when they do not like the conditions in the factory. It also gives them the freedom to work for less than minimum wage when they enjoy the work or are too proud to go on the public dole. But when trouble strikes, as it always does, they can't obtain loans on decent terms.[540]

Ethnographic and sociological studies reveal similar patterns. Many poor whites live in tight-knit communities, like in the mountains of eastern Kentucky, where the population changes little and kin ties are all important. In such places, family and friends frequently lend small sums of cash or marketable goods (like eggs, cigarettes, or milk) to each other for short periods. I vividly recall an uncle once asking my father if he could "hold a sawbuck" until payday and my mother was known to "hold" packs of cigarettes for neighbors for up to a week. The poor use the verb to "hold" instead of to borrow because that makes it seem like they are just "holding onto" the money or the goods, almost like they were doing the lender the favor of relieving them of the burden of "holding" the money themselves. In some trailer park communities, relatives sometimes aided each other in times of need with sizable loans at low or no cost. Sometimes, though, they did not want to help because of old squabbles/bad blood, often over money or other resources, or because they were simply unable to render assistance.[541]

Trashy whites also had a difficult time getting credit from hospitals and other healthcare providers. A 1955 survey revealed that four out of five families with incomes over $5,000 had medical insurance but only two in five families with incomes below $3,000 had coverage. And fewer than half of rural residents, regardless of income level, had health insur-

---

540 Carolyn Chute, *The Beans of Egypt, Maine,* (New York: Ticknor & Fields, 1985).
541 Schwarzweller, Brown, and Mangalam, *Mountain Families,* 211, 229; Edwards, "We're Decent People," 523.

ance.[542] Little wonder then, that most of the people in Alabama who went to loan sharks did so in order to pay for medical treatment. In 1960, Guy Sparks, executive assistant to the Alabama Commissioner of Revenue, noted that "hospitals demanded a cash deposit to secure admittance. They convinced most low-income families that the patient could not leave the hospital until the bill was paid in full. Doctors became almost impossible for these families to get unless they were assured of payment. Drugs could not be secured by these families without payment."[543]

Throughout the postwar period, many poor farmers could not obtain health insurance and ended up losing their farms when medical emergencies struck. They then moved into trailer parks or other cheap housing even if they were not technically white trash.[544] And they were the fortunate ones. Mary Farwell, director of a church-based rural support group in eastern Iowa, "saw many people die, because they didn't have the money to pay for a doctor," so they let relatively minor conditions worsen into emergencies that led to death, dismemberment, or disability.[545]

Today, many poor white Americans cannot obtain credit or health insurance for any sum, while others must pay exorbitant rates for paltry sums or coverage. Before passage of the Affordable Healthcare Act, low income women were much more likely to be underinsured than women with higher incomes.[546] For most poor whites, the healthcare and insurance situation remains dire.

---

542 Christy Ford Chapin, *Ensuring America's Health: The Public Creation of the Corporate Health Care System* (New York: Cambridge University Press, 2015), 62.

543 Hillel Black, *Buy Now, Pay Later* (New York: William Morrow and Company, 1961), 155.

544 Davidson, *Broken Heartland*, 75.

545 Davidson, *Broken Heartland*, 83.

546 Joint Economic Committee, *Invest in Women, Invest in America: A Comprehensive Review of Women in the U.S. Economy* (Washington, DC: U.S. Government Printing Office, 2011), 156.

Immobile Mobile Homes

*Most Americans ... never visit underclass neighborhoods. ... They are
unaware of the real face of economic deprivation. — "The Underclass," Hearing Before the Joint Economic Committee, Congress of
the United States, 100 First Congress, 1st Sess., May 25, 1989, 1.*

Trailers, later rechristened mobile homes, certainly have their place
in the menu of American housing options. When they first came
into widespread use in the 1930s, they were truly mobile, though more
practical for vacationing than permanent living. Tens of thousands of
trailers, however, were pressed into service during World War II in areas
with wartime housing shortages and, though only eight feet wide, lost
their recreational roots. Starting in 1954, with the introduction of the "ten
wide," and the adoption of the homey-sounding mobile home moniker,
they became longer, wider, heavier, and more livable but at the cost of
lost mobility.[547] By the 1970s, one in five new houses were classified as
mobile homes, and most were owned by low income Euroamericans.[548]
By the 1990s, ownership was more diverse and over 2 million mobile
homes served as primary residences. Many Appalachians (and some
coastal Carolina African-Americans) use them when adult children form
families of their own but want to stay on the homestead or cannot find
alternative affordable forms of housing, like apartments, available nearby.
Mobile homes can also be appropriate choices for singles (with or without

547 Frank D. Boynton, "Financing the Mobile Home Industry," *Financial Analyst Journal* 16,
2 (March-April 1960): 87; Robert Mills French and Jeffrey K. Hadden, "Mobile Homes: Instant
Suburbia or Transportable Slums?" *Social Problems* 16, 2 (Autumn 1968): 219, 221; Dina Smith,
"Lost Trailer Utopias: *The Long, Long Trailer* (1954) and Fifties America," *Utopian Studies* 14,
no. 1 (2003): 116–17; Kenneth K. Baar, "The Right to Sell the 'Im'mobile Manufactured Home
in Its Rent Controlled Space in the 'Im'mobile Home Park: Valid Regulation or Unconstitutional Taking?" *The Urban Lawyer* 24, no. 1 (1992): 162–68; Irby, "Taking Out the Trailer
Trash," 185–86; James Magid, "The Mobile Home Industry," *Financial Analyst Journal* 25, no.
5 (1969), 30.

548 In 1970, only about 65,000 African-Americans and Hispanics owned mobile homes. Phillip Weitzman, "Mobile Homes: High Cost Housing in the Low Income Market," *Journal of
Economic Issues* 10, no. 3 (1976): 588.

children), retirees, and young or childless older couples with modest incomes.[549]

Despite their name, mobile homes can turn into traps because many become *economically* immobile, as evidenced by the construction of attached breezeways, cabanas, car ports, decks, garages, or porches. Some, generally called prefabricated or manufactured homes, are built in a factory and shipped to a site where they are pretty much designed to remain, sometimes attached to other buildings or even basements. Even small trailer homes with attached wheels, however, often become stuck in the same place. That is because while it is possible to put manufactured homes and trailers on private land, many end up on rented plots, exposing their owners to monopolistic landlords and social conditions that can deteriorate over time to the level of inner city "slums" because mobile home owners have little money for lawyers and even less political clout among policymakers. Unlike condominium owners, they have no ownership stake in the "parks" in which their trailers are parked and no say in their management.[550]

Mobile homes are affordable in the sense that they cost fewer dollars than traditional houses do and hence have much lower entry costs. In the 1990s, for example, the average mobile home cost $25.75 per square foot, compared to $61.47 per square foot for traditional housing. As a result, owners spend less of their monthly budget on housing than they would if they bought a comparable traditional house. In the end, however, mobile homes can be extremely costly, especially holding square footage con-

549 Baar, "The Right to Sell," 157; Kate Porter Young, "Rural South Carolina: An Ethnographic Study of Homeownership, Home Financing, and Credit," *Cityscape* 3, no. 1 (1997): 14; Beaver, *Rural Community*, 96–97; Pamela Twiss and Thomas Mueller, "Housing Appalachians: Recent Trends," *Journal of Appalachian Studies* 10, 3 (2004): 390–91; G. C. Hoyt, "The Life of the Retired in a Trailer Park," *American Journal of Sociology* 59, no. 4 (1954): 361–70; L. C. Michelon, "The New Leisure Class," *American Journal of Sociology* 59, no. 4 (1954): 371–78; Amy J. Schmitz, "Promoting the Promise Manufactured Homes Provide for Affordable Housing," *Journal of Affordable Housing and Community Development Law* 13, no. 3 (2004): 386.

550 Michelon, "New Leisure Class," 372; Frederick H. Bair, Jr. "Mobile Homes: A New Challenge," *Law and Contemporary Problems* 32, 2 (Spring 1967): 287, 291; Baar, "The Right to Sell," 158, 170–72; French and Hadden, "Mobile Homes," 219–26; Schmitz, "Promoting the Promise," 384, 390.

stant. One study completed in 1974, for example, showed that a mobile home held for seven years cost all told an average of $3.25 per square foot per year, compared to about $2.50 for a traditionally built house. And mobile home ownership could be just as costly as renting.[551]

People bought mobile homes despite their high net cost out of a combination of ignorance of their true costs, a dearth of alternative detached dwellings friendly to low-income people, and an inability to obtain credit from mortgage lenders.[552] Many trashy types do not trust banks, preferring to stash their cash in safer places, like their grandmother's safe. Such actions make it difficult for banks to establish the source of down payments, to verify income, and so forth. The following is an actual letter, written in 1994 (with the Savings and Loan debacle clearly still fresh), from a trashy grandma to a bank that her son applied to for a mortgage:

It has come to my attention that my grandson's method of handling money does not suit you. My grandson takes most of his practices from me, specifically not placing every dime he has in a bank for someone else to watch over. For years I have maintained a small safe in my home. Both [my grandson] and I routinely use the safe as opposed to the bank to hold our money. For me this makes more sense than showing the world what you have got. Also my safe has never gone bankrupt through foolish management practices. ... Maybe you should spend more time managing your own affairs.[553]

Mobile homes are expensive for four reasons, the first of which is because they are so cheap, i.e., shoddily built. National codes have eliminated the worst fire hazards, like aluminum wiring, and some warranty standards exist but physical durability still woefully lags that of traditional housing. Four out of five mobile homes suffer from manufacturing or

551 Weitzman, "Mobile Homes," 589; Smith, "Lost Trailer Utopias," 128–29; Twiss and Mueller, "Housing Appalachians," 398–99; Schmitz, "Promoting the Promise," 385; Jack Gaumnitz, "Mobile Home and Conventional Home Ownership: An Economic Perspective," *Nebraska Journal of Economics and Business* 13, 4 (Autumn 1974): 138–40; French and Hadden, "Mobile Homes," 223.

552 Weitzman, "Mobile Homes," 576–97.

553 Young, "Rural South Carolina," 30.

installation defects and it is all downhill from there. In the most rural parts of Appalachia, where mobile homes make up 30, 40, even 45 percent of the housing stock, mobile homes are often pressed into service for decades longer than the 15 to 20 years they were designed to last, turning into dilapidated eyesores and heating/cooling nightmares in the process.[554] "Unlike a well-kept 25- or 30-year old car," one wit observed, vintage mobile homes "rarely make interesting or valuable antiques."[555] (There was an urban analog to this in the early postwar period, the traditionally built but shoddy ghetto house marketed mainly to African-Americans and Hispanics.[556])

Second, only about one in five mobile homes are sited on land owned by the owner of the home. The rest end up on rented land, sometimes as standalones but often in "parks" designed to accommodate scores, hundreds, or occasionally even thousands of trailers on small lots. Rental payments, which often include trash removal, sewerage, road maintenance, and sometimes recreational amenities, come in addition to the cost of the mobile homes themselves.[557]

Third, financing mobile homes is relatively expensive because they are traditionally financed with chattel loans rather than mortgages. Some mortgage products became available in the 1950s but four out of five mobile home loans remained chattel loans and hence do not qualify for the federal mortgage interest tax deduction, which has always helped the rich and middle class much more than the poor. Chattel financing is almost always at a higher interest rate and for shorter periods (12 years or less) than mortgages on traditional homes, which makes economic sense because traditional homes on average last much longer than mobile homes and are better collateral. (Half of the mobile homes occupied

---

554 Schmitz, "Promoting the Promise," 396; Weitzman, "Mobile Homes," 580; Twiss and Mueller, "Housing Appalachians," 392–94; Smith, "Lost Trailer Utopias," 129; French and Hadden, "Mobile Homes," 225.

555 Young, "Rural South Carolina," 27.

556 Davis McEntire, *Residence and Race: Final and Comprehensive Report to the Commission on Race and Housing,* (Berkeley: University of California Press, 1960), 154–55.

557 Weitzman, "Mobile Homes," 580, 584; Magid, "Mobile Home Industry," 30.

in 1960 were discarded by 1970.) In and of themselves, which is to say detached from any lot, used mobile homes have little market value (Their relative lack of value is due to the old adage that what matters in real estate is 'location, location, location.') so repossession of a mobile home is not like driving off an automobile or boat; it is more like an eviction or foreclosure though based on repossession laws rather than more owner-friendly mortgage foreclosure laws. While mortgage lenders are entitled to deficiency payments only in certain circumstances and states, mobile home lenders can always try to recoup any remaining sums after sale under UCC 9, which also renders repossession a much quicker process than foreclosure. Mobile home repossessions sometimes occur *en masse* after periods of too easy financing because lenders know that, generally speaking, mobile homes quickly depreciate in value over time like an automobile rather than appreciating as traditional houses do, which is another reason why financing them is so relatively expensive.[558]

Making matters worse, relatively few lenders want anything to do with the mobile home financing market and many of those that do appear to have predatory intentions in a market where default rates are four times higher than traditional house financing. The lack of a secondary market for mobile home loans has allowed the market to remain segmented so borrowers in each region of the nation have little choice but to pay rates two to five percentage points (200 to 500 basis points) higher than comparable mortgage borrowers. Many borrowers are relatively uneducated and get duped into paying higher than market rates for credit and homeowner's insurance as well. Due to various unneeded tack on fees, many mobile home borrowers start off under water, i.e. owing more than their house is worth.[559]

---

558 Smith, "Lost Trailer Utopias," 121–22; Gaumnitz, "Mobile Home," 130–31; Weitzman, "Mobile Homes," 580–81; Schmitz, "Promoting the Promise," 388, 393–95; Baar, "The Right to Sell," 159; Twiss and Mueller, "Housing Appalachians," 394; Laura Sullivan, Tatjana Meschede, Thomas Shapiro, and Maria Fernanda Escobar, "Misdirected Investments: How the Mortgage Interest Deduction Drives Inequality and the Racial Wealth Gap," Institute on Assets and Social Policy and National Low Income Housing Coalition (October 2017).

559 Schmitz, "Promoting the Promise," 396–98; Allen F. Jung, "Dealer Pricing Practices and Finance Charges for New Mobile Homes," *Journal of Business* 36, no. 4 (1963): 430, 434;

Fourth, and most ironically, moving mobile homes has become extremely expensive, often the equivalent of several years' rent due to the need for special trucks and crews, and hence only 3 to 4 percent of mobile homes are moved after their initial siting. So while they can technically be moved to a new location if necessary, in practical terms mobile homes are almost as immobile as traditional homes (which can also be moved but only at great expense). That, combined with a general dearth of mobile home lots due to restrictive zoning, building and health codes, and even outright bans on trailer parks, allows landlords, the owners of the lots on which mobile homes sit, much market power, i.e. the ability to raise lot rents *a lot*. Many trailer park residents suffered from sudden large rent increases according to a 1998 survey by *Consumer Reports*. Because many landlords abused their market power, many jurisdictions slapped rent controls on mobile home lots. Of course that just led to the invention of workarounds where the controls were not vigorously enforced (e.g., new fees or cuts in service quality), and lot shortages (demand > supply) due to lot closures and a slowdown or cessation of new park creation where the new rules were enforced. Where rents were not controlled or legally changeable upon sale, mobile homes lost much of their resale value as nothing protected new owners from large rent increases. That, in turn, led to titanic legal battles.[560]

Many of the restrictions placed on mobile homes were motivated by their close association with white trash. As recently as 1940, the U.S. Census lumped trailer residents into the same category as those who lived in railroad cars, tents, and shacks. Community leaders assumed that trailer parks, or "Hillbilly Havens" as they were sometimes termed because so many served as ghettos for migrants from the rural or mountainous South, would cause fiscal problems because they would generate

Gaumnitz, "Mobile Home," 132.

560 Jung, "Dealer Pricing Practices," 430; Baar, "The Right to Sell," 158, 160–62, 172–76, 180–83; Schmitz, "Promoting the Promise," 385, 388–89; Bair, "Mobile Homes," 288; Rolfe A. Worden, "Zoning – Townships – Complete Exclusion of Trailer Camps and Parks," *Michigan Law Review* 61, no. 5 (1963): 1010–14; Anon., "Regulation and Taxation of House Trailers," *University of Chicago Law Review* 22, 3 (Spring 1955): 738–51.

less in new taxes than in new expenditures for jails, schools, welfare, and the like. That was especially the case when mobile homes were taxed at lower vehicle rates but even after they were re-classified as real estate in many states (i.e., for municipal tax purposes, not for the IRS), they were still seen as fiscal drains. Many communities fought the establishment of trailer parks tooth and nail, even after developers informed them that most of the residents would be little old ladies from decidedly non-trashy families. Living in a trailer, it seems, constituted *prima facie* evidence of trashiness, even for grandma.[561]

For those reasons, family identity management, the construction and reconstruction of each family's social position, is particularly important and difficult work for trailer park mothers who wish to differentiate their families from their trashy or "no good" neighbors. They cite employment and relationship stability, long residence, well-behaved children, a clean house and yard, and an absence of government intervention in their lives (from police or social workers) as major indicators of their non-trash ("good") status, at least within their communities.[562]

The sad truth, however, is that even if those non-trashy mothers had purchased traditional houses in 2000, before the subprime debacle, they would have benefited little from price appreciation. The housing bubble, bust, and recovery were largely a coastal phenomenon. In the vast spaces between, where the majority of America's white trash dwell (though of course not everyone living between the eastern edge of the Alleghany and the western edge of the Rocky mountains is trashy), home prices barely budged. Were it not for the mortgage interest deduction, there would be little economic reason to own a house or the land upon which it sits in America's vast middle.[563]

---

561 French and Hadden, "Mobile Homes," 220, 222, 224; "Regulation and Taxation of House Trailers," *University of Chicago Law Review* 22, 3 (Spring 1955): 738–51; Schmitz, "Promoting the Promise," 395; Gaumnitz, "Mobile Home," 131; Irby, "Taking Out the Trailer Trash," 182–83, 189.

562 Edwards, "We're Decent People," 515–29.

563 Laura Kusisto, "Housing Gains Highlight Economic Divide," *Wall Street Journal*, 28 December 28, 2016.

CHAPTER SIX

Females and Finance: Gender Discrimination in Lending, Insurance, and Employment

Discrimination does not just hurt the underclass, the darkest skinned, trashiest, and least educated among us; it also negatively impacts females, independently of their race, ethnicity, or the reputed color of their necks. Relatively wealthy white women not subject to coverture, the rules governing the rights of married women, were not always completely shut out of the financial system, however, especially in the late eighteenth and early nineteenth centuries. If unmarried or of *feme sole* status, well-to-do females were often welcomed at America's banks, brokerages, and insurers. A *feme covert*, a married women, was not welcomed, unless acting as her husband's agent, because she was a poor credit risk "not legally responsible for her obligations" as the authors of an early credit textbook put it. Major financial institutions rejected poor, Amerindian, and African-American women regardless of their marital status, but marginal financial institutions would lend to them, albeit at a steep price. Women of all classes and races also interacted with the financial system as borrowers and lenders, savers and entrepreneurs, and insureds and insurers, in the late nineteenth and early twentieth centuries to a surprising degree only recently come to light.[564]

Readers shocked by the revelation that some women could finance their homes and businesses in the eighteenth and nineteenth centuries need to understand that progress is not always linear. Women gradually lost access to finance in the late nineteenth and twentieth centuries, only to regain it in the second half of the latter century, so the standard narrative about the importance of the women's rights movement of the 1960s is understandable, if somewhat incomplete. Most of the gains in recent years have been in the area of female management of financial institutions, though the almost complete dearth of female leadership at the top levels of the industry remains a serious issue.

Businesswomen

Yet the very fact that women ... appeared at all in the Dun ledgers, and in great numbers, deserves some comment. Had these individuals been dismissed as undeserving of credit by the fact of their sex ... alone, the credit-reporting agencies would not have wasted the resources to report on them. — Rowena Olegario, A Culture of Credit: Embedding Trust and Transparency in American Business *(Cambridge: Harvard University Press, 2006), 115.*

In the colonial period, women were active in the economy in myriad ways. If they remained single or were widowed, they enjoyed most of the property rights of men. Many ran their own businesses, often by assuming control of those of their fathers, brothers, or husbands. Eleana Wright of Charleston, for example, proved as litigious and business savvy as her deceased husband John, an important merchant in early eighteenth century South Carolina. The common law rules of coverture

---

564 Anon., "The Underclass," Hearing Before the Joint Economic Committee, Congress of the United States, 100 First Congress, 1st Sess., May 25, 1989, 1; Peter P. Wahlstad and Walter S. Johnson, *Credit and the Credit Man,* (New York: Alexander Hamilton Institute, 1917), 9.

proscribed the property rights of married women but they often took over *de facto* management when their husbands were absent, physically and sometimes mentally. Deborah Franklin ran Benjamin's print shop during his many absences, for example, as did Margaret Bache, wife of printer Benjamin Franklin Bache. Some married women also asserted *feme sole* status, which essentially gave them the same property rights as single women. Indian women even engaged in the fur trade in colonial New York and received mercantile credit just as male Indian and male Euroamerican fur traders did.[565]

Between 1740 and 1775, over 300 women owned retail shops in New York and Philadelphia alone. Numerous others ran taverns, schools, boardinghouses, millineries, and other ventures considered open to women but, interestingly, many also owned "masculine" businesses like print shops, tanneries, farms, plantations, and even international wholesale import-export businesses. Female entrepreneurs sometimes ran such businesses as placeholders until minor brothers or sons came of legal age but often they remained partners or even sole proprietors. From the 1720s to the 1760s, for example, Mary Alexander was a powerful "she-merchant" who, for and on her own account, imported large orders of manufactured goods from Britain and sold them, wholesale, to colonial retailers. Upon her death, Alexander's estate was valued at over a quarter of a million dollars, a very large sum in the colonial era.[566]

Most colonial businesswomen, large and small, extended credit to their customers and received trade credit in turn from their suppliers. A

565 Alan Gallay, *The Indian Slave Trade: The Rise of English Empire in the American South, 1670–1717*, (New Haven: Yale University Press, 2002), 248; Susan Branson, "Women and the Family Economy in the Early Republic: The Case of Elizabeth Meredith," *Journal of the Early Republic* 16, no. 1 (1996): 55; Kees-Jan Warren and Jan Noel, "Not Confined to the Village Clearings: Indian Women in the Fur Trade in Colonial New York, 1695–1732," *New York History* 94, 1–2: 40–58; George Robb, *Ladies of the Ticker: Woman and Wall Street from the Gilded Age to the Great Depression*, (Champaign: University of Illinois Press, 2017).

566 Robert E. Wright, "Banking and Politics in New York, 1784–1829," (Ph.D. Diss., SUNY Buffalo, 1997), 658–59; Susan Ingalls Lewis, *Unexceptional Women: Female Proprietors in Mid-Nineteenth Century Albany, New York, 1830–1885*, (Columbus: Ohio State University Press, 2009), 165–66; Rowena Olegario, *A Culture of Credit: Embedding Trust and Transparency in American Business*, (Cambridge: Harvard University Press, 2006), 110.

list of debts drawn up by a major lender in November 1763, for example, listed several female debtors, including Elizabeth Allair of West Chester (13 shillings), Mary Cornwell of Long Isle (£1 11s. 3d.), Elizabeth Johnston of Amboy (£13 17s. 10d.), Catherine Livingston of New York (£2 18s. 5d.), and a Mrs. Pinhome of New York, who repaid the £1 she owed the lender and was rewarded with a line drawn through her name.[567]

When women could not save enough capital themselves, they often went into business with siblings, other relatives, or friends and co-religionists. Matters stayed much the same during the Early Republic, when Elizabeth Meredith, a married woman, ran a tannery, kept the business's accounts, obtained loans from the Bank of Pennsylvania, and collected debts due the company. Meredith, like many other women in early national Pennsylvania, was essentially her husband's partner, not a mere "deputy" or agent. Many widows were able to take over their husbands' businesses because they had been *de facto* partners all along.[568]

About two in every five widows in southeastern Pennsylvania in the early national period, of those widows who could be tracked, certainly managed to increase their personal wealth. (We cannot conclude, however, that three in five lost assets because some widows gave away wealth before dying or never received as much as their husbands specified in their wills.) Stories like that of Margaret Holman, who turned around the fortunes of a tavern after her drunkard husband passed, abound. It was publicly acknowledged that "she did the money business" and much of the rest of the work even before his death. Her estate was valued at $18,000 upon her death in 1844.[569]

---

567 Wright, "Banking and Politics," 659; "Recoverable Outstanding Debts," 4 November 1763, New York Historical Society.

568 Patricia Cleary, "'She Will Be in the Shop': Women's Sphere of Trade in Eighteenth-Century Philadelphia and New York," *Pennsylvania Magazine of History and Biography* 119, 3 (July 1995): 181–84, 194–96; Branson, "Women and the Family Economy," 47–48, 54, 59–60; Lisa Wilson Waciega, "A 'Man of Business': The Widow of Means in Southeastern Pennsylvania, 1750–1850," *William and Mary Quarterly* 44, 1 (January 1987), 42; Claudia Goldin, "The Economic Status of Women in the Early Republic: Quantitative Evidence," *Journal of Interdisciplinary History* 16, 3 (Winter 1986): 401.

569 Waciega, "Widow of Means," 57–58.

Meredith was not unusual in receiving bank loans. "She-merchants" like Hannah Holland and other females running sizable operations regularly discounted commercial paper at banks in the 1790s. In fact, in the 1790s up to 5 percent of the Bank of North America's 1,600 customers were women. Sarah Wistar also borrowed from the Bank of North America numerous times between 1809 and 1815. It of course helped that she was wealthy and a stockholder in the bank. In 1831, at least five women received loans at the Farmers' Bank in Reading, Pennsylvania. Other female bank customers, like Anne and Sarah Ashbridge, mostly used banks to hold their deposits and make payments by check. Such women composed 11 percent of the Bank of Germantown's customers in 1830.[570]

Josephine Antweiler, Maria L. Butz, Delphina Bowen, Mary B. Boognard, Eliza H. Bulkley, Elizabeth Bable, Anna Bushing, Julia Biedleman, Sarah A. Cochran, Mary Crothers, Eliza Jane Duffy, Eliza Ann Edwards, Helen Freeman, Anna L. Frick, Susan Gibbs (by her mark), Mary Gibson, Ann Goodier, Mary Graw, Lydia A. Geiger, Mary Anne Griffin, Caroline P. Jaffee, Mrs. E. Hunter, Mrs. Matilda Hahn, Mary Ann Hardwick, Isabella T. Jones, Miss Mary Ann Johnson, Nancy E. Johnson, Amanda S. King, Ann C. Knight, Louisa Kopehofer, Elizabeth Kurtz (by her mark), Margaret Kurtz (by her mark), Mary Magee (by her mark), Christianna McCamman (by her mark), Hannah McClure, Mary A. McLean, Mrs. George P. McLean, Esther T. McElroy, Emily R. Marcher, Ann C. Morriss, Catharine Ott, Anna M. Peters, Elizabeth Pilkington, Catharine Rubicam, Louisa Seeger, Mary Smith, Sarah L. Snyder, Lydia H. Springer, Marsha U. Sprogell, Hannah Stump, Anna H. Taylor, Mary Amanda Wakeling, Emily D. Way, Caroline J. Wetherill, Margaret Wiley, Elizabeth Willday, Caroline Williamson, Hannah Williamson, Mary C. Wister, Ann Jane Yewdall, and undoubtedly others (reading signatures is difficult, many signed with just initials or partnership names, and some pages were missing or damaged) signed the customer signature book of

570 Robert E. Wright "Women and Finance in the Early National U.S.," *Essays in History* 42 (2000) online: www.essaysinhistory.com/articles/2012/100; Robert E. Wright, *Hamilton Unbound: Finance and the Creation of the American Republic* (New York: Greenwood Press, 2002), 189.

the Philadelphia (National) Bank between 1856 and 1868. Some, like Antweiler, Jaffee, Kopehofer, Morriss, and Yewdall were just large depositors
but the others appear to have been borrowers.[571]

Businesswomen who could not borrow at a bank received trade
credit from their suppliers or wholesalers. Women also sometimes sold
promissory notes into the market to raise funds. They could also borrow
on mortgage. In 1831, for example, Mary Walters borrowed $700 from
the Northern Dispensary, a charitable hospital for the poor located in
northern Philadelphia. She repaid the principal and interest in February
1833. In 1844, that same institution lent $500 on mortgage to Elizabeth S.
Nichols.[572]

By the Civil War, very few women ran artisanal shops or other
"masculine" businesses. Over the antebellum period, however, women
became more prominent in retail. In 1791, women owned 28 percent of
the shops in Philadelphia but by 1860 they owned 43 percent of them.
Of course the retail sector was very diverse by the mid-nineteenth century. Between 1830 and 1885, women owned almost 100 different types
of businesses in Albany, New York alone, including root beer vendors,
pawnbrokers, wig makers, livery keepers, milliners, and milk delivery
companies.[573] Even in the antebellum and Civil War South, women can
be found in banking records in various roles.[574]

The female labor force participation rate dropped in Philadelphia,
and presumably in other settled areas, from about 50 percent in 1800 to
about 35 percent by 1860. Of course the population over that same period
grew very rapidly so the absolute number of women in the workforce,

571 Philadelphia National Bank Signature Book, 1856–1868, Historical Society of Penn
sylvania.

572 Wright, "Women and Finance"; Wright, "Banking and Politics," 679; Northern Dispensary for the Medical Relief of the Poor, Minute Book #1, Ms. #1687, Historical Society of
Pennsylvania.

573 Goldin, "The Economic Status of Women," 398, 402; Lewis, Unexceptional Women,
165–66; Olegario, Culture of Credit, 110.

574 See, for example, 22 April, 6 May, and 9 May entries in the Daily Cashier's Settlement
Book, Bank of Athens, 1857 and the letters of 19 November 1860 and 27 May 1862 in the
Edward Remington Bank of Savannah Letters, 1860–1862, University of Georgia Libraries.

laboring for others or in their own businesses, grew. The same could be said for the rest of the century, when the population continued to rise rapidly and female labor force participation rates remained in the vicinity of 40 percent. Nonetheless, many fewer women were actively engaged in business pursuits than would have been had their labor force participation rate held up at half. One reason for the change was that wealthier women, increasingly caught up in Victorian social mores and the notion of the "separate sphere," no longer served their husbands as business partners or even helpers. Such women found it difficult to obtain bank loans or insurance because they did not have sufficient experience or education to run increasingly complex businesses. By the time of the Great War, for example, typical grocery stores carried between 750 and 1,000 different brands, advertising had become more complex, and recordkeeping technologies were more variegated. Increasingly devoid of business education, experience, or connections, wealthier women opted to become rentiers who lived off of interest and dividend payments instead of active participants in business.[575]

Nevertheless, in the nineteenth century throughout the rapidly growing nation hundreds of thousands of women owned and operated their own businesses. That astonishing figure extrapolates from case studies of urban areas, like Minnesota's Twin Cities, where the number of women operating their own small businesses in the late 1870s and early 1880s exploded. The same could be said of San Francisco, which by 1870 was home to over 1,100 female business owners. A decade later, that number had swelled to about 1,975. By 1920, almost 2,800 females owned businesses in the Golden City. Women business owners as a percentage of all employed women, however, peaked at around 10 percent in 1880, and shrank to just 5 percent after the Great War.[576]

---

575 Goldin, "The Economic Status of Women," 385–92; Edith Sparks, *Capital Intentions: Female Proprietors in San Francisco, 1850–1920* (Chapel Hill: University of North Carolina Press, 2006), 149, 169–70; Wright, *Hamilton Unbound*, 173–94.

576 Lewis, *Unexceptional Women*, 2; Jocelyn Wills, *Boosters, Hustlers, and Speculators: Entrepreneurial Culture and the Rise of Minneapolis and St. Paul, 1849–1883* (St. Paul: Minnesota Historical Society, 2005), 209; Sparks, *Capital Intentions*, 215.

Most nineteenth century businesswomen were widows or never married "old maids" but some were married women with *feme sole* status. Most ran very small businesses but a few achieved significant scale. In the latter half of the century, credit reporting agencies tracked the creditworthiness of tens of thousands of those businesswomen. As pointed out in the head quote to this section, if businesswomen were automatically disqualified from borrowing, nobody would have bothered creating and selling credit reports covering their business operations. That does not mean, of course, that women did not face discrimination, just that they clearly were not excluded from business finance.[577]

When and where women found it difficult to borrow, a law ostensibly designed to help them often lurked. In early national Baltimore, for example, women could not be imprisoned for debt, which of course only made it more difficult for them to borrow. After 1862, *feme sole* traders in California were barred by law from investing more than $500 in their businesses out of the estates they owned in common with their husbands. That forced many to pawn their personal effects, like clothes and jewelry, to obtain startup funds.[578]

Of course most financing came from friends and relatives, not formal financial institutions, especially at startup. Women found it relatively difficult to save money to fund entrepreneurial ventures. Men earned more and had more control over expenditures than women, especially married ones. So many women had to borrow to start their businesses, usually from close male family members like fathers, brothers, and in-laws, and also from other women.[579]

As earlier in the century, businesswomen in the late nineteenth century also received loans from banks and wealthy individuals. Nancy C. Noyes, for example, borrowed $3,000 from San Francisco's Hibernia Bank in 1877. Others borrowed from wealthy individual "capital-

577 Olegario, *Culture of Credit*, 115.

578 Seth Rockman, *Scraping By: Wage Labor, Slavery, and Survival in Early Baltimore* (Baltimore: Johns Hopkins University Press, 2009), 186; Sparks, *Capital Intentions*, 92–93.

579 Sparks, *Capital Intentions*, 90–91.

ists," some male and some female. In good times, ample competition allowed businesswomen to borrow from whomever offered the best terms. Increasingly, that meant specialized factoring houses that bought accounts receivable for cash.[580]

Most female business owners in places like Albany and San Francisco were able to secure one or two lines of credit from their suppliers, even when credit evaluators warned against it because they were too small and had too little capital. They were able to do so as members of networks of friends, family, neighbors, and co-religionists who vouched for them and sometimes signed on as sureties or co-signors on notes and mortgages. Credit in Albany seemed to flow to those worthy of it. Women with substantial savings or who received inheritances, insurance checks, or gifts from relatives received commensurate credit. So, too, did those few who ran large businesses. Widow Ann Beck, who dealt in boots and shoes, was able to borrow $2,500 against her shop, which was valued at $6,500, plus another $500 on additional property assessed at $1,500. With the help of rational credit, some businesswomen thrived. For example, Lucretia Blessing over 15 years was able to save $1,500 from her small confectionery and toy shop after paying off an $800 mortgage.[581]

Businesswomen in San Francisco also appear to have received their just due. As in Albany, the biggest problem identified by credit evaluators was not gender per se but small scale, which of course signaled greater risk of late repayment and bankruptcy. Credit raters also probed women's private lives looking for signs of potential credit weakness like lazy husbands, drunkard sons, or spendthrift personal habits. Men, though, were subject to similar inquisitions as creditors looked for signs of moral hazard. Those women who merited credit got what they needed. Mrs. Mary A. Soper, for example, was considered "worthy of all the credit [she] will ask" because she had a net worth of $15,000 accumulated over a flawless career spanning a dozen years. After a recession and a move to San

---

580 Sparks, *Capital Intentions*, 93, 97.

581 Lewis, *Unexceptional Women*, 61, 67, 77–79, 102–3, 111–12.

Francisco rendered her not "as prompt as formerly," her credit standing understandably decreased.[582]

A few businesswomen even received too much credit. It does not appear that the intent was predatory on the part of lenders as most of them took "haircuts" during bankruptcy proceedings. Aided by overeager creditors, many failed female retailers simply stocked up on goods that did not sell fast enough to turn a profit. Others spent too much on new gadgets, like cash registers, that provided no return for a low-volume business where traditional paper-based transaction records worked just fine. To speed turnover, women could sell goods on credit but that exposed them to the creditworthiness of their customers, some of whom thought nothing of paying six months late, if at all. Many a female proprietor succumbed to bankruptcy with substantial accounts receivable.[583]

Credit evaluators were certainly products of their times and hence harbored various stereotypes, but mostly against racial and ethnic minorities, like African-Americans, Jews, Catholic Irish, and southern and eastern Europeans. The most pernicious gender-based stereotype was that female-owned businesses suffered higher failure rates than male-owned ones because females were less interested in business. Most evaluators, however, were not perceptively prejudiced against businesswomen in their reports. Gender was identified but the core analysis remained on the Three Cs of character, capacity, and capital. Sometimes the credit reports noted that the woman in a partnership could be trusted but not the drunkard or laggard man. Credit evaluators were more likely to rate women highly in terms of their character than they were men, largely because women were, in fact, less likely to be drunkards, scoundrels, and scammers.[584]

We cannot conclude that lenders discriminated against businesswomen in the nineteenth and early twentieth centuries simply because they received fewer loans than male-owned businesses did because

---

582 Sparks, *Capital Intentions*, 154–55, 186–87.

583 Sparks, *Capital Intentions*, 155–58, 160–62.

584 Sparks, *Capital Intentions*, 89; Olegario, *Culture of Credit*, 108–18; Lewis, *Unexceptional Women*, 71, 145.

women may have demanded fewer loans than men *ceteris paribus*. Historian Edith Sparks makes a good case that the median businesswoman may have been more risk averse than her male counterpart. Among her evidence is that within seven years of the creation of a Women's Banking Department by Bank of America in 1921, 20,000 women became depositors but many fewer applied for loans.[585]

The agricultural crisis of the 1920s and the Great Depression were not kind to anyone's small businesses and appear to have hit female entrepreneurs particularly hard. During World War II, many women entered the labor force as employees rather than as business proprietors. By the mid-twentieth century, such female business owners as remained found it very difficult to obtain bank loans due to a variety of factors, including outright discrimination. Business credit was included in the Equal Credit Opportunity Act, which took effect in October 1975 and which made it unlawful to discriminate against applicants for any form of credit on the basis of, among other factors, gender or marital status. But women still faced a subtler form of discrimination based on their preference for smaller, more local types of businesses.[586]

Female entrepreneurship was on the rise again in the 1960s and 1970s. Female business owners found it difficult to obtain appropriate financing but so too, a Treasury report based on 30,000 questionnaires and six roundtables found, did male entrepreneurs. Entrepreneurs of both genders, it claimed, lacked "management experience, marketing expertise, financial planning ability, and knowledge of the money and banking systems in the United States." In addition, big banks avoided making loans to small entrepreneurs because they lost money on loans for less than $50,000 due to fixed administrative costs. Smaller banks, however, often made much smaller loans to finance startups. If females had a

---

585 Sparks, *Capital Intentions*, 93–94, 171.

586 Treasury Department Study Team, *Credit and Capital Formation: A Report to the President's Interagency Task Force on Women Business Owners* (April 1978), 51–52; Enrico Beltramini, "Consumer Credit as a Civil Right in the United States, 1968–1976," in *The Cultural History of Money and Credit: A Global Perspective*, ed. Chia Yin Jus, Thomas Luckett, and Erika Vause (New York: Lexington Books, 2016), 82.

more difficult time obtaining start-up funds, the study concluded, it was because more of them wanted to start home-based nano-businesses or micro-businesses like a "boutique-type of operation." Females "interested in a true entrepreneurial venture," by contrast, received the same treatment as male entrepreneurs *"all other things being equal"* (emphasis in original). The Treasury study blamed women's penchant for micro- and nano-entrepreneurship on their socialization. "Traditionally," the study claimed, "women have been socialized to achieve in directions other than owning and managing their own businesses." So the problem was not with the financial system, it was with "society," which "still seems to believe that women are not as serious as men about handling financial and business matters."[587]

By the mid-1980s, women owned at least part of one in every three American businesses. Millions of female entrepreneurs offered products and services, many of which were designed for women. Some, though, ventured into more general markets. Sandy Kurtzig, for example, turned a small business, Ask Computer, into a $65 million business. About the same time, Phyllis Murphy established one of the most successful computer service companies in the Los Angeles market.[588] Barbara Isenberg of Greenwich, Connecticut grossed $5.5 million designing and manufacturing toy bears with names like Elvis Bearsley and William Shakesbear.[589]

Most female-owned businesses remained micro-sized and retail-oriented into the Third Millennium and that explained much of why women-owned businesses started off with lower levels of capitalization and less debt than male-owned startups. The residual was partly due to discrimination by lenders, partly to debt/risk aversion on the part of female entrepreneurs, and partly due to gender differences in loan negotiation styles.[590]

---

587 Treasury Department Study Team, *Credit and Capital Formation*, 1–4, 29, 51–52.

588 Jeffrey R. Yost, *Making IT Work: A History of the Computer Services Industry* (Cambridge, Mass.: MIT Press, 2017), 218–221.

589 John Naisbitt and Patricia Aburdene, *Re-inventing the Corporation: Transforming Your Job and Your Company for the New Information Society,* (New York: Warner Books, 1985), 109–11.

590 Sara Carter, Eleanor Shaw, Wing Lam, and Fiona Wilson, "Gender, Entrepreneurship, and Bank Lending: The Criteria and Processes Used by Bank Loan Officers in Assessing

Few of the 110 female entrepreneurs surveyed in rural South Dakota in 2006, however, believed that their gender negatively impacted their businesses and a surprising percentage, almost half, believed that being female even *helped* to secure financing. That sentiment appears to have been due to government policies rather than the "leg loans" allegedly made to especially attractive and flirtatious women in the postwar period or to the chivalrous loans of the Early National period referred to by Elizabeth Meredith after bragging to her son about her "reputation Especially in the Financing business. You know," she wrote, "'tis hard for any Gentleman to refuse the request of a Lady."[591]

That female entrepreneurs generally received relatively equal access to business credit is perhaps not surprising because simply by entering business they showed themselves to be extraordinary and signaled their creditworthiness. Businesswomen, in other words, were less subject to prevailing stereotypes long used to justify denying credit to female consumers and homeowners; namely that single women would marry and quit their jobs, that married women would get pregnant, and that postmenopausal, widowed, or divorced women were emotionally unstable.[592]

Access to Credit for Female Consumers and Homeowners

According to scholars Robert Schafer and Helen Ladd, single women were long discriminated against because of "outdated myths that women are inherently unstable, are incapable of conducting their own affairs, and need the protection of a male." Divorced women, the duo also explained, were considered "emotionally unstable; and … the inability of an unmarried woman to find a man demonstrates that something

Applications," *Entrepreneurship Theory and Practice* 31, no. 3 (2007): 427–44.

591 Abbigail A. Meeder, "Entrepreneurial Activity by Women in Rural South Dakota," (M.S., Economics, South Dakota State University, 2007), 40–44; Treasury Department Study Team, *Credit and Capital Formation*, 66; Branson, "Women and the Family Economy," 59.

592 Treasury Department Study Team, *Credit and Capital Formation*, 51.

must be wrong with her."[593] Despite the persistence of crude stereotypes
questioning their pecuniary faculties, females were not entirely excluded
from consumer credit or home financing, perhaps because most lenders
realized, as the Florida National Bank of Jacksonville did, that "women
today make most of the family purchases, control most of the money
in the country."[594] Wealthier, white women had an easier go of it and
of course mortgages, which by definition were collateralized by real
property, were easier to obtain, all else equal, than unsecured consumer
financing.[595] From the colonial era through the formation of the modern
mortgage market during the Great Depression, women could borrow on
mortgage if they owned real estate. Even females of color could receive
mortgage loans. In the 1820s, 1830s, and 1840s, Elleanor Eldridge, who
was definitely half African-American and perhaps half Amerindian as well,
obtained numerous mortgages. She also suffered several lawsuits and
foreclosures but it does not appear that the loans were predatory in the
sense defined at the outset of this book because they were made on terms
typical in that era, i.e., short-term, interest-only at 10 percent made by a
bank director with personal knowledge of Eldridge. The loss of property
is more accurately attributed to a combination of Eldridge's own financial
problems and a biased legal system than to predatory lending.[596]

Women borrowed from the loan offices set up by various colonial
governments. Pennsylvania's General Loan Office (GLO), for example,
lent to at least 69 different female borrowers. Their average loan size,
£65.39 Pennsylvania currency ($1 = 7s 6d; £1 = $2.667), was almost

---

593 Robert Schafer and Helen F. Ladd, *Discrimination in Mortgage Lending* (Cambridge: MIT Press, 1981), 6–7.

594 "4 Good Reasons Why You Should Want to Attend All 3 Sessions of the Women's Finance Forum," 27 March 1956, Scrapbook, Florida National Bank Records, 1887–1989, University of Florida Smathers Libraries. See also Lendol Calder, *Financing the American Dream: A Cultural History of Consumer Credit*, (Princeton: Princeton University Press, 1999), 182.

595 U.S. Commission on Civil Rights, *Mortgage Money: Who Gets It? A Case Study in Mortgage Lending Discrimination in Hartford, Connecticut* (Washington: U.S. Government Printing Office, 1974), 18.

596 Jacqueline Jones, *A Dreadful Deceit: The Myth of Race from the Colonial Era to Obama's America* (New York: Basic Books, 2013), 108, 124–30, 142.

precisely the average of all loans granted by the GLO. Most female GLO borrowers were widows, some were never-married "spinsters," and a few were *feme sole*.[597]

Throughout the nineteenth and early twentieth centuries, female land owners regularly borrowed on mortgage. In the 1870s, for example, the Pennsylvania Fire Insurance Company made numerous mortgage loans to women, including one for $4,000 to Armenia Bartlett on a 4-story brick property on Vine Street appraised at $10,000, one for $10,000 to Mary A. Hunter on ten 3-story brick houses and lots on 11th Street between Spruce and Pine appraised at $20,000, one for $2,000 to Laura Lane on two properties appraised at $5,000, one for $4,000 to Ellen Mahoney on a 4-story brick store and dwelling appraised at over $10,000, and others too numerous to detail. Female borrowers might have paid higher interest rates or had to post more collateral than their male counterparts did, *ceteris paribus*, but they certainly were not excluded from the mortgage market.[598]

The downside to financial inclusion was that female mortgagors suffered right along with everybody else during the Depression. In 1939, the widow Mrs. Robert B. Wright (no relation, I hope) turned over the keys of her home in Rochester, New York, to the mortgagee, the East Side Savings Bank. The market price of the place was then around $12,000, far less than the $18,000 mortgage. Rather than sink the rest of her inheritance into the property, she left it to the bank in the most honorable way possible and moved across Lake Ontario to Toronto. But the Depression did not mean that lenders ceased lending, just that their appraisals got tighter. So when Elizabeth Alden asked for a $1,900 mortgage loan on her

---

597 Mary Schweitzer, *Custom and Contract: Household, Government, and the Economy in Colonial Pennsylvania*, (New York: Columbia University Press, 1987), 157; Edwin J. Perkins, *The Economy of Colonial America*, 2nd ed. (New York: Columbia University Press, 1988), 145.

598 Pennsylvania Fire Insurance Company Mortgages, 1881, Historical Society of Pennsylvania.

Highland Avenue house in 1937, East Side Savings sent over an appraiser to scrutinize the property and those around it.[599]

During World War II, property values stabilized and even increased, making it easier for East Side Savings to lend. It still had to reject some applicants, however, and some of its files noted why. For example, in March 1943 it approved loans to three men and one woman but rejected the applications of two men and one woman. One of the men would have been approved for $2,500, only half of what he asked for. The other's property, though, was too old and its "immediate environment" was found unsuitable. Mrs. Carl Maier's $3,700 application was rejected due to the "Condition of Property." In August of that same year, Josephine Syracuse received a $950 mortgage while four male applicants and one female applicant were rejected because their properties were old, in bad condition, or "poorly laid out." The bank later wished that it had rejected the $25,000 mortgage application of Tina Hert, which in October 1944 it settled for $14,418.49.[600]

The bank later rejected other applicants, male and female, due to bad credit and insufficient income as well as poor location. Obviously, no firm conclusions can be drawn from such thin explanations. They could have been concocted out of whole cloth, but that seems unlikely given the lack of incentive to distort their own records in an age when they could have expressed bigoted sentiments without legal repercussion. The impression left is that the bankers were not prejudiced against female applicants in any obvious, overt, or systematic way.[601]

Later in the postwar period, by contrast, bankers began to explicitly discount the incomes of married, fertile women who applied for mortgages to account for the risk of pregnancy and subsequent income reduction. Some discounted their incomes by 25 percent, others by 50,

599 J. H. Zweeres (president) to Arthur A. Barry (trustee), May 3, 1939; Henry B. Allen to Arthur A. Barry, October 16, 1937, Real Estate Correspondence, East Side Bank, Rush Rhees Library.

600 Agendas/Minutes: Exec. Committee East Side/Community, Rush Rhees Library.

601 Mortgage Loan Applications, East Side Bank, Rush Rhees Library.

and others would not count it at all. Before 1973, the VA, but not the FHA, applied a similar rule. (The FHA, however, did not keep records on rejected applications so assessing its practices has proven difficult.) By the 1970s, scholars argued that bankers were "unwise" to make such a large deduction because more mothers were returning to the labor market, and doing so more quickly, than ever before.[602]

Postwar bankers also imposed onerous requirements on female mortgagors like "the payment of all outstanding debts, the purchase of mortgage insurance, the taking of monthly payments directly from the applicant's paycheck, and the cosigning of the mortgage by an appropriate man."[603] Whether those impositions were unequally applied to women, however, remained unclear and some studies found that lenders were most wary of single and divorced applicants, male or female.[604]

As the case with poor whites and African-Americans, it never became absolutely clear that mortgage lenders systematically and unfairly discriminated against women. (Calculating the probability that a woman would bear children and have a lower income after that, for example, could be considered prudent lending.) So rather than punish discriminatory lenders, the government induced them to loosen their credit standards so that more women could obtain mortgages. Unsurprisingly, in the runup to the financial fiasco of 2008, women were 32 percent more likely than men to receive subprime loans.[605]

Women were also recipients of all the various forms of consumer credit outlined in Chapter 2, but they were especially prominent customers of pawnshops, composing up to three quarters of all pawners. While husbands worked, wives were supposed to see to the family's expenses

---

602 Beltramini, "Consumer Credit," 89; Schafer and Ladd, *Discrimination*, 5–6; U.S. Commission on Civil Rights, *Mortgage Money*, 20, 25.

603 Schafer and Ladd, *Discrimination*, 7.

604 Schafer and Ladd, *Discrimination*, 287; U.S. Commission on Civil Rights, *Mortgage Money*, 26.

605 U.S. Commission on Civil Rights, *Mortgage Money*, 22–24; Joint Economic Committee, *Invest in Women, Invest in America: A Comprehensive Review of Women in the U.S. Economy* (Washington, DC: U.S. Government Printing Office, 2011), 20.

and if expenditures exceeded income, as they often did, the local pawnshop was a convenient place to obtain a little spending money. Some
pawned their family's Sunday best every Monday, only to redeem the
clothes each Saturday in time for Sunday services the next morning. In
addition to the loan, such families also received storage services. Women
also borrowed from loan sharks, salary buyers, and other illegal lenders. Between 1891 and 1893, for example, a widow in Philadelphia paid
$142.50 for the use of $75. The lender tried to get an additional $112.50
out of her until lawyers got involved and put the miserable contract out
of its misery.[606]

Many retail account books abound with female customers, married
and single. Factoring accounts and collateral agreements also show the
extent of female consumer credit. In 1900, for example, Florida Cycle
Company secured its $1,000 loan with the Mercantile Exchange Bank
by pledging its accounts receivable as collateral. The detailed schedule
it provided the bank showed that the company sold cycles on credit to
Lilly Branch, Emma Wright, Mrs. M. E. Pons, Mrs. E. McDonald, Flora
McCoy, Ethel M. Bateman, Eliza B. Cheney, Della Mosely, Rebacka
Nolan, Mrs. S. F. Hall, Clara Miles, Miss M. Hankins, Mrs. M. A. Hankins,
and Mrs. B. H. Pyke. Many of their credit purchases were for sums greater
than those made to male purchasers and the loan to value ratios were
comparable.[607]

The personal finance industry also catered to women. According to
one authority, in 1914 at least four out of every five dollars lent to consumers for non-durables was signed for by a woman because they were
the primary shoppers in most households. At the same time, men were
the biggest borrowers for consumer durables, especially automobiles.[608]

Women could also obtain personal bank loans once banks began to
make such loans. In 1936, for example, a South Dakotan woman was able

606 Calder, *Financing*, 42–49, 119.

607 Agreement, Florida Cycle Company and Mercantile Exchange Bank, 20 July 1900, Florida
National Bank Records, 1887–1989, MS 069, University of Florida Smathers Libraries.

608 Calder, *Financing*, 218–20.

to obtain a $1,500 loan from a bank in Rapid City without any questions asked because the banker knew the sum "was well within her ability to pay." After the business was transacted, the borrower revealed that her daughter had run up the debt gambling in one of the infamous and then-illegal casinos in nearby Deadwood. In 1955, another South Dakotan woman explained to her banker that she was late on her loan because within a few days she had gallbladder surgery, her husband accidentally cut off 3 fingers at work, and her elderly parents were in a serious automobile collision. "This all seems crazy but its [sic] the truth." The banker verified her story and extended the loan.[609]

Females also took part in the charge and credit card revolutions in the postwar period, though typically only with the approval of a father or husband. Most famously, Diners' Club gave a gold card (gratis) to Mrs. Ivy Baker Priest when she was U.S. Treasurer (not to be confused with the much higher ranking Secretary of the Treasury). In addition to waiving the $5 annual fee, Diners' did not even check her credit rating. Diner's Club president Alfred Bloomingdale reportedly asked her, "What's your bank?" to which she glibly responded, "Fort Knox." Other women (as well as other African-Americans, Hispanics, and members of other oppressed groups), by contrast, fell victim to the petty prejudices of low-level loan officers. In the case of respectable white females, however, stiff competition appears to have kept discrimination down. Teenagers of both sexes were able to obtain cards before 1960 even though in most states they were not legally required to repay (unless a parent cosigned but that was not always insisted upon if the minor had a job).[610]

Married women also received consumer credit, sometimes to the chagrin of their husbands, one of whom wrote a lengthy, learned response to two dunning letters from Bloomingdale's that noted that "for far too many years ... my wife has been a thrall to Bloomingdale's,

---

609 A. E. Dahl, *Banker Dahl of South Dakota: An Autobiography* (Rapid City: Fenske Book Company, 1965), 89–90, 179.

610 Louis Hyman, *Debtor Nation: The History of America in Red Ink* (Princeton: Princeton University Press, 2011), 201; Hillel Black, *Buy Now, Pay Later* (New York: William Morrow and Company, 1961), 21–22, 99–107.

and this relationship has been an incubus whose power has freighted my dreams with visions worthy of a Baudelaire, a Poe, a Verlaine." His wife Alice "wandered monthly and blithely through Bloomingdale's plucking goods from the glittering counters much as a child plucks daisies and buttercups from a vernal hillside." But those days were over as the financially stressed husband had agreed with his "darling wife" to pay one last bill of $42.32 if she would hang up her charga-plate in "a place of honor in our home."[611]

In fact, one San Francisco merchant claimed that the Bank of America had surmised, correctly as it turned out, that women would lead the charge for bank-issued credit cards featuring revolving credit. Wives, they believed, "would rather argue with the old man after charging a purchase than try to get money from him in advance." In the postwar period, banks eager to attract female customers made their branches more architecturally appealing to women and plied them with free shows, concerts, newsletters, and tea parties. "And in Cleveland," one observer noted, "the fashion-minded housewife can sign checks printed in four tweed-patterned colors to match her dresses."[612]

Whether single women were more likely to be denied credit or charged higher rates than men, all other factors equal, was never clearly shown but widely suspected. Clearly, though, divorced women and widows complained that their marital credit records were wiped out when they became single so that, unlike men, they were treated by credit card issuers and other lenders as new borrowers, which of course meant higher interest rates, lower credit lines, greater likelihood of mortgage application rejection, and so forth. Equally as clearly, women were subject to all the tricks of the credit gouger and predatory lender, the perennial bane of all poor borrowers. Around 1960, for example, one elderly woman in Cleveland fell victim to a balloon payment scam when financing a car for $2,543. She made monthly payments of $50 only to be hit with a final bill for $1,993, which she had to refinance on onerous terms. In the end, she

611 Black, *Buy Now*, 71–73.

612 Black, *Buy Now*, 118, 169.

paid $650 to reduce her principal balance by only one percent. Banks, like Bowery Savings in New York, that adopted anti-discrimination policies promising not to base loan decisions on "race, religion, or national origin," failed to mention gender![613]

For those reasons, feminists in the late 1960s began pushing for fairer access to consumer credit and they won several important victories, including the Consumer Protection Act of 1968, state gender credit equality laws, the Fair Credit Reporting Acts of 1970 and 1973, and the Equal Credit Opportunity Act (ECOA) of 1974. A careful econometric study, however, found that even before the passage of ECOA commercial bankers did not discriminate against female borrowers seeking loans for new or used automobiles, household goods, or debt consolidation after controlling for risk variables.[614]

Widows, Orphans, and Other Feminine Investors

I am able to manage my affairs better than any man can manage them. — Hetty Green, as quoted in Sheri J. Caplan, Petticoats and Pinstripes: Portraits of Women in Wall Street's History (Denver: Praeger, 2013), 45.

The most famous early American female investor is probably Abigail Adams, wife of the second president of the United States. While John helped to found the nation, Abigail tended to the family's business and did a heck of a good job. In the troubled 1770s and 1780s, before the United States emerged from the ashes of revolution, default, and bankruptcy, she persuaded her husband to buy dirt cheap government bonds instead

---

613 U.S. Commission on Civil Rights, *Mortgage Money*, 29; Beltramini, "Consumer Credit," 88; Lewis Mandell, *The Credit Card Industry: A History*, (Boston: Twayne Publishers, 1990), 58; Black, *Buy Now*, 149–50; Davis McEntire, *Residence and Race: Final and Comprehensive Report to the Commission on Race and Housing* (Berkeley: University of California Press, 1960), 227.

614 Hyman, *Debtor Nation*, 191–219; Richard L. Peterson, "An Investigation of Sex Discrimination in Commercial Banks' Direct Consumer Lending," *Bell Journal of Economics* 12, no. 2 (1981), 550, 552, 555, 560.

of cheap dirt farms. Her speculations paid off handsomely, with nominal returns well into the double digits. She also had her diplomat husband ship her various fineries that she profitably retailed to the ladies of eastern Massachusetts by consigning them to a cousin in the mercantile line.

After profiting on their joint account, Abigail asserted her financial independence from John by buying government bonds on her own account via her uncle Cotton Tufts. After adoption of Treasury Secretary Alexander Hamilton's funding and assumption programs, Abigail scored again, while her husband seethed at the notion of profiting from mere paper investments. She was at it again on her own account in the late 1790s, when the federal government issued bonds bearing an attractive eight percent coupon, using accumulated interest to buy new bonds whenever prices were favorable. She sat out the War of 1812, however, perhaps because over the years she had seen too many of her friends go bankrupt by making too many risky investments.[615]

Abigail was clearly the principal in those transactions, not a shill or agent like Kitty Duer, wife of infamous speculator William Duer was. Abigail was more akin to the women, most apparently of middling means, who bought Duer's promissory notes during his failed attempt to corner the securities markets in 1791 and 1792. The wives of other public figures also speculated on their own accounts. Mary Parker Norris, widow and second wife of important Pennsylvania legislator Charles Norris, speculated in rental properties with the hope that Congress would return to Philadelphia in 1785. When it did not, house rents moved lower so Norris changed strategies and tried to sell the houses and lots on ground rent (perpetual interest-only mortgage) to the highest bidder instead of leasing the properties to government officials. Sarah Livingston Jay also bought bank stock and made collections on behalf of herself and

615 Woody Holton, "Abigail Adams, Bond Speculator," *The William and Mary Quarterly* 64, no. 4 (2007): 821–38; Woody Holton, *Abigail Adams* (New York: Free Press, 2009), 133, 145, 189–90, 212–14, 238, 249, 252, 272–77, 280–82, 310, 322–24, 340, 351–52, 374–75, 397–98, 407.

her husband, John Jay, co-author of the *Federalist Papers* and principal American negotiator of the infamous treaty that bore his name.[616]

Abigail was also not the only female to invest in government bonds. Of the 1,781 economic entities (individuals, partnerships, corporations, governments) that registered U.S. government bonds in Virginia between 1790 and 1834, 120 (6.7%) were women. Of the 1,878 individuals who owned U.S. government bonds throughout the country on January 1, 1795, 161 (8.6%) listed their occupation as "spinster" or "widow." Unfortunately, few of these early female bondholders have left much trace in the historical record.[617]

Abigail was also not the first woman to buy public securities. During the French and Indian War, 19 of the 31 investors who subscribed to Pennsylvania's Indian Commissioner Loan were women. Women also bought Continental bonds during and after the Revolution. Of the 2,696 entities that purchased Connecticut Loan Office certificates between January 1777 and March 1780, for example, 202 (7.5%) were women. The numbers were similar for New Jersey loan office certificates, where of the 1,915 different investors between March 1777 and August 1781, 187 (9.75%) were female. Some women, like Marian Maxwell, later speculated by accepting state securities in payment of debts owed to them. Women continued to buy state bonds throughout the antebellum period and beyond. Hellen Ellice, for example, owned a large sum of Pennsylvania state bonds in the 1830s.[618]

---

616 Wright, "Banking and Politics," 673–74; Waciega, "Widow of Means," 53; Sheri J. Caplan, *Petticoats and Pinstripes: Portraits of Women in Wall Street's History* (Denver: Praeger, 2013), 24–25.

617 Robert E. Wright, *One Nation Under Debt: Hamilton, Jefferson, and the History of What We Owe* (New York: McGraw Hill, 2008), 187, 213–14, 248, 307.

618 For female investors in seventeenth and eighteenth century British securities, see Anne L. Murphy, *The Origins of English Financial Markets: Investment and Speculation Before the South Sea Bubble* (New York: Cambridge University Press, 2009), 201–207. For female investment in Europe in the nineteenth century, see Robert Beachy, Beatrice Craig, and Alastair Owens, eds. *Women, Business and Finance in Nineteenth-century Europe: Rethinking Separate Spheres* (New York: Berg, 2006). For America, see Wright, *Hamilton Unbound*, 182–83; Loan Office Certificate Books, Connecticut, M1005, Roll 1; Loan Office Certificate Books, New

Abigail was also not the most astute early female investor. Some women engaged in a far wider range of investment activities. In the late 1840s, for example, Judith Bogert lent directly to individuals, men and women, by mortgage and on bond. She owned U.S. bonds and also those of New York state, New York City, and several churches. She also rented real estate to both men and women tenants.[619] Elizabeth Willing Powel owned considerable amounts of real estate and once referred to herself in a letter to a tenant delinquent on his rent as a "man of business."[620] She also owned tens of thousands of dollars of U.S. bonds upon her death and had an account with the Bank of the United States, though perhaps only because she was a large stockholder.[621] She sold out in January 1811 at a high price before Congress denied the bank a new charter.[622]

Thanks to her shrewd moves, Powel died in 1830 worth over $140,000, a princely sum at the time. But that sum was a pittance compared to the fortune of several hundred million dollars amassed by Henrietta Howland Robinson, a.k.a. "Hetty" Green, during the Civil War and Gilded Age. By being extremely miserly in her expenditures and shrewdly investing in paper money, government bonds, real estate, and railroad securities, Green became, with the help of family seed money earned out of New Bedford, Massachusetts in the China and whaling trades, the nation's first female "tycoon." By following strategies that would later be called value investing, "The Witch of Wall Street" became so wealthy that the great investment banker J.P. Morgan reportedly summoned her to his lair in November 1907 to seek her help in staving off the financial panic then sweeping through the nation.[623]

Jersey, M1006, Roll 1, RG 53, Records of the Bureau of the Public Debt, National Archives and Records Administration II.

619 Judith Bogert Memorandum Book, 1843, Historical Society of Pennsylvania.

620 As quoted in Waciega, "Widow of Means," 52.

621 Elizabeth Willing Powel Estate Books, Historical Society of Pennsylvania.

622 Waciega, "Widow of Means," 53–54.

623 Waciega, "Widow of Means," 54; Charles Slack, *Hetty: The Genius and Madness of America's First Female Tycoon* (New York: Ecco, 2004); Caplan, *Petticoats*, 45–54.

Many more modestly endowed female investors also acquired equities, or shares in joint-stock business corporations, by buying or inheriting them. Of the almost 73,000 investors in Pennsylvania DPOs (direct public offerings of stock, similar to today's IPO but not intermediated by an investment bank) between 1814 and 1859 for which we have records, almost 6,500, or 8.85 percent, were female. Females subscribed, though, for only about 2 percent of the 2.4 million total shares purchased. The largest female subscriber, Margaret H. Baxter, subscribed 2,000 shares in the Merchants and Mechanics Mutual Insurance Company of Philadelphia. That was impressive but she was only the 180th largest investor in terms of total shares subscribed.[624]

As in Europe, female investors in America represented a sizable portion of some financial markets. To invoke the specter of the many "widows and orphans" who would be hurt by corporate taxes and regulations was a cliché by the 1830s, but one grounded in reality.[625]

Women invested extensively in bank and insurance stocks, particularly those, like the Bank of the United States, that paid good, regular dividends. Of the 89 people who owned stock in the Insurance Company of North America between 1792 and 1799, 11 were women. Of the first 388 subscribers in the Manhattan Company, 53 were women. Of the first 69 investors in the Commercial and Farmers Bank of Baltimore, 14.5 percent were women and they owned 12.5 percent of the bank's capital stock. Females owned 45 shares in the Bank of Utica in 1812. Many other early banks also had female stockholders. Five different females owned shares in the Bank of Gettysburg in 1814. Each possessed a taxable estate

---

624 Records of the Department of State, Corporation Bureau, Letters Patent, 1814–1874, Boxes 1–13, RG-26, Pennsylvania State Archives.

625 Alastair Owens, "'Making Some Provision for the Contingencies to Which Their Sex Is Particularly Liable': Women and Investment in Early Nineteenth-century England," and Tom Petersson, "The Silent Partners: Women, Capital and the Development of the Financial System in Nineteenth-century Sweden," in Beatrice Craig, Robert Beachy, and Alastair Owens, eds., *Women, Business and Finance in Nineteenth-century Europe: Rethinking Separate Spheres* (New York: Berg, 2006), chapters 2 and 3; Robert E. Shalhope, *The Baltimore Bank Riot: Political Upheaval in Antebellum Maryland* (Chicago: University of Illinois Press, 2009), 63, 65; Rockman, *Scraping By*, 154–55.

greater than $500, a sizeable sum for that time and place, and two were among the borough's richest farmers with estates valued above $5,000. In the 1830s, 1840s, and 1850s, women comprised between 7.5 and almost 25 percent of stockholders in Maine banks and females owned between 4 and 16 percent of Maine bank stock. While females made no investment in some Maine banks, they owned over a quarter of the shares of a few. In 1841, women owned 7.8 percent of the dollar value of bank stock in Ohio, while about the same time they owned an impressive 38.5 percent of the total banking capital in Massachusetts.[626]

Females owned bank shares throughout the nineteenth and into the twentieth century. Between 1880 and 1892, 343 of the 776 different economic entities (people and institutions) that owned shares in the Merchants National Bank of New Bedford, Massachusetts were women and they owned more shares than the average male stockholder did. In the early 1890s, 40 of the 200 stockholders in the Germania Savings Bank of Georgia were female. In the early twentieth century, Eliza J. Macduff owned shares in the Mercantile Exchange Bank of Florida. Like many other stockholders, male and female, she assigned her proxy rather than voting in person at the annual stockholder meetings.[627]

Even more women invested in banks by holding their banknotes or deposits. Lydia R. Bailey, for example, held a checking account with the United States Bank of Pennsylvania in 1840. Females essentially lent to banks whenever they held a banknote, as most did at some point in their lives as we know from various theft notices and lost and found advertisements, and instances where women were duped by counterfeits, as the First Female Beneficial Society of Philadelphia was in 1820 when it took

---

626 Wright, *Hamilton Unbound*, 183; Robert E. Wright, *The Wealth of Nations Rediscovered: Integration and Expansion in American Financial Markets, 1780–1850* (New York: Cambridge University Press, 2002), 68–69, 102, 104–9; James Karmel, "Banking on the People: Banks, Politics, and Market Evolution in Early National Pennsylvania, 1781–1824," (Ph.D. dissertation, SUNY Buffalo, 1999), 209–10, 217–21.

627 Robert E. Wright, "New Bedford, Massachusetts and the Importance of Local Sources of Capital," *Financial History* 110 (Spring 2014), 30; Germania Savings Bank, Stockholders Records, 1891–93, Georgia Historical Society; 1904 Stockholders Meeting, Florida National Bank Records, 1887–1989, MS 069, University of Florida Smathers Libraries.

"a bad note" during "the Collection" of its dues. Women, white, black, and of every other hue, were also avid investors in savings banks throughout the nineteenth and into the twentieth century.[628]

Women were somewhat less likely to invest in shakier, non-financial corporations like turnpikes. Only 1 of the original 66 investors in the James River Company was female. Only 10 of the 85 initial investors in the Albany and Schenectady Turnpike were women and only 22 of the first 427 investors in the Permanent Bridge, near Philadelphia, were women. They became more avid investors later, after that company established a good record of dividend payments. After it established itself as one of the nation's leading railroads, the Pennsylvania Railroad became known as the "Petticoat Line" because more than half of its shareholders were female. Women also invested in manufacturing companies, though generally less readily than they purchased bank shares. Women in San Francisco in the latter part of the nineteenth century purchased stock for investment and sometimes for speculation, for example in mines in the Comstock Lode. Unfortunately, many held shares that were valued at zero dollars in their bankruptcy or estate files.[629]

Some of this widespread investment in corporations by "ladies of a 'certain age,' widows, and orphans," however, was encouraged by unscrupulous men bent on controlling their money. "This class of stockholders," one former stock broker noted in 1838, were "particularly favored and acceptable, because they never want to borrow, and never find fault with the management; and if by chance they should suspect themselves to be badly used, a tear shed in secret is the only complaint they ever make."[630]

---

628 Elizabeth Steele Accounts, Historical Society of Pennsylvania; Wright, "Banking and Politics," 681–82; First Female Beneficial Society of Philadelphia Minutes, 1814–1840, Historical Society of Pennsylvania; Jonathan Levy, *Freaks of Fortune: The Emerging World of Capitalism and Risk in America* (Cambridge: Harvard University Press, 2012), 137.

629 James River Company Account Book, 1785–1789, Virginia Historical Society; Wright, *Hamilton Unbound*, 184–85; Caplan, *Petticoats*, 31, 67; Wright, *Wealth of Nations*, 68–69; Sparks, *Capital Intentions*, 167.

630 A Reformed Stock Gambler, *Stocks and Stock-Jobbing in Wall-Street, with Sketches of the Brokers, and Fancy Stocks* (New York: New-York Publishing Company, 1848), 27.

Some women put their savings out to loan, often to other women at interest, via brokers. Antebellum free black women entrepreneurs too owned shares in corporations, including banks when allowed, and government bonds. When rich enough they could borrow from banks, especially if they owned slaves. Some acted as private bankers, even shaving notes.[631]

Madame Eulalie d'Mandeville Macarty, for example, shaved notes at 10 percent discount. Although herself an African-American, she owned 32 slaves as well as shares in corporations, banks, and government bonds. By the 1840s, she was worth over $150,000, all due, as a court decided, to her own efforts. Anna Martin also established her own lending operation in Texas in 1901.[632] Other women made personal loans directly to borrowers. Banker Alexander Bryan Johnson told of a widow who loaned her husband's small estate "on interest." The arrangement, he claimed, "added greatly to her resources, small as the income seems to persons in a different society."[633] Matters did not go so well for Mary Vredenburgh, however, because she had to sue Benjamin Thomas when he defaulted on his loan from her. In the late nineteenth century, female purchasers of mortgage bonds issued by J. B. Watkins Land Mortgage Company of Lawrence, Kansas were as numerous as male purchasers.[634]

Many financial securities were left to widows by deceased craftsmen, shopkeepers, merchants, professionals, and even farmers. According to historian Lisa Wilson Waciega, "Wealthy widows knew the nature of their material worth and how to use it. In letters and diaries, affluent widows demonstrated familiarity with real estate values, the nuances of stock investments, and even subtle indicators of change in the economy." A "separate estate" was a married woman's assets kept separate from

---

631 Sparks, *Capital Intentions*, 96–97; Juliet E. K. Walker, *The History of Black Business in America: Capitalism, Race, Entrepreneurship*, 2nd ed., Vol. 1 (Chapel Hill: University of North Carolina Press, 2009), 164–93.

632 Walker, *History of Black Business*, 171; Caplan, *Petticoats*, 59.

633 As quoted in Wright, "Banking and Politics," 679–80.

634 Wright, "Banking and Politics," 681; Lance E. Davis, "The Investment Market, 1870–1914: The Evolution of a National Market," *Journal of Economic History* 25, no. 3 (1965), 385–86.

the property of her husband. Such trusts, which came with the colonists from English equity law, allowed fathers and brothers to give or bequeath property to daughters and sisters without fear that it would expropriated by their husbands. Equity law, however, varied greatly from state to state. (Connecticut, for example, never even establish an equity court.) The biggest shortcoming of the system was that the husband had to give his consent and the only time he had a strong incentive to do so was when trying to protect assets from his creditors. Some women, like Elizabeth Murray of Boston, signed prenuptial agreements that protected business assets accumulated during spinster- or widowhoods from their new husbands but not all women had such foresight or bargaining power.[635]

In response to those problems and other pressures, most states between the 1830s and 1880s passed legislation that automatically recognized the property rights of married women in assets they owned prior to marriage or inherited during marriage. Later versions also recognized the wages and business profits of married women. Some newer states rejected common law marriage altogether and adopted instead community property systems that recognized separate estates for both men and women and also recognized the wife's ownership of half of the property acquired during marriage. One major impetus for the change, historian Carole Shammas has argued, was to allow male relatives to transfer corporate shares to their women folk. Such passive investments could be lucrative but demanded much less attention than real property or small businesses did.[636]

In 1860, women and children combined composed only 5.6 percent of all wealth holders in the United States and they owned only 7.2 percent of the nation's total wealth. By 1900, thanks to the adoption of

---

635 Waciega, "Widow of Means," 49, 52; Winifred Barr Rothenberg, *From Market-Places to a Market Economy: The Transformation of Rural Massachusetts, 1750–1850*, (Chicago: University of Chicago Press, 1992), 136–42; Branson, "Women and the Family Economy," 52.

636 Carole Shammas, "Re-Assessing the Married Women's Property Acts," *Journal of Women's History* 6, no. 1 (1994): 9–15, 25; Jane E. Simonsen, *Making Home Work: Domesticity and Native American Assimilation in the American West, 1860–1919*, (Chapel Hill: University of North Carolina Press, 2006), 46, 49.

community property and married women's property acts, women composed one third of all wealth holders and females owned about a quarter
of all property, at least as measured by probate records.[637]

Women also owned an unknown percentage of corporate stock
through their control of numerous charities, benevolent societies, and
other non-profit organizations. As historian Johann Neem notes, "By
the 1820s, reform work was an integral part of a middle-class woman's
identity." Not all non-profits had significant reserves to invest, of course.
For example, the New York Exchange, one of the largest of the women's
exchanges (consignment stores), never enjoyed four digit reserves. Many
female-controlled non-profits, however, owned considerable assets that
had to be invested. Some, like the Ladies' Benevolent Society of the First
Baptist Church of St. Paul, Minnesota, purchased "wild lands" on speculation. Others made loans to individuals or purchased corporate stock, corporate bonds, or government bonds depending upon their goals and the
state of the money and capital markets. The Association for the Relief of
Respectable Aged Indigent Females, for example, purchased shares in the
Mechanics Bank and used the dividends to provide its wards with cash,
wood, and tea. The First Female Beneficial Society of Philadelphia split
its monies among its several stewards, who disbursed them to members
with valid claims, like sickness or the death of a spouse. Funds that might
be needed it kept in the Bank of the Northern Liberties. Any long-term
excess funds, by contrast, were lent at interest to individuals. Some of the
organizations controlled by women were enormous. Established in 1873,
the Woman's Christian Temperance Union (WCTU) came to dominate
the U.S. temperance movement and hence fundamentally influenced
American history for half a century.[638]

---

637 Shammas, "Re-Assessing," 20–21.

638 Johann N. Neem, *Creating a Nation of Joiners: Democracy and Civil Society in Early
National Massachusetts*, (Cambridge: Harvard University Press, 2008), 103–7, 177; Kathleen
Sander, *The Business of Charity: The Woman's Exchange Movement, 1832–1900* (Chicago:
University of Illinois Press, 1998), 98; Anne Firor Scott, *Natural Allies: Women's Associations
in American History*, (Urbana: University of Illinois Press, 1992), 26; Lori D. Ginzberg, *Women
and the Work of Benevolence: Morality, Politics, and Class in the Nineteenth-Century United
States*, (New Haven: Yale University Press, 1990), 52; Wills, *Boosters*, 88; Wright, *Wealth of*

It is well known that women formed and ran non-profit corporations without any male guidance or control whatsoever. Their minute books are indistinguishable from those of male-run corporations and, if anything, their officer elections were even more rancorous and contested.[639] "As the wives and daughters of merchants and lawyers," historian Lori Ginzberg explained, "these women knew well the advantages of corporate status."[640] Less well understood is that females were also occasionally incorporators of for-profit businesses. Of the 88,105 unique individuals and partnerships that successfully chartered businesses corporations by special act of the legislature before the Civil War, only 343 (0.4%) were women. Females never comprised the majority of incorporators in any one corporation but in some instances they provided a surprisingly large contingent. In 1836, for example, Catherine Stanber, Magdelena Fransu, Elizabeth Spach, Margaret Waterson, Louisa Thamsh, Johanna E. Shultz, and 23 men incorporated the Salem Manufacturing Company of North Carolina.[641] The company, which ceased operations in 1849, produced textiles. The women, though, apparently had no say in its operation.[642]

Many women continued to invest in the securities markets after the Civil War and some were quite active traders. When Teresa Holden of San Francisco went bankrupt in 1873, she owed the coal company, an attorney, and her wholesalers but also a stock broker for unpaid commissions.[643] By the late nineteenth century, many communities throughout the land were home to so-called "bucket shops" where people of

---

Nations, 70; First Female Beneficial Society of Philadelphia Minutes, 1814–1840, Historical Society of Pennsylvania; Jed Dannenbaum, *Drink and Disorder: Temperance Reform in Cincinnati from the Washingtonian Revival to the WCTU*, (Urbana: University of Illinois Press, 1984), 180–233.

639 See, for example, First Female Beneficial Society of Philadelphia Minutes, 1814–1840, Historical Society of Pennsylvania.

640 Ginzberg, *Women*, 48–49.

641 North Carolina *Statutes* (1836), 324–26.

642 Michael Shirley, *From Congregation Town to Industrial City: Culture and Social Change in a Southern Community*, (New York: New York University Press, 1994), 60–93; Frank Tursi, *Winston-Salem: A History*, (USA: John F. Blair, 1994), 77.

643 Sparks, *Capital Intentions*, 160.

all descriptions, "man or woman, boy or girl, white, black, yellow or bronze" as the *Chicago Tribune* put it, could bet on the direction of stock prices without actually owning any shares whatsoever.[644] In bigger cities, like New York, people had long been able to make similar gambles in the so-called "privileges" market that operated on the curb outside of the stock exchange. Outright bets could also be made and by 1838 were "too well understood to need any particular explanation."[645] Bucket shops brought the action indoors and extended it. Bucket shops that catered exclusively to women even appeared in uptown Manhattan. The little shops of speculation numbered in the hundreds and remained quite popular until they were run out of business by authorities before the Great War.[646]

Between 1900 and 1922, the number of American stockholders trebled from about 4.4 to 14.4 million, or from about 5 to 12 percent of the population, largely due to the proliferation of employee stock option plans, a fringe benefit extended to many female employees, like the "human switches" responsible for AT&T's fasting growing telephonic network. Thanks to their experience in the bucket shops as well as buying Liberty Loans during the Great War, many more Americans purchased shares during the ebullient bull market of the 1920s. Many of them were women who frequented the over 5,000 brokerages that specialized in female investors that cropped up in the vacuum left by the bucket shops. Many women sold out during and following the 1929 Crash but there were plenty of exceptions, including FDR's secretary, Missy LeHand, who owned shares in gold mining companies.[647] Many men behaved likewise but some observers sought to blame the crash on panicked selling by women because the notion of emotion-laden decision-making fit well

644 As quoted in David Hochfelder, "'Where the Common People Could Speculate': The Ticker, Bucket Shops, and the Origin of Popular Participation in Financial Markets, 1880–1920," *Journal of American History* 93, no. 2 (2006), 337, 341.

645 A Reformed Stock Gambler, *Stocks and Stock-Jobbing*, 9, 11–12.

646 Hochfelder, "Bucket Shops," 337, 341–42, 355.

647 Sebastian Edwards, *American Default: The Untold Story of FDR, the Supreme court, and the Battle Over Gold* (Princeton: Princeton University Press, 2018), 172.

with prevailing gender stereotypes. Decades later, some prominent members of the brokerage community still doubted whether women could invest rationally so attempts to entice them into the market were tempered with appeals for investor education and expert (male) guidance.[648]

In the 1940s, in an effort to rebuild from the horrors of the Depression, brokers like Merrill Lynch proclaimed that, "No account is too small! Regardless of size, we'll give it the best service we can." About a quarter of the account holders in its Los Angeles branch about that time were women. Soon after, it began to actively seek out female investors as reports showed that less than 10 percent of American families owned stock directly and that women could induce their husbands to buy stock. By the early 1950s, about half of all individual shareholders were women, but they did not own anything like half of all shares by value. By 1975, however, women owned 47 percent of the nation's wealth, including about half of the common stock of the nation's largest publicly traded businesses. Throughout the postwar period, however, women controlled much less than they nominally owned because most of their wealth was inherited and entrusted to various institutional asset managers or their husbands made them stockholders solely as a tax dodge.[649]

In the twentieth century, far more women turned to financial intermediaries rather than the stock market for their investment needs. Lori Charla Edwards, for example, held a savings account in the Union National Bank of Little Rock, Arkansas between April 1959 and June 1977 and earned over $700 interest in the process. Mrs. F. E. Mackle earned considerably less on the $5 she held in a Florida savings bank on the eve of the Great War. But many women held sizeable certificates of deposits in the Florida Bank & Trust Company. Mrs. Lena A. Ottinger,

---

648 Hochfelder, "Bucket Shops," 336–38; Caplan, *Petticoats*, 67, 73–82; Janice M. Traflet, *A Nation of Small Shareholders: Marketing Wall Street After World War II* (Baltimore: Johns Hopkins University Press, 2013), 153–58.

649 Edwin Perkins, *Wall Street to Main Street: Charles Merrill and Middle-Class Investors* (New York: Cambridge University Press, 1999), 153, 157; Traflet, *Nation of Small Shareholders*, 64, 146, 152; Caplan, *Petticoats*, 140; Treasury Department Study Team, *Credit and Capital Formation*, 10.

for example, bought a $5,000 certificate of deposit in that bank in January 1905. Rebecca Miller bought $1,000 in March of that same year, as did Ida K. Stausell. All three investors received 4 percent interest by foregoing the right to draw on the money for 3 months. In the postwar period, many banks sponsored special ladies' day promotions. One such event held by Community Savings Bank of Rochester, New York at the end of February 1952 attracted 970 new female depositors who brought over $88,000 of cash into the bank's coffers. Women also invested by purchasing insurance policies.[650]

Women and Insurance

The Home Mutual Insurance Company ... charged higher premiums in 1865 for any business that utilized cooking or heating equipment or whose stock was considered highly flammable. Among the enterprises singled out were bakeries, confectioneries, crockery and drug stores, hotels, restaurants, laundries, tobacco and cigar retailers, toy stores, and millinery shops – all business that were frequently operated by women. — Edith Sparks, Capital Intentions: Female Proprietors in San Francisco, 1850–1920 (Chapel Hill: University of North Carolina Press, 2006), 191–92.

Women were also major players in all three major segments of the insurance industry, the one that guarantees income (life and disability insurance and annuities), the one that hedges against large medical bills (health insurance), and the one that reimburses property losses (fire, auto, and other property and casualty lines). From the start of the modern U.S. life insurance industry in the early nineteenth century, women were the primary beneficiaries of life insurance. They, and their children, were the main reasons that men, husbands and fathers anyway, were supposed

650 Union National Bank Records, Passbooks, MSS 02–07, Butler Center for Arkansas Studies; Savings Account Number 6091, Florida National Bank Records, 1887–1989, MS 069, University of Florida Smathers Libraries; Agendas/Minutes: Board Meetings Community, Rush Rhees Library.

to buy life insurance. In fact, starting in the 1840s wives in some states could lawfully insure their husbands' lives without their consent.

It was more difficult, however, for women to insure their own lives. Although insurers realized that women were likely to live longer than men, they also knew that childbirth raised female mortality risks significantly. By the end of the 1860s, after decades of indifference toward female applicants, most life insurers refused to insure women at any premium due to a study that showed a high level of adverse selection, i.e., that insured females died at much higher rates than uninsured women. Those companies that did write female business mostly underwrote widows with dependent children and at a higher premium than charged men of the same age for the same policy.[651]

By the end of the nineteenth century, however, most British insurers were insuring female lives (single, married, and widowed), many without any additional premium, which they realized only exacerbated the adverse selection problem noticed a few decades earlier. By 1900 or so, most American life insurers were again covering women though some, like Acacia Mutual (est. 1867) continued to demur. Moreover, many U.S. insurers continued to insist on an extra premium if the insured woman was capable of bearing children, which remained the leading cause of death in younger women. Essentially, insurers were saying that motherhood was a hazardous occupation because they added the same premium surcharges as men working as coal miners and in other dangerous jobs.[652]

Prior to World War II, Guardian Life Insurance Company of America, like many other major life insurers, insured some married women but did not press for the business. Housewives, the thought went, should carry enough insurance to cover "final expenses" but no more, lest greedy

---

651 Sharon Ann Murphy, *Investing in Life: Insurance in Antebellum America* (Baltimore: Johns Hopkins University Press, 2010), 42–44, 142–151.

652 Anon., "The Practice of Life Offices in Regard to Assurances on Female Lives," *Journal of the Institute of Actuaries* 29, no. 1 (1891): 75–78; Howard Kacy, *A Unique and Different Company*, (Princeton, N.J.: Newcomen Society 1964), 18–19; R. Carlyle Buley, *The American Life Convention, 1906–1952: A Study in the History of Life Insurance*, 2 vols. (New York: Appleton-Century-Crofts, 1953), 1:70.

husbands or children hasten their demise. Women who were employed
or active in business, however, could be safely covered at several years'
salary without increasing familial moral hazard. After World War II,
the industry realized that the ever-growing number of working wives
deserved coverage. Guardian took the logic a step further and began to
cover housewives, too, because it realized that it was costly to replace the
services they provided the household, especially given their increasingly
important role as a tax deduction. No sane hubby, in other words, would
kill off his Mrs. just to cash in on her life insurance. By the 1960s, management was actively encouraging Guardian's sales force to sell insurance on
the wife as well as on the husband as industry analysts believed that "the
primary consideration in underwriting married women and children is
that the father be insured to a reasonably adequate extent, then possibly
the mother for a small amount, and then the children."[653]

Women also faced some exclusionary discrimination in the disability insurance market due to widespread perceptions that females were
frail or would feign disability so they could remain at home, where they
were thought to feel the most comfortable. Matters improved in the final
decades of the twentieth century but, ultimately, the private disability
market is too small to matter much.[654]

Dramatic improvements in female mortality rates during childbirth
(eventually combined with lower birthrates), helped life insurers to
reverse the gender penalty. Men now pay more than women for the same
insurance coverage, as well they should given their higher rate of mortality at every adult age. At the same time, however, and often at the same
companies, women had to pay more for healthcare insurance due to the
costs associated with reproduction: childbirth, abortions, contraceptives,

---

653 *Proceedings of the Forty-Ninth Annual Meeting of the Life Insurance Association of America.*
(New York: 1955), 159; Robert E. Wright and George David Smith, *Mutually Beneficial: The
Guardian and Life Insurance in America* (New York: New York University Press, 2004), 21,
142–43; *The Guardian,* 12 November 1962, 27 April 1964; Pearce Shepherd, "Principles and
Problems of Selection and Underwriting," in *Life Insurance Trends at Mid-Century,* ed. David
McCahan (Philadelphia: University of Pennsylvania Press, 1950), 66.

654 Treasury Department Study Team, *Credit and Capital Formation,* 21.

and so forth. The New York Insurance Department, the most important insurance regulator in the nation throughout the twentieth century, studied the matter and confirmed, in the words of one insurance executive, "That claim costs for women are much higher than for men in most age groups and all occupational groups."[655] Perhaps because of the very personal nature of health insurance, the female premium issue became politicized and many states forced insurers to stop charging females more for health insurance. (The fact that men paid more for life insurance and automobile insurance than women, *ceteris paribus*, was ignored.) That, in turn, led some insurers, like Guardian, to exit some of the markets, which led to large numbers of uninsured Americans, male and female, though females bore the brunt of the dearth of supply. Hispanic and Native American women had even higher rates of non-insurance, about one in three in each case in 2011. Because health insurance in the U.S. is uniquely, and very oddly, tied tightly to employment by corporate tax rules and other public policies, women, especially poorer women, have often had to go without health insurance entirely.[656]

Property insurance has, generally speaking, not been so problematic. In the 1850s through the 1880s, for example, the Pennsylvania Fire Insurance Company regularly insured the property of women against fire. Elizabeth Savage recovered $15 after her property, insured for $500, was lightly damaged in a fire in 1855. The next year, Mary Tisdall recovered $210 and Eliza Cox $50, after fires damaged their properties, insured under policy numbers 11,637 and 5,593, respectively. Females were only a small percentage of claimants but rather than discrimination that might have been because fewer of them insured with the company than men did and/or that female-owned property suffered fires at a lower rate than those owned by men. While insurers charged many of the businesses typically owned by females extra premiums, as noted in the head quote by

---

655 Gerald S. Parker to All Agencies in New York State, 26 April 1978, Circular Letters, Agency Communication and Sales Promotion, Box 212, GLICA Archives.

656 Joint Economic Committee, *Invest in Women*, 149–51, 153, 156; Christy Ford Chapin, *Ensuring America's Health: The Public Creation of the Corporate Health Care System* (New York: Cambridge University Press, 2015), 62–63.

historian Edith Sparks, the extra premiums were not applied to women but rather to situations thought to pose extra risk. Men running those or similar businesses also had to pay extra for coverage.[657]

In the first decade of the twentieth century, most of those insured by the St. Paul Mutual Hail & Cyclone Insurance Company were men but women, even married women, obtained coverage when appropriate. Mary Smasal and Mary Faeber, both of Boyd, Minnesota, each had policies worth over $3,000. One of the largest policies, for $9,100, was that of Lizzie Struve of Chippewa Falls. And while Mrs. Phillip Willet of Cadott may have simply followed her husband, who was also insured by St. Paul Mutual, Mrs. Ida F. Tucker, also of Cadott, was insured by the company even though her husband was not.[658]

Loss of insurance was a serious matter for both businesses and homeowners. In 1940, the East Side Savings Bank of Rochester, New York, felt compelled to discharge a $7,500 mortgage on Terrace Gardens nightclub, owned by Sarah Martin, for $4,600 when Martin's fire insurance policies were cancelled and she was "unable to obtain additional fire insurance." The reasons for the insurance cancellation are unknown but the bank's correspondence showed no animus toward Martin as a woman or as a person. "Assets of this character," the president explained to the board chairman, "have no place on our books."[659] Despite the setback, the business, which one observer called "the liveliest night club in the city," survived until at least December 1943, when *Billboard* noted that burlesque dancer Francine had just wound up a 10-week gig there.[660]

---

657 Pennsylvania Fire Insurance Company, Claim Book, 1855–1881, Historical Society of Pennsylvania.

658 "List of Wisconsin Cyclone Members Written by Agents F. N. Robinson & Guy R. Cooper," August 13, 1908, "Examination Reports, Domestic Companies, 1908–1910," Insurance Department, Examining Division, Box 2, Series 1049, State Historical Society of Wisconsin Archives, Madison, Wisconsin.

659 Joseph H. Zweeres (president) to Arthur A. Barry (chairman), August 20, 1940, Business Correspondence East Side Bank, Rush Rhees Library.

660 Several documents attribute ownership to Butch Martin, presumably Sarah's husband. Henry W. Clune, "Remembering Front Street," *Rochester History* 55, no. 3 (1993), 14.

Little evidence of gender-specific predation has been found either, perhaps because most insurance is written through commissioned agents and brokers, rather than insurers directly, and female insurance agents and brokers actively sought the business of women and female-owned businesses. Nevertheless, some women bought too much coverage while others purchased too little. Both suffered the consequences.[661]

Female Employment in the Financial Sector

He has monopolized nearly all the profitable employments, and from those
she is permitted to follow, she receives but a scanty remuneration.
— *Declaration of Sentiments, Seneca Falls, New York, 1848.*
It is a shameful fact that women own companies but can't get top jobs in them.
— *"Pressure Group," New Yorker (June 25, 1949), 16.*

Given the extensive participation of women in the financial sector as borrowers, lenders, policyholders, and, to a lesser extent, owners, it is unsurprising to find that females were also employed in the financial sector, although until recently not to the degree that males were. Moreover, female financial workers typically received far less money than men doing comparable jobs. In July 1948 in Rochester, New York, for example, male bank employees received $46.73 per week on average while women received just $34.58. Two years later, both men and women earned slightly more on average but the pay gap persisted, though it was smaller at some institutions than others. By 1952, male bank employees averaged $61.21 per week for 36.7 hours of work, versus $44.71 for women for 35.9 hours of work. The pay gap persists to this day partly due to the custom, already prevalent in postwar Rochester, of increasing wages across the board by percentages rather than fixed dollar amounts. Under such a sys-

---

661 Treasury Department Study Team, *Credit and Capital Formation*, 21; Sparks, *Capital Intentions*, 164.

tem, those at the bottom of the distribution can earn more over time but never gain on those above them.[662]

Determining the causes of the wage gap are especially difficult in the higher echelons of finance, where piece rate comparisons are impossible or undesirable. (Nobody at the Community Savings Bank of Rochester, New York, for example, thought it fair to pay bank tellers for each deposit or withdrawal because some branches were busier than others, a situation largely out of the control of the tellers.) For stockbrokers, commissions could be equal but the biggest, best clients were steered to the male brokers, leaving the females with smaller, less lucrative accounts.[663]

Moreover, gaps were sometimes not in the absolute number of dollars paid, but in effort. Over the years, many women in finance have claimed that they had to work twice or thrice harder than men holding the same job.[664] "People think Wall Street is terribly glamorous," one female investment banker explained, "and sometimes it is. But it's also … sitting at your desk sending out for pizza at 5 a.m. when you've been working all night."[665] And as we will see, female financiers suffered, and continue to suffer, much more gender-related grief at work than their male counterparts.[666]

The earliest employment for females in finance came from ownership of their own firms. For example, Sara Millem owned and operated a pawn shop in Baltimore in the early 1830s and she was far from alone as

---

662 Executive Committee Meeting, August 9, 1948; Executive Committee Meeting, August 7, 1950; Executive Committee Meeting, January 7, 1952, Agendas/Minutes: Exec. Committee Community; Industrial Management Council, Labor Turnover Report, July 1952, Documents: Employee/Public Relations, Community, Rush Rhees Library.

663 Glenn W. Miller, *The Problems of Labor*, (New York: Macmillan Company, 1951), 414–15; Recommendations, Exam. Com., East Side/Community, Barry (Arthur) Papers, Special Collections, Rush Rhees Library; Susan Antilla, *Tales from the Boom-Boom Room: The Landmark Legal Battles that Exposed Wall Street's Shocking Culture of Sexual Harassment*, (New York: HarperBusiness 2003), 66.

664 Caplan, *Petticoats*, 98, 156; Sue Herera, *Women of the Street* (New York: John Wiley & Sons, 1997), 130, 171.

665 As quoted in Anne B. Fisher, *Wall Street Women* (New York: Alfred A. Knopf, 1990), vii.

666 See, for example, Herera, *Women*.

female-owned pawnshops have been detected in antebellum Philadelphia, Jersey City, New York, and Chicago. Nevertheless, most pawnbrokers were male and pawn brokering, despite the large contingent of female customers, was not considered well suited to women because some borrowers were presumed to be desperate or deranged men. Loan sharks, by contrast, almost always hired women to make their loans and even sometimes to do collection work because females were less likely to be assaulted by irate customers.[667]

In 1870, sisters Tennessee Claflin and Victoria Woodhull, backed by their friend (friend with benefits in the case of Claflin), the magnate Cornelius Vanderbilt, established a brokerage at 44 Broad Street, not far from the New York Stock Exchange. The duo, dubbed the "Queens of Finance," thrived at first due to publicity (some of it even favorable), novelty, and their association with Vanderbilt. The *New York Times* predicted "a short, speedy winding up of the firm Woodhull Claflin & Co.," but it was overly pessimistic. Jay Gould began paying the ladies $1,000 a day to do some of his dirty work while novice female investors flocked to the Queens for advice, though not much of it turned out to be any good. Victoria's husband actually did most of the work while the sisters focused their attention on Victoria's presidential bid and the weekly newspaper, *Woodhull and Claflin's Weekly*, that supported it.

By May 1871, the sisters had lost Vanderbilt's friendship and patronage and Victoria concentrated more on her unlikely political career than on the business. When financial panic struck the Street in 1873, the already teetering brokerage fell, just as Victoria's presidential campaign and Tennessee's bid for Congress had the year before. The sisters found themselves in jail on election night facing obscenity charges for a detailed article about adultery that appeared in their paper. They were eventually cleared of the charges but their liberal views on sexuality hurt their popularity in the increasingly prudish, Victorian circles in which they had

667 Rockman, *Scraping By*, 186; Wendy A. Woloson, *In Hock: Pawning in America from Independence through the Great Depression* (Chicago: University of Chicago Press, 2009), 15, 57, 73–74, 163; Calder, *Financing*, 53.

previously garnered support. Victoria divorced, the paper folded, Vanderbilt passed away, and the sisters slipped off to England, where they lived,
one hopes at least sometimes happily, the rest of their natural lives.[668]

Before the dethroned Queens of Finance died in the 1920s, 22 Wall
Street brokerage firms employed at least one female partner and one of
those, Rich, Clark & Company, was headed by a woman, Ethel G. Rich.
None of those ladies worked on the NYSE trading floor, however, until
Helen Hanzelin became a telephone clerk there in April 1943. Within
weeks, scores of females, adorned in carefully chosen, conservative uni-
forms, worked as "quote girls" and "carrier pages" on the floor. Soon
after, women began working on the New York Curb Exchange and the
San Francisco Stock Exchange and probably other exchanges as well.
Most of them, however, lost their jobs after the war.[669]

Female participation in the labor force, including the financial sector,
increased during wars, starting with the Civil War when the U.S. Treasury began to employ them to cut and trim paper for use as Greenbacks,
the Union's fiat paper currency. World War I brought another boost. For
instance, Irma Dell Eggleston started selling Liberty Bonds thanks to a
vacancy at C. F. Childs & Co. created by the call for doughboys to fight in
the Great War in France and Belgium. Over the next decade, she traded
bonds worth $30 billion. In the 1930s, Marjorie Elizabeth Eggleston had
taken over the leadership role and women made more strides in bond
brokerage than any other field of finance, partly because men wanted
little to do with such seemingly staid, feminine products.[670]

In the first half of the nineteenth century, clerks in all sorts of businesses were almost invariably males because such jobs were essentially
apprenticeships for partnership. As businesses grew larger and more
complex, however, they needed many more clerks than could ascend
the ranks of management. About the same time, new machines, like

668 Caplan, *Petticoats*, 33–44.

669 Caplan, *Petticoats*, 68, 95–98, 103.

670 Caplan, *Petticoats*, 30–31, 97–98; Tracy Lucht, *Sylvia Porter: America's Original Personal Finance Columnist* (Syracuse: Syracuse University Press, 2013), 37–38.

typewriters and cash registers, began to appear, allowing clerkships to be deskilled. Business colleges caught on to the trend and began offering courses in basic office skills that were open to both men and women. Thus began the transition from male to female back office workers. Before automation and computerization, life insurers and banks hired scads of women, young and old (but few in between), to update account cards. After successive waves of automation, they continued to hire women to do simple, repetitive tasks like data input. Many sales jobs, especially those requiring extensive interaction with female customers, were also staffed by women. By the early 1870s, for example, female insurance agents peddled fire insurance to female businesswomen in San Francisco.[671]

In the late nineteenth century, however, most banks that established women's departments still used male tellers, who were presumably more "convincing" to female depositors. Such banks often had separate facilities for the ladies, even dressing rooms where they could remove or stash cash in their stockings. They also offered ladies fancy checks and crisp new currency. Starting in the 1910s and 1920s, some banks found it worthwhile to hire females to work in and even to manage the special departments and branches. The Columbia Trust Company of New York hired Virginia Furman to run its new women's department in 1919, for example, and soon after the Bank of America hired a woman of Chinese birth to run its branch in San Francisco's Chinatown. Others followed suit under pressure from Elizabeth Ellsworth Cook, who in 1921 founded the Women's Bond Club as a place where women could share advice and complain about banks that did not hire females to manage their women's departments.[672]

Between 1920 and 1960, women's participation in paid employment increased dramatically economy-wide. African-American women, who in 1944 had a labor force participation rate of 2 in 5, compared to 1 in 3 for Euroamerican women, led the way though their average pay

---

671 Wills, *Boosters*, 209–10; Sparks, *Capital Intentions*, 164.

672 Caplan, *Petticoats*, 68, 84–93.

lagged. The overall female labor force participation rate jumped from less than a quarter in 1920 to a third in 1960 when working married women outnumbered single female employees for the first time. By 1960, more women held Master's degrees than had held Bachelor's, Master's, and Doctorates in 1920. Most of those degrees, however, were not in higher paying "masculine" fields like engineering and business management.[673] And they certainly were not in finance. As recently as the late twentieth century, many college deans still believed that finance was "not a proper subject for girls."[674]

Factory work remained the major type of paid employment for women but farm and household work became less important as female office workers became increasingly common. One New York city bank that employed only 2 females at the outset of the Great War employed 1,000 before the onset of the Great Depression. In 1952, the number of female workers at eight Rochester, New York area banks was 1,339 compared to 753 men. The city's manufacturing sector at that time employed over 53,000 men compared to 26,000 women. In the early 1970s, women were "abundantly represented" in the lower echelons of banks in Hartford, Connecticut, constituting almost three in every five workers overall. Only 5 percent of managers, however, were women.[675]

By 1936, 72 women were partners in brokerages that held NYSE seats. But it was during World War II that female participation in brokerage soared, when Betty the Broker joined Rosie the Riveter at brokerages like Merrill Lynch as male employees left to fight Fascism. By war's end, the number of African-American women employed as real estate or insurance agents or brokers almost doubled, to 1,300. During the war, women

---

673 United States Department of Labor, Women's Bureau, *Negro Women War Workers*, Bulletin No. 205 (1945), iii; Talitha LeFlouria, *Chained in Silence: Black Women and Convict Labor in the New South* (Chapel Hill: University of North Carolina Press, 2015), 31, 64; Miller, *Problems of Labor*, 425; Treasury Department Study Team, *Credit and Capital Formation*, 6.

674 As quoted in Anne B. Fisher, *Wall Street Women* (New York: Alfred A. Knopf, 1990), 8 (hereafter Fisher, *Wall Street Women*).

675 Caplan, *Petticoats*, 90; Industrial Management Council, Labor Turnover Report, July 1952, Documents: Employee/Public Relations, Community, Rush Rhees Library; U.S. Commission on Civil Rights, *Mortgage Money*, 31–32.

also proved proficient at clerical and other back office work at companies that had not yet transitioned to female clerical workers.[676] Many women lost their jobs after the war but others remained in the labor force in more traditionally female roles, or, as a 1958 *New York Times* article put it, "as secretaries, stenos, bookkeepers, receptionists, ticker operators, file clerks, messengers and pages."[677] A government study concluded in 1960 that "some of these differences [in occupation] are undoubtedly due to differences in the nature of the work, its requirements and its suitability or attractiveness to women, but others persist largely because of conventional attitudes toward women and work."[678] Whatever its causes, "occupational segregation by sex" proved remarkably resilient. A 1978 Treasury study noted that "women still remain in traditional sectors and female jobs such as clerical-sales."[679]

After World War II, women continued to find employment in financial companies in the back office despite the persistence of stereotypes that questioned the ability of females to handle mathematics. In his autobiography, South Dakota banker Art Dahl tells several stories about how some of his "girls" made clerical mistakes that required his male banking prowess to fix. Paradoxically, computer programming was initially considered women's work, which allowed Janet Norman to get a good job at the American Stock Exchange (AMEX) helping it to transition from punch card to electronic data entry. In 1958, AMEX became the first major stock market to appoint a woman (Mary Roebling) as a governor (director).[680]

---

676 Lucht, *Sylvia Porter*, 37; United States Department of Labor, *Negro Women*, 17, 22; Perkins, *Wall Street to Main Street*, 171–72.

677 As quoted in Melissa S. Fisher, *Wall Street Women* (Durham: Duke University Press, 2012), 35 (hereafter Fisher, *Wall Street*).

678 Alice K. Leopold, *Highlights, 1920–1960* (U.S. Department of Labor, 1960).

679 Treasury Department Study Team, *Credit and Capital Formation*, 9.

680 Calder, *Financing*, 166; Dahl, *Banker Dahl*, 128–30, 145–46; Fisher, *Wall Street*, 36–37; Wilma Soss, Pocketbook News, 3 November 1958, Box 8, Wilma Soss Papers, American Heritage Center.

By 1960, female bank officers numbered 10,923, female bank directors numbered 1,583, and 164 banks had female presidents. That was far ahead of Canada, probably because the latter nation's banking system was controlled by a dozen or fewer megabanks that were male bastions into the 1990s. One's ability to play hockey was, no joke, a major factor in employment up there.[681]

Women also increasingly took up gendered publicity, writing, and sales roles. Brokerages like Merrill Lynch that tried to attract female investors, for example, hired female account representatives to work with them. The first black female stockbroker, Lilla St. John, quit her singing and television career in Milwaukee to join Oppenheimer & Company in 1953. Four years later, African-American broker Wilhelmina B. Drake began an annual series called "Women's Day on Wall Street" designed to entice mutual fund investments from black women. By 1958, about 45 women were partners in NYSE-member firms.[682]

Ferris & Company of Washington, D.C. also hired women and had the great fortune of hiring Julia Walsh (nee Montgomery nee Curry) as a broker in 1956. She became a partner in 1959 despite the death of her husband after the arrival of their fourth child. After receiving advanced training at Wharton and Harvard Business School's Advanced Management Program, she became an even better broker and investor of her own money. By the mid-1960s, her earned income was the highest of any woman in the Washington, D.C. area. It was a good thing, too, because her marriage to real estate executive Thomas Walsh brought with it eight additional children, seven from Thomas's previous marriage and one from their own union.

In 1965, Walsh and Phyllis S. Peterson became the first female full members of AMEX. Three years later, a *Time* magazine feature article

---

681 Pocketbook News, 25 December 1960, Box 8, Wilma Soss Papers, American Heritage Center; Duncan McDowall, *Quick to the Frontier: Canada's Royal Bank*, (Toronto: McClelland & Stewart, Inc., 1993), 75, 106–7, 392–93.

682 Fisher, *Wall Street*, 155–56; Gregory S. Bell, *In the Black: A History of African Americans on Wall Street*, (New York: John Wiley & Sons, 2002), 40, 50–51; Wilma Soss, Pocketbook News, 3 November 1958, Box 8, Wilma Soss Papers, American Heritage Center.

revealed that Walsh's annual income had swelled to $200,000, a small fortune at the time. Soon after, she served on a number of corporate boards, at first as a token but later as a valued team member. In 1972, she followed Mary Roebling, of whom more below, onto Amex's board of directors. In June 1977, she established the brokerage Julia Walsh & Sons. It quickly managed over $100 million in assets and soon joined the New York Stock Exchange. She sold the company for $6 million in 1983.[683]

Few women rose in the corporate hierarchy in the 1960s or 1970s, however, due to "conventional attitudes" that limited women to supervisory roles only over other women. In the 1960s, for example, Liberty Mutual Insurance Company was sued because it systematically funneled female college graduates into "claims representative" positions that paid less than the equivalent "claims adjuster" positions awarded to male college graduates. Moreover, "claims representatives" could only be promoted to roles supervising "claims representatives" while "claims adjusters" could be promoted to "claims supervisor" and from there all the way up the corporate ladder. Liberty Mutual reformed itself, at least on the surface; in the early 1990s, when the author went through the company's "claims adjuster" training in classes that included female college graduates. Other insurers, however, continued to create "glass ceilings" for women and of course pay them less. Even the federal government has engaged in such tracking: every Treasurer of the United States since 1949 has been female but the holder of the post does not set policy; only implements it. No woman has yet to serve as Secretary of the Treasury, a cabinet-level position.[684]

A 1965 study in the *Harvard Business Review* concerning senior executives concluded that "in the case of both Negroes and women, the barriers are so great that there is scarcely anything to study."[685] The exceptions

---

683 Caplan, *Petticoats*, 123–33.

684 Treasury Department Study Team, *Credit and Capital Formation*, 9–10; Barbara Bergmann, *The Economic Emergence of Women*, (New York: Basic Books, 1986), 107–8; Pocketbook News, 25 December 1960, Box 8, Wilma Soss Papers, American Heritage Center; Caplan, *Petticoats*, 184.

685 As quoted in Caplan, *Petticoats*, 137.

proved the rule. Mary Roebling became president of the Trenton Trust Company in 1937 a year after she had stepped into the directorship of her husband, who was also a major stockholder, when he died. Although the shares were almost worthless, Mary used those bequeathed to her and her infant son to oust the incompetent male president of Trenton Trust and become the first female president of a major urban bank. (The 74 other female bank presidents then in office oversaw much smaller institutions.) Under her management the bank, beaten down by the Depression, turned around and eventually thrived. Many considered her the "first lady of finance" by the 1950s.[686]

In fact, widows' succession, like the custom of the U.S. Congress to replace deceased Senators and House Representatives with their spouses until the expiration of their terms, was the route that most women bank directors and presidents took to the top in the early days. In 1883, for example, Louisa Stephens assumed the presidency of the First National Bank of Marion, Iowa after the death of the president, her husband. Jessie Gillespie Herndon took a vice presidency in Atlanta Life after her husband died. In 1949, Claire Hoffman assumed the seat of her father, bank founder Amadeo Giannini, on the board of Bank of America. In 1964, Mrs. H. C. Couch, Jr. became the first female director of the Union National Bank of Little Rock, also assuming the spot held by her husband from 1937 until his death. She served until 1967 when Donald P. Couch took her place. Two other men with the surname Couch became active on the board about the same time, suggesting that Mrs. Couch's ascension was about maintaining the family's presence on the board and nothing more. No other woman served as director of that bank until Mrs. Anne S. Holmann in 1975.[687]

---

686 Patricia R. Faulk, "Gender and Power in the Twentieth Century: Mary G. Roebling, Pioneer Woman Banker," (Ph.D. Diss., University of Pennsylvania, 1992), 29–36, 95, 136, 206; Caplan, *Petticoats*, 113–21.

687 Caplan, *Petticoats*, 59, 116; Shennette Garrett-Scott, "To Do a Work that Would Be Very Far Reaching: Minnie Geddings Cox, the Mississippi Life Insurance Company, and the Challenges of Black Women's Business Leadership in the Early Twentieth-Century United States," *Enterprise & Society* 17, no. 3 (2016), 488; "Autobiography of a Bank," Union National Bank Records, Mss. 02–07, Butler Center for Arkansas Studies.

By the Depression era, however, some had suggested that women could become financial leaders on their own merits. The first woman to serve as a trustee in a mutual savings bank in New York may have been Miss Anna Stone, who served the Chenango Valley Savings Bank in Binghamton in the 1930s. About the same time, Miss Genzlinger, a Yonkers attorney, "started a movement to interest savings banks in considering the election of women as trustees." Genzlinger argued that "women have shown outstanding ability in the world of finance and business, that they control a large part of the wealth of the country and comprise a majority of [mutual savings bank] depositors." The Savings Banks Association of the State of New York responded "that there is nothing in the law at the present time preventing the election of any qualified woman to serve as trustee and that ... there is no opposition on the part of our bank officials to women trustees as such."[688]

About that same time, women were finally beginning to appear as "officers" in the middle management of banks and insurers. Before World War II, only Mary Vail Andress of Chase National Bank had become a general (i.e., without gender-typed authority) officer of a major money center bank and received so much attention that she even refused an interview with famous financial reporter Sylvia Porter, whom she directed to previously published press clippings. Female officers, however, were fairly abundant at smaller institutions in the 1930s. Dorcas Campbell, for example, was a vice president of the East River Savings Bank by 1939. New York City alone was home to three other bank presidents, another veep, and about 250 other female officers of sufficient rank to join the Association of Bank Women.[689]

The number of female bank officers nationwide increased from about 4,500 in 1937 to over 5,600 in 1946. Madelyn H. Sullivan became Public Relations Director of the Community Savings Bank of Roches-

---

688 Paul W. Albright, Bulletin Letter #565, August 16, 1940, Correspondence, Savings Bank Association of New York, Rush Rhees Library.

689 Treasury Department Study Team, *Credit and Capital Formation*, 9–10; Caplan, *Petticoats*, 92; Lucht, *Sylvia Porter*, 34, 37–40.

ter, which also listed several other women as assistant secretaries (not secretaries or assistants to officers but junior officers essentially), in 1950. Sullivan had been on the rise since the Depression, when she served as advertising manager of the East Side Savings Bank, an institution that also made Viola Erickson and Leah Woodruff junior officers in 1939. "For a woman bank employee," Erickson wrote in "appreciation, … this is indeed a promotion." East Side Savings was not much ahead of the times when it came to gender equality, however, because when the president learned that Dorothea Philipps was sleeping with an unnamed married male colleague, he fired Dorothea even though she broke off the affair.[690]

By the late 1970s, when a Treasury report claimed that women "have invaded the corporate hierarchy," women were serving as bank loan officers and branch managers.[691] On the West Coast, 40 to 50 percent of loan officers were female but in other parts of the country they were still rarely encountered.[692] Moreover, the higher echelons of management continued to evade them. In 1983, none of the directors or officers of the bank holding company Florida's National Banks of Florida were women. Some of its subsidiaries, however, did have limited female leadership. On the board of directors of Florida National Bank, the bank holding company's operating flagship, sat Joanne H. Miller, a securities analyst. Its list of vice presidents included Betty D. Bocher, Joyce Indingaro, Cynthia P. Runnion, Elizabeth M. Slate, and Cynthia C. Zerbe. Female assistant vice presidents were even more numerous. The Jacksonville affiliate had on its board Alberta C. Drummond, the president of Drummond Press, but no officers above the assistant VP level. Several of its branches, however, were headed up by women like Grace Williamson and Joyce Beauchamp. Moreover, a majority of its banking officers were women. The Miami affiliate, by contrast, had no female directors but five female VPs and 14

690 Caplan, *Petticoats*, 102, 114; Regular Board Meeting, October 11, 1950, Agendas/Minutes: Board Meetings; Madelyn H. Sullivan to Arthur A. Barry, December 26, 1936, Viola Erickson to Arthur A. Barry (trustee), January 15, 1939, Dorothea Philipps to Arthur A. Barry (trustee), February 2, 1939, Business Correspondence East Side Bank, Rush Rhees Library.

691 Treasury Department Study Team, *Credit and Capital Formation*, 4.

692 Treasury Department Study Team, *Credit and Capital Formation*, 67.

female assistant VPs. The executive suite of Florida's National Banks of
Florida mirrored that of most companies at the time. As a 1985 Conference Board study showed, only one in ten college-educated women
held management jobs compared with one in four comparably educated
men.[693]

The deregulation of brokerage commissions in May 1975 ("May
Day") helped women to penetrate the trading floors of big Wall Street
firms — investment banks and brokerages — which had long relegated
women to research divisions, marketing, and other "women's ghetto"
departments. For example, Patricia Riley, one of the most senior women
in global finance by 1994, entered Wall Street in the early 1970s via the
research department, which was then considered a strictly supportive or
"back office" affair.[694]

In the pre-May Day world of fixed commissions, brokerages could
afford to shunt female applicants away by telling them that they were
"much too pretty to work here" or would be happier at Bloomingdale's.
In the newly competitive marketplace, however, it behooved brokerages
and investment banks to become more meritocratic and cast a wider talent net, even when their recruiters did not want to, because the game was
no longer rigged in favor of incumbents and the status quo. (Most infamously, Goldman Sachs recruiters in 1984 asked female MBA graduates
at Stanford if they would have abortions to remain on the "fast track" in
investment banking.) Early female financiers, some of whom helped each
other to endure the anomie engendered by Wall Street's hyper-masculine
culture by joining the Financial Women's Association of New York (est.
1956), had valuable insights to offer.[695]

---

693 Statement of Condition and Directory of Officers and Directors, Florida National Banks
of Florida, Inc., 1983, Florida National Bank Records, 1887–1989, MS 069, University of Florida
Smathers Libraries; Naisbitt and Aburdene, *Re-inventing the Corporation*, 206.

694 Melissa Fisher, "Wall Street Women's Herstories," in *Constructing Corporate America:
History, Politics, Culture*, ed. Kenneth Lipartito and David B. Sicilia (New York: Oxford University Press, 2004), 294–320; Fisher, *Wall Street Women*, 14; Fisher, *Wall Street*, 1, 40.

695 Fisher, *Wall Street Women*, 9, 11; Fisher, *Wall Street*, 3.

In 1980, for example, a young stockbroker named Amy Domini helped to invent a whole new way of investing called socially responsible investing (SRI). Instead of picking stocks based solely on the expected return, SRI funds consider the impact of their investments on individuals, ecosystems, and societies. Quakers had always avoided defense stocks, Methodists had eschewed investing in alcohol, gambling, and tobacco companies, and so forth, and in 1972 Dreyfus introduced a fund that avoided investment in companies with poor environmental and employee-relation records. In 1982, Calvert Investments launched a fund that would not invest in companies associated with apartheid. Building on such precedents, Domini wrote the book, literally, on *Ethical Investing* in 1984. In the book, which she followed up with *The Challenges of Wealth: Mastering the Personal and Financial Conflicts* in 1988, Domini also pushed for shareholder activism to shame corporations into giving up environmentally or socially damaging activities.

In 1989, Domini joined with Peter Kinder (her husband) and Steven Lydenberg to form KLD Research & Analytics, which monitored and evaluated corporate community, customer, environmental, and labor practices and policies. The following year, the company launched the Domini 400 Social Index and, in 1991, the Domini Social Equity Fund to track it. By 1996, the fund, which was outperforming the S&P 500, had swelled to $100 million. Tech-heavy, it really soared during the tech boom in the late 1990s, hitting $1.5 billion before the bubble burst in March 2000. It survived that bust but became an actively managed fund in 2006. It also survived the subprime debacle and stood at about $675 million at the end of 2011. The surest sign of the fund's success, however, was the number of competitors it spawned, with a total of about $3 trillion under management by 2010.[696]

In 1985, Patricia Jehle figured out how to securitize consumer automobile loans for Salomon Brothers. Soon, First Boston and GMAC started doing it as well. Within a year, $8 billion worth of CARS (Certificates for Automobile Receivables) had been traded. About the same time,

696 Caplan, *Petticoats*, 169–79.

Ann Kaplan at Goldman invented a new type of municipal bond that helped New York City build subsidized housing when federal aid disappeared during the Reagan years. Her insights lifted Goldman from sixth to second place in the munibond rankings within a year. Meanwhile, the quant work that Stanford Ph.D. Leslie Daniels did for Chase Manhattan, before she became the first woman on its trading floor, was so important that she was "really not supposed to say what" it was, and didn't![697]

Other women became respected economic prognosticators. Philadelphia native, Drexel alum, and NYU Ph.D. Elaine Garzarelli, for example, built a name for herself accurately predicting the economy's and the market's ups and downs in the 1980s, including the 1987 stock market crash, which saw the Dow Jones Industrial Average plummet 22.6 percent in a single day, a week after Garzarelli had warned of a 1929 magnitude collapse on *Moneyline*. With a five percent boost that day alone, her investment fund by the start of 1988 had grown to over $770 million. Garzarelli also did something that few women on Wall Street had dared to do; she dressed and behaved like a woman, a winking, pearl nibbling, flirty, fashionably attired "wax doll" looking Italian-American princess of a woman. Despite being named the top quantitative analyst by *Institutional Investor* for eleven consecutive years, her fund shrank and she was ousted from Lehman. So in 1995 she formed the money management and research firm Garzarelli Capital.[698]

Other women, though, stuck it out and eventually made partner at the big bulge bracket firms. Marilyn LaMarche, for example, became a partner in Lazard Freres in the late 1980s. By then, Morgan Stanley boasted six female managing directors and Salomon Brothers had two female managing directors and six female directors. In 1998, Abby Cohen, a razor-sharp analyst, became a partner at Goldman, a leading investment bank with 246 partners, 17 of whom were female, up from just one female (Jeanette Loeb) out of 106 partners a decade earlier. Goldman went public the following year. The year after that, the bull market that

---

697 Fisher, *Wall Street Women*, 32, 48–51.

698 Fisher, *Wall Street Women*, 38–41; Caplan, *Petticoats*, 151–57.

Cohen had helped to create met its ignominious end. Cohen's career continued as head of Goldman's Global Markets Institute, though apparently her analysis was not found useful during the subprime mortgage debacle or subsequent financial crisis. She retired in 2017.[699]

But even now, many female financial executives feel openly discriminated against on Wall Street, the culture of which has long been permeated by gender myths and outright misogyny. In a sex discrimination suit filed against Goldman in 1987, for example, it was demonstrated that Goldman's female employees were the butt of jokes too sophomoric to bear repetition. Unfortunately, Goldman was, in the words of a female former employee, "a typical investment bank" when it came to gender issues, especially on the raucous trading floors. Sometimes progress was really regress, as in the case of one investment banker who liked to hire women, but only to make them part of his "harem."[700]

"Wall Street has been discriminating against women for decades," former investment banker Frank Partnoy noted in his 1997 exposé of Wall Street, "and getting away with it." "The work environment may be getting less hostile, slowly, but just a few examples of allegations which became public this past year will make you cringe," Partnoy opined. "At Smith Barney, women were called lapdogs, bitches, and whores. Male brokers groped women, demanded sex, and gave women genital-shaped food. At Merrill Lynch, women were humiliated by strippers at office parties. ... At Lew Lieberbaum, there were strippers, cat calls, and demands for oral sex. ... When one woman complained, a manager whipped out his penis and asked the woman to suck it."[701]

Partnoy wrote partly from personal experience and partly from the publicity surrounding some high-profile lawsuits directed at Wall Street's largest and most prestigious firms in the mid-1990s. At Smith Barney

---

699 Fisher, *Wall Street Women*, 7–8; Caplan, *Petticoats*, 159–68, Paul Vigna, "'The Prophet of Wall Street' to Retire," *Wall Street Journal*, 13 February 2017.

700 Fisher, *Wall Street Women*, 12–13, 71.

701 Frank Partnoy, *F.I.A.S.C.O.: The Inside Story of a Wall Street Trader*, (New York: Penguin Books, 1997), 278–79. For additional details, see Antilla, *Tales*, 92–94.

(and predecessors like Shearson Lehman), men regularly referred to their female colleagues with the c-word as well as the b, t, and w words and used the f-word as a noun, adjective, verb, and adverb. They flashed their genitals, showed lewd pictures around the office, and put their hands on female employees. Those were not isolated incidents but rather an integral part of the corporate culture. According to one study, one third of the women at Smith Barney had been sexually coerced on the job. The same percentage had been called a b-word, c-word, or d-word by a colleague and two in five had been forced to view pornographic images in the office. Almost one in ten had had to physically or verbally fight off unwanted sexual advances at work. More than nine in ten believed that their statements and opinions were systematically ignored and their work purposefully demeaned. Women who complained were harassed and, eventually, let go on the grounds that they could not get along well with men.[702]

One particularly notorious Smith Barney branch in Garden City, Long Island was run by Nick Cuneo, a quintessential "good old boy" who believed that a woman's place was in her home or in his bed. He was, of course, beloved by the many men he helped to enrich over the years but the "slits and tits," as he called the women under his charge, were put off, to say the least, as were the male employees Cuneo called "faggots" or wimps. It was Cuneo's idea to build a party room, christened the Boom-Boom Room, in the basement of the branch's new digs in 1982.[703]

It was also Cuneo's idea to hire and retain brokers with less-than-perfect regulatory records because they were the ones who generated trading activity, and hence large commissions that far outweighed the fines they incurred and the settlements the company paid to avoid lawsuits filed in response to their sundry securities shenanigans. The outsized profits insulated Cuneo from pressure from headquarters when female employees began complaining about their boss, like his propensity to flash a handgun, and about the activities taking place in the Boom-Boom Room. "Just

---

702 Antilla, *Tales*, 1–2, 265.

703 Antilla, *Tales*, 8–12.

try to get along with Nick," the company's head of human resources, Jodie-Beth Galos, advised.[704]

Later, during an investigation of Cuneo directed from the company's headquarters, chief counsel advised disgruntled female employees that they sounded like hysterical women and that they should just quit. Instead, the women finally sued. Those still with the company were fired or forced to quit but the momentum shifted once the media widely publicized their accusations, which helped women being harassed at other brokerages and other Smith Barney offices nationwide to speak up and join the fray. By October 1996, 23 women in 10 states had joined their class action suit (which was needed to circumvent arbitration, which was mandatory for workers in the securities industry at that time) and other women instituted suit against Merrill Lynch, then the nation's largest brokerage. The negative media attention and settlement costs induced those companies, and other players in the securities industry, to implement sexual harassment training and reform outdated policies and procedures that prevented qualified women from rising through the ranks.[705]

Industry-wide reforms were necessary because, unfortunately, Smith Barney had not been an outlier. At broker-dealer Rodman & Renshaw, one executive VP regularly groped female employees, calling them objects whose job was to satisfy him sexually. When they thwarted his physical advances, he harassed them verbally by saying, publicly, that he liked "the pussy that you are wearing." Other male employees regularly propositioned the company's *head of human resources*, Susan Jaskowski. Rodman ended up being one of the first firms to settle sexual discrimination lawsuits.[706]

The very few African-American women on Wall Street had an even worse time of it. Cuneo called an African-American sales assistant "the watermelon kid." During her tenure at Smith Barney in New York, Marianne Spraggins was called, in addition to the usual misogynist sobriquets,

704 Antilla, *Tales*, 12–16, 68.

705 Antilla, *Tales*, 122, 161–70, 174, 186–93, 226–27.

706 Antilla, *Tales*, 88–89.

an n-word. One company executive even publicly speculated about the size of her penis. With help from Jesse Jackson, Spraggins received a $1.35 million settlement.[707]

Olde Discount Company of Detroit, Michigan was explicit in its rationale for hiring "studly males" and avoiding "broads": young, good-looking males had more incentive to earn big commissions because "they want to drive fancy sports cars so they can pick up the girls." Women were not as ambitious and should stay at home with their children. Single women should be avoided, too, as they were too much of a distraction for the studly males. To rid themselves of unwanted applicants, Olde Discount interviewers would ask exceptionally difficult questions or quote salaries below the actual pay grade for the position. At the same time, company bosses encouraged the women they had already hired, and in more liberal times even promoted, by taking their clients, cutting perks, demoting them, and publicly humiliating them at meetings. Not coincidentally, those policy changes occurred as Olde transformed itself from an honest discount brokerage into a fraud-riddled affair modeled after Smith Barney. It later settled the discrimination complaints and sold itself to H&R Block.[708]

In 2004, the Equal Employment Opportunity Commission (EEOC) socked Morgan Stanley with a $54 million fine for sexually discriminating against its female employees. All told, Smith Barney, Merrill, and Morgan each paid out over $100 million for their employee's misogynist behaviors. Those were paltry sums for the giant investment banks but in the eyes of many observers proved their guilt. Wall Street was "forever changed" by such verdicts but just how much remains unclear and of course contested, though clearly the worst abuses are no longer flaunted publicly. According to sociologist Louise Marie Roth, by 2006 "you would

707 Antilla, *Tales*, 95, 115.

708 Antilla, *Tales*, 99–104.

be hard-pressed to find a 'boom-boom room' associated with any of the major or minor firms" in the financial sector.[709]

Sometimes, it was difficult to tell where sexism ended and regular old rivalry began. Emma Hemmes, the first woman to serve as cashier (COO) of a Wall Street bank (1936), believed that women faced little discrimination; they just misinterpreted the financial system's strict pecking order. For example, one CEO of a major bank, a male from an "old" family who went to all the "right" schools, felt that he could not speak at the meetings of one of the corporate boards on which he sat because he was seated at the bottom of the table, signaling his low status in this group of financial alpha males, and, with just three years on the board, he was still a "new guy." Even leading female financiers were known to turn away female applicants who were too "ladylike" or shy because those traits suggested that they would be insufficiently assertive, inquisitive, or acquisitive to thrive on the Street.[710]

Important early female stockbroker Muriel Siebert admitted that she "never knew when the acrimony and ill will was gender-based." Women put up with abuse on Wall Street, which Siebert called "absolutely the last bastion of male supremacy," because they earned more there than they could elsewhere.[711] A "golden muzzle" was better than an iron one, Siebert believed, dismissing the notion that women should just avoid investment banking altogether.[712]

And not all of the discrimination was Wall Street's fault *per se*. Until the late 1980s, the Links Club, the Racquet Club, the New York Athletic Club, and other elite meeting places routinely denied entry to female financiers, even partners. In 1942, for example, the University Club denied entry to the General Mills stockholder meeting to female stockholders as well as female financial reporter Sylvia Porter. The New York Finan-

---

709 Louise Marie Roth, *Selling Women Short: Gender Inequality on Wall Street* (Princeton: Princeton University Press, 2006), 1; Caplan, *Petticoats*, 182–83; Antilla, *Tales*, 229, 293–302.

710 Lucht, *Sylvia Porter*, 34; Fisher, *Wall Street*, 79; Fisher, *Wall Street Women*, 72.

711 As quoted in Fisher, *Wall Street Women*, 8.

712 Caplan, *Petticoats*, 141–43; Fisher, *Wall Street Women*, 13, 87–88.

cial Writers Association would not admit Porter or other women into membership until 1972.[713]

Conditions for most rank-and-file women in the wider financial services sector, by contrast, improved markedly in the 1980s, by which time working women were so numerous that they were able to change corporate cultures to make them more amenable to parents. Daycare, for example, became a "work issue" rather than "a woman's problem." In January 1983, Chemical Bank, then the nation's sixth largest commercial bank, introduced a flexible benefit program that included daycare. Women were also able to obtain flex time, work-from-home assignments, and so forth. Insurers and commercial banks led the way with female-friendly work policies but even in those sectors the gender pay gap remained a wide one.[714]

Female participation in the sector, however, had certainly increased. By 2010, three out of every five people employed in the financial sector were women, and that figure was lower than its pre-financial crisis peak. Hiring women made much sense because they were, on average, cheaper to hire than men despite being more educated. (Females received 40 percent of the bachelor's degrees granted in the United States in 1970 but 60 percent by 2010.)[715]

Women, "however, remained underrepresented in corporate leadership,"[716] a fact that Abby Cohen attributed to the small pool of women who "express interest in investment banking"[717] and others chalked up to an exodus of experienced women from Wall Street in the late 1990s and the early 2000s. The latter had grown tired of the harassment and perturbed at the newer, transactional (as opposed to relational), gambling casino-like atmosphere prevalent at many firms. Whatever

713 Fisher, *Wall Street Women*, 9–10; Lucht, *Sylvia Porter*, 35–36.

714 Naisbitt and Aburdene, *Re-inventing the Corporation*, 203–5, 214, 218.

715 Fisher, *Wall Street*, 163–64; Joint Economic Committee, *Invest in Women*, 5.

716 Joint Economic Committee, *Invest in Women, Invest in America: A Comprehensive Review of Women in the U.S. Economy* (Washington, DC: U.S. Government Printing Office, 2011), 8.

717 As quoted in Caplan, *Petticoats*, 167.

the reasons, in 2011 women represented 46.4 percent of all employees at Fortune 500 companies but held just 15.7 of board seats and 14.4 percent of executive positions. They were only 7.6 percent of the top earning executive officers and 2.4 percent of CEOs. Those numbers had improved somewhat by 2016, but the *Wall Street Journal* reported that year that 76 significant U.S. companies had not had a single female on their boards over the previous decade.[718]

In the financial sector, even though women composed the majority of the workforce, women held only about 16.5 percent of board seats in the years leading up to and including the financial crisis. About a third of all managers were women but most remained in lower-paid, less prestigious "staff" jobs rather than the "line" jobs that produced most top leaders. That was far from parity, but also far better than in 1988, when only about 1 percent of Wall Street's highest ranking jobs were held by women.[719]

Apparently, as with financial discrimination, gender discrimination in finance has become more subtle and hence harder to detect in individual cases. Overall, though, the effects are crystal clear. To this day, women remain underrepresented in corporate suites. A widely reported 2016 study by McKinsey showed that while 46 percent of entry level workers (across the economy) are women, only 37 percent of managers are female. At the VP level that percentage drops to 29 percent and hits 19 percent at the top levels. To combat stats like those, in 2015 investment bank KKR instituted human resources policy changes designed to make it easier for women to juggle career and family in a business where 70-hour work weeks are commonplace.[720]

---

718 Fisher, *Wall Street*, 136–54, 165–74; Allen N. Berger and Gregory F. Udell, "The Future of Relationship Lending," in *The Future of Banking*, ed. Benton Gup (Westport, Conn.: Quorum Books, 2003), 203–228; Joann S. Lublin, "Dozens of Boards Excluded Women for Years," *Wall Street Journal*, 28 December 2016.

719 Joint Economic Committee, *Invest in Women*, 11; Melissa S. Fisher, *Wall Street Women* (Durham: Duke University Press, 2012), 75; Fisher, *Wall Street Women*, 76; Fisher, *Wall Street*, 71.

720 Roth, *Selling Women Short*, 7; Joint Economic Committee, *Invest in Women*, 104–5; Nathan Bomey, "Promotions Are Mostly a Guy Thing," *USA Today*, 28 September 2016;

KKR might be on to something as some studies have shown that companies with more women at the top achieve higher profits, other factors constant, and the best way to attract more women executives is to employ more women throughout the management chain. Indeed, the few women who have already made it to the C-suite in the hyper-competitive financial system include Deanna M. Mulligan of Guardian Life, a company that since the 1970s, at the urging of its longtime actuary Armand DePalo, has tried to induce qualified women to take up senior management positions as they became available.[721]

Other top-level female financiers include Catherine Kinney, who served as president of the NYSE from 2002 until 2008. Beth Mooney became CEO and Chairman of KeyCorp, a major bank holding company, in 2012, about the same time that JPMorgan Chase named Marianne Lakes its CFO, the same position that Ruth Porat took up at Morgan Stanley in 2010. Also in 2012, Fidelity Investments named Abigail Johnson president, but then again she was the CEO's daughter. Whether female bosses alone can make a difference in how major financial institutions treat female customers, however, is an open question. Some have assumed that merely placing women (or other "minorities") into positions of power would be sufficient to reduce discrimination but that may not be the case.[722]

While women on average earn more in the financial sector than anywhere else in the economy, equal pay for equal work never was Wall Street's mantra. Bonuses, everybody's bonuses, were kept as quiet as possible, lest clients figure out they were being hornswoggled. Even within departments, salaries and bonuses varied wildly from person to person and perhaps were best seen as signals about how bosses viewed

Rachel Silverman, "High Finance and Family-Friendly? KKR Is Trying," *Wall Street Journal*, 27 September 2016.

721 Joann S. Lublin, "The More Women in Power, The More Women in Power," *Wall Street Journal*, 27 September 2016; Robert E. Wright interview of Armand DePalo, January 27, 2003, GLICA archives.

722 Caplan, *Petticoats*, 182, 184–85; U.S. Commission on Civil Rights, *Mortgage Money*, 32.

particular individuals.[723] "It's highly subjective," Sarah Gopher-Stevens noted. "Either someone higher up likes you and decides to take good care of you, or not."[724] According to sociologist Louise Marie Roth, Wall Street is not, and never was, a meritocracy where pay equaled performance. She has shown "that women who were equal to their male counterparts as a group made less money."[725] That may surprise people who think of Wall Street as the hotbed of capitalist competition but in fact most competition in investment banking occurs at only a few margins. Because male and female talents are equally distributed along a bell curve (*if* women are more risk averse than men, a claim sometimes even made by women but one that I strongly doubt, they would of course deserve less remuneration), and the number of key jobs is small enough that either gender could fill all of them, gender discrimination does not necessarily affect profits.[726] What women in search of pay parity need to do is to establish their own brokerages and investment banks, and some of them, as we will see in the final chapter, already have.

723 Fisher, Wall Street Women, 81–83; Antilla, Tales, 42; Roth, Selling Women Short, 181–84.

724 As quoted in Fisher, Wall Street Women, 87.

725 Roth, Selling Women Short, 179, 181.

726 Bharat N. Anand and Alexander Galetovic, "Relationships, Competition and the Structure of Investment Banking Markets," Journal of Industrial Economics 54, no. 2 (2006): 151–99; Fisher, Wall Street, 2–3.

CHAPTER SEVEN

Avoiding Past Mistakes

Clearly, African-Americans, American Indians, trashy poor whites, and women have suffered from discrimination at the hands of various components of the financial system. Sometimes, the discrimination was outright exclusionary: members of discriminated-against group X need not apply. Other times, the discrimination occurred at the margins and was difficult to detect: X can apply and will be serviced *unless* s/he will crowd out a ~X applicant. Still more subtly, discrimination can be probabilistic: X can apply but the model used to evaluate his/her application is, unintentionally or not, slanted against his/her success. Local, state, and federal governments largely succeeded in stamping out exclusion but, for the most part, they failed to defeat the subtler forms of discrimination by direct interdiction. Instead, they offered lenders incentives to lower credit standards for minorities, with predictably disastrous results. Instead of punishing financial firms for engaging in behaviors that are difficult to detect or parse from legitimate business activities, or encouraging them to run large risks, governments should encourage competition, especially via the formation of financial institutions dedicated to ending discriminatory practices. That, as we will learn in the final chapter, is the traditional American way of handling discrimination.[727]

---

727 John Taylor, Josh Silver, and David Berenbaum, "The Targets of Predatory and Discriminatory Lending: Who Are They and Where Do They Live?" in *Why the Poor Pay More: How to Stop Predatory Lending*, ed. Gregory D. Squires (Westport, Conn.: Praeger, 2004), 25–37.

Encouraging the entry of non-discriminators leads to the creation of numerous, relatively small financial institutions, some of which will go bankrupt. Failure, however, should not dissuade policymakers from this path because the bankruptcy of small financial institutions does not represent a systemic threat to the economy. Moreover, thanks to technological improvements, minimum efficient scale in most financial services is quite small. If a bank that specializes in serving members of group X fails, it is probably because X is not really being exploited by the incumbent providers. This market-based solution to discrimination (and predation) is imperfect, but far better than the alternatives for both X and the overall economy. Most importantly, the market can respond much more quickly than the government can to new groups that feel discriminated against. Members of the LGBTQ community, for example, have been discriminated against in many areas of life for a long time. Instead of waiting until politicians and voters eventually come to their aid, they ought to be able to do what numerous other Xs have done in the past, form their own financial service providers. The same goes for any "minority" group that may arise in the future, including mine — balding, overweight, middle-aged males – and untold others. If the discrimination is real, the new entrants should thrive. If the purported discrimination is economically justified, as it apparently is in the case of base-jumping wingsuit pilots who cannot buy life insurance, then the startups will fail and humanity will be the wiser for it.[728]

Command and Control: Been There, Done That

Because the remaining problem is more one of de facto rather than de jure discrimination, the solution is more complicated than merely passing more laws. — Treasury Department Study Team, Credit

---

728 John Clarke, "Wingsuit Test Pilot Defies Physics, Has Trouble Getting Life Insurance," *Wall Street Journal*, 6 December 2016.

and Capital Formation: A Report to the President's Interagency Task Force on Women Business Owners (April 1978), 53.

Unfortunately, governments cannot stop bad behaviors merely by outlawing them. Sometimes, the bad behavior is just too lucrative. Dealing illicit drugs is a good example. Sometimes, as in crimes of passion, people behave irrationally and hence do not respond to (dis)incentives no matter how well-designed. Sometimes, the bad behaviors are so complicated or diverse that attempts to stop them are easily sidestepped. Most attempts to regulate financial institutions and markets, for example, can be, and are, worked around in myriad ways. Many financial regulations, therefore, end up doing more harm than good and can actually hurt those they purport to help.[729]

The hoariest and most infamous financial regulation is the usury law, a maximum rate of interest that lenders can lawfully charge borrowers. Ostensibly, such laws or interest caps should help borrowers by outlawing a bad behavior, the charging of "high" rates of interest. In reality, usury laws encourage discrimination by encouraging lenders to engage in credit rationing, i.e., to lend only to the best borrowers. Usury laws, Hillel Black noted, therefore "fostered organized loan sharkery" just as Prohibition had given "rise to organized crime." Unsurprisingly, the biggest supporters of usury laws were loan sharks, individuals and companies that made high-interest rate loans.[730]

What authorities considered "too high" varied over time and place. The British colonies of mainland North America adopted usury statutes

---

729 Brimmer, "Statutory Interest Rate Ceilings," 1–3.

730 J. B. C. Murray, *The History of Usury from the Earliest Period to the Present Time … And an Examination into the Policy of Laws on Usury and Their Effect Upon Commerce* (Philadelphia: J. B. Lippincott & Co., 1866), 11–62; James M. Ackerman, "Interest Rates and the Law: A History of Usury," *Arizona State Law Journal* (1981): 61–79; Thomas W. Miller, Jr., and Harold A. Black, "Examining Arguments Made By Interest Rate Cap Advocates," in *Reframing Financial Regulation: Enhancing Stability and Protecting Consumers*, ed. Hester Peirce and Benjamin Klutsey (Arlington, Va.: Mercatus Center, George Mason University, 2016), 343–45, 351; Lendol Calder, *Financing the American Dream: A Cultural History of Consumer Credit*, (Princeton: Princeton University Press, 1999), 112–23; Hillel Black, *Buy Now, Pay Later* (New York: William Morrow and Company, 1961), 154.

similar in form to that of the Mother Country but, at 6 to 8 percent per year, one to three percentage points higher. They were widely evaded anyway. After the Civil War, most Northern states capped interest at six percent, while Southern and Western states often allowed interest of 7, 8, and even 10 percent per annum. The penalty for usury also varied widely, from forfeit of usury only (any interest taken above the cap), to forfeiture of three times the usury and costs, to forfeiture of all interest and principal. By 1900, 11 states had repealed their usury laws and many others decreased penalties until by 1921 only six states still inflicted the loss of principal. Disgust with salary lenders and loan sharks, however, led to a reaction whereby many states reimposed usury caps, though often ones allowing higher interest rates on shorter, smaller loans that recognized the high fixed cost inherent in lending. By the early 1960s, only four states had no usury laws. Starting in the 1980s, some states, including most infamously South Dakota, and the federal government repealed usury caps in response to the high inflation/high nominal market interest rates then prevalent.[731]

Whenever deregulation of interest rates occurred, empirical evidence that usury caps did not help borrowers, especially of the poorer sort, emerged.[732] In 1981, Robert Schafer and Helen Ladd stated the majority consensus with crystal clarity:

Usury ceilings are an inappropriate and counterproductive means of protecting unsophisticated mortgage seekers ... it leads to credit rationing, that is, the restriction of ... credit, whenever the usury ceiling falls below the market yield. The lower-income and less-sophisticated borrowers bear the burden of this law through reduced opportunities for mortgage credit.[733]

---

731 Ackerman, "Interest Rates and the Law," 85–94; Murray, *The History of Usury*, ix.; Elisabeth Anderson, "Experts, Ideas, and Policy Change: The Russell Sage Foundation and Small Loan Reform, 1909–1941," *Theory and Society* 37, no. 3 (2008): 292; Black, *Buy Now*, 152; Brimmer, "Statutory Interest Rate Ceilings," 6; Robert E. Wright, *Little Business on the Prairie: Entrepreneurship, Prosperity, and Challenge in South Dakota*, (Sioux Falls: Center for Western Studies, 2015), 98–104.

732 Black, *Buy Now*, 154.

733 Robert Schafer and Helen F. Ladd, *Discrimination in Mortgage Lending*, (Cambridge: MIT Press, 1981), 302. See also William Trufant Foster, *Loan Sharks and Their Victims*, (New

Of course most lenders and borrowers simply worked around usury laws, most of which contained numerous loopholes. Interest charges could be easily disguised as insurance premiums, as discounts for cash payment for goods, as foreign exchange differentials, or as sundry fees. Or lenders and borrowers agreed that the latter would overpay the former for some asset of nominal value. Jurisdictional arbitrage was also possible, especially in the United States. Pawnbrokers and commercial paper were often explicitly exempt, as were "salary buyers," which today go by the name payday lenders.[734] Some legal subterfuges could be overturned unilaterally by the borrower but that was, in the words of one nineteenth century student of usury laws, simply "another risk encountered by the creditor, for which the borrower must pay."[735] In the end, then, borrowers ended up paying more than they would have in the absence of the usury stricture, i.e., the market rate plus the cost of exploiting the loophole plus the risk of legal sanction.[736]

In a few cases, usury laws were binding, or in other words they could not be easily or cheaply dodged. In those instances, lenders engaged in "nonprice rationing." In other words, they lent to the "best" borrowers, i.e., those most likely to repay and those with the personal traits they found most attractive. "The banks," one rejected female loan applicant noted, "serve their favorites first ... the men who are able to make large cash deposits."[737] The borrowers who were turned away were spared paying "high" rates of interest but denied the benefits of borrowing, which presumably outweighed any interest charge they would willingly consent to. So in cases where usury laws were binding, and below the prevailing market rate, all but the best borrowers lost access to credit.

York: Public Affairs Committee, 1940), 6–9.

734 Ackerman, "Interest Rates and the Law," 96–99; Murray, *The History of Usury*, 107–21, 130–31; Calder, *Financing*, 49–55.

735 Murray, *The History of Usury*, 134–36.

736 Ackerman, "Interest Rates and the Law," 86.

737 As quoted in Susan Branson, "Women and the Family Economy in the Early Republic: The Case of Elizabeth Meredith," *Journal of the Early Republic* 16 (Spring 1996): 60.

After World War II, for example, Arkansas passed a very strict usury cap and its courts plugged most of the traditional loopholes. The binding cap helped to keep Arkansas impoverished relative to its neighbors. Despite being part of the Sun Belt, Arkansas remained economically depressed, suffering from a dearth of venture and other forms of risk capital. At the same time in nearby Alabama, another economic backwater, usury laws effectively prevented banks and other large-scale institutional creditors from lending to the poor, who consequently found themselves preyed upon by a large school of loan sharks. Delinquents were harassed at all hours of the night and even "beaten, shot, crippled for life," because Alabama legislators would not allow markets to function unimpeded by price regulations.[738]

One takeaway from all this is that high-interest lending is not necessarily, or even usually, predatory lending. Triple and even quadruple digit annual interest rates are necessary to induce lenders to lend small sums for short periods to risky borrowers. Prospera Credit Union teamed up with Good Will Industries to offer the cheapest possible unsubsidized payday loans and even they had to charge $9.90 for the use of $100 for two weeks, or about half the going rate at for-profit payday lenders. "Its experiment," payday lending expert Robert Mayer noted, "offers clear proof that two-week or one-month loans could never be viable if the usury limit were reduced to 36%."[739]

Most "command and control"-type regulations lead to similarly perverse outcomes. For example, attempts by six states to force banks to offer low-cost accounts to poor people, called "lifeline" banking, have also been minimally effective as measured by the change in the percentage of unbanked households.[740] It may seem strange that any adult head

---

738 Ackerman, "Interest Rates and the Law," 103–5; Black, *Buy Now*, 154–56.

739 Robert Mayer, *Quick Cash: The Story of the Loan Shark*, (DeKalb: Northern Illinois University Press, 2010), 225.

740 John P. Caskey, *Fringe Banking: Check-Cashing Outlets, Pawnshops, and the Poor*, (New York: Russell Sage Foundation, 1994), 129–33; Ebonya Washington, "The Impact of Banking and Fringe Banking Regulation on the Number of Unbanked Americans," *Journal of Human Resources* 41, 1 (Winter 2006): 107–8.

of household would forgo a simple checking account but some people do not want one for a variety of reasons ranging from privacy concerns to inconvenience to cost. "Bounce protection programs are a closer approximation to the short-term check loan," payday lender expert Robert Mayer noted, "but this product is usually more costly than payday credit."[741] And since the end of Regulation Q, which capped the interest rates that banks could pay to depositors, and other regulatory changes, banks have not been eager to attract or retain small depositors. As checking account fees increased (essentially from zero or even negative due to the doling out of free toasters and so forth), consumers sensitive to price, privacy, and so forth opted for check cashing offices rather than traditional bank checking accounts. Lifeline legislation induced bankers to exit (reduce supply) by closing branches in low income areas, leaving little, if any, net benefit for the poor.[742]

Similarly, bank solvency supervision is notoriously difficult for regulators to do well because bankers quickly became adroit at "window dressing," or giving the appearance of some required balance statement condition. During the Depression, for example, the East Side Savings Bank of Rochester, New York, regularly "sold Government bonds under a repurchase agreement to increase our cash position for a temporary period."[743]

The problem is not that policymakers are bumbling idiots, that regulators are lazy, and so forth. The problem is that government bureaucrats simply do not have sufficient information and incentive to achieve desired outcomes. Given that fact, governments should not attempt to control prices or quantities. When they do, disasters, like that of 2008, result.

Many factors contributed to the financial crisis of 2008 but at its root were governmental attempts to create an "ownership society" where

---

741 Mayer, *Quick Cash*, 226.

742 Washington, "The Impact of Banking," 111–13, 132.

743 J. H. Zweeres (president) to Arthur A. Barry (trustee), June 27, 1936, Business Correspondence East Side Bank, Rush Rhees Library.

everyone "owned" their own home. The problem was that President Bush and other policymakers confused real ownership (no "encumbrances" as the colonists used to say, i.e., free and clear of mortgage debt, liens, etc.) with "renting from the bank," the expression used to describe nominal ownership with little or no equity actually invested in the home. Historically, Americans well knew the difference. In 1937, for example, East Side Savings Bank issued a short pamphlet called "No More Mortgage Interest: The Goal of Every Home-Owner!" During World War II, however, most Americans began paying income taxes for the first time and of course continue to do so to this day. The mortgage interest deduction, a fixture of the income tax code from its earliest days, changed their incentive from that expressed in the quaint pre-war pamphlet to 'More Mortgage Interest Please.' So many Americans began "renting from the bank" rather than paying off their mortgages and owning their homes outright.[744]

Another major cause of the financial crisis in 2008 was the GSEs, Fannie and Freddie. Those institutions were literally financial chimeras, privately-owned but publicly-backed behemoths with huge incentives to assume massive risks. If all went well, the GSEs, especially their managers, would get filthy rich. If everything fell apart, as it did, they would get just plain rich. Academics like Nouriel Roubini clearly warned everybody about those ticking time bombs but the government sat idly by, which suggests that turning over consumer finance (home mortgages, consumer lending, individual insurance) to the government is not an optimal reform strategy.

744 Jo Becker, Sheryl Gay Stolberg, and Stephen Labaton, *New York Times*, 21 December 2008; John Leland, "Facing Default, Some Walk Out on New Homes," *New York Times*, 29 February 2008; Mechele Dickerson, *Homeownership and America's Financial Underclass: Flawed Premises, Broken Promises, New Prescriptions*, (New York: Cambridge University Press, 2014), 24; Printed Ephemera, East Side and Community Savings, Rush Rhees Library.

Some Problems with Government Banking and State Insurance

From corporate banking, we have suffered more in the United States than from all other causes of evil put together, and yet there is one evil that is worse than even corporate paper money banking. It is government banking ... the evil without any checks. — William Gouge, The Fiscal History of Texas (Philadelphia: Lippincott, Grambo, and Co., 1852), 91.

I f ending financial exclusion, discrimination, and predation is so important to the economy and to the welfare of individual Americans, why
not simply create government-owned and controlled financial institutions
to bank the unbanked and insure the uninsured? The idea is not as crazy
as it might sound at first, especially given the presumed success of government banks in Brazil. A postal savings banking system that did not make
loans, like that of Japan and many western European countries (as well as
the United States from 1911 to 1967), could help provide convenient, low-
cost, plain vanilla deposit and check cashing services. But the notion of
Uncle Sam, Financier (the government as a lender in other words) should
be jettisoned in favor of a superior alternative.[745]

For starters, the formation of a government bank runs directly counter to the prevailing *Zeitgeist*, or spirit of the times. Correctly or not, most
Americans no longer trust the federal government, the approval ratings
of which are at all-time lows. Even lifelong Democrats like law professor
Peter Schuck believe the federal government is dysfunctional and despair
the successful implementation of substantive reforms. State governments
are generally considered more highly and one, North Dakota, has owned
and operated its own bank since 1919. That bank, however, transacts

---

745 Kurt E. von Mettenheim, *Federal Banking in Brazil: Policies and Competitive Advantages*,
(London: Pickering & Chatto, 2010); Caskey, *Fringe Banking*, 137–38; Mehrsa Baradaran, *How
the Other Half Banks: Exclusion, Exploitation, and the Threat to Democracy*, (Cambridge: Harvard University Press, 2015).

mostly with other banks and not directly with the public and the federal government already has a bank like that, the Federal Reserve.[746]

History, in fact, is rife with examples of successful provision of a variety of services by governments. Even Adam Smith, who argued that most of the time government efforts fail due to "slothful and negligent profusion" and "thoughtless extravagance," recognized the success of government postal offices, postal banking systems, pawnshops, and banks. The key to the success of government enterprises, scholars have discovered, is very Smithian: competition and careful alignment of the organization's goals with the internal incentives it provides its leaders and other employees.[747]

One of the successes that Smith pointed to, in fact, were the loan offices established by the colonial governments of mainland British North America. Essentially banks, the offices lent paper money, called bills of credit, on conservative loan-to-collateral terms and at below market rates of interest. Most succeeded and some, like colonial Pennsylvania's General Loan Office (GLO), have been credited with stimulating economic growth. The poorest of the poor did not receive loans as they owned nothing to post as collateral, but some loans went to households with very modest taxable wealth and even women received 2.3 percent of its loans. Free blacks and American Indians were so few and generally so poor that their apparent absence from the borrower lists cannot be taken as definitive evidence of their purposeful exclusion. So while the GLO may have engaged in discrimination in the modern sense, it did not

746 Dan Immergluck, *Credit to the Community: Community Reinvestment and Fair Lending Policy in the United States*, (New York: M. E. Sharpe, 2004), 4, 10–11; Peter H. Schuck, *Why Government Fails So Often and How It Can Do Better*, (Princeton: Princeton University Press, 2014); Josh Harkinson, "How the Nation's Only State-Owned Bank Became the Envy of Wall Street," *Mother Jones*, 27 March 2009; Raghuram G. Rajan and Rodney Ramcharan, "Land and Credit: A Study of the Political Economy of Banking in the United States in the Early 20th Century," *Journal of Finance* 66, no. 6 (2011): 1,898; Eric Hardmeyer, "Why Public Banking Works in North Dakota," *New York Times*, 1 October 2013.

747 Adam Smith, *Wealth of Nations*, Book V, Chapter 2, Part I, "Of the Funds or Sources of Revenue Which May Peculiarly Belong to the Sovereign or Commonwealth"; Robert E. Wright, "On the Economic Efficiency of Organizations: Toward a Solution of the Efficient Government Enterprise Paradox"; *Essays in Economic and Business History* 25 (2007), 143–54.

systematically exclude female or poor borrowers and its forms, created by
none other than Benjamin Franklin himself, were even printed so as to be
gender neutral. For the most part, after gaining some experience, colonial
loan offices managed to align the incentives of their managers with their
organizational goals. No commercial banks were established to compete
with them, but they faced considerable competition from individual
mortgage lenders resident both in the colonies and the Mother Country.[748]

After the Revolution, several states created loan offices that lent bank
money rather than their own notes, issuance of which the Constitution
forbade. Too little is known about them to come to any definitive conclusions about their performance but it appears that over time for-profit,
joint stock corporations supplanted them. Several states in the South, for
example, established so-called "property banks," like the Consolidated
Association of Planters and the Real Estate Bank of Arkansas, that issued
bank notes but made longer term mortgage loans rather than the short-
term trade-based loans favored by commercial banks.[749]

The government loan office of Missouri proved disastrous because,
right after achieving statehood in 1821 ironically enough, it tried to circumvent the Constitutional ban on state paper money by issuing its own
bills of credit. Although ostensibly modeled on the successful colonial
loan offices, Missouri's loan office allowed what one chronicler called

---

748 Theodore Thayer, "The Land-Bank System in the American Colonies," *Journal of Economic History* 13, no. 2 (1953): 145–59; Donald L. Kemmerer, "The Colonial Loan-Office
System in New Jersey," *Journal of Political Economy* 47, no. 6 (1939), 867–74; Mary Schweitzer,
Custom and Contract: Household, Government, and the Economy in Colonial Pennsylvania,
(New York: Columbia University Press, 1987); Keith Arbour, "Benjamin Franklin's First Gov-
ernment Printing: The Pennsylvania General Loan Office Mortgage Register of 1729, and Sub-
sequent Franklin Mortgage Registers and Bonds," *Transactions of the American Philosophical
Society* 89, no. 5 (1999), 28–30; Robert E. Wright, *Origins of Commercial Banking in America,
1750–1800,* (Lanham, Md.: Rowman & Littlefield, 2001); Robert E. Wright, *The First Wall
Street: Chestnut Street, Philadelphia, and the Birth of American Finance,* (Chicago: University of
Chicago Press, 2005).

749 John Kaminski, *Paper Politics: The Northern State Loan-Offices During the Confederation,
1783–1790,* (New York: Garland, 1989); Littleton Teackle, *An Address to the Members of the
Legislature of Maryland, Concerning the Establishment of a Loan Office for the Benefit of the
Landowners of the State,* (Annapolis, 1817), 29–31; Earl S. Sparks, *History and Theory of Agricultural Credit in the United States,* (New York: Thomas Y. Crowell Co., 1932), 83–111.

"much irregularity in the method of issuing the loan office certificates."
Counterfeiting was rampant, loans were made on poor collateral, over-
due loans were not vigorously collected, and no specie redemption
reserve, promised to bill holders in the law, was accumulated. Within 18
months, the loan office fell under attack and "the erstwhile friends of the
system failed to defend it." It took 15 years to unwind the mess. The U.S.
Supreme Court declared the act creating the bills of credit unconstitutional and relieved the borrowers of further obligation but forced the state
(i.e., its taxpayers) to redeem the bills with good money.[750]

Although it ran several successful businesses, including a cement
factory, South Dakota formed a loan office in 1917 that proved a costly
disaster. In the early twentieth century farmers across the nation, but
especially in the three Ota states, believed that they were being discriminated against by mortgage lenders and commercial banks. In several
states, including South Dakota, they had enough political clout to do
something about it and Peter Norbeck, a well driller from Redfield turned
politician, concluded that a government agricultural credit system like
that established in New Zealand would work best. The basic idea was
sound: the state would borrow cheaply at a relatively low rate by selling
bonds to investors, then relend the money, at cost plus expenses, in small
batches to numerous farmers throughout the state. Cheap credit would
allow farmers to make the prairie bloom like a rose so repayment would
be no problem.[751]

Norbeck, a progressive Republican, could not have been more
wrong. Although the law stipulated conservative lending standards – it
capped loans at $10,000 per borrower and at 70 percent of the value of the
land plus 40 percent of the insured value of improvements – many borrowers defaulted on interest payments during the agricultural depression
that struck the heartland after World War I. That posed serious problems

750 Albert J. McCulloch, "The Loan Office Experiment in Missouri, 1821–1836," *University of Missouri Bulletin* 15, no. 24 (1914), 10–13.

751 Robert E. Wright, *Little Business on the Prairie: Entrepreneurship, Prosperity, and Challenge in South Dakota*, (Sioux Falls: Center for Western Studies, 2015).

for the state because the holders of the bonds that it sold to fund the loans to farmers expected timely repayment.[752]

South Dakota was clearly a victim of adverse selection. The best (least risky) borrowers had already received loans from private lenders, leaving the riskiest farmers and ranchers to borrow from the state. The demand for loans was heavy and the members of the loan board did not have sufficient incentive to reject unworthy applicants or to reduce the loan requests of marginal ones, so they rarely personally examined properties or applicants, relying instead on the advice of a few of the applicant's neighbors for information and advice. By 1926, nearly half of the loans were delinquent. Not coincidentally, almost four out of five South Dakotan voters rejected the establishment of a state-owned and operated bank in a 1922 ballot measure.[753]

After officials realized their mistake and tried to enact stricter controls, farmers and ranchers who had not yet received loans raised a stink by asking why they were not entitled to loans on the same terms as their neighbors. Additional reforms were also sunk by politics as Norbeck, by then a U.S. senator, fought to maintain his system and reputation. Then the Depression hit, land values plummeted, and even more loans went into default. State officials had already proved themselves to be inept landlords and real estate dealers when they leased or tried to sell foreclosed farms and the greatly depressed commodity and land prices of the 1930s only made matters worse. South Dakota taxpayers ended up paying bondholders $57 million.[754]

On the eve of the Great Depression, 17 states had special rural credit systems but most were tiny. Vermont, for example, lent out less than $100,000 and Maine only a little more than $200,000. South Dakota's experience suggests that governments did not often engage extensively

---

752 Gilbert C. Fite, "South Dakota's Rural Credit System: A Venture in State Socialism, 1917–1946," *Agricultural History* 21, no. 4 (1947): 239–49.

753 Alan Clem *South Dakota Political Almanac,* 2nd ed. (Vermillion: Dakota Press, 1969), 37.

754 Gilbert C. Fite, "The History of South Dakota's Rural Credit System," *South Dakota Historical Collections* 45 (1949): 220–75.

in retail banking (i.e., lending directly to citizens) because the politics involved were tricky. A government bank with strict lending standards would not be very popular. One that lent on easy terms would be, at least until the defaults started to pile up, when it would find the urge to let the borrowers slide virtually irresistible. As one cotton farmer put it, "The government is the best place to owe money to" because it charges less interest and will take longer to foreclose. A government bank operated on strictly commercial principles would behave just like private institutions, so it might well engage in the same sorts of seemingly discriminatory lending practices. A government bank operated on political principles, by contrast, might be even more discriminatory than a commercial one. As we learned above, the federal government has not always served as a bastion for civil rights and party politics often trump common sense or common decency.[755]

Attempts to directly fund minorities with government money have generally failed to spur economic development. The Alaska Reorganization Act of 1936, for example, lent $600,000 to Tlingit and Haida fishers for nets and other fishing equipment in southeast Alaska. The loans, however, came at an unpropitious moment, when both fishing yields and prices declined. Losses rather than gains naturally resulted.[756]

The federal government nominally privatized the non-farm mortgage lender that it established during the Depression, Fannie Mae, along with its more recent cousin and ostensible competitor, Freddie Mac. As explained above, the government induced those GSEs to loosen their credit standards in the 1990s and 2000s, with disastrous results. Policymak-

---

755 Ivan Wright, *Farm Mortgage Financing*, (New York: McGraw-Hill, 1923), 303–14; Sparks, *History and Theory of Agricultural Credit*, 198–221; Margaret J. Hagood, *Mothers of the South: Portraiture of the White Tenant Farm Woman*, (Chapel Hill: University of North Carolina Press, 1939), 32.

756 David Arnold, "Work and Culture in Southeastern Alaska: Tlingits and the Salmon Fisheries," in *Native Pathways: American Indian Culture and Economic Development*, eds. Brian Hosmer and Colleen O'Neill (Boulder: University Press of Colorado, 2004), 173–74.

ers had forgotten their own 1978 dictum: *"equal credit" does not mean "easy credit."*[757]

U.S. governments, especially the federal one, have also entered the insurance business. Some government insurance is a wash, with benefits nearly equaling costs. Federal deposit insurance is a prime example. It reduces the incidence of bank runs while simultaneously inducing banks to assume more risk. The true cost of deposit insurance was revealed in the wake of the Savings and Loan debacle of the 1980s and the financial fiasco of 2008. By 1982, almost all states insured insurers by creating guaranty funds designed to protect policyholders from insurer insolvency. Like deposit insurance, guaranty funds increase risk-taking on the part of insurers and also expose taxpayers to the risk of having to bail out insolvent guaranty funds, almost all of which rely upon post-insolvency assessments.[758]

---

757 Treasury Department Study Team, *Credit and Capital Formation: A Report to the President's Interagency Task Force on Women Business Owners,* (April 1978), 70.

758 Loftin Graham and Xiaoying Xie, "The United States Insurance Market: Characteristics and Trends," in *Handbook of International Insurance: Between Global Dynamics and Local Contingencies,* ed. J. David Cummins and Bertrand Venard (New York: Springer, 2007); Scott E. Harrington, "Public Policy and Property-Liability Insurance," in *The Financial Condition and Regulation of Insurance Companies,* ed. Richard E. Randall and Richard W. Kopcke (Boston: Federal Reserve Bank of Boston, 1991); Peter M. Lencsis, *Insurance Regulation in the United States: An Overview for Business and Government,* (Westport, Conn.: Quorum Books, 1997); Thomas E. Moloney, "Discussion," in *The Financial Condition and Regulation of Insurance Companies,* ed. Richard E. Randall and Richard W. Kopcke (Boston: Federal Reserve Bank of Boston, 1991); David Moss, *When All Else Fails: Government as the Ultimate Risk Manager,* (Cambridge: Harvard University Press, 2002); Richard E. Randall and Richard W. Kopcke, "The Financial Condition and Regulation of Insurance Companies: An Overview," in *The Financial Condition and Regulation of Insurance Companies,* ed. Richard E. Randall and Richard W. Kopcke (Boston: Federal Reserve Bank of Boston, 1991); Al H. Ringleb and Steven L. Wiggins, "Institutional Control and Large-scale, Long-term Hazards," in *Government Risk-Bearing: Proceedings of a Conference Held at the Federal Reserve Bank of Cleveland,* ed. Mark S. Sniderman (Boston: Kluwer Academic, 1993); Joseph E. Stiglitz, "Perspectives on the Role of Government Risk-Bearing within the Financial Sector," in *Government Risk-Bearing: Proceedings of a Conference Held at the Federal Reserve Bank of Cleveland,* ed. Mark S. Sniderman (Boston: Kluwer Academic, 1993); Kenneth Wright, "The Structure, Conduct, and Regulation of the Life Insurance Industry," in *The Financial Condition and Regulation of Insurance Companies,* ed. Richard E. Randall and Richard W. Kopcke (Boston: Federal Reserve Bank of Boston, 1991); Brian Wright, "Public Insurance of Private Risks: Theory and Evidence

Other government forays into the provision of insurance distort privately provided alternatives and effectively redistribute wealth from taxpayers to special interests. That is because premiums paid to the government are lower than those private insurers would charge, or the government pays out more in benefits than private insurers would. Unlike private insurers, the government does not invest the premiums it receives, so any difference between premiums received and claims paid ultimately come from taxpayers.[759]

Government insurance that works well initially may degenerate later if the government adapts too slowly to changing market conditions, including increases in asymmetric information brought on by the existence of government insurance itself. For example, in the wake of the Employee Retirement Income Security Act (ERISA) of 1974, stronger corporations avoided paying premiums by switching from defined benefit to uninsured defined contribution pension plans while weaker corporations shifted their pension liabilities onto the new Pension Benefit Guaranty Corporation (PBGC) and profited from the transaction.

Similarly, government flood insurance programs induced construction in areas, like southern Louisiana, where human habitation weakened natural defenses against flooding and increased the damage inflicted by hurricanes. Repeated government bailouts of hurricane and other victims have taught American consumers, businesses, and insurers that buying catastrophe insurance or reinsurance is unnecessary. Farmers adversely affected by large scale events, for example, often receive government payouts even if they are not enrolled in government crop insurance programs. Unsurprisingly, farmers favored with government-subsidized

---

from Agriculture," in *Government Risk-Bearing: Proceedings of a Conference Held at the Federal Reserve Bank of Cleveland*, ed. Mark S. Sniderman (Boston: Kluwer Academic, 1993).

759 Kenneth J. Meier, *The Political Economy of Regulation: The Case of Insurance*, (Albany: State University of New York Press, 1988), 37; Mark S. Sniderman, "Preface," in *Government Risk-Bearing: Proceedings of a Conference Held at the Federal Reserve Bank of Cleveland*, ed. Mark S. Sniderman (Boston: Kluwer Academic, 1993); Stiglitz, "Perspectives on the Role of Government."

insurance, price supports, and disaster assistance take more financial and production risks than unsubsidized farmers do.[760]

State governments also offer various types of loan guarantees and insurance. Maryland once offered automobile insurance, for example, and Wisconsin sells small life insurance policies. Government officials have incentives to provide insurance because it appears to be free. People laud politicians for helping, forgetting that when disaster strikes the true cost of the insurance will be revealed. In the meantime, however, politicians gain popularity because they seemingly aided constituents without raising taxes.

Moreover, government insurance programs are rarely actuarially sound. Governments find it politically difficult to charge premiums based on differences in risk and they face pressures from rent seekers, special interest groups that wish to displace risks onto taxpayers while retaining the rewards of their risky activities. Governments therefore often subsidize risk-taking, sometimes heavily. While governments in theory may be able to solve market failures, in practice they rarely do so, often creating problems as costly as those they solve.[761]

---

760 Edward J. Kane, "Commentary," in *Government Risk-Bearing: Proceedings of a Conference Held at the Federal Reserve Bank of Cleveland*, ed. Mark S. Sniderman (Boston: Kluwer Academic, 1993); Howard Kunreuther, "Ambiguity and Government Risk-Bearing for Low-Probability Events," in *Government Risk-Bearing: Proceedings of a Conference Held at the Federal Reserve Bank of Cleveland*, ed. Mark S. Sniderman (Boston: Kluwer Academic, 1993); Moss, *When All Else Fails*; Zvi Bodie, "Commentary," in *Government Risk-Bearing: Proceedings of a Conference Held at the Federal Reserve Bank of Cleveland*, ed. Mark S. Sniderman (Boston: Kluwer Academic, 1993); Meier, *Political Economy of Regulation*; Justine Rodriguez, "Information and Incentives to Improve Government Risk-Bearing," in *Government Risk-Bearing: Proceedings of a Conference Held at the Federal Reserve Bank of Cleveland*, ed. Mark S. Sniderman (Boston: Kluwer Academic, 1993); Kathleeen P. Utgoff, "The PBGC: A Costly Lesson in the Economics of Federal Insurance," in *Government Risk-Bearing: Proceedings of a Conference Held at the Federal Reserve Bank of Cleveland*, ed. Mark S. Sniderman (Boston: Kluwer Academic, 1993); Wright, "Public Insurance of Private Risks."

761 Dennis R. Connolly, "Government Risk-Bearing: What Works and What Doesn't," in *Government Risk-Bearing: Proceedings of a Conference Held at the Federal Reserve Bank of Cleveland*, ed. Mark S. Sniderman (Boston: Kluwer Academic, 1993); Mark V. Pauly, "Commentary," in *Government Risk-Bearing: Proceedings of a Conference Held at the Federal Reserve Bank of Cleveland*, ed. Mark S. Sniderman (Boston: Kluwer Academic, 1993); Ringleb and Wiggins,

Consider, for example, Social Security. In the first third of the twentieth century industrial pension plans grew, primarily as a response to labor unrest. Companies gained by tying workers' long-term interests to their employers rather than to their unions and inducing pensioners to act as strikebreakers. Nevertheless, some elderly Americans were impoverished, causing considerable consternation among progressives on both sides of the aisle. The plight of the impoverished elderly worsened as the Depression deepened and many philanthropists reduced rather than expanded their charitable giving. Poverty among the elderly and widowed, many argued, was due partly to their failure to save. That failure, in turn, was largely due to regulatory impediments that prevented life insurers from educating as many people about income risks as thoroughly as they would have liked to have done. Regulations also kept administrative costs higher than insurers would have preferred. Instead of addressing those problems, however, the government rushed to take direct action. Threat of social unrest or implementation of more disruptive schemes, like those of Francis Townsend, Huey Long, or Charles Coughlin, played a major role in Social Security's passage.[762]

Compared to private insurance, Social Security is deeply flawed. "Premiums" – really just payroll taxes — are based solely on income, not life expectancies. While the taxes are progressive to a point, higher

---

"Institutional Control"; Rodriguez, "Information and Incentives"; Stiglitz, "Perspectives on the Role of Government"; Utgoff, "The PBGC"; Wright, "Public Insurance of Private Risks."

762 Grace Abbott, *From Relief to Social Security: The Development of the New Public Welfare Service*, (Chicago: University of Chicago Press, 1941); Barbara Armstrong, *Insuring the Essentials: Minimum Wage Plus Social Insurance – A Living Wage Program*, (New York: Macmillan Company, 1932); Joseph Belth, "Discussion," in *The Financial Condition and Regulation of Insurance Companies*, ed. Richard E. Randall and Richard W. Kopcke (Boston: Federal Reserve Bank of Boston, 1991); Gerard M. Brannon, "Public Policy and Life Insurance," in *The Financial Condition and Regulation of Insurance Companies*, ed. Richard E. Randall and Richard W. Kopcke (Boston: Federal Reserve Bank of Boston, 1991); Blanche Coll, *Safety Net: Welfare and Social Security, 1929–1979*, (New Brunswick, N.J.: Rutgers University Press, 1995); Abraham Epstein, *Insecurity, a Challenge to America: A Study of Social Insurance in the United States and Abroad*, 3rd ed. (New York: Random House, 1936); Jill Quadagno, *The Transformation of Old Age Security: Class and Politics in the American Welfare State*, (Chicago: University of Chicago Press, 1988); I. M. Rubinow, *The Quest for Security*, (New York: Henry Holt and Co., 1934).

mortality among certain minorities and the poor more generally mean that in practice the system is highly regressive, biased against African-American males and other groups. Nothing but a paltry death benefit is left to heirs, so Social Security exacerbates intergenerational wealth disparities by reducing the bequests of the less affluent. People married for fewer than 10 years and numerous other groups also suffer under its provisions. Benefits are not guaranteed and reserves are nominal only. The existence of the benefits for three quarters of a century have weakened markets for private insurance, life annuities, and a variety of retirement products. That, in turn, makes reforming or eliminating the program more difficult because opponents of change argue, not without evidence, that Americans do not know how to save for retirement or purchase income insurance.[763]

Not even government terrorism insurance is strictly necessary. The U.S. government began subsidizing terrorism insurance soon after the September 2001 terrorist attacks on the World Trade Center. Insurers fear that another major attack could bankrupt them and the federal government is likely to rush to the aid of victims anyway. Government aid may be justified here because terrorist attacks are unpredictable and potentially many times more devastating than a natural disaster. That makes pricing tricky, especially given that insurance company managers tend to be more risk averse than the stockholders they serve. Without the federal backstop, terror insurance might not be available at a price anyone would be willing to pay due to budget constraints and/or their inability to compute an actuarially fair rate. Government intervention seems warranted as well because moral hazard is small, it being difficult to imagine that the existence of terrorism insurance would induce businesses to behave in ways that would increase the risk of attack or reduce

763 Henry Aaron, Jr. and John B. Shoven, *Should the United States Privatize Social Security?* (Cambridge: MIT Press, 1999); Robert Eisner, *Social Security: More, Not Less,* (New York: Century Foundation Press, 1998); Moss, *When All Else Fails*; Sylvester Schieber and John B. Shoven, *The Real Deal: The History and Future of Social Security,* (New Haven: Yale University Press, 1999).

their incentives to take measures to prevent an attack or mitigate its effects.[764]

Mutual pools, however, offer a better remedy. Mutual pools, some with an initial government risk-sharing backstop that decreased as the pool built its reserves, worked in nuclear accident insurance, where uncertainty and high-impact loom as large as in terrorism insurance. Regardless of the details, making premiums retrospective, like participating life policies or old school ex post assessments, is a key provision. Unfortunately, interest in mutual solutions appears to be waning.[765]

Finally, the federal government has failed to reduce financial discrimination by subsidizing certain types of credit, most importantly the financing of small, minority-owned businesses. One federal program run by the Small Business Administration in operation from 1969 to 1973 had a 70 percent default rate and did little but bolster the notion that black-owned businesses were inherently risky.[766]

Another program started soon after encouraged the creation of 301(d) Small Business Investment Companies, which were initially known by the more revealing name of Minority Enterprise Small Business Investment Companies, or MESBICs. Those privately-owned companies were essentially venture funds that helped small businesses at least half-owned by "socially or economically disadvantaged individuals" by selling them financial and management advice and by taking equity stakes in them. They were designed to offset the failure of the Small Business

---

764 Robert Hartwig and Claire Wilkinson, "An Overview of the Alternative Risk Transfer Market," in *Handbook of International Insurance: Between Global Dynamics and Local Contingencies*, ed. J. David Cummins and Bertrand Venard (New York: Springer, 2007); Holman W. Jenkins, "Terror Insurance Is Here to Stay," *Wall Street Journal*, 8 August 2007; Kunreuther, "Ambiguity and Government Risk-Bearing"; Ringleb and Wiggins, "Institutional Control."

765 Dan R. Anderson, "Commentary," in *Government Risk-Bearing: Proceedings of a Conference Held at the Federal Reserve Bank of Cleveland*, ed. Mark S. Sniderman (Boston: Kluwer Academic, 1993); Connolly, "Government Risk-Bearing"; Kunreuther, "Ambiguity and Government Risk-Bearing"; Meier, *Political Economy of Regulation*.

766 Immergluck, *Credit to the Community*, 63.

Administration (SBA) to jumpstart minority-owned small businesses in ghettos and on Indian Reservations.[767]

MESBICs did not advertise, instead relying on word-of-mouth networks that rarely included women. The women who did find out about MESBICs and applied for funds rarely had large enough financing needs in a financing model where $150,000 constituted the lowest rung. "Where is the woman who will walk through the door asking for money to set up a computer software company?" one MESBIC analyst asked. "I'd fund her in a minute. All I get are boutique owners." Another MESBIC manager claimed that he had "never seen a woman with a fundable idea." Other MESBIC managers did not think that women legally qualified for their assistance unless they were also "a member of a racial minority."[768]

The program could not help black entrepreneurs either because most MESBICs were chronically "under-capitalized and illiquid. Very few of those surveyed," in 1978 were making new investments and some were eager for a Small Business Administration bailout. They had difficulty hiring and retaining quality analysts so many of their deals "have gone sour" as one MESBIC manager put it. "The concept behind MESBICs," another manager argued, "was more social than economic and we're having to live through the experience of being a social solution."[769]

That MESBIC manager was right. The best solution to social problems like discrimination is a purely economic approach that relies primarily on self-interest, not on charity, government subsidy, or government ownership. A much better way than government financial institutions to reduce exclusion, discrimination, and predation is to encourage the very people being discriminated against to form their own financial institutions. America has a very long history of just this type of self-help, the best of which was purely private in origin. As the sordid history of the

---

767 Treasury Department Study Team, *Credit and Capital Formation*, 43–44; David Benson, Aaron Lies, Albert Okunade, Phanindra Wunnava, "Economic Impact of a Private Sector Micro-Financing Scheme in South Dakota," *Small Business Economics* 36 (2011): 158.

768 Treasury Department Study Team, *Credit and Capital Formation*, 45–47.

769 Treasury Department Study Team, *Credit and Capital Formation*, 47.

Freedman's Bank shows, however, too much government involvement in the self-help process can prove pernicious.

The Freedman's Savings and Trust Company

As described in Chapter 3, most African-Americans did not enjoy ample access to the financial system before the Civil War. The war itself, however, increased blacks' incomes and savings due to liberation, emancipation, and employment, particularly with the Union Army, which saw fit to create a number of military savings banks for Union soldiers and for the denizens of occupied cities like New Orleans, Louisiana, Norfolk, Virginia, and Beaufort, South Carolina. The Free Labor Bank, as one such institution was named, was successful but short-lived because in 1865 Congress congealed all the military savings banks into the Freedman's Savings and Trust Company, a mutual savings bank that soon came to have branches in almost 3 dozen cities in every section of the country except New England. The bank's goal was to introduce former slaves to the financial system by providing them with a safe and steady six percent return on their deposits. In a fateful move, the bank's books were overseen by Congress itself, not the newly formed Office of the Comptroller of the Currency. (The Bank's records are now available in the Records of the Comptroller of the Currency and accessible online via FRASER, an online archive of financial records maintained by the Federal Reserve Bank of St. Louis.)[770]

At first, the Freedman's Bank, as it came to be known, adhered to safe and sound banking principles, including investing primarily in U.S. government bonds. Many freedpersons believed that the bank was part

---

770 Arnett G. Lindsay, "The Negro in Banking," *Journal of Negro History* 14, 2 (April 1929), 127–28, 162, 164; Jonathan Levy, *Freaks of Fortune: The Emerging World of Capitalism and Risk in America* (Cambridge: Harvard University Press, 2012), 104–13; John Sibley Butler, *Entrepreneurship and Self-Help Among Black Americans: A Reconsideration of Race and Economics,* (Albany: State University of New York Press, 1991), 127–28; Abby Gilbert, "The Comptroller of the Currency and the Freedman's Savings Bank," *Journal of Negro History* 57, 2 (April 1972): 127, 130.

of the Freedman's Bureau or some other part of the federal bureaucracy. Some passbooks even asserted that "the government of the United States has made this bank perfectly safe," and Lincoln's beloved face was leveraged to the hilt. Its fate, though, was really in the hands of its 50 private trustees. It was, in other words, a bank *for* rather than *of* freed slaves, very few of whom served above the level of tellers or clerks in the bank's early years.[771]

As yields on government bonds dropped well below the six percent promised to depositors, and as expenses continued to run high, the bank had to assume more risks, and that meant making commercial and real estate loans. That may have worked but the bank's first trustees, mostly abolitionists with little financial experience, were not bankers and there were so many of them it was easy for them not to feel any individual responsibility for the bank's operations. When new faces stepped in to 'help,' it was with the intent of bilking the bank. Despite early difficulties, the bank had grown, attracting during its eight years of operation some 72,000 different individual depositors, the vast majority of whom were black. At its height, deposits reached $4.2 million, a tempting pot of cash indeed. (Many sources claim $57 million but that was the total deposited over the life of the institution and hence, due to constant withdrawals, far more than the balance due depositors and available to lend, or steal, at any given moment.)[772]

So over time the bank became a tool for surreptitiously extracting rents from poor blacks, who, like other savings bank depositors, were not considered acceptable risks as borrowers. After 1871, nary a single trustee remained unconnected to a large borrower. Unsurprisingly, shenanigans abounded and some, like that of Jay Cooke, who borrowed $500,000 from the bank at 5 percent interest, a full point *below* the rate paid to depositors,

---

771 Gilbert, "Comptroller of the Currency," 136; Lindsay, "Negro in Banking," 161, 163, 163 n19; Levy, *Freaks of Fortune*, 126, 132; Abram L. Harris, *The Negro as Capitalist: A Study of Banking and Business Among American Negroes* (New York: American Academy of Political and Social Science, 1936), 28, 30.

772 Gilbert, "Comptroller of the Currency," 126; Levy, *Freaks of Fortune*, 107–8, 115, 117, 126–29; Lindsay, "Negro in Banking," 165–66; Harris, *Negro as Capitalist*, 29.

were quite transparent. It helped that Cooke's relative Henry came to be in charge of the bank's investments. Other schemes were more complex but the charter prescribed no penalties or performance bonds for trustees and only a few of the shenanigans led to prosecutions, so the defalcations continued.

Moreover, many of the branches were maintained more for political than business reasons. By the time the examiners of the Comptroller of the Currency were called to help in 1873–74, unprofitable and ill-managed branches had impaired the bank's capital to such a degree that the bank proved unsalvageable.[773]

Near the end, blacks, including Frederick Douglass, were brought into leadership positions so they could be blamed for the bank's failure. Runs finished the job, reducing deposits to just $3.3 million by January 1874 and $2.9 million by its final day in operation on June 29 of that year. After decades of liquidation, the remaining depositors received only 62 cents on the dollar and, despite the urging of the Comptroller of the Currency, the government never made good on its implied backing of the institution.[774]

In addition to casting additional doubt on the efficacy of government-influenced lending, the Freedman's Bank episode warns that aggrieved groups need to respond to discrimination on their own. If the government had simply left African-Americans to their own devices, like the leading white citizens of Durham, North Carolina would later do, free blacks and freed slaves would have established appropriate financial institutions for themselves. Numerous bottom-up efforts are much more likely to find a formula for success than large, top-down plans or institutions are and, even if they fail, grassroots endeavors will be smaller and hence cause less pain if they do not pan out. The same general lessons can

---

773 Levy, *Freaks of Fortune*, 138, 140; Harris, *Negro as Capitalist*, 32, 34, 36–41; Lindsay, "Negro in Banking," 166; Gilbert, "Comptroller of the Currency," 127, 130.

774 Lindsay, "Negro in Banking," 167–68; Gilbert, "Comptroller of the Currency," 129, 131–32, 136–43.

be drawn from the history of government involvement in agricultural credit systems.[775]

The Curious Case of Farm Credit

Farming in a new country is always in crying need of more capital. ...
The great economic problem is, therefore, to induce capital to flow
from older centers of accumulation to these new areas of deficit. —
Thomas N. Carver, "Foreword," in Earl S. Sparks, History and
Theory of Agricultural Credit in the United States (New York:
Thomas Y. Crowell Co., 1932), xi.

Farmers, qua farmers, have long complained about a dearth of access to the financial system.[776] African-American, Amerindian, female, and "dirt" (read white trash) farmers, especially those who were tenants (cash or share), had an especially hard time of it but even farmers of Euroamerican descent who owned their own farms and equipment, even those who were landlords of one or more tenant farmers, often found financing and insuring their farming operations a challenge. Before the Great War, wrote one student of the subject, "few, if any, banks encouraged the farmers to borrow from them." Instead, banks lent to those with more liquid capital, like cotton factors, who in turn lent to planters and other agriculturalists.[777]

Objectively, farming is risky business because bad weather in specific locales can crush an individual farmer's output while good weather over a broad swathe can increase the yields of many farmers, decimating prices. Those struck with misfortune did not have much to bring to market while in the second instance bumper crops did not always mean bumper income. Long-term credit can help to smooth out year-to-year

---

775 Butler, *Entrepreneurship and Self-Help*, 176–77.

776 For a dated but still solid overviews of farm financing before the FCS, see Sparks, *History and Theory of Agricultural Credit* and Wright, *Farm Mortgage Financing*.

777 B. M. Gile, *The Farm Credit Situation in Southwestern Arkansas*, (Fayetteville: University of Arkansas Agricultural Experiment Station, 1929), 29–30.

fluctuations in farm incomes but one disastrous year, or a short succession of bad ones, can wipe out a farmer's equity before markets and the weather again bring good prices and a bountiful yield.[778]

Farmers responded to the lack of credit and insurance privately, as all groups that felt put upon do when regulators allow them to, by establishing their own mutual insurers and specialized farm lenders, typically in the form of local unit commercial banks, which provided seasonal credit, livestock loan companies, which provided intermediate credit to develop herds, and specialized farm mortgage banks. Wealthy individuals, some local and others distant, provided mortgages, as did institutional investors like large eastern life insurance companies. By the end of the nineteenth century, the farm credit system was good enough to allow roughly 7 out of 10 farmers to own their farms. Even mortgages offered by most institutional lenders, however, generally ran for only a few years and were interest-only (non-amortizing). They were far from ideal because they subjected borrowers to interest rate and refinancing risk. In other words, a borrower might have to pay a higher interest rate or not be able to obtain a new loan at all, leaving the maturing one subject to default. Longer-term amortizing mortgages, like those offered by building and loan societies, might have spread more widely privately but the government interceded before they did.[779]

In terms of seasonal credit, agriculturalists became discontented with the high prices charged by factors and merchants, especially as competition from chain stores and mail order catalogs grew more intense, so they began to ask banks for cash loans. Bankers, in turn, came to see the benefits of making consumption loans to successful farmers, whose land could always be mortgaged, and then seized if necessary. By 1927, almost

---

778 Wright, *Farm Mortgage Financing*, 17–18.

779 William J. Collins and Robert A. Margo, "Race and Home Ownership from the End of the Civil War to the Present," *American Economic Review* 101, 3 (May 2011), 357; Sparks, *History and Theory of Agricultural Credit*, 3–11, 158–60, 169–75, 177–87, 372–77, 429; Wright, *Farm Mortgage Financing*, 17–18, 96–141, 297–302, 315–23.

3 in 4 farm owners and cash tenants obtained seasonal credit from banks even in relatively backwards places like Arkansas.[780]

The farm credit problem, as it was termed, had macro and microeconomic dimensions, both of which gained saliency in the aftermath of the Panic of 1907. Roosevelt's Country Life Commission (1908), the National Monetary Commission (1909), the American Commission on Agricultural Credit and Cooperation (1912), and the United States Commission (1913) all addressed farm credit in one way or another, as did a joint public-private commission sent to Europe in 1913 to study German *landschafts* and other agricultural cooperative lenders in 13 other European nations. Formation of the Federal Reserve System in 1913–14 ostensibly settled the macroeconomic issues. The microeconomic ones, which came in the form of complaints that farm mortgage interest rates were too high, varied too much from region to region, and that loan maturities were too short, were thought to require a more focused approach. In 1916, average rates on farm mortgages were 8 or more percent per year in about half the country and average maturities varied from 3 to 10 years.[781]

Rather than make loans directly to farmers, like colonial governments, Missouri, and South Dakota did, the federal government in 1916, in its first major foray into the credit market since the dissolution of the second Bank of the United States in 1836, established a public-private (government-cooperative) hybrid now called the Farm Credit System (FCS). Due to the widespread belief that governments should standardize business methods rather than actually lend money, the federal government initially planned to support the system only by supplying it with startup capital for its first few formative years. Due to the agricultural depression of the 1920s, the general Depression of the 1930s, and World

---

780 Gile, *Farm Credit Situation*, 30.

781 W. N. Stokes, Jr., *Credit to Farmers: The Story of Federal Intermediate Credit Banks and Production Credit Associations*, (Washington, D.C.: Federal Intermediate Credit Banks, 1973), 3; W. Gifford Hoag, *The Farm Credit System: A History of Financial Self-Help*, (Danville, Ill.: Interstate Printers & Publishers, 1976), 1, 212; Sparks, *History and Theory of Agricultural Credit*, 315–31; Jerome J. Hollenhorst, "An Analysis of the Federal Land Bank System's Debt Management, 1947–1961," (Ph.D. Diss., Iowa State University, 1965), 8–10.

War II (when the government came to control vast swathes of the economy), however, the government greatly expanded its financial support.
So only in 1953 was the FCS completely privatized, though overseen by
an independent federal agency called the Farm Credit Administration,
and government capital, which had been reduced in 1947, was slowly
replaced with private capital and completely repaid by the end of 1968.
The government never received a dividend on its stock and even left the
accumulated surplus with the FCS.[782]

The FCS was divided into 12 districts, each with a Federal Land
Bank (FLB) that supported numerous, small Federal Land Bank Associations (FLBAs), co-operative ventures that made loans secured by first
mortgages on farmland and rural real estate. (Joint-stock land banks were
allowed at first too but they died during the Depression and were not
reintroduced.) To obtain (and keep) a loan, a farmer had to own stock,
with a par value of at least 5 percent of his loan, in his local FLBA. Non-
real estate lending (for equipment, etc.) was conducted in a similar way,
via local Production Credit Associations (PCAs) and each district's Federal
Intermediate Credit Bank (FICB). The FCS also lent to farm co-ops and
rural banks via the Bank for Cooperatives located in each district, as well
as a national Central Bank for Cooperatives.[783]

The entire system was funded by its own operational profits, commercial bank loans, and, most importantly, the sale of securities (notes
and bonds) to investors by the Federal Farm Credit Banks Funding Corporation (FFCBFC). The securities were backed by the combined financial resources of all the banks in the FCS, so buying one offered investors
a safe, liquid, diversified, divisible method of investing in farm mortgages
relative to making individual farm mortgage loans. Thus investors were

---

782 Sparks, *History and Theory of Agricultural Credit*, 11; Stokes, *Credit to Farmers*, 99–128,
142–43; Hoag, *Farm Credit System*, 19, 25; Hollenhorst, "The Federal Land Bank System's
Debt," 12.

783 Hollenhorst, "The Federal Land Bank System's Debt," 11; Sparks, *History and Theory of
Agricultural Credit*, 140–51; Stokes, *Credit to Farmers*, 5; Richard M. Todd, "Taking Stock of
the Farm Credit System: Riskier for Farm Borrowers," *Federal Reserve Bank of Minneapolis
Quarterly Review* 9, 4 (Fall 1985): 14–24; Hoag, *Farm Credit System*, xiii–xiv, 221–22.

willing to accept a lower yield on the bonds than on individual farm mortgages, which of course was key to the entire system. The securities did
not, however, enjoy an explicit federal government guarantee. Because
top level policy decisions were the bailiwick of the Farm Credit Administration Board, the structure of which has changed over time but which
has always been essentially controlled by POTUS, however, investors
always believed that the government would support the FCS if necessary.
The FFCBFC's obligations, in other words, have long been considered
the first "agency" bonds and traded at yields not far above those of the
bonds issued by the U.S. Treasury itself.[784]

Scale economies and federal subsidies, in the form of almost $10.5
million of free startup capital and initial operating costs, additional infu-
sions during the Depression totaling $638 million, the implied guarantee
of its debt, a federal income tax exemption on both its bonds and its
profits, and the use of the facilities of the Treasury and Federal Reserve at
cost, allowed the FCS to offer highly competitive products. The system's
loans were capped at 6 percent, for example, and amortization mandated
at between 5 and 40 years (most mortgages were amortized over 20 years
or more). Unsurprisingly, demand for FSC mortgages was strong at first.
(Due to stringent standards, low capital, and weak management, it took
the intermediate credit and other parts of the system some decades to
become important.) By the end of 1928, the FCS had lent over $1.5 billion
secured by over 480,000 mortgages, about 20 percent of the overall market.[785] Those were numbers that impressed contemporaries, especially
those who saw the effects of the FCS on the ground, as did one farm
credit researcher in Arkansas, who noted that the FCS had "been of great
assistance" to farmers, especially smaller ones. "Since the federal land
banks are cooperative and not operated primarily for profit, they, unlike

---

784 Hollenhorst, "The Federal Land Bank System's Debt," 22–32; Todd, "Taking Stock of the
Farm Credit System," 14–24; Hoag, *Farm Credit System*, 33–39.

785 Hoag, *Farm Credit System*, 19; Hollenhorst, "The Federal Land Bank System's Debt," 25,
31–32, 88; Sparks, *History and Theory of Agricultural Credit*, 137, 153, 160–62; Stokes, *Credit
to Farmers*, 13–19; James B. Morman, "Cooperative Credit Institutions in the United States,"
Annals of the American Academy of Political and Social Science 87, no. 1 (1920): 179.

the joint-stock land banks, would not especially seek the large and hence more profitable loans," he explained. "Furthermore," the land banks were "obligated" as non-profit cooperatives "to give the same service to the small farmer as to the larger operator."[786] At 2.8 percent, however, loan losses were an order of magnitude higher than expected and in 1925 the Spokane district bank had to be bailed out, to the tune of $2.8 million, by the other 11 district banks. Other districts cut back in response and farm mortgage interest rates increased in many places, including southern Arkansas where they settled at about 8 percent by the time the Depression hit.[787]

After World War II, America's agricultural sector boomed due to strong demand and rising yields thanks to technological advances in farm equipment, fertilizers, insecticides, and seeds. Agricultural real estate prices generally increased due to suburbanization but also because farmers combated the so-called cost-price squeeze, the unfavorable reduction in the ratio of the costs of farm inputs to the prices for farm products, by scaling up (buying more land to farm with high fixed-cost machinery). In an attempt to slow down the advance in real estate prices, the FCS kept interest rates low but rationed credit heavily by lending only on conservative assessments about three-fifths of current market prices. That policy kept defaults at extremely low levels but it also meant that the FCS supplied only about 10 percent of a rapidly growing market dominated by insurers, commercial banks, and, especially, individuals. After its privatization in the mid-1950s, however, the FSC began to ease up on appraisals in order to make more loans and gain market share. The tactic worked. By 1961, individuals still supplied $1.1 billion (38.1%) of the $2.9 billion farm mortgage market, but the FSC supplied $.64 billion (22.3%), beating out both insurers (17.7%) and banks (21.6%). The gains did not jeopardize the FCS, however, as its average interest rate was always the lowest of all major lenders, though at times the spread was only a few basis points

---

786 Gile, *Farm Credit Situation*, 31–32.

787 Sparks, *History and Theory of Agricultural Credit*, 135–37; Gile, *Farm Credit Situation*, 33–36.

(100ths of a percent). In 1947, for instance, the FCS average rate was 4.10% while the rate charged by individual lenders averaged 4.12%. In 1961, the FCS rate, 5.64%, was only 10 basis points better than the average of individual lenders and only 15 basis points better than the average of all lenders. Other times, though, the average FCS rate was more than 1 percent (100 basis points) better than that of its major competitors.[788]

The 1970s was also a period of growth and prosperity for the FCS as the agricultural sector continued to boom and at least two self-congratulatory commemorative histories of the system appeared. Inflation-adjusted farm equity, for instance, grew 82 percent and FCS's loan losses ranged from low to negative (i.e., collections on loans already written off exceeded new write-offs). By 1985, the FCS lent over $60 billion, making it the country's largest agricultural lender in a market of about $200 billion. About that time, however, some farm lending cooperatives started to go bankrupt because depressed agricultural conditions in the first half of the 1980s, among the worst reversals in U.S. agricultural history, increased loan defaults well above expectations while rapidly declining agricultural real estate prices quickly eroded the equity in the 85 percent loan-to-value mortgages made legal in 1971 (up from 65 percent previously). Farmers who feared that their co-op stock might lose value applied to banks for refinancing so they could pay off their co-op loan and redeem their stock at par. Banks happily accommodated the best 20 percent or so of the applicants, leaving the riskiest borrowers to their fate. That, of course, hurt the co-ops, which began to suffer from yet higher default rates at the same time that investors demanded higher yields on FCS's bonds and notes.[789]

While the FCS clearly increased nominal competition in the farm mortgage sector and demonstrated the value of the amortizing mortgage, it is not clear that it was able to significantly reduce interest rates or

788 Hollenhorst, "The Federal Land Bank System's Debt," 45–49, 52; Stokes, *Credit to Farmers*, 129–43.

789 Stokes, *Credit to Farmers*, iii, 160; Hoag, *Farm Credit System*, v-viii; Todd, "Taking Stock of the Farm Credit System," 14–24; Hollenhorst, "The Federal Land Bank System's Debt," 25.

regional discrepancies in mortgage rates. Early FCS critics warned that because real estate prices do not always increase and the FCS did not improve the system of farm appraisal, it might lead to over-borrowing, followed by a real estate market bubble and subsequent crash. "It is small comfort," a professor of agricultural credit at the University of South Dakota noted at the outset of the Great Depression, "to the borrowing farmer to know that farm incomes and farm values may increase over the century if they happen to decrease during his lifetime."[790]

In fact, the FCS fomented the Farm Crisis of the 1980s ($36 billion of farm loans were delinquent by 1986, causing the failure of some 60 agricultural lenders) by lending based on market prices, rather than more fundamental land values based on realistic discounted cash flow or similar valuation models that take into account soil quality, farm location, cost of transportation, availability of water, overall climate, farm elevation, land contour, and the value of improvements, as well as the state's tax and business policies. After all, due to the perennially illiquid nature of real estate, many agricultural properties changed "hands at far more or far less than their value."[791] When farm prices, unchecked by short selling and buoyed by low real interest rates or overly optimistic forecasts (weather or financial), soared too high, private borrowers prudently stopped lending to protect themselves from losses. Despite the claim that "the System has been very careful to avoid lending for speculative projects," the FCS took up the slack, which allowed prices to go even higher.[792] Investors continued to buy the FCS's bonds because of the implied government guarantee backing them. So the Farm Crisis of the 1980s was very much a dry run for the subprime mortgage debacle because the unholy mixture of public risk-taking and private profits led to irrational lending, just as it did at Fannie and Freddie two decades later. The government's response was similar, too, as it bailed out the FCS while leaving its structure and incentives largely intact. The only major reform was the establishment in

---

790 Hollenhorst, "The Federal Land Bank System's Debt," 61, 68–69, 451.

791 Wright, *Farm Mortgage Financing*, 186, 187–200.

792 Hoag, *Farm Credit System*, 15.

1987 of Farmer Mac, a joint stock corporation and GSE that made a secondary market in farm mortgages much like Fannie and Freddie did for home mortgages.[793]

Despite reduction of the number of districts (from 12 to 8 to 5), the amount of stock borrowers must purchase (from 5% to 2% of the loan amount), and other operational details, the FCS continues to operate as a GSE, a standalone network of rural credit cooperatives sponsored by the federal government. It does not receive regular government appropriations but it still receives the tax exemptions and implicit guarantee of its debt discussed above, in return for which it is subject to close federal supervision. In 2004, when a member cooperative tried to sell itself to Rabobank, a private rural cooperative credit network based in the Netherlands that entered the United States early in the Third Millennium, the deal fell through amid much controversy. Until recently, the FCS was the second largest lender to agriculturalists after only commercial banks.[794]

As the head quote to this section shows, it is a hoary canard that farmers, as a group, cannot finance the operation of the agricultural sector. "No matter how desperate the need," wrote W. N. Stokes, Jr. in his history of Federal Intermediate Credit Banks, "farmers were not able to supply the capital necessary to organize their own financing institutions."[795] But their high average savings rate and eventual ownership of the FCS suggest that farmers *would not* supply the necessary capital, not that they *could not* do so. In retaliation for half a century of high tariffs on manufactured goods, they were happy to squeeze the subsidies out of the federal government detailed above, and many more besides, including generous (to farmers that is) crop insurance programs. In 2015,

---

793 Mark Steven Carey, "Feeding the Fad: The Federal Land Banks, Land Market Efficiency, and the Farm Credit Crisis," (Ph.D. Diss., University of California, Berkeley, 1990); Jim Monke, "Farm Credit System," *Agricultural Finance and Credit*, ed. J. M. Bishoff (new York: Nova Science Publishers, 2008), 83–89.

794 Monke, "Farm Credit System," 75–81, 83–89; Robert E. Wright and Richard Sylla, *Genealogy of American Finance*, (New York: Columbia University Press, 2015), 296–99; Jim Monke, "Agricultural Credit: Institutions and Issues," *Agricultural Finance and Credit*, ed. J. M. Bishoff (new York: Nova Science Publishers, 2008), 67–73.

795 Stokes, *Credit to Farmers*, 11, 18–19.

subsidies to American agriculturalists totaled $20 billion. Most groups do not have enough political pull to pull off that much rent-seeking, so they must engage in private self-help, and, as we will see in the next chapter, they will do so whenever their entrepreneurial predilections are not quashed by regulators.[796]

---

796 Dale W. Adams, "Mobilizing Household Savings Through Rural Financial Markets," *Economic Development and Cultural Change* 26, no. 3 (1978): 547–60; Mark R. Rosenzweig, "Savings Behaviour in Low-Income Countries," *Oxford Review of Economic Policy* 17, no. 1 (2001): 40–54; Richard D. Rippe, "No Savings Crisis in the United States," *Business Economics* 34, no. 3 (1999): 47–55; Hoag, *Farm Credit System*, 3, 19; Wright, *Farm Mortgage Financing*, 8; Calvin Iglehart and Grant J. Zsofka, eds. *Farming and Farmland in the United States: Changes and Trends, Agriculture Issues and Policies*, (New York: Nova Science Publishers, 2012); Barry K. Goodwin, *The Economics of Crop Insurance and Disaster Aid*, (New York: AEI Press, 1995); Anon., "Milking Taxpayers: As Crop Prices Fall, Farmers Grow Subsidies Instead," *Economist*, 14 February 2015.

CHAPTER EIGHT

The Self-Help Solution

I see a need for po' peoples – white, black, blue, brown, yellow or pink.

Puerto Rico or anybody. For all po' peoples. I see a great need for

improvement. — Audrey Olsen Faulkner, Marsel A. Heisel, Wendell

Holbrook, and Shirley Geismar, When I was Comin' Up: An Oral

History of Aged Blacks (Hamden, Conn.: Archon Books, 1982), 172.

Economists Stephen Ross and John Yinger argue persuasively that fair-lending enforcement agencies "are incapable of identifying many, if not most, instances of discrimination in loan approval," and offer their own set of diagnostic tools for identifying and extirpating discriminatory behaviors. Their methodology is impressive on paper but it may or may not work in the real world and in any event it is limited to mortgage lending and may well be specific to African-American and Hispanic borrowers. The solution offered here, by contrast, is time-tested and will aid any group in any field of finance.[797]

For all its faults and foibles, America's financial system has done a pretty darn good job of stimulating the nation's economic growth and development. That system is the product of over two centuries of innova-

---

797 Stephen Ross and John Yinger, *The Color of Credit: Mortgage Discrimination, Research Methodology, and Fair-Lending Enforcement,* (Cambridge: The MIT Press, 2002), 313–68.

tion, much of it driven by and for people previously excluded from specific sectors of the system. In fact, the history of the U.S. financial system, from the colonial period to the present, can be told from the perspective of "outsiders" forcing their way in via innovative new financial institutions or products.

Innovative Self-Help: An American Tradition

People are constantly using the tradition of self-help and entrepreneurship to make their lives better. — John Sibley Butler, Entrepreneurship and Self-Help Among Black Americans: A Reconsideration of Race and Economics (Albany: State University of New York Press, 1991), 330.

British Imperial authorities prevented colonists from forming their own joint-stock commercial banks, so the colonists proclaimed their independence and chartered the Bank of North America. After actually winning independence from the Mother Country, Americans formed additional commercial banks in the new nation's major seaport cities. When frontier farmers found it difficult to obtain loans from those institutions, they formed their own commercial banks. When urban artisans and mechanics found it difficult to obtain commercial banks loans, they also established their own banks. (The exact number cannot be stated with certainty because not all banks with names like "Mechanics Bank" or "Mechanics and Tradesmen Bank" were actually owned by, and operated in the interests of, such groups. But internal records show that some were.) In addition, Benjamin Franklin created loan funds dedicated to urban artisans in Philadelphia and Boston.[798]

798 Robert E. Wright, "Banking and Politics in New York, 1784–1829," (Ph.D. Diss., SUNY Buffalo, 1997); Howard Rock, *Artisans of the New Republic: the Tradesmen of New York City in the Age of Jefferson*, (New York: New York University Press, 1984), 166–69; Dan Immergluck, *Credit to the Community: Community Reinvestment and Fair Lending Policy in the United States*, (New York: M. E. Sharpe, 2004), 20; Bruce Yenawine, *Benjamin Franklin and the Invention of Microfinance*, (New York: Routledge, 2010).

After the poor discovered that they were not even welcomed to lodge deposits in most commercial banks, they, with help from philanthropists, formed mutual savings banks. When in some areas not enough mutual banks formed to meet depositor demand, joint-stock savings banks appeared. Depositors in savings banks of both varieties learned that even the wealthiest among them could not borrow from their banks of deposit. Between 1832 and 1897, for example, the Cheshire Provident Institution for Savings of Keene, New Hampshire made only about 12 percent of its loans to people reported to have a net worth of less than $1,000. Most of its loans went to wealthy individuals, insiders, and corporations. Not until after World War II could mutual savings banks legally make personal loans. Moreover, most savings banks capped the size of deposits they would accept so as not to become mutual funds for the wealthy.[799]

Working people of middling means responded by teaming up with each other to create building and loan societies that helped the less-than-wealthy to both save and borrow to build new homes or improve old ones. First established (from British precedents) in Philadelphia in the 1830s, building and loans proliferated, numbering over 5,800 in 1893 with half a billion dollars on loan. Mutual organizations owned by their borrowers and run on shoestring budgets, they offered the best, cheapest mortgage financing available. Building and loans would not lend to those who wanted to borrow for other reasons, however, so consumers created credit unions, non-profit depository institutions for everyday folks interested in affordable, plain vanilla banking.[800]

Originally introduced into the United States, from Germany via Britain and Canada, in late 1908, the credit union movement got off to

---

799 Wright, *Corporation Nation*; Andrew Beveridge, "Local Lending Practice: Borrowers in a Small Northeastern City, 1832–1915," *Journal of Economic History* 45, no. 2 (1985): 393–403; Recommendations, Exam. Com., East Side/Community, Rush Rhees Library.

800 Lendol Calder, *Financing the American Dream: A Cultural History of Consumer Credit*, (Princeton: Princeton University Press, 1999), 66–68; Herman E. Krooss and Martin R. Blyn, *A History of Financial Intermediaries*, (New York: Random House, 1971), 122–24; James M. Ackerman, "Interest Rates and the Law: A History of Usury," *Arizona State Law Journal* (1981): 91–92.

a slow start because each required a state charter and state regulators prevented them from growing large by restricting their membership to small, tightly defined groups. By 1930, 1,000 or so had formed in 32 states. The movement received a boost in 1934, when the federal government began to charter credit unions as well. By the start of 1940, 2.5 million Americans were members of some 8,700 credit unions.[801] Two decades later, over 11 million Americans were members of almost 20,000 credit unions nationwide. Why membership did not grow even more quickly is unclear. "Wherever possible," Hillel Black enjoined his readers in 1961, "join or start a credit union," which he explained was "simply a group of people who save their money together and make loans to each other at low interest rates." Consumer loans required only a signature and mortgages were also available. Default rates were low, about 0.5 percent, though their loan officers accepted "risks" that no banker would dare touch, because borrowers realized that default would hurt their friends, neighbors, and co-workers.[802]

Some of the remaining demand for individual consumer banking was supplied by so-called Morris Plan banks, for-profit enterprises that did hundreds of millions of dollars of business annually by the 1930s. They lent from $50 to $5,000 on the basis of character, income, and co-signers. The institutions were named after Arthur J. Morris, the son of a North Carolina storekeeper who became a financial innovator par excellence. It was Morris who sold the first car "on time" in 1910 and who organized the first credit life insurance company in 1917. He developed his "industrial" bank for the working poor in 1912 after discovering, while working in a law office, that banks did not lend to poor people, even if they had good jobs. "I began to investigate several of these applicants [for loans from the attorney] and found them to have the human need for money.

---

801 Matthew Cropp, "The Origins of US Credit Unions," *Financial History* (Spring 2014): 24–27; Earl S. Sparks, *History and Theory of Agricultural Credit in the United States*, (New York: Thomas Y. Crowell Co., 1932), 362–67; Calder, *Financing*, 281; Rowena Olegario, *The Engine of Enterprise: Credit in America*, (Cambridge: Harvard University Press, 2016), 130.

802 Hillel Black, *Buy Now, Pay Later*, (New York: William Morrow and Company, 1961), 225–27.

They held steady jobs with fair earning power and were persons of good character." So he co-signed their loans while thinking of ways to subvert the usury laws that the bankers all cited as the major barrier preventing their entry into the small loan market. The innovative work around he developed was an investment certificate that the borrower purchased in order to cancel the principal of his or her loan. Eventually, some 170 Morris Plan banks lent $90 billion to millions of the working poor.[803]

Credit unions and "remedial loan societies" were part of a coordinated response to loan sharking and other predatory lending practices identified by the Russell Sage Foundation early in the twentieth century. The solution was a model bill that allowed licensed lenders to charge higher rates of interest for small loans. By 1945, with more than 90 per cent of the population covered by small-loan laws, the Russell Sage Foundation moved on to other areas of concern. (Though it has occasionally circled back, as with its publication of John Caskey's *Fringe Banking* in 1994.)[804]

When Westerner mortgagors discovered that Easterner mortgagees were discriminating against them by charging interest rates greater than the higher default rate on Western mortgages warranted, they responded in a variety of ways, most importantly here by establishing their own mortgage companies.[805]

Self-help also reached Wall Street. When in the mid-nineteenth century brokers found it difficult to join the "Old Board," the original New York Stock Exchange, they formed the "New Board" and encouraged wider membership. In addition to charging a $400 entrance fee for one of its "seats," the Old Board members voted on whether to accept new

---

803 Olegario, *Engine of Enterprise*, 128–29; Black, *Buy Now*, 164–68.

804 Elisabeth Anderson, "Experts, Ideas, and Policy Change: The Russell Sage Foundation and Small Loan Reform, 1909–1941," *Theory and Society* 37, 3 (June 2008): 271–72, 289; Black, *Buy Now*, 163–64; John P. Caskey, *Fringe Banking: Check-Cashing Outlets, Pawnshops, and the Poor,* (New York: Russell Sage Foundation, 1994).

805 Kenneth Snowden, "Mortgage Rates and American Capital Market Development in the Late Nineteenth Century," *Journal of Economic History* 47, 3 (September 1987): 671–91; D. M. Frederiksen, "Mortgage Banking in America," *Journal of Political Economy* 2, 2 (March 1894), 207.

members. Only three vetoes disqualified ("blackballed") an applicant so
there were "several applicants refused for one admitted." Because the bal-
lots were secret, applicants were "as likely to be *refused* from private pique
or prejudice as anything else." The New Board charged only $25 per seat
and beyond that required only the payment of all obligations that fell due
to other members in the course of trading. But often more business was
"done in the open air," i.e., outside both boards and, in fair weather, literally outside where "all other operators and interested persons, assemble
promiscuously at the corner of Wall and Hanover streets." On the curb,
"offers to sell or buy are made by any and every one, as his inclination
may prompt."[806]

A similar story can be told about both major parts of the insurance
sector. When joint-stock fire insurers appeared to discriminate against
farmers and factory owners alike, they formed their own mutual fire and
wind storm insurers.[807] In many cases, regulations constrained companies
from writing policies covering new risks. In other instances, insurers had
not developed methods for determining rational premiums for new risk
types. As a result, specialized firms arose to underwrite new types of risks
or to insure new types of businesses. Originally, fire insurance covered
"every possible loss by fire" but insurers over time began to "specify particular losses by fire for which they would not be answerable."[808] New
companies arose to fill the void. When the new companies took the
mutual form, as most did, they were called "class mutuals" because they
underwrote only one or a few classes of risks, including those peculiar to
bakers, canners, factories, florists, millers, and manufacturers.[809]

806 A Reformed Stock Gambler, *Stocks and Stock-Jobbing in Wall-Street, with Sketches of the Brokers, and Fancy Stocks*, (New York: New-York Publishing Company, 1848), 8.

807 Sara E. Wermiel, *The Fireproof Building: Technology and Public Safety in the Nineteenth-Century American City*, (Baltimore: Johns Hopkins University Press, 2000), 104–37.

808 Joseph B. Ecclesine, *A Compendium of the Laws and Decisions Relating to Mobs, Riots, Invasion, Civil Commotion, Insurrection, &c., as Affecting Fire Insurance*, (New York: Grierson and Ecclesine, 1863), 96.

809 John E. Pierce, *Development of Comprehensive Insurance for the Household*, (Homewood, Ill.: Richard D. Irwin, 1958).

New England textile mill owners, for example, became frustrated when fire insurers would not rate their mills by assigning lower premiums to safer ones. In the mid-1830s mill owner Zachariah Allen responded by establishing a mutual fire insurance company that specialized in insuring textile mills. Allen kept rates low by vigorously screening and monitoring policyholders to ensure that they minimized the risk of loss. In the 1850s, mill mutuals proliferated and cooperated closely with each other, reinsuring by sharing the risks posed by their largest policyholders. In addition to charging lower initial premiums than stock insurers, mutuals returned premiums in the form of dividends when losses fell below expectations. That induced mill owners to welcome inspections and to consider carefully the safety advice their insurers dispensed. Urged on by the lure of lower net premiums, mill owners installed fire hoses, sprinklers, firefighting towers and reservoirs, and adopted the fire-resistant architectural techniques of mutual mill insurance president Edward Atkinson. More cost effective than "fireproof" construction based on the British iron and brick arch system, Atkinson's "slow-burning" construction system sought via fire-resistant materials and architectural improvements to slow the progress of a fire until workers could effectively respond to the blaze. Mill mutuals also engaged in fire prevention research, operating America's only fire prevention research lab until the 1890s.[810]

Other specialized companies also arose to underwrite new risks that fire insurers refused. The risks associated with steam boiler explosions, for example, were long covered by specialized companies. Similarly, farmers' fire insurance mutuals arose in the 1820s to insure farm buildings and their contents. By 1920 there were almost 2,000 such companies in operation throughout the United States, with the largest concentrations in the Northeast and Midwest. The reluctance of most fire insurers, including farmers' mutuals, to cover wind damage spurred the creation of yet other mutual insurance companies that specialized in underwriting wind damage risks. From the first such company, formed in 1884, the industry

810 F. C. Oviatt, "Historical Study of Fire Insurance in the United States," *Annals of the Academy of Political and Social Science* 26 (1905):155–78; Wermiel, *Fireproof Building*.

grew to over three score companies by 1920. By the end of 1935, farmers' mutual windstorm-insurance companies numbered 65 and had $2.74 billion insurance in force in 13 states. Like the mill mutuals, they owed their success to some extent to their loss prevention programs. Nothing could stop claims arising from powerful tornadoes but the mutuals sought to reduce the losses from less severe storms by refusing insurance on dilapidated or rickety buildings, encouraging the erection of buildings of wind-resistant construction, insisting upon proper bracing of lightly constructed buildings, requiring timely repair of damaged buildings, and by salvaging partially damaged buildings and personal property.[811]

Similarly, almost every ethnic group formed their own life insurance companies, as names like Germania and Hibernia attest. Jews, Catholics, Mormons, and members of other religious groups did likewise. They also formed their own commercial banks, mutual savings banks, building and loans, credit unions, and even investment banks.[812]

For the poorest of the poor emerged industrial life insurance. For pennies a week, tens of millions of American families received modest protection from the death of a breadwinner or other family member, usually enough to ensure a proper burial. Industrial policies were not as flexible as standard policies, largely due to government regulations forbidding policy loans and assignments. Other restrictions were put in place by the companies themselves to reduce adverse selection. Most companies, for example, would not insure dependents unless the main breadwinner was already insured. Dollar for dollar, industrial insurance was expensive

---

811 Gordon Bubolz, *Farmers'-Mutual Windstorm-Insurance Companies*, (Washington, DC: Farm Credit Administration, 1938); W. F. Moore, "Liability Insurance," *Annals of the American Academy of Political and Social Science* 26 (1905): 319–39; Robin Pearson, "Insurance: Historical Overview," in *The Oxford Encyclopedia of Economic History*, ed. Joel Mokyr (2003); Pierce, *Development of Comprehensive Insurance*; Victor N. Valgren, *Farmers' Mutual Fire Insurance in the United States*, (Chicago: Chicago University Press, 1924).

812 Anita Rapone, *The Guardian Life Insurance Company, 1860–1920: A History of a German-American Enterprise*, (New York: New York University Press, 1987); Robert E. Wright and Richard Sylla, *Genealogy of American Finance*, (New York: Columbia University Press, 2015); Susie Pak, *Gentlemen Bankers: The World of J. P. Morgan*, (Cambridge: Harvard University Press, 2013); Cropp, "Origins."

compared to ordinary whole life because mortality rates among the poor were higher and the costs of collection were greater. Scale economies were important to keep costs as low as possible so relatively few insurers wrote industrial life and some smaller ones that tried, like Germania (now Guardian), exited quickly. Industrial insurance remained a fixture of life in heavy industrial areas and the South until after the middle of the twentieth-century, when it was largely supplanted by group plans.[813]

Numerous assessment and fraternal life insurance associations also appeared in the nineteenth century. The former failed, largely for economic reasons. As their initial membership aged, assessments became frequent and large, inducing members to withdraw and making it difficult to attract new ones. By contrast, fraternal insurance companies that offered mostly industrial-style insurance on a mutual basis competed successfully against large corporate rivals, mostly due to their informational and associational advantages and their comparatively low operating and claims costs. Fraternals faded only after governments began to regulate them closely during the Great Depression. In some states, like Massachusetts and New York, savings banks also began offering life insurance policies of modest size.[814]

---

813 Malvin E. Davis, *Industrial Life Insurance in the United States*, (New York: McGraw-Hill Book Company, 1944); Marquis James, *The Metropolitan Life: A Study in Business Growth*, (New York: Viking, 1947); Rapone, *Guardian*; Robert E. Wright and George David Smith, *Mutually Beneficial: The Guardian and Life Insurance in America*, (New York: New York University Press, 2004); James Oates, *Business and Social Change: Life Insurance Looks to the Future*, (McGraw-Hill Book Company: New York, 1968), 18.

814 Miles Dawson, "Fraternal Life Insurance," *Annals of the American Academy of Political and Social Science* 26 (1905):128–36; Loftin Graham and Xiaoying Xie, "The United States Insurance Market: Characteristics and Trends," in *Handbook of International Insurance: Between Global Dynamics and Local Contingencies*, ed. J. David Cummins and Bertrand Venard (New York: Springer, 2007); William G. Lehrman, "Diversity in Decline: Institutional Environment and Organizational Failure in the American Life Insurance Industry," *Social Forces* 73 (1994):605–35; Sharon Ann Murphy, "Life Insurance in the United States through World War I," in *EH.Net Encyclopedia*, ed. Robert Whaples (2002); George Zanjani, "The Rise and Fall of the Fraternal Life Insurer: Law and Finance in U.S. Life Insurance, 1870–1920," Working paper, 2003; How Is Life Insurance Business Likened to Savings Bank Business?, Documents: Life Insurance, Community, Rush Rhees Library.

Despite the proliferation of savings banks, many poorer folks found it difficult to save enough to see themselves or their families through periods of illness. For a variety of complex reasons, employers and governments were slow to help.[815] Workers took matters into their own hands, informally by "passing the hat" to help sick co-workers, and formally by forming mutual insurance, friendly associations, or employee benefit associations that provided "modest but nonetheless welcome relief in cases of disability arising from accident or sickness."[816]

Between 1880 and 1920, from one quarter to one half of all industrial workers had some form of sickness coverage, mostly underwritten by industrial sickness funds like mutual benefit associations and labor union-sponsored plans. Fraternal associations that formed in the late nineteenth century along class, caste, gender, and occupational lines supplemented those plans.[817]

Unlike commercial insurers, which provided top-shelf benefits at commensurate prices, fraternals and industrial sickness funds provided modest benefits at low cost. Adverse selection and administrative costs were low because, rather than paying agents and staffers, members recruited new members and handled paperwork themselves. They also minimized cheating by regularly visiting sick members to verify illness while providing comforting non-monetary assistance. Few members attempted malfeasance because they knew who they were stealing from, their friends, neighbors, and co-workers. Precisely because they were

---

815 Herb Emery, "Fraternal Sickness Insurance," in *EH.Net Encyclopedia*, ed. Robert Whaples. (2001); Beatrix Hoffman, *The Wages of Sickness: The Politics of Health Insurance in Progressive America*, (Chapel Hill: University of North Carolina Press, 2001); Gerald Morgan, *Public Relief of Sickness*, (New York: Macmillan Company, 1922); David Moss, *When All Else Fails: Government as the Ultimate Risk Manager*, (Cambridge: Harvard University Press, 2002); John E. Murray, *Origins of American Health Insurance: A History of Industrial Sickness Funds*, (New Haven: Yale University Press, 2007); I. M. Rubinow, *Standards of Health Insurance*, (New York: Henry Holt and Co., 1916).

816 Anon., *The Present Status of Mutual Benefit Associations*, (New York: National Industrial Conference Board, 1931), v.

817 Murray, *Origins*; Robert Whaples and David Buffum, "Fraternalism, Paternalism, the Family, and the Market: Insurance a Century Ago," *Social Science History* 15, no. 1 (1991): 97–122.

organized into local lodges, however, fraternals could not adequately diversify their risks, subjecting themselves to financial distress. Although few associations exited for financial reasons, government regulators increasingly scrutinized their activities, thus increasing their capital and regulatory costs. Increased competition from commercial insurers, especially their burgeoning group health lines, government programs, union plans, and mutual benefit associations sealed their fate. Hundreds of local labor unions and scores of nationals also offered medical reimbursement and/or sick pay insurance. In 1916, about one quarter of unionized workers were covered by union healthcare plans.[818]

Non-union workers also often formed industrial sickness or mutual benefit associations to relieve themselves of the uncertainties, unfairness, and free riding associated with informal "hat" assessments. When the worker associations proved their value in tangible terms like reduced worker turnover, management reciprocated by providing them with advice, administrative help, and, to widely varying degrees, money, transforming them by degrees into so-called establishment funds. Like their workers, managers preferred making a single contribution to an association "rather than to respond to a series of small solicitations" for aid from employees.[819] By the Great Depression, hundreds of mutual benefit associations and establishment funds, most in companies with 100 or more employees, provided benefits to millions of employee-members. As mutual concerns, they paid more liberally in case of real hardship than commercial insurers did. The associations also believed they could keep costs lower than insurance companies could because they had better information with which to detect "attempted malingering or fraud."[820] With death benefits, however, where fraud was much less of an issue, industrial life and, beginning circa 1912, group insurance ruled, with mutual benefit associations rarely providing more than basic burial

---

818 Emery, "Fraternal Sickness Insurance"; Graham and Xie, "United States Insurance Market"; Hoffman, *Wages of Sickness*; Morgan, *Public Relief*; Murray, *Origins*.

819 Anon., *Mutual Benefit*, 3.

820 Anon., *Mutual Benefit*, 2.

coverage averaging $150. Commercial insurers also dominated the sale of annuities and group annuities used to fund company pension plans.[821]

Success in health insurance required mitigating adverse selection by signing up as many workers as possible or denying coverage to the riskiest workers, those over a certain age or with pre-existing health problems as determined by physical examination. Compulsion was rarely resorted to, even in establishment funds, because it was illegal in some jurisdictions, because it destroyed workers' morale and their incentive to minimize free riding, and because insurers had other techniques to reduce asymmetric information. Setting benefit levels just right, not so low as to be of little aid but also not so high as to make the coverage unaffordable to all but malingerers, ensured wide participation while discouraging shirking. Best practice was to set the sickness benefit at one-half to two-thirds of full pay. To reduce adverse selection, new employees could not receive benefits, usually for the first month, and to discourage shirking benefits generally ceased after 13 weeks. To further discourage cheating, many associations withheld the first week of benefits in case of sickness, which was relatively easy to fake, but not in case of accident. They also hired their own doctors rather than relying on those hired by the workers themselves, who tended to be more sympathetic to the workers' woes, real or otherwise.[822]

Recognition that medical care reduced the length of disability increasingly drew industrial sickness funds into providing medical benefits too, including well visits, vaccinations, inoculations, and other prophylactic services. Here, too, commercial life insurers offered a group product that had difficulty competing on a cost-benefit basis due to the superior information available to the associations. Mutual aid societies continued to thrive into the 1920s but faded during the 1930s, due largely to improvements in commercial insurers' group health insurance actuarial

---

821 Anon., *Mutual Benefit*; Graham and Xie, "United States Insurance Market"; Murray, *Origins*.

822 Anon., *Mutual Benefit*; Murray, *Origins*.

tables and the emergence of sick leave, a fringe benefit paid directly by employers to sick workers.[823]

Each of the financial innovations described above was accompanied by a do-gooder or crusade-like mentality. The first commercial bankers, like Thomas Willing and Alexander Hamilton, believed they were cementing the new nation's independence from Britain. Savings bankers and building and loan managers thought they were saving the poor from the wolves of want, the bites of sharks, and the stings of slumlords. Credit union leaders saved their members from high cost bankers and predatory lenders. "No group has impressed me as much as those associated with the credit union movement," wrote Hillel Black in 1961. "These are selfless individuals with one purpose – helping people help each other."[824] Similarly, the proponents of every new stock market and insurer claimed to be saving some group or another from the oppression of some other group. Savings banks, for example, called their life insurance policies an integral "part of a complete thrift program."[825] Such proclamations may sound like promotional hot air, but in the end who are we to judge who truly felt the sting of exclusion, discrimination, or predation and who was merely drumming up business?

One thing is clear, though. Every group was in it for themselves as most excluded or discriminated against outsiders. The Boston Workingmen's Loan Association, for example, would "not loan to persons who frequently change their residence and are of disreputable character or to certain nationalities among immigrants, races that have not yet evolved a sense of honor, and to persons who have recently become residents of the

823 Anon., *Mutual Benefit*; Kenneth J. Meier, *The Political Economy of Regulation: The Case of Insurance*, (Albany: State University of New York Press, 1988); Morgan, *Public Relief*; Murray, *Origins*; Noel Whiteside, "Insurance: Health and Accident," in *The Oxford Encyclopedia of Economic History*, ed. Joel Mokyr (2003).

824 Black, *Buy Now*, 225.

825 How Is Life Insurance Business Likened to Savings Bank Business?, Documents: Life Insurance, Community, Rush Rhees Library.

city."[826] So every group had to form their own institutions. And, for the most part, they did.

***

Women, Indians, and African-Americans Help Themselves

One of the best hopes for the Negro in America is the growing co-oper-ative movement through which Negroes, and others, can organize their economic resources to help themselves. — Edwin Embree, Brown Americans: The Story of a Tenth of the Nation (New York: Viking Press, 1943), 132.

Like slaves and other oppressed persons, those discriminated against in the financial system fought back whenever and however they best could. Often, that entailed forming their own institutions. Sometimes, relatively little is known of their efforts. Women, for example, formed their own mining stock exchange in San Francisco in the late nineteenth century but little is known about it other than it was short-lived. Likewise, little is known about the informal lending pools that Chinese, Japanese, West Indian, and members of other ethnic groups used to start small businesses and finance homes. Other times, tales of resistance are well-documented and occasionally as inspiring as the slave or Civil Rights narratives with which they are intertwined.[827]

Born in Civil War Richmond to an ex-slave mother and a white abolitionist father, Maggie Walker was the first African-American woman to incorporate a bank. First a laundress, then a teacher, Walker early in life joined a black fraternal society, the Independent Order of the Sons and Daughters of St. Luke. She also worked part-time for an insurance company that insured black women. In 1899, she was elected the Right

---

826 As quoted in Olegario, *Engine of Enterprise*, 118–19.

827 Sheri J. Caplan, *Petticoats and Pinstripes: Portraits of Women in Wall Street's History*, (Denver: Praeger, 2013), 31; John Sibley Butler, *Entrepreneurship and Self-Help Among Black Americans: A Reconsideration of Race and Economics*, (Albany: State University of New York Press, 1991), 25–26.

Worthy Grand Secretary of St. Luke's, where she soon engineered a turnaround in its fortunes. By 1901, Walker had become convinced that African-Americans needed a bank of their own. "Let us put our moneys together; let us use our moneys; let us put our money out at usury among ourselves, and reap the benefit ourselves," she prayed in one speech. Tutored by the managers of the white-owned Merchants' National Bank of Richmond, Walker learned the banking business and raised capital. In July 1903, the St. Luke Penny Savings Bank was born with Walker as the first president. Press coverage was favorable and she was invited to join the Virginia Bankers' Association. By 1919, the bank, rechristened St. Luke Bank and Trust Company in 1910, had almost $400,000 on deposit and loans spread throughout Richmond's African-American community. By 1929, it was the oldest active black-owned bank in the country and had assets of almost half a million. During the Depression, Walker's bank consolidated with two struggling African-American banks to prevent their failure. She served as chairperson of the new entity until her death in December 1934. Fittingly, Walker's bank was purchased in 2005 by Adams National Bank, the first national bank owned and led by women. Its identity as a bank for minorities, however, was lost after Adams merged with Premier Financial Bancorp in 2010.[828]

The first state banks to specialize in lending to women formed around the time of the Great War in big cities like New York, Chicago, Kansas City, and Dallas, as well as in rural Wyoming, Colorado, Iowa, and Kansas. One of those pioneers was the First Woman's Bank of Tennessee, established in 1919 by Brenda Runyon. Shortly after, a savings and loan run entirely by women and 90 percent female-owned was established in the Midwest.[829]

Women also joined the credit union movement. By 1978, 17 female-controlled credit unions were in operation, along with 4 savings and loans

828 Arnett G. Lindsay, "The Negro in Banking," *Journal of Negro History* 14, 2 (April 1929), 177–79; Caplan, *Petticoats and Pinstripes*, 55–64.

829 Edith Sparks, *Capital Intentions: Female Proprietors in San Francisco, 1850–1920*, (Chapel Hill: University of North Carolina Press, 2006), 171; Caplan, *Petticoats and Pinstripes*, 87, 90.

and 7 commercial banks.[830] One of those commercial banks had been established the year before by Mary Roebling, erstwhile head of Trenton Trust (discussed in Chapter 6). The goal of her Women's Bank was "to translate the economic power of our women into a more productive and profitable resource for the whole community," by ensuring that women who deserved loans received them. Many of the bank's 50 co-founders believed that they had been denied credit unfairly and sought redress. The bank, which granted credit to worthy men as well, opened the following year and by 1981 had deposits in excess of $21 million.[831] Like other minority-owned financial institutions, female banks often found it difficult to raise outside capital, largely because female investors, of which there were many as detailed in Chapter 6, did not actively seek out female-owned companies. A 1978 Treasury study, for example, found "no evidence ... of women-owned wealth in businesses owned by other women, e.g., through mechanisms such as capital pools for investment."[832]

That was despite the fact that women have also been active fighting discrimination on the securities side of the financial system. In 1947, Wilma Soss asked U.S. Steel to appoint a female director. Rudely rebuffed, she responded by founding the Federation of Women Shareholders in American Business, which accumulated the proxies of female shareholders into a block that Soss used to verbally bludgeon corporate executives who dared oppose liberal reforms until her death in 1986 at age 86. According to New York Times report Michael Norman, Soss was "persistent, direct and unflinching. Yet," he admitted, "she earned the respect of many of the executives she challenged."[833]

An important early female broker, Muriel Siebert, got her big break at Bache & Co. by lying about having completed college, not by disguising her gender. Truth was, she dropped out after her father was diag-

---

830 Treasury Department Study Team, *Credit and Capital Formation: A Report to the President's Interagency Task Force on Women Business Owners*, (April 1978), 54.

831 Caplan, *Petticoats and Pinstripes*, 120.

832 Treasury Department Study Team, *Credit and Capital Formation*, 11.

833 Caplan, *Petticoats and Pinstripes*, 172; Michael Norman, "Wilma Porter Soss, 86, A Gadfly at Stock Meetings of Companies," *New York Times*, 16 October 1986.

nosed with cancer and she never went back. After a three-year ordeal, her father died and Siebert moved to New York in search of a change. Rejected by the United Nations and Merrill Lynch because she lacked a degree, not because she was a woman, Siebert lied during her Bache interview and soon was analyzing the aviation and motion picture industries in its research department. Those assignments proved fortuitous for Siebert, who foresaw the implications of televised movies and jet engines before others did. She managed to jump to Shields & Co. in 1958, where she obtained her license to sell stocks, where gender still mattered more than qualifications, by giving her name on her résumé as "M. Siebert."

A succession of jobs followed, as did a rapidly escalating portfolio of her own. In 1967, after concluding that existing firms were too stodgy to allow a woman to rise to prominence, Siebert decided to invest some of her investment earnings in an NYSE seat. The hitherto all-male club looked for legal ways of denying her application, which told the truth about her limited college credentials, but finding none accepted her just after Christmas. Despite the stunning success of Muriel Siebert & Co., which earned nearly $1 million in commissions its first year, Siebert remained the sole female in the 1,365-member organization for almost a decade, except for a two-month period when Jane R. Larkin also held a seat.

After the 1975 deregulation of fixed commissions, Siebert repositioned her company as a deep discount brokerage. In 1977, she placed it into a blind trust so she could become New York's Superintendent of Banking. No state bank failed during her tenure because she forced reorganizations and mergers at the first signs of real trouble. After her stint, she returned to find her company a wreck. Rather than sell, she revivified it by embracing investment banking and new technologies like telephone stock quotations and online trading platforms. While the company catered to women with its Siebert Women's Financial Network, it also accepted male clients. "We're not sexist," Siebert noted in an interview.[834]

834 Caplan, *Petticoats and Pinstripes*, 135–43.

After two of Maria Fiorini Ramirez's employers failed, she started her own eponymous global advisory and money management firm. Born in Italy but raised and educated in the U.S., Ramirez started at American Express in 1967, which gave her tremendous international experience and prepped her for the globalization of finance that took place in the 1970s and 1980s. After achieving success at Merrill Lynch, she moved on to A.G. Becker Paribas, which quickly failed, and then Drexel Burnham Lambert, which failed after a spectacular run that propelled the company to the top of the investment banking industry. "That's when I decided to start my own firm," she later recalled. "I can do this on my own."[835]

When Linda Bradford Raschke smacked into Wall Street's "glass ceiling," pretty much before her career even started, she too set off on her own, first as an independent trader backed by a private investor, and then by forming her own "group" embossed with just her initials. A top futures market trader, perhaps once the very best in the world, her *Street Smarts* remains one of the few books penned by a female trader. Her funds were so successful that she stopped accepting new money in her pools and managed accounts. Importantly, she also limited them so she could work out of her suburban New Jersey home more often, where her dogs, children, and husband, an ex-trader, were often underfoot. Many other women, including Robin Wiessmann, who founded the investment bank Artemis Capital Group, have also fought discrimination by going into business for themselves.[836]

Indians have attempted self-help as well. On the Pine Ridge Reservation, women formed a peer lending group designed to aid members who needed short-term access to cash on reasonable terms when their immediate friends and family could not help out. Informal pawning is also common but borrowers do not always redeem their chattels or repay their peer groups. Loans of food or other necessities are common on many reservations, especially within kin groups. On the Rosebud Reservation, the

835 Sue Herera, *Women of the Street*, (New York: John Wiley & Sons, 1997), 127–37.

836 Herera, *Women*, 163–81; Melissa S. Fisher, *Wall Street Women*, (Durham: Duke University Press, 2012), 75.

local Catholic mission will lend money to help people start businesses but it imposes social and financial strings that many Lakota find too onerous. "Sometimes I think the Father thinks this is his project," complained one borrower.[837]

In 1986, a private fund called the Lakota Fund (LF) became the first Native Community Development Financial Institution (NCDFI). In its first two decades it made over $1 million in loans to over 300 tribal members, many of whom also received business training from LF. By 2008, it had made $4.1 million in loans and trained some 3,600 aspiring or active entrepreneurs. A recent study showed econometrically that the LF has significantly increased small business activity and real per capita income on the Pine Ridge Reservation. Sicangu Enterprise Fund tried but failed to replicate its success on the Rosebud Reservation but the Four Bands Community Fund has been helping small business on the Cheyenne River Sioux Reservation for over a decade now and by 2006 had made 53 loans totaling $140,000.[838]

Several other tribes, including the Hupa, Penobscot, and Hopi, also formed their own formal lending organizations. In fact, community development financial institutions (CDFIs) blossomed in the 1990s, especially after regulators counted loans to CDFIs toward banks' CRA requirements. By 2008, CDFIs throughout the nation had $2.7 billion in outstanding loans, only 0.3 percent of which was in default, but only a

---

837 Kathleen Ann Pickering, *Lakota Culture, World Economy*, (Lincoln: University of Nebraska Press, 2000), 30, 33, 70–71; Tressa Berman, "'All We Needed Was Our Gardens': Women's Work and Welfare Reform in the Reservation Economy," in *Native Pathways: American Indian Culture and Economic Development*, ed. Brian Hosmer and Colleen O'Neill (Boulder: University Press of Colorado, 2004), 146–47.

838 Pickering, *Lakota Culture*, 75–76; Kyle Smith, *Predatory Lending in Native American Communities* (Fredericksburg, Va.: First Nations Development Institute, 2003), 27; David Benson, Aaron Lies, Albert Okunade, Phanindra Wunnava, "Economic Impact of a Private Sector Micro-Financing Scheme in South Dakota," *Small Business Economics* 36 (2011): 157–68; Robert J. Miller, *Reservation "Capitalism": Economic Development in Indian Country*, (Denver: ABC-CLIO, 2012), 129; Robert Miller, "Indian Entrepreneurship," in *Unlocking the Wealth of Indian Nations*, ed. Terry Anderson (New York: Lexington Books, 2016), 252–53; Jennifer Malkin and Johnnie Aseron, *Native Entrepreneurship in South Dakota: A Deeper Look* (CFED, December 2006), 64.

small portion of that was loaned out to Indian entrepreneurs. As recently as 1999, only two NCDFIs were in operation. That number had grown to 49 by 2008 but most were small and, obviously, new and inexperienced and only 21 were owned by tribes. Since then, the number of NCDFIs has continued to grow across Indian Country. In 2008, several individual Indians purchased a bank, possibly the first Indian-owned bank in the country, on the Turtle Mountain Reservation in North Dakota. Pine Ridge added a mortgage lender in 2004 and its own credit union, Lakota Federal (LFCU), in 2012. In November 2016, exactly four years after its opening, LFCU had 1,856 members with $3.5 million on deposit and had made 351 loans worth $2.2 million.[839]

Owned by 26 tribes, the Denver-based Native American Bank is one of the largest NCDFIs. Another, Blackfeet National Bank, helped about 200 Indian businesses in its first years of operation. The most successful NCDFIs, like South Dakota's Lakota Fund and the Seneca Nation of Indians Economic Development Company in upstate New York, provide pragmatic financial literacy and business training while also building on native concepts like generosity (wawokiye, or helping without expecting a return) and wisdom.[840]

African-Americans have also fought discriminatory practices by forming and running their own financial institutions. As noted above, black men had run their own unincorporated private banks since the 1830s. Drawing on African precedents, free blacks in the antebellum North and South shut out of jobs, banks, and insurance companies formed numerous benevolent and mutual benefit societies. For a small weekly sum, free blacks received payments when they became unemployed or ill or when a loved one passed on. The Free African Society, formed in Philadelphia in 1778, was the first such organization. Black

---

839 Miller, "Indian Entrepreneurship," 248, 256. http://lakotafcu.org/about/about-lfcu/ Accessed 13 November 2016.

840 Miller, Reservation "Capitalism,", 149; Sandy Gerber, "Native CDFIs Work Toward a New Economic Reality in South Dakota," Federal Reserve Bank of Minneapolis Community Dividend (2008), 1, 6, 8; Naomi Schaefer Riley, The New Trail of Tears: How Washington Is Destroying American Indians, (New York: Encounter Books, 2016), 47.

women formed their own societies but a few, like the Union Bond Society of New Orleans, enrolled both genders. The number of such societies was impressive. Philadelphia alone was home to almost a dozen by 1811, more than 50 in 1832, 119 in 1838, and 106 in 1849. About half the free black population of that city reported being a member of at least one of the societies by 1849.[841]

Baltimore was another major center of African-American mutual aid societies. Over two dozen formed before the Civil War and by 1890 Charm City was home to more African-American beneficial societies than any other city in the nation, with the possible exception of New York. Black fraternals and secret societies, including the Odd Fellows, Masons, the Black Knights of Pythias, the Knights and Daughters of Tabor, and hundreds of smaller organizations maintained large membership rolls well into the twentieth century.[842]

In the late antebellum period, several calls for a black-owned chartered bank were made but before the war broke out only a single black-owned savings institution formed, in California in 1859. Out of the Civil War, as we learned in Chapter 7, came a government-sponsored savings bank that whites looted before turning over to African-Americans. The failure of that so-called Freedman's Bank dampened enthusiasm for black-owned banks until 1888, when the Capitol Savings Bank of Washington, D.C. opened. In 16 years of independent existence, this black-owned and run commercial bank was able to weather several financial panics while increasing its capital from $6,000 to $50,000. It failed in 1904, however, due to some bad loans and insufficient internal controls.[843]

841 Lindsay, "The Negro in Banking," 156–57; Butler, Entrepreneurship and Self-Help, 40–41; Immergluck, Credit to the Community, 54–55; Leonard P. Curry, The Free Black in Urban America, 1800–1850: The Shadow of the Dream, (Chicago: University of Chicago Press, 1981), 196–215.

842 Butler, Entrepreneurship and Self-Help, 99–109; Audrey Olsen Faulkner, Marsel A. Heisel, Wendell Holbrook, and Shirley Geismar, When I was Comin' Up: An Oral History of Aged Blacks, (Hamden, Conn.: Archon Books, 1982), 213; Carole Merritt, The Herndons: An Atlanta Family, (Athens, Ga.: University of Georgia Press, 2002), 77.

843 Rhoda Golden Freeman, The Free Negro in New York City in the Era Before the Civil War, (New York: Garland Publishing, 1994), 219; Juliet E. K. Walker, The History of Black

In 1890, the Alabama Penny Savings Bank of Birmingham began operations. More than 10,000 people, mostly African-Americans, made deposits in the institution, which eventually established branches in Montgomery, Selma, and Anniston. It failed during a Christmas run in 1915 after a bad merger, the death of the president, and an unfortunate rumor.[844]

Due to those and other failures, several black fraternal organizations entered savings banking in the two decades before 1900. Most failed but some only after gaining reputations as the "Gibraltar of Negro Business," and so forth, because of their initially strong, conservative management. Eventual bankruptcy does not mean that those banks were failures in the broader sense as the average bank in that era lasted only a quarter of a century. Many black-owned banks provided tens of thousands of depositors and borrowers with valuable services for years or decades before they were forced to wind up business or sell themselves to larger or stronger institutions.[845]

Between 1900 and the Great Depression, African-Americans formed an additional 88 commercial and savings banks from Alabama to Illinois and Florida to Massachusetts. All told, 134 black-owned banks formed before the early 1930s, most in the South. Several, including the Douglass National Bank, the largest black-owned bank in the nation with $2 million in assets, even joined the Federal Reserve System. Providing banking services for blacks was considered so lucrative that the Rockefellers established the Dunbar National Bank in New York to cater to them. They employed blacks in many positions throughout the rank and file, from tellers to typists, and even placed three African-Americans on its board. It soon had assets of almost $2 million and counted numerous

---

Business in America: Capitalism, Race, Entrepreneurship, 2nd ed., Vol. 1 (Chapel Hill: University of North Carolina Press, 2009), 115–17; Abram L. Harris, The Negro as Capitalist: A Study of Banking and Business Among American Negroes, (New York: American Academy of Political and Social Science, 1936), 23, 42–46; Butler, Entrepreneurship and Self-Help, 126; Immergluck, Credit to the Community, 55, 88; Lindsay, "The Negro in Banking," 169–70.

844 Lindsay, "The Negro in Banking," 170–72.

845 Lindsay, "The Negro in Banking," 172–87.

Euroamericans amongst its depositors [846] Most African-American controlled banks, however, failed or merged before the Depression. The great
bank runs of the early 1930s terminated most of those that remained.
Jesse Binga's Binga State Bank, which had lent widely on mortgages to
black churches and fraternal orders in Chicago, went down in 1930 after
failing to obtain an emergency loan from white bankers, most of whose
banks soon failed too. American Mutual Savings Bank of Louisville had to
merge with First Standard Bank in 1932 but the combined entity collapsed
during the 1933 runs anyway. The Metropolitan Bank and Trust of Norfolk, Virginia, also succumbed in 1933 as many of its customers lost their
jobs. Even Rockefeller's Dunbar National was forced to close, in 1936.
Several black-owned banks, however, made it through the Depression
and even the merger waves of the last thirty years. The Citizens Savings
Bank and Trust Company of Nashville, for example, thrives to this day on
$100 million in assets, as does the Citizens Trust Bank of Atlanta, which is
led by African-American banker Cynthia N. Day.[847]

The story of black-owned building/savings and loan associations
is similar. They were always too few to have a dramatic impact and the
Great Depression proved a major setback as their number shrank from 70
in 1930 to about 50 just eight years later. The same could be said of credit
unions. While Paragon Progressive Federal Credit Union greatly aided
some blacks in Brooklyn, its assets, which topped out at $4.7 million in
1969, were but a small drop in an economic ocean.[848]

---

846 Andrew F. Brimmer, "The Black Banks: An Assessment of Performance and Prospects," Speech by Member of the Federal Reserve System's Board of Governors, December 28, 1970, 5; Immergluck, *Credit to the Community*, 55; Lindsay, "The Negro in Banking," 194, 198–99; Harris, *Negro as Capitalist*, 163; "Staff of the Dunbar National Bank, Harlem, New York City, circa 1930," New York Public Library, http://digitalcollections.nypl.org/items/a5730750-bf32-0131-e260-58d385a7b928 Accessed 10 Dec. 2016.

847 Brimmer, "The Black Banks," 38; Harris, *Negro as Capitalist*, 162, 165, 191–92, 194; Lindsay, "The Negro in Banking," 192–93; Thomas C. Parramore, Peter C. Stewart, and Tommy L. Bogger, *Norfolk: The First Four Centuries*, (Charlottesville: University Press of Virginia, 1994), 322. http://www.bankcbn.com/about-us/general-information/. Accessed 10 Dec. 2016. https://ctbconnect.com/ctb-management/. Accessed 10 December 2016.

848 Immergluck, *Credit to the Community*, 88–89; Craig Wilder, *A Covenant with Color: Race and Social Power in Brooklyn*, (New York: Columbia University Press, 2000), 199–200.

Black-owned and operated industrial banks also sprang up in the 1920s, beginning in 1922 with the formation of the Peoples Finance Corporation of St. Louis. By 1929, it boasted assets of $537,000 and had inspired the formation of copycats in Cleveland, Detroit, Kansas City, Newark, and elsewhere. The Depression hurt them, too. Only 3 black-owned banks of any sort formed in the 1930s and 1940s and none in the 1950s.[849]

By 1963, only 11 black-owned banks were in operation in America. By 1967, however, 17 black-owned banks controlled $122 million of assets and "taken as a group ... [were] not appreciably different from other banks of comparable size" in terms of their operating histories and ratios. The more established banks, like those that survived the Depression discussed above, tended to have more conservative lending practices and hence a better loan loss record than the new black-owned banks, which had pushed into unsecured loans, automobile paper, and loans to lower income borrowers. By 1969, 5 more black-owned banks had opened for business and several more were in the process of formation so that by the end of 1971 there were 29 in operation.[850]

African-Americans also formed their own insurers. In 1810, the African Insurance Company formed in Philadelphia in response to discrimination from white-controlled insurers. It failed in 1813 and no other black-owned insurers formed until the early 1880s, when African-Americans were pushed into the formal life insurance industry because of discrimination in the form of higher premiums or, in some cases, outright exclusion. Upper and middle class African-Americans knew that only impoverished blacks suffered the high mortality rates that the incumbent life insurers so feared. The association of several insurance agents with lynchings fueled further resentment, leading some African-Americans to

---

849 Lindsay, "The Negro in Banking," 197–98; Brimmer, "The Black Banks," 5.

850 Andrew F. Brimmer, "Financial Institutions and Urban Rehabilitation," Speech by Member of the Federal Reserve System's Board of Governors, September 22, 1967, 11–13; Brimmer, "The Black Banks," 1; Andrew F. Brimmer, "Recent Developments in Black Banking: 1970–1971," Speech by Member of the Federal Reserve System's Board of Governors, July 31, 1971, 3, 11–23.

beef up existing fraternal life insurance while others formed formal legal reserve insurers.[851]

One leader of an early all-black life insurer was Minnie Geddings Cox. Born to former slaves in 1869 Mississippi, Cox graduated from Nashville's Fisk University in 1888. After serving as a teacher and postmistress, Cox, with the aid of her husband, organized the Delta Penny Savings Bank, which opened for business in 1905. Three years later, the couple opened the Mississippi Beneficial Life Insurance Company, which became the first black-owned insurer to offer whole life policies. She took over the company after her husband died in 1916 and sold out to Heman Perry, "The Daddy of Negro High Financing" and founder of the Standard Life Insurance Company of Atlanta, in 1923. When Perry sold out to the white-owned Southern Life of Nashville a few years later, black policyholders revolted, lapsing their policies en masse.[852]

In Atlanta, Alonzo Herndon used his own private fortune, saved and invested over five decades, to save the Atlanta Mutual from regulatory homicide in 1921, when the white insurance commissioner demanded that the company, tainted by a minor embezzlement scandal, immediately increase its capital from $25,000 to $100,000. The commissioner was stunned when Herndon responded, "I can have it before morning," and successfully raised the $75,000 needed overnight.[853]

During the Great War, observers interested in the exodus of African-Americans from the rural South to the urban South and North often polled black insurance companies for information as their weekly debit

851 Butler, *Entrepreneurship and Self-Help*, 109–111; Shennette Garrett-Scott, "To Do a Work that Would Be Very Far Reaching: Minnie Geddings Cox, the Mississippi Life Insurance Company, and the Challenges of Black Women's Business Leadership in the Early Twentieth-Century United States," *Enterprise & Society* 17, 3 (Sept. 2016), 474, 482; Arnold Rose, *The Negro in America: The Condensed Version of Gunnar Myrdal's An American Dilemma*, (New York: Harper & Row, 1948), 110.

852 Garrett-Scott, "Minnie Geddings Cox," 478–79, 488, 496, 501.

853 Merritt, *The Herndons*, 198.

rolls recorded the loss of established customers as well as the advent of customers newly arrived in cities like Atlanta and Valdosta, Georgia.[854]

By the 1920s, several "Black Wall Streets," including Beale Street in Memphis, Tennessee, Greenwood Avenue in Tulsa, Oklahoma, and Parrish Street in Durham, North Carolina, had emerged. Parrish Street in particular was dominated by financial institutions, including the Mechanics and Farmers Bank, which had a branch in Raleigh, the North Carolina Mutual, the largest of the African-American-owned life insurers, and a dozen other financial companies, including a rare black-owned fire insurer.[855]

By the Great Depression, black-owned life insurers numbered over two dozen and most, despite the economic downturn, remained prosperous though they captured only about a quarter of the African-American market for industrial insurance. By 1947, 211 insurers, exclusively owned by blacks, were in operation. Collectively, they had 5.2 million policies in force and over $100 million in assets. By 1966, 48 black-owned insurers had $2.2 billion of policies in force and assets approaching $400 million. Because black-owned insurers were systematically kept out of the group insurance market, however, they became increasingly marginalized over the postwar period as the life insurance market became increasingly reliant on term policies and group insurance.[856]

Perversely, Jim Crow laws aided the establishment of financial companies run by African-Americans, for African-Americans, because it furthered the goals of segregationists and racists, who delighted whenever a black-owned institution tumbled. Of course the failure of black-owned enterprise often reflected as much on the general state of race relations as

---

854 R. H. Leavell, T. R. Snavely, T. J. Woofter, Jr., W. T. B. Williams, and Francis D. Tyson, *Negro Migration in 1916–17*, (Washington: U.S. Department of Labor, 1917), 97; Emmett J. Scott, *Negro Migration During the War*, (New York: Oxford University Press, 1920), 61, 64.

855 Garrett-Scott, "Minnie Geddings Cox," 492–93, 502; Quincy Mills, "Black Wall Street," *Encyclopedia of African American Business History*, ed. Juliet E. K. Walker (New York: Greenwood, 1999), 81–83; Butler, *Entrepreneurship and Self-Help*, 174–76, 182–92, 195.

856 Butler, *Entrepreneurship and Self-Help*, 111–15, 116–20, 123–24; Brimmer, "Financial Institutions," 8, 10; Christy Ford Chapin, "'Going Behind with that Fifteen Cent Policy': Black-Owned Insurance Companies and the State." *Journal of Policy History* 24, no. 2 (2012): 644–74.

it did on the financial acumen of African-Americans. In Chicago in 1947, for example, 21 lending companies with assets of almost $8.9 million were run by African-Americans. According to one chronicler, they found raising adequate capital "all but impossible" because "non-Negro institutions" would not buy, or lend on the collateral of, their mortgages. Savers therefore tended to eschew them for the higher rates or greater safety afforded by "the white companies."[857] At about the same time in Philadelphia, however, black banker Edward C. Brown experienced no difficulty getting loans from white bankers because Brown had developed a reputation for financial wizardry.[858]

In 1943, Edwin Embree summarized the history of black financial enterprise prior to World War II:

The insurance companies, which grew out of the widespread burial and mutual societies, have flourished because of the discrimination against Negro policyholders by the large white companies. Banks, which despite a number of failures rank close to insurance in financial importance, have as one of their chief reasons for existence the refusal of general banking institutions to give credit on equal terms with others to Negro individuals and businesses.[859]

The war did not change the situation immediately. One early postwar chronicler noted that African-Americans were "completely insignificant as a banker. There were not even 1,000 Negro proprietors and managers of financial, real estate, and insurance establishments in 1940, or much less than 1 percent of white workers in such occupations."[860] Another noted that there was "no Negro bank" in all of Harlem, though "local branches of the great white banks employ Negro personnel." Insurance companies owned and operated by blacks, by contrast, were numerous and largely responsible for the fact that by 1970 blacks were slightly

---

857 Charles Abrams, *Forbidden Neighbors: A Study of Prejudice in Housing*, (New York: Harper & Brothers, 1955), 176.

858 Harris, *Negro as Capitalist*, 143.

859 Edwin Embree, *Brown Americans: The Story of a Tenth of the Nation*, (New York: Viking Press, 1943), 131–32.

860 Rose, *The Negro in America*, 110.

more likely to own life insurance than Euroamericans were, though they paid more for it.[861]

Postwar prosperity and the Civil Rights Movement eventually brought some gains. Between 1947 and 1964, African-American owned savings and loan associations tripled their assets while black-owned commercial bank assets increased from a total of $5 million in 1940 to $53 million in the mid-1960s. Between 1951 and 1964, the assets of African-American controlled insurance companies assets doubled to $320 million. Most wealth owned by African-Americans, however, remained invested in white-controlled banks and insurers.[862] The largest African-American owned bank was Freedom National Bank in New York. At its height, it boasted deposits of $30 million, making it the 1,734th largest bank in a country with over 10,000 banks. The wealthiest black man in the U.S. after World War II may have been the president of North Carolina Mutual in Durham, North Carolina.[863]

After the long-forgotten reign of the Dark Prince Jeremiah G. Hamilton in the 1830s, Wall Street remained lily white, or Jewish, until 1952, when the first NASD registered black-owned broker-dealer, McGhee & Company, opened for business. Three years later, Special Markets, Inc. opened on Liberty Street after no landlord would rent it digs on Wall Street proper.[864] Only in 1960 was the black-owned investment bank H. L. Wright & Company allowed to rent on the Street, in the building numbered 99. One stockbroker in the firm joked that "the only Negroes on Wall Street before us were either sweeping it or shining shoes on it."[865]

---

861 John Gunther, *Inside U.S.A.*, (New York: Harper Brothers, 1947), 575; Andrew F. Brimmer, "Small Business and Economic Development in the Negro Community," Speech by Member of the Federal Reserve System's Board of Governors, July 25, 1969, 6.

862 Thomas Pettigrew, "White-Negro Confrontations," in *The Negro Challenge to the Business Community*, ed. Eli Ginzberg (New York: McGraw-Hill Book Company, 1964), 42–43, 46.

863 Louis Hyman, *Debtor Nation: The History of America in Red Ink*, (Princeton: Princeton University Press, 2011), 184–85; Gunther, *Inside U.S.A.*, 284.

864 Gregory S. Bell, *In the Black: A History of African Americans on Wall Street*, (New York: John Wiley & Sons, 2002), 31–38.

865 As quoted in Bell, *In the Black*, 17.

The joke was unfunny because it was only a slight exaggeration, one that downplayed the role of black speculators like H. R. George, the "Black Wolf of Wall Street" in the heady 1920s. Several other black-owned securities firms opened in subsequent years but they all had to mutate into mutual funds due to a dearth of blacks interested in stock speculation. Several failed in the late 1960s and early 1970s anyway. After the demise of Wright & Company in 1962, 99 Wall soon became a sort of mini-ghetto for black-owned securities firms.[866]

No new milestones were reached until 1965, when Merrill Lynch hired its first three black stockbrokers. Then, in 1968, Russell L. Goings, Jr. convinced broker-dealer Shearson Hammill to open a branch in Harlem. A few years later, in 1970, Travers Bell Jr. and Willie Daniels, under the partnership name Daniels & Bell, managed to form with help from timely and sympathetic articles on their capital plight by young financial journalist Myron Kandel. Daniels & Bell was soon opened and admitted to the NYSE; First Harlem Securities followed just four months later. Despite pushback from racist organizations like SPONGE (Society for the Prevention of Negroes Getting Everything), market-shaking regulatory reforms, and a volatile macroeconomic climate, black-owned investment banks and securities dealers grew in number, to about 20, and importance in the 1970s and 80s.[867]

Most minority-owned commercial and investment banks, however, either failed or were gobbled up by larger financial institutions during the great failure and merger waves of the last several decades. The number of commercial banks owned and operated by African-Americans, for example, fell from 48 to 21 between 2000 and 2016. Few observers felt a need to replace them because financial discrimination appeared to be a remnant of the past as credit qualifications eased in the 1990s and 2000s and financial predation was not yet viewed as a pervasive problem. As

866 Bell, *In the Black*, 23–25, 35–40, 51–52, 54.

867 Bell, *In the Black*, 9–12, 45, 57–151.

financial discrimination appears to be on the rise again, however, a return to self-help is in order.[868]

Defending the Self-help Solution

The blueprint [of self-help] is neither conservative nor liberal, but draws its strength from the adjustment of oppressed groups throughout history. — John Sibley Butler, Entrepreneurship and Self-Help Among Black Americans: A Reconsideration of Race and Economics *(Albany: State University of New York Press, 1991), 324.*

In short, the best way to reduce financial discrimination and predation is to reduce barriers to entry and encourage members of groups that feel discriminated against to form their own financial services companies. To do nothing will result in increased levels of discrimination, predation, or both.

In the 1980s, the number of various "fringe banks," a term coined by financial theorist Hyman Minsky in conjunction with Swarthmore economist John P. Caskey, more than doubled to provide short-term loans and check cashing facilities to the growing number of unbanked Americans, most of whom were non-white and/or poor. In 1977, the level of unbanked households was just under 10 percent. By 1989, almost 14 percent of households were unbanked. Fringe check cashing outlets arose because they were relatively unregulated so entry was cheaper and faster than establishing *de novo* banks. Moreover, fringe banks were not subject to the Community Reinvestment Act (CRA), which induced some traditional depository institutions to be careful not to extend their presence into the neighborhoods of the downtrodden lest the government force them to lend to those same people. The problem with the extension of fringe banks was that they were usually not owned or even managed

---

868 Ruth Simon and Paul Overberg, "Credit Gap for Black-Owned Firms," *Wall Street Journal*, 10 November 2016; Bell, *In the Black*, 152–277; David Star, "Black Dollars Matter," *Atlanta Black Star*, 19 June 2016.

by members of the communities that they served, so many engaged in predatory behaviors as circumstances permitted. Real banks owned and staffed by members of the underserved communities themselves would have provided better service, at lower cost.[869]

Self-help still exists but it is relatively muted, largely due to entry barriers. Between 2000 and 2014, the number of minority-owned banks in operation increased only modestly, from 162 to 173, thanks to substantial increases in the number of Asian-owned banks, from 69 to 85, Hispanic-owned banks, from 31 to 41, and American Indian-owned banks, from 14 to 19. Over that same period, however, almost as many minority-owned banks exited via failure or merger.[870]

The existence, or possible existence, of minority-owned financial companies should never be taken as an excuse for discriminatory practices but only as a real-world test for discrimination. To that end, the startups should do a wide range of business with customers from the putatively discriminated against groups as well as others. If a group does not have sufficient human or financial capacity to start its own company, which is a significant barrier for many minority groups, regulators and NGOs (like the Russell Sage Foundation) need to kickstart the process by helping the community to build capacity through education, relevant work experience, and maybe even startup capital. The Minority Bank Depository Program initiated by President Nixon in 1969, for example, increased deposits at minority-owned banks by incentivizing (white-owned) corporations to park some money with them.[871]

869 Caskey, *Fringe Banking*, xii-xiii, 72, 86, 90–97, 133–39.

870 Russell Kashian, Fernanda Contreras, and Claudia Perez-Valdez, "The Changing Face of Communities Served by Minority Depository Institutions: 2001–2015," Community Banking in the 21st Century Research and Policy Conference, St. Louis Federal Reserve, St. Louis, MO, (September 28–29, 2016), 20–21, 30–31.

871 Immergluck, *Credit to the Community*, 59–62; Kashian, Contreras, and Perez-Valdez, "Changing Face of Communities," 2; Amanda Bayer and David Wilcox, "The Unequal Distribution of Economic Education: A Report on the Race, Ethnicity, and Gender of Economics Majors at US Colleges and Universities," Finance and Economics Discussion Series 2017–105 (Washington: Board of Governors of the Federal Reserve System, 2017).

If, having achieved minimum efficient scale, a group cannot turn a profit, it should be allowed to wind up its operations as clearly its services were unneeded. The Lumbee Guaranty Bank (LGB), for example, charges its borrowers a higher interest rate than the local "white" bank. So Dobbs Oxendine, a Lumbee entrepreneur, borrows from the latter. The very fact that he can do so suggests that the LGB may no longer be necessary, that its formation was enough to induce incumbent institutions to reform their practices. Regulatory approaches that rely on markets have a far better chance of success, of actually helping those groups regulators purport they would like to help, than those that try to repress markets.[872]

Some regulators, like the Minneapolis and Philadelphia districts of the Federal Reserve, recently have implemented programs that are helping African-Americans and Indians to create their own financial institutions, but much more remains to be done. Moreover, regulators face headwinds from incumbent financial institutions that would rather have regulators implement ineffective top-down regulations than to suffer additional competition. I discovered that the hard way when I investigated becoming part of a group that wanted to establish a bank designed specifically to cater to physically and mentally challenged individuals in the Chicagoland area. The project flamed out after the financial crisis as regulators clamped down on the formation of de novo banks nationwide. For almost a decade after the financial crisis, about the only way for a group to break into banking was to take over a troubled existing institution, which naturally was risky business.[873]

One key reason to expect self-help to work is that people, and the institutions they own and run, are unlikely to exclude, discriminate against, or prey upon members of their own group, hence the criticism

872 Riley, *The New Trail of Tears*, 73; Hester Peirce and Benjamin Klutsey, "Introduction: Market-Based Financial Regulation," in *Reframing Financial Regulation: Enhancing Stability and Protecting Consumers*, ed. Hester Peirce and Benjamin Klutsey (Arlington, Va.: Mercatus Center, George Mason University, 2016), 1–9.

873 George J. Benston, *Regulating Financial Markets: A Critique and Some Proposals* (Washington, D.C.: AEI Press, 1999), 11; Immergluck, *Credit to the Community*, 79–81; Rachel Witkowski, "Banks Are Sprouting Anew in the U.S.," *Wall Street Journal*, 9 February 2017.

of the long domination of banks and insurers by white males. There of course have been some exceptions, but they tend to prove the rule. Most examples of women swindling other women, for example, turn out to be women swindling African-Americans, Amerindians, Hispanics, trailer park trash, or members of other minority groups who happened to be women. And this is not to say that self-help institutions are necessarily charitable or generous, especially if they are organized as for-profit businesses. Many, like black life insurers in Chicago, offered African-Americans tough mortgage deals: big down payments, points, and 7 percent interest. But they lent when most white-owned institutions would not. A black insurer in Georgia, Industrial Life and Health Insurance Company, even tried to prevent the rise of black-owned competitors so that it could enjoy some degree of market power.[874]

The key is that self-help institutions are more likely to employ "culture brokers," people who understand both the needs of the financial institution and the people it is trying to help, at high enough levels to make a difference in the corporation's culture and standard operating procedures. The intuitions of culture brokers are based on subtle cultural clues that no algorithm or generic loan officers can replicate. The best culture brokers are expert at communicating with applicants in terms that they can understand. The fact that only 8 of the 1,300 mortgage brokers operating in the country in 1967 were African-American, and none of those had a correspondent relationship with a major life insurer, goes a long way toward explaining the charges of mortgage discrimination ubiquitous in that era.

---

874 U.S. Commission on Civil Rights, *Mortgage Money: Who Gets It? A Case Study in Mortgage Lending Discrimination in Hartford, Connecticut*, (Washington: U.S. Government Printing Office, 1974), 31; Martha Olney, "When Your Word Is Not Enough: Race, Collateral, and Household Credit," *Journal of Economic History* 58, no. 2 (1998), 425; Lindsay, "The Negro in Banking," 158; Gregory D. Squires, "Community Reinvestment: An Emerging Social Movement," in *From Redlining to Reinvestment: Community Responses to Urban Disinvestment*, ed. Gregory D. Squires (Philadelphia: Temple University Press, 1992), 17; Sparks, *Capital Intentions*, 95–96; Karen Orren, *Corporate Power and Social Change: The Politics of the Life Insurance Industry*, (Baltimore: Johns Hopkins University Press, 1974), 141; Merritt, *The Herndons*, 83, 169, 230 n20.

The banks' penchant for hiring scads of minorities, but only at the lowest level jobs, also helps to explain the persistence of discrimination.[875]

Consider how self-help could help to reduce other types of discrimination as well. For example, some people dislike the fact that auto insurers use non-driving variables like occupation and education in their decisions about insurability and premium level. They want regulators to ban the practice but insurers point to a high correlation between education, occupation, and other non-driving related variables on the one hand, and claim levels on the other. If the aggrieved believe there is a better way to price automobile insurance, they should be encouraged to try out their model in the real world. Maybe they are on to something. Or maybe they are simply looking for the government to lower their premiums by diktat. The former may help improve industry efficiency while the latter can only serve to redistribute wealth from safer to riskier drivers. Ditto with Indians who want health insurance that covers traditional native treatments. Maybe they are on to something or maybe they just want something for nothing. The only way to tell is to test the notion in the real world.[876]

Self-help solutions can be a source of great pride. Robert L. Smith, an African-American banker in Waco, Texas, had this to say about black-owned banks in 1920:

To my way of thinking, the history of our Negro banking institutions reveals more than any other business or profession, the great and wonderful progress our race has made since the war. The very idea that men and women who were chattels about fifty years ago, or whose mothers and fathers were denied an education and were owned and sold as slaves,

875 Kate Porter Young, "Rural South Carolina: An Ethnographic Study of Homeownership, Home Financing, and Credit," *Cityscape* 3, 1 (March 1997): 31; Sandro Ambuehl, B. Douglas Bernheim, Fulya Y. Ersoy, and Donna Harris, "Social Transmission of Financial Decision Making Skills. A Case of the Blind Leading the Blind?" (December 30, 2016). Available at SSRN: https://ssrn.com/abstract=2891753; Brimmer, "Financial Institutions," 2–3, 18–19; Andrew F. Brimmer, "Equal Opportunity in Banking: An Urban Perspective," Speech by Member of the Federal Reserve System's Board of Governors, 11 July 1968, 1–3.

876 Leslie Scism, "Insurance Practice Questioned," *Wall Street Journal*, 17 November 2016; Pickering, *Lakota Culture*, 34–35.

without previous apprenticeship or experience in banking, have been able to establish and conduct successfully nearly sixty (60) Negro banking institutions now operating in this country – I say such a record of progress has no parallel in the annals of human history. …. Instead of being put up for a loan and being sold themselves, as chattels, they are lending money, making deposits, owning and selling stocks and chattels in bonds and many other forms of securities.[877]

To the extent that financial exclusion, discrimination, and predation still exist, self-help innovations have proven insufficient to fully combat those problems. To reject self-help as a viable solution to discrimination, as historian Louis Hyman does, however, is to go too far. For starters, entry has been far from free. Moreover, as shown above, self-help has worked in numerous instances to reduce and even eliminate discrimination across the financial system. It is not a panacea, however, for groups that face broader forms of discrimination because the minority-owned institutions themselves are discriminated against, or their customers are. Importantly, the self-help approach can be used in conjunction with other policies, so policymakers should not use it as an excuse for dismissing other proposals, like those of Mehrsa Baradaran.[878]

In the limit, minority communities have faced existential threats due to their very success. As noted above, Tulsa, Oklahoma was home to numerous successful black-owned businesses, and the financial institutions to match. African-Americans first came to Oklahoma as the slaves of members of the so-called Five Civilized Tribes forced to resettle there as Euroamericans pushed westward in the decades following the American Revolution. The slaves numbered 7,603 in 1860. More African-Americans arrived voluntarily after the Civil War as rumors swirled that the lands of the Choctaw, which sided with the Confederacy during the conflict, would be turned over to freedpersons from throughout the South. A

---

877 Alson L. Holsey, "Progress in Industries: Farms, Homes and Business Enterprises," in *Progress of a Race, or the Remarkable Advancement of the American Negro*, eds. J. L. Nichols and William H. Crogman (J. L. Nichols & Company, 1920), 265–66.

878 Mehrsa Baradaran, *The Color of Money: Black Banks and the Racial Wealth Gap*, (Cambridge: Harvard University Press, 2017).

Financial Exclusion

black colony in Oklahoma never materialized but several all-black towns were formed by private groups. So by 1900 almost 19,000 African-Americans lived in Oklahoma and formed the basis for the expansion of black-owned businesses based in Tulsa.[879]

As elsewhere, most of those businesses were small and catered exclusively to other African-Americans. A few, however, broke out into the larger economy. Jay Cola, for example, was guzzled down by whites and blacks alike and nobody seemed to care that the telephone system was owned by a black man named W. C. Reed. Ditto Sydney Lyons, whose East India Toilet Goods and Manufacturing Company earned an international reputation for quality. And when World War II broke out, Walter Edwards' salvage yard became worth a small fortune, much of which he poured into an all-black hospital in Oklahoma City.[880]

North and east of Oklahoma's eponymous metropolis lay Tulsa, which was just a small Indian town until the oil strike of 1905 turned it into a classic boomtown. African-Americans flocked to the rapidly growing area in search of jobs and a few of them, like auto mechanic John Williams, hit it big, despite high levels of racial animosity. Williams, a successful printer, and other black entrepreneurs helped to develop the much vaunted "Little Africa" or "Negro Wall Street" section of town around Greenwood Avenue. By May 1921, that neighborhood was home to numerous black-owned professional offices and businesses, including hotels, restaurants, stores, and theaters.[881]

In a fit of racial pique, Euroamericans destroyed the district after Tulsa blacks displayed the audacity to prevent the lynching of a young black man accused of attempted sexual assault upon a divorcee described by her ex-husband as a "notorious character." A police-sanctioned lynching, of a white man no less, the previous year convinced about 75 African-Americans that they needed to arm themselves and protect the accused. An altercation took place, shots were fired, and a full-scale race riot broke

---

879 Butler, *Entrepreneurship and Self-Help*, 199–202.

880 Butler, *Entrepreneurship and Self-Help*, 203–4.

881 Butler, *Entrepreneurship and Self-Help*, 204–9.

out, then escalated into all-out war as enraged whites attacked the Greenwood neighborhood and soon there was a skirmish line along the Frisco railroad tracks. Aided by the police and the National Guard, the white mob broke through the defenses. While the police arrested every African-American they could lay their hands on, the mob began to loot and burn black-owned businesses.

As the National Guard arrived at the height of the battle, the mob threatened to shoot any firefighters who tried to put out any of the blazes and a murdered black man was dragged around the neighborhood behind an automobile. A. C. Jackson, one of the most able surgeons in the nation, was killed after he surrendered himself to a group of whites who swore they would protect him from other whites. One of the estimated 25,000 rampaging whites even took to the air in his private plane and bombed and strafed the neighborhood while a machine gun in the granary also rained lead down on the district in a scene that makes any clip from *The Purge* movie franchise seem tame by comparison.[882]

Martial law was declared in Tulsa on 1 June and blacks were rounded up into camps, tagged, and released only on the recognizance of employers. Many, understandably, fled Tulsa as soon as they could discover the fate of loved ones and retrieve any surviving pieces of personal property. The Euroamerican rioters, meanwhile, were excused and even applauded for ridding the city of crime, vice, and n-words who did not know their proper place.[883]

The Greenwood district was rebuilt and repopulated but very slowly because white banks refused to lend to borrowers in the area. Moreover, the lesson of the riot was not soon forgotten in the African-American community. Although never prominent in Euroamerican history books, the Tulsa riot taught interwar African-Americans throughout the nation never to challenge the white power structure. So when the North Carolina Mutual Company put up a high rise home office building, its presi-

---

882 Butler, *Entrepreneurship and Self-Help*, 209–14.

883 Butler, *Entrepreneurship and Self-Help*, 215–17.

dent made certain that it would not be taller than any of the white-owned buildings in Durham.[884]

Most minority-owned financial institutions faced obstacles that were more quotidian but ultimately just as limiting. Early commercial banks owned by African-Americans, for example, had difficulty achieving scale economies because there were so few large black-owned businesses to lend to. By 1970 or so, black-owned banks were considerably less profitable than other banks because their costs were higher and their efficiency lower. Loan loss rates were two to three times higher than average and average account size was much lower than in other banks because black consumers were on average poorer and black businesses were on average smaller. The solution to such problems was to accept lower or no profits (as credit unions do), to improve costs and efficiency, or to admit that lending to some groups was indeed costlier, no matter who ran the bank. The last-mentioned conclusion was indeed reached by Andrew F. Brimmer, an African-American member of the Federal Reserve's Board of Governors when he concluded in 1969 after careful study that "black banks trying to do business in urban ghettos appear to operate at a substantial disadvantage (even when compared with other banks of the same size)." As a result, many black-owned banks invested higher than average portions of their deposits in U.S. government bonds and in overnight loans to other banks (the so-called federal funds market).[885]

In particularly severe cases, it may behoove regulators to pay lenders to make loans or extend insurance in specified areas or to members of specified groups while holding the lenders or insurers responsible for any losses. That would induce the lenders to make as many prudent loans (insurers to extend prudent insurance coverage) in such areas or to such groups as possible, minimize the need for costly command and control-

---

884 Butler, *Entrepreneurship and Self-Help*, 218–23.

885 Lindsay, "The Negro in Banking," 179; Brimmer, "The Black Banks," 2–3, 9, 12; Brimmer, "Recent Developments in Black Banking," 6–8.

type regulations, and keep the government out of the business of making loan and insurance decisions.[886]

Another problem is that otherwise well-meaning bureaucrats and regulations can unintentionally inflict severe damage on minority-owned financial services companies. As Hyman argues, banks owned by African-Americans suffered from higher operating costs because their accounts tended to be smaller and less commercial than those of other banks but the dearth of commercial accounts was itself rooted in bigotry on the part of businesses and social structures, many supported by the government, that prevented African-Americans from spawning entrepreneurs engaged in lawful activities. In some cases, regulators colluded with white-owned businesses to intimidate African-American entrants into the insurance industry.[887]

Similarly, credit unions did not meet the "credit needs of the ghetto," as Hyman put it, not because of structural problems with credit unions or low-income communities but because not enough credit unions were formed. As Hyman himself points out, between 1965 and 1968 Project Moneywise organized only 218 credit unions across the country. Because credit unions then could not grow very large due to regulatory restrictions on membership, 21,800 new credit unions would have been a more appropriate goal.[888]

Hyman also argues that the poor simply cannot save enough to fund a sufficient number of credit unions or banks but he also notes that many "ghetto credit unions reinvested in white suburbia." In 1960, Eunice and George Grier pointed out that no African American-run bank could be induced to invest in early privately developed inter-racial housing tracts. In both cases, the real problem was again with regulations, this time ones that restricted the types of loans that credit unions and banks (regardless of ownership) could make. The record of the Urban League's credit union

---

886 Jack M. Guttentag and Susan M. Wachter, *Redlining and Public Policy*, (New York: Salomon Brothers Center, 1980), 4, 47–48.

887 Garrett-Scott, "Minnie Geddings Cox," 474.

888 Hyman, *Debtor Nation*, 186.

in Washington, D.C. shows that minority-run depository institutions could succeed when given the proper incentives and allowed a freer reign. Moreover, the number of black banks was limited by stringent entry barriers that were only loosened, in the case of national and some state banks, in the 1960s. Unsurprisingly, the number of black-owned and run banks increased rapidly in that decade.[889]

When not shackled by regulations, self-help institutions could definitely significantly reduce discrimination to a palpable extent. When women in the nineteenth century realized that they could no longer sell their handmade wares in dry goods and department stores, for example, they organized "exchanges" or consignment shops in 72 cities, including Baltimore, Boston, New Orleans, New York, Philadelphia, and Saint Louis. Run by wealthy women as non-profit charities, the exchanges gave female producers a place to consign their tea cozies and doilies, shawls and other types of clothing, jewelry boxes and woodcarvings, and innumerable other useful and ornamental handmade household items. The women's exchange movement remained important for decades because no regulators had sufficient authority to prevent it from adapting to variation over space or change over time.[890]

The same could be said of African-American churches. Free blacks in antebellum Manhattan and elsewhere who felt discriminated against in white-led churches left to form their own congregations. Unencumbered by regulations, they proliferated and thrived and continue to do so to this day.[891]

When poor workers living in inner cities in New Jersey got fed up with their impossibly long commutes using public transit systems designed to bring suburbanites into the cities each morning, they formed

889 Eunice Grier and George Grier, *Privately Developed Interracial Housing: An Analysis of Experience*, (Berkeley: University of California Press, 1960), 119; Hyman, *Debtor Nation*, 186–89; Brimmer, "The Black Banks," 6.

890 Kathleen Sander, *The Business of Charity: The Woman's Exchange Movement, 1832–1900*, (Chicago: University of Illinois Press, 1998), 55–58.

891 Richard C. Wade, *The Urban Frontier: The Rise of Western Cities, 1790–1830*, (Cambridge: Harvard University Press, 1959), 224–25; Freeman, *The Free Negro*, 281.

their own private transportation company based around vans and solved their commuting problems. Other examples abound.[892]

Even more to the point here, while political battles over housing segregation raged in the 1950s and beyond, many private housing developers identified a demand for desegregated housing and voluntarily met it. The movement for interracial housing tracts, begun in 1937 by a group of Quakers in Pennsylvania's coal country, grew slowly. Of about 10 million new units constructed between 1946 and 1955, inclusive, only about 8,000 were open to all races. Successful early experiments in Minnesota, Wisconsin, California, and New York City, however, led to the construction of yet more open occupancy developments in the late 1950s and 1960s.[893]

The movement picked up speed after laws banning housing discrimination were passed in some locales in the later 1950s though developers continued to encounter a variety of obstacles. In some places they were outright banned while other communities relegated their projects to what one study termed "areas of inferior residential quality." Sometimes land owners refused to sell, while other times zoning laws were changed or governments threw up other technicalities. Obtaining financing was also sometimes difficult as lenders refused to give up the notion that mixed neighborhoods inevitably degenerated into minority-only slums. (It did not help that most of the mixed-race developments offered modest houses in the $11,000 to $15,000 purchase range or a rental range of $70 to $100 per month.) Financing, however, was never the biggest obstacle that developers faced. Some developers discovered that the best tactic was to approach lenders with a record of funding African-American housing. Those lenders typically assumed the interracial projects would soon become all black and learned valuable lessons when they did not.[894]

---

892 Butler, *Entrepreneurship and Self-Help*, 323.

893 Davis McEntire, *Residence and Race: Final and Comprehensive Report to the Commission on Race and Housing*, (Berkeley: University of California Press, 1960), 199–201; Richard Plunz, *A History of Housing in New York City: Dwelling Type and Social Change in the American Metropolis*, (New York: Columbia University Press, 1990), 256.

894 McEntire, *Residence and Race*, 199–203, 207; Grier and Grier, *Privately Developed*, 125, 245.

By proving time and again that building mixed-race housing could be profitable if properly managed and that desegregated neighborhoods did not create significant social problems, private developers opened financial spigots originally clogged with a strong lender preference for the status quo, i.e., financing either all-white or all non-white developments. After the federal government finally stopped blocking FHA and VA mortgages in racially mixed housing developments, years after postwar laws and court decisions banned government enforcement of race-restrictive covenants, private lenders of course became more willing (due to the federal subsidies inherent in the programs just mentioned) to back the open-occupancy developers, though often in exchange for higher interest rates justified by the higher risks involved. By 1970, segregated housing was for the most part an issue in public housing only.[895]

It might also be supposed that self-help financial institutions would be prone to be too lenient with their own kind. To the extent that decision-makers want their organizations to continue in operation, be it for pecuniary or charitable reasons, however, they have incentives to take only rational risks. In 1823, for example, the First Female Beneficial Society of Philadelphia rejected the $100 mortgage loan application of one of its own members, Mrs. S. Prealls, with only six members voting in favor. "Consequently the Money remains in Bank," the minutes stated, earning no interest but in hands believed to be much safer than those of Prealls. Similarly, female-owned banks did much more for women than MESBICs ever did because they were "business-oriented and ... not cause-oriented" so their leaders had strong incentives to become good bankers, not pushovers.[896]

---

895 McEntire, *Residence and Race*, 207–209; Enrico Beltramini, "Consumer Credit as a Civil Right in the United States, 1968–1976," in *The Cultural History of Money and Credit: A Global Perspective*, ed. Chia Yin Jus, Thomas Luckett, and Erika Vause (New York: Lexington Books, 2016), 83; Grier and Grier, *Privately Developed*.

896 Smith, *Predatory Lending*, 16; First Female Beneficial Society of Philadelphia Minutes, 1814–1840, Historical Society of Pennsylvania; Treasury Department Study Team, *Credit and Capital Formation*, 54.

Many non-profits possessed a desire for self-preservation so strong that they were ultimately quite conservative lenders. The Provident Loan Society of New York, the largest of the non-profit pawnshops, did not, due to the high fixed costs of making small loans, lend to the poorest of the poor as evidenced by the fact that its average loan was 5 times larger than that of the average for-profit pawnshop. Similarly, remedial loan societies, some that provided loans at no interest and others at discounted rates that capped their profits at 6 percent, remained small institutions with lending volumes best characterized as a "drop in the bucket."[897]

Financial self-help can actually help to improve financial system efficiency for several reasons. First, it increases competition and exactly at the margin to address the problem. Irrational redlining and other irrational forms of discrimination must give way to competitive forces. Educating borrowers and helping them to "shop around for the best set of mortgage terms available" also increases effective competition by lowering transaction costs and encouraging price discovery.[898]

Financial self-help also improves system efficiency because people tend to understand the needs of their own group best, thereby ensuring that loan and insurance decisions are in the Goldilocks zone, neither too harsh nor too lenient. Women are more likely to understand a female product line than men are; African-Americans are more likely to understand a product or service designed for other blacks than a white person would be, and so forth. The same holds when it comes to finance. Who better to interpret the credit and employment history of a member of group X than another member of group X? Indeed, a 2014 FDIC study concluded that minority-owned banks in fact do originate more mortgages in high-poverty areas and to minority individuals than white-owned banks do.[899]

---

897 Calder, *Financing*, 49, 120–22.

898 Guttentag and Wachter, *Redlining*, 13–14; Robert Schafer and Helen F. Ladd, *Discrimination in Mortgage Lending* (Cambridge: MIT Press, 1981), 301.

899 Susan Peck and David Saffert, *Lending on Native American Lands: A Guide for Rural Development Staff*, (Washington, DC: Housing Assistance Council, June 2006), 36; Trea-

Consider, for example, the Borinquen Federal Credit Union (BFCU), which several women, including Carmen Echavarri and Veronica Melgar, formed in July 1974 to provide basic banking services to Philadelphia Hispanics, who most financial institutions then considered an "unbankable community." The institution grew slowly but surely. By 1980, despite being open only a few hours for three days each week, the BFCU, the first thrift in Philadelphia run by and for Hispanics, boasted 600 active members, assets of $350,000, and a delinquency rate below one percent. To help more families, it applied for, and received, an $85,000 grant that allowed it to lend to low income homeowners who needed to make home repairs worth up to $2,500. After its bilingual, bicultural staff successfully lent the initial allotment, it received $41,000 more, which enabled it to help about 70 poor Hispanic families in all. "We are proud to state," BFCU officers announced after completion of the program in 1985, "that we have been able to serve our community by providing them services which they may be otherwise unable to obtain in a local bank thru this program."[900]

BFCU was able to "bank" the otherwise "unbankable" because it understood Hispanic borrowers better than other institutions did. Its loan officers, for example, understood that frequent job and residency changes were common in the Hispanic community, not signs of untrustworthiness as loan officers at traditional lenders believed. The BFCU also understood that Hispanic borrowers would not willingly or easily default on loans funded by other members of the Hispanic community. (That was one of the main reasons credit unions were long restricted to some affinity group or another.) To ensure that it was not lending to the few bad apples that infest every community, the BFCU partnered with community-based organizations to pre-screen applicants. And, of course,

sury Department Study Team, *Credit and Capital Formation*, 46; Kashian, Contreras, and Perez-Valdez, "Changing Face of Communities," 21.

900 OHCD Public Hearings, June 21, 1982, Hispanic Federation for Social and Economic Development, Administrative Series, Box 4, Folder 5; BFCU Memorandum, March 5, 1985, Hispanic Federation for Social and Economic Development, Administrative Series, Box 4, Folder 3.

it took proper precautions, such as a second mortgage or co-signer, whenever appropriate.[901]

Self-help also aids efficiency by increasing effective demand. People often feel more confident about approaching "their own" for loans, so women's banks actually increased overall loan demand by females. Some of the same effect could be obtained by having female or black loan officers handle loan applications from members of their own group, but only when the applicants believed the loan officers have the authority to approve their loans.[902]

Corporations have unique cultures and business historians have repeatedly shown that corporate cultures are important factors in corporate performance. Minority-owned and -led corporations have more room to create cultures attractive to their leaders, employees, and customers. Susan Byrne's asset management company Westwood Management, for example, developed an easygoing culture more like that of a Silicon Valley tech startup than a money manager. Founded in 1983, it remains in operation today and was named one of the "Best Places to Work in Money Management" by *Pensions & Investments* in 2015.[903]

Personal confrontation with discrimination also can motivate people to fight for reform. Rudolph Severa headed up the Credit Bureau of Greater New York, for example, because he experienced credit discrimination at a tailor in the early 1920s. "Because I was a minor," Severa complained, "I had to get my father's signature" even though he earned more than his father. "Then I told him to call my employer. But he still wouldn't give me credit. I told him right then and there that if I ever became a credit manager I would institute a more elastic policy based on

---

901 William Trufant Foster, *Loan Sharks and Their Victims*, (New York: Public Affairs Committee, 1940), 4; Various documents, Hispanic Federation for Social and Economic Development, Administrative Series, Box 4, Folders 2–14, Historical Society of Pennsylvania.

902 Treasury Department Study Team, *Credit and Capital Formation*, 54, 63, 66.

903 Anne B. Fisher, *Wall Street Women*, (New York: Alfred A. Knopf, 1990), 74–75. http://westwoodgroup.com/our-firm/. Accessed 20 May 2016.

character and earning power." He did so two decades later as credit manager at Macy's.[904]

The only other two major objections to the "self help" approach to financial discrimination and predation that I have encountered are also both flawed. The first is that self-help appears to be akin to segregation. The resemblance is only superficial as all the anti-discrimination laws (like the Fair Housing Act of 1968 and the Equal Credit Opportunity Act of 1974, as amended) should remain on the books and everyone should remain free to bank or insure at whatever company they wish. Self-help aims to increase competition in specific underserved geographical markets and market segments so it is about inclusion, not exclusion, a point grasped by David Love, writing in the *Atlanta Black Star*, when he called for the formation of more black-owned banks in a 2016 article, and sociologist John Sibley Butler in his groundbreaking *Entrepreneurship and Self-Help Among Black Americans*.[905]

Bigger Is Not Better

Ignorance is bad public policy. — George C. Galster, "Use of Testers in Investigating Discrimination in Mortgage Lending and Insurance," in Michael Fix and Raymond J. Struyk, eds. *Clear and Convincing Evidence: Measurement of Discrimination in America* (Washington, DC: Urban Institute Press, 1993), 328.

The other, final objection to self-help is that minority-owned financial institutions are bound to be much smaller, and hence less profitable and efficient, than their competitors. Without government or charitable support, therefore, they will be more likely to fail than their competitors. That would be a weighty objection if it had any basis in fact, but it does not. Once an institution has achieved minimum efficient scale, it is just

904   Black, *Buy Now*, 39–40.

905   Ross and Yinger, *Color of Credit*, 30–32; Star, "Black Dollars Matter"; Butler, *Entrepreneurship and Self-Help*.

as efficient, and sometimes more efficient, than its largest competitors. Thankfully, minimum efficient scale has been decreasing in real (inflation-adjusted) terms thanks to various network and computer technologies that provide even the smallest financial intermediaries, like credit unions, with access to state-of-the-art communication and transaction systems.[906]

What sometimes happens is that minority-owned financial institutions thrive when discrimination exists but when it wanes those institutions come into direct competition with institutions that are more efficient. That is what apparently happened to most black-owned financial institutions in the 1960s and 1970s as financial exclusion gave way to subtle discrimination. Those institutions either increased efficiency or exited, via failure or merger, just as they should have. As noted above, although they no longer exist, such companies should be counted as successful enterprises because they serviced customers for years or decades and in the process helped to reduce discrimination.[907]

Although they went about it the wrong way, Ben Bernanke, Timothy Geithner, and other policymakers were right to try to put the kibosh on the financial panic that swept across the nation and globe in September 2008. The simultaneous destruction of numerous large financial institutions would have injured the economy severely and perhaps irreparably. That is not to say, however, that the U.S. economy, or any other economy for that matter, needs big banks or insurers in order to thrive. In fact, history tells the opposite story. Most years since 1790, the U.S. economy has grown robustly in inflation-adjusted per capita terms. Yet only since the mid-1990s has America possessed mammoth financial institutions like Bank of America, Citigroup, Goldman Sachs, J.P. Morgan Chase, and Wells Fargo.

Americans have never liked megabanks. During the colonial period most held an abiding distrust and even hatred of the Bank of England, even though the vast majority of colonists never interacted with it directly. One reason was ideological: many Brits distrusted the big bank

---

906 Immergluck, *Credit to the Community*, 59.

907 Brimmer, "Financial Institutions," 2; Butler, *Entrepreneurship and Self-Help*, 224–26.

and made no bones about it. The great classical economist Adam Smith, for example, was no fan of big, powerful banks. He favored the proliferation of banks in Britain because he feared that the safety of the nation's financial system rested too squarely on the Bank of England. Should the credit of the Bank of England's notes fall victim to panic, he warned, "confusion" would reign. Barter or credit would be the only mechanisms for making exchanges and the government would be unable to raise taxes sufficient to repel invaders. Colonists also disliked the Bank of England because its policies helped to cause a major recession in the colonies after the French and Indian War. Tight money meant high interest rates which made colonial land prices puffed up during the wartime boom plummet. Instead of extending aid, British policymakers clamped down harder, sending thousands of colonists into bankruptcy and even prison. What followed were remonstrances and protests, then boycotts on imported goods, then a massacre, a Tea Party, and Lexington and Concord.[908]

Following this drubbing, Americans so distrusted big banks that it was only at the tail end of the Revolution that they created their own, much smaller version of the Bank of England, the Bank of North America. After ratification of the Constitution, many Americans opposed the creation of the Bank of England's true American heir, the Bank of the United States (BUS). As historian David Cowen, now the president of the Museum of American Finance, showed over a decade ago, the BUS did a fine job preventing financial disruptions from becoming systemic panics by following Hamilton's Rule, i.e., lending at a penalty rate to all those who could post sufficient collateral. After the federal government sold off its ownership stake in the institution, the BUS was wholly private, and the only bank in the nation that could branch across state lines. Capitalized at $10 million, it remained the nation's largest, and by far most hated, bank until its 20-year charter expired in 1811 and was not renewed.[909]

---

908 Adam Smith, *An Inquiry into the Nature and Causes of the Wealth of Nations*, (New York: Modern Library, 1937), 304 (Book II, Chapter 2), 452 (Book IV, Chapter 3).

909 David Cowen, *The Origins and Economic Impact of the First Bank of the United States, 1791–1797*, (New York: Garland Publishing, 2000); David Cowen, "The First Bank of the United States and the Securities Market Crash of 1792," *Journal of Economic History* 60, no.

The government regretted its decision not to renew the BUS's charter when it found it difficult to borrow enough money to fight the British in the War of 1812. It managed to bumble its way through that conflict but in the process lost Washington, DC to British troops brandishing torches and the monetary system to chaos. After the war, the political stars aligned to create a second Bank of the United States (SBUS). Capitalized at $35 million, the SBUS was much larger than its predecessor and also more under the thumb of the government, which owned $7 million of its stock and controlled five board positions. The government essentially selected the bank's first president, a drunkard named William Jones, who soon led the institution to the brink of bankruptcy. Instead of thwarting financial crises like its predecessor did, the SBUS was a leading cause of the Panic of 1819 and the debilitating recession that followed. Andrew Jackson was one of thousands of Americans hurt by that downturn and he never forgave the SBUS for it.

Jackson and many other Americans also worried about the SBUS's large size and the economic and political power they assumed that it wielded. It established over two dozen branches, some in states, including Maryland and Ohio, that did not want the behemoth bank's presence within their borders. Several SCOTUS cases, including the infamous *McCulloch v. Maryland* (1819), upheld the bank's right to establish branches pretty much wherever it saw fit. After jettisoning Jones and hiring a competent replacement named Langdon Cheves, the SBUS's stockholders found a real dandy to lead the institution, a Philadelphian named Nicholas Biddle. The SBUS thrived financially under his stewardship and also protected the nation's economy from the bursting of a stock market bubble in Britain in 1825.

4 (2000); Richard Sylla, Robert E. Wright, and David Cowen, "Alexander Hamilton, Central Banker: Crisis Management During the U.S. Financial Panic of 1792," *Business History Review* 83, no. 2 (Spring 2009), 61–86; Robert E. Wright, *The First Wall Street: Chestnut Street, Philadelphia, and the Birth of American Finance*, (Chicago: University of Chicago Press, 2005); Robert E. Wright and David J. Cowen, *Financial Founding Fathers: The Men Who Made America Rich*, (Chicago: University of Chicago Press, 2006).

Despite the successful turnaround, Biddle fretted that the 20-year charter of the SBUS was set to expire in 1836, the last year of Jackson's putative second term as president. Biddle pushed for recharter early, in 1832, hoping to make the renewal of his big bank an issue in the presidential election that fall. The tactic backfired when Jackson vetoed the recharter bill on the grounds that it aided the rich at the expense of the poor:

It is to be regretted that the rich and powerful too often bend the acts of government to their selfish purposes. ... When the laws undertake ... to make the rich richer and the potent more powerful, the humble members of society — the farmer, mechanics, and laborers — who have neither the time nor the means of securing like favors to themselves, have a right to complain of the injustice of their Government.[910]

Jackson was re-elected by a landslide and began draining the SBUS of the government's deposits. Biddle put the final nail in the coffin of big U.S. banks when he chartered the tattered remnants of the SBUS in Pennsylvania and within a few years ran the new bank out of business, forever associating the institution with the financial crises of the late 1830s and the nasty economic downturn of the early 1840s. Subsequent calls for the establishment of a Third BUS all fell short and even the Civil War could not resurrect interest in behemoth banks or central banking.

From 1836 until 1913, the United States relied on the automatic mechanisms of the gold standard to determine its domestic monetary policy (money supply and interest rates). During that period, capital (including gold) flowed in and out of the country freely and exchange rates varied hardly at all but the government was largely powerless to stop domestic shocks, like financial crises, from occurring or from wrecking the economy for a few years after they struck. For the most part, Americans were content with that painful tradeoff, demonstrating just how much they disliked and distrusted large financial institutions.

---

910 As quoted in Robert Remini, *Andrew Jackson and the Bank War: A Study in the Growth of Presidential Power*, (New York: W. W. Norton and Company, 1967): 83.

Fear of financial concentration reappeared with a vengeance in the late nineteenth century in the Populist and Progressive movements.[911] Democracy and massive concentrations of wealth were incompatible, many Americans believed, following ancient thinkers like Phaleas of Chalcedon. "For any democracy to be successful," Phaleas argued, "its citizens must have neither so much personal wealth and power as consistently to be able to dominate others, nor so little as to be dominated consistently by others."[912] In his impassioned "Cross of Gold" speech, Democratic presidential hopeful William Bryan Jennings warned that "on the one side stand the ... moneyed interests, aggregated wealth and capital, imperious, arrogant, compassionless. ... On the other side stand an unnumbered throng," the 99 percent in today's parlance.[913] Theodore Roosevelt, Robert La Follette, Louis Brandeis, Franklin Delano Roosevelt, and other Progressives also inveighed against bigness, particularly big financial institutions, and throughout the early twentieth century state and national investigatory committees like Armstrong, Pujo, Pecora, and TNEC probed the financial sector repeatedly and not always superficially.[914]

Unsurprisingly, banking remained largely a small-time affair. Some banks in New York, and later Chicago and San Francisco, grew large enough to squeak onto the bottom of international rankings but branching restrictions purposely prevented them from becoming megabanks. Some southern states had large state-controlled banks or other large banks allowed to branch within the state but interstate branching died

---

911 The Sherman Antitrust Act was certainly part of this general movement, but its legal application to large financial institutions is tenuous. That is why a suit brought under it against investment bankers in 1947 failed miserably. The judge dismissed the case with prejudice and scolded the government for bringing suit. See Horace Robbins, "'Bigness', the Sherman Act, and Antitrust Policy," *Virginia Law Review* 39 (1953): 907–948; Vincent Carosso, "The Wall Street Money Trust from Pujo through Medina," *Business History Review* 47, no. 4 (1973): 432.

912 Adrian Kuzminski, *Fixing the System: A History of Populism, Ancient and Modern,* (New York: Continuum, 2008), 3.

913 Mark Roe, "A Political Theory of American Corporate Finance," *Columbia Law Review* 91 (1991): 31–34.

914 Robert La Follette, *La Follette's Autobiography,* (Madison: University of Wisconsin Press, 1911), 196–203.

with the SBUS. Many states banned all branching, even within the state, or allowed only a handful of banks to branch on a case-by-case basis. The so-called national banks that became numerous after the enactment of Civil War banking reforms could not freely branch. (They were called national because the federal government chartered them, not because they had a national presence.) The prevalence of small unit banks explains why America had so many banks, especially compared to Canada and Great Britain after those two nations began to encourage bank amalgamation in the late nineteenth century. It also explains the long persistence of the untrained country banker lending by the seat of his intuition instead of formal rules or actuarially sound formulas.[915]

Despite a dearth of megabanks, the U.S. economy grew steadily in real per capita terms after 1790, recessions of course excepted. The unit banking system probably made the Great Depression worse than it otherwise would have been because in the absence of an effective lender of last resort tens of thousands of little banks could not withstand the strain of the prolonged downturn and failed. That shrank the money supply and placed more downward pressure on prices and the economy. Two entities that allowed branching, California and Canada, fared much better than unit banking states did. (That is why the Joads of *Grapes of Wrath* fame and most flesh and blood Okies fled to California instead of to hard-hit Illinois, which did not allow branching.) The dearth of private megabanks, however, did not prevent the economy from rebounding after Roosevelt devalued the dollar (against gold) and World War II stimulated aggregate demand.

America also did not need private megabanks to finance either world war or the Cold War. The securities markets, the markets for stocks and bonds, took up any slack by linking large numbers of investors to large entrepreneurs and numerous small savers to the biggest

---

915 Robert E. Wright, "Banking System Stability/Fragility: The Roles of Governance and Supervision in Canada and America," in Mark S. Bonham, ed., *Becoming 150: 150 Years of Canadian Business History*, (Toronto: Canadian Business History Association, 2018): 226–38; B. M. Gile, *The Farm Credit Situation in Southwestern Arkansas*, (Fayetteville: University of Arkansas Agricultural Experiment Station, 1929), 6.

borrowers. Americans were not too keen on investment banks or the stock market, particularly after the Stock Market Crash of 1929 eventually took the blame for the Depression, but viewed them with somewhat less trepidation after Glass Steagall, part of the Banking Act of 1933, separated commercial (taking deposits and making loans) from investment (selling securities and helping with mergers) banking.

Between the death of the SBUS in 1836 and the mid-1990s, the only megabank in operation in the United States worthy of the name was the Federal Reserve System (the Fed). Established in 1913 and operational by the end of 1914, the Fed is technically owned by its member banks, which own dividend-paying but resale-restricted shares of its stock. Ultimately, however, the Fed is the tool of the federal government, which controls appointment of its most important leaders, such as Chairman of the Board of Governors. The Fed's adoption was made possible by political compromise, public disgust with repeated panics and recessions, and fear of J. P. Morgan, the investment banking titan who twice (in 1893 and 1907) seemed to rescue the economy from the throes of financial crisis. Any man with enough power to stop a financial panic, the common wisdom held, certainly had enough power to start one. Fearful that some mega-capitalist like Morgan would hold the nation's economy hostage someday, Americans agreed to the creation of a central bank with the power to thwart panics by acting as a lender of last resort.

To keep the mighty beast from turning on its masters, the American people, the Fed was divided into 12 districts, each endowed with independent policy capabilities. (That Missouri, not exactly a financial powerhouse then or now, ended up headquartering two of the district banks, the ones in St. Louis and Kansas City, is believed to have been the result of some congressional horse trading.) The districts remain to this day, but their independent powers for the most part do not. By the 1950s, if not earlier, the Federal Reserve had become the monster megabank that Jackson and his multitudinous followers so feared. And it would play a leading role in the creation of the private megabanks that wrecked the economy in 2008.[916]

Here, briefly, is the story. After exacerbating the Great Depression, the Fed fudged up badly again in the 1970s. The Arab oil embargoes of 1973 and 1979 did not help matters but neither alone could have caused the stagflation, the simultaneous high levels of inflation and unemployed, that plagued the economy throughout most of that malaise-laden decade.[917] As a direct result of the nation's economic difficulties, a group of small banks called Savings and Loans (S&Ls for short) asked for demutualization (to sell shares in themselves to stockholders) and deregulation (less stringent rules). Granted both concessions, hundreds of them soon were technically bankrupt because their executives, freed from the restrictions of regulators and depositors, took excessive risks in a failed effort to pad their own wallets and egos. Regulators who did not want to admit that they had been asleep at the switch, however, refused to shut down the failed S&Ls. Called zombies because they were economically dead but still in operation, the bankrupt S&Ls took even bigger risks that sank most of them even deeper into the red. The end result was the infamous S&L crisis and bailout of the late 1980s and early 1990s.[918]

That crisis created two very unfortunate consequences. Foremost, it confirmed regulators' prior belief, inherited from the banking panics of the nineteenth century and the experience of the Great Depression, that small and even medium-sized banks were inherently shaky. Small

916 For a general overview of the Federal Reserve System, see Robert E. Wright, *Money and Banking*, 3rd ed., (Boston: Flat World Knowledge, 2017). For the most detailed history of its early years yet published, see Allan Meltzer, *A History of the Federal Reserve, Vol. 1: 1913–1951*, (Chicago: University of Chicago Press, 2003).

917 The best treatments of the Fed's policies and practices since the 1950s include Stephen H. Axilrod, *Inside the Fed: Monetary Policy and Its Management, Martin Through Greenspan to Bernanke*, (Cambridge: MIT Press, 2009); Robert P. Bremner, *Chairman of the Fed: William McChesney Martin, Jr. and the Creation of the American Financial System*, (New Haven: Yale University Press, 2004); Robert Hetzel, *The Monetary Policy of the Federal Reserve: A History*, (New York: Cambridge University Press, 2008).

918 The best description of the S&L crisis is still probably Meir Kohn, *Money, Banking, and Financial Markets*, 2nd ed. (New York: Harcourt Brace, 1993), 447–80.

banks were thought to attract small minds and loans from geographically limited areas. A small but localized shock, like the failure of a major
employer, could quickly put even a well-managed small bank into trouble
and sink a typical one. Bigger banks, it was believed, attracted better managers and also a geographically wider portfolio of loans. That is true, but
only to a point. As discussed below, ever bigger is not ever better. In addition, bigger banks tend to take on higher levels of risk than small banks
do, effectively canceling any gains from geographical dispersion of their
loan portfolios.

The S&L crisis also helped to spur the failure of Continental Illinois, a
Chicago unit bank with a national (that is to say federal) banking charter.
In 1973, Continental Illinois began a period of aggressive growth under
new chairman Roger Anderson, whose goal was to get the bank into the
very top tier of money center banks in the country and to earn for himself
the fame and wealth commensurate with such a feat. To accomplish it,
he told his bank's loan officers to lend large sums on attractive terms.
They obliged and drove Continental to the seventh spot in the U.S. commercial bank size rankings. By 1983, Continental had accumulated some
$42 billion in assets, up from $12.5 billion in 1972. Funds for the loans
came partly from deposits but mostly from the sale of NCDs, uninsured
institution-sized certificates of deposit.

The rapid growth, however, came at the cost of the bank's safety.
Its long list of borrowers included Latin American dictators of dubious creditworthiness and shaky corporations like Penn Square, Braniff,
International Harvester, Massey-Ferguson, and Chrysler, all of which
eventually defaulted or sought bankruptcy protection. The purchasers
of Continental's NCDs soon realized that the big bank was in trouble,
so they stopped rolling the instruments over and demanded the return
of their principal. The bank's borrowing costs therefore mounted just
as its gross revenues slipped due to the bad loans. In a desperate attempt
to dig itself out of a hole of its own creation, Continental Illinois made
more risky loans, most of which went bad by April 1984. On May 10, a
rumor that regulators were going to close the bank quickly spread. Its
remaining creditors refused to renew their loans, so the bank was forced

to ask the Fed for a $3.5 billion loan. Confidence in the banking system began to waver, so J.P. Morgan and 15 other banks provided Continental with a $4.5 billion line of credit. It was not enough. All the Fed's horses and all J.P. Morgan's men could not put Continental Illinois back together again. The FDIC took it over on July 26, 1984 and promptly promised to pay all of the bank's creditors, not just the depositors covered by its insurance program. The government believed it had to protect all the bank's creditors because Continental Illinois owed money to over 2,000 banks nationwide. At least 66 of those banks would have gone bankrupt if not repaid and another 113 would have been crippled. The failure of Continental Illinois therefore cost U.S. taxpayers several billion dollars but more importantly, in retrospect, it induced government regulators to develop a policy, called Too Big to Fail (TBTF), that essentially told bankers that they should endeavor to grow their banks as big as possible, as quickly as possible, if they wanted to enjoy free insurance of their liabilities. (Free to the biggest banks, that is. Very expensive for everyone else.) In 1991, TBTF policy was engraved in statutory stone as part of the Federal Deposit Insurance Corporation Act (FDICIA), a series of reforms initiated in response to the S&L crisis.[919] It didn't take bankers long to catch on. If they got really big, they could, thanks to the federal backstop, take on significantly more risk and hence earn much higher profits. And get bigger they did, beginning right after TBTF became explicit policy. The cause and effect is not difficult to discern. Financial institutions grow larger (through merger or organic growth) for six basic reasons:

    (1) economies of scale (more output per unit of input due to higher production levels);

---

919 Kohn, *Money*, 455–457; Alan Gart, *Regulation, Deregulation, Reregulation: The Future of the Banking, Insurance, and Securities Industries*, (New York: John Wiley and Sons, 1994), 94–97, 159–161; Jane W. D'Arista, *The Evolution of Finance, Volume II: Restructuring Institutions and Markets*, (Armonk, N.Y.: M.E. Sharpe, 1994), 162–163; Benton E. Gup, ed. *Too Big to Fail: Policies and Practices in Government Bailouts*, (Westport, Conn.: Praeger, 2004); Charles Calomiris, *The Postmodern Bank Safety Net: Lesson from Developed and Developing Economies*, (Washington, D.C.: The AEI Press, 1997), 17–18.

(2) economies of scope (more output per unit of input due to the production of a broader range of products);

(3) X-efficiency (managerial efficiency);

(4) market power (ability to extract more of the exchange surplus triangle created by trading);

(5) managerial agency (increase the entrenchment and/or pay of managers);

(6) better access to government regulators and the safety net (like TBTF).

The first three reasons for bank growth are "good" ones because they increase the size of the economic pie. The last three are "bad" because, at best, they simply redistribute pieces of the pie from consumers to financial institutions and/or their executives. At worst, the last three actually reduce the size of the overall economic pie. That four, five, and six were the real reasons for the rapid growth of big banks is clear from two facts, the timing of their growth spurt and the lack of compelling evidence for any of the three "good" reasons for banks to grow or merge.[920]

In the late 1980s and early 1990s, the biggest banks began to grow bigger by inducing the Fed, the primary supervisor of bank holding companies (the form that the largest banks tended to take), to relax restrictions against interstate branching and combining investment and commercial banking activities under one balance sheet. About the same time, they induced many states to loosen branching restrictions both within state and, with the proliferation of regional reciprocal branching agreements, across state lines. Formal legislative repeal of interstate branching restrictions by national banks and Glass Steagall took place in

---

920 Gregory Hanc, "The Future of Banking in America: Summary and Conclusions," in *FDIC Future of Banking Study* (Washington, D.C.: FDIC, 2004), 9; Stephen Pizzo, "Minneapolis Fed: Bank Consolidation Won't Cause Economies of Scale," *National Mortgage News*, 7 October 1991, 29; Allen Berger, Rebecca Demsetz, and Philip Strahan, "The Consolidation of the Financial Services Industry: Causes, Consequences, and Implications for the Future," *Journal of Banking and Finance* 23 (1999): 135–94; Kenneth Carow, Edward Kane, and Rajesh Narayanan, "How Has Financial Modernization Affected Corporate Customers?" NBER Working Paper No. 11256 (March 2005), 2, 19; Calomiris, *Postmodern Bank Safety Net*, 6–12.

1994 and 1999, under the Riegle-Neal Interstate Banking and Efficiency Act and the Gramm-Leach-Bliley Financial Services Modernization Act, respectively.[921]

The effects of those new policies and laws were immediate, palpable, and pernicious. The biggest banks immediately began gobbling up smaller banks, driving banking sector concentration up to levels not seen in the United States since the early 1790s, when the BUS overshadowed the handful of state institutions then in existence. In 1920, the top 10 banks controlled about 10 percent of the nation's deposits. That figure increased to over 25 percent after the Great Depression shakeout (a lot of failures and mergers) but subsequently dropped to about 20 percent in 1959 and actually trended slightly lower through the 1970s and 1980s. Today, by contrast, the ten biggest banks control half of Americans' deposits. To add a new twist to a famous quotation by Winston Churchill, *never have so few owed so much to so many*. The story reprises itself on the other side of the balance sheet as well. In the mid-1980s, the 10 largest banks owned about 15 percent of the banking industry's total assets but by 2010 they owned fully half.

Financial conglomeration, the combining of formerly disparate financial services under one roof, also increased significantly. LCFIs (large, complex financial institutions) have grown in importance when compared to the overall economy. From the end of the World War II until the early 1990s, the assets of the nation's 10 largest financial companies consistently equaled about a quarter of GDP. In the early 1990s, that figure began to skyrocket. It exceeded 100 percent of GDP by the early 2000s, a four-fold increase in a single decade. The big ten's share of total financial system assets also exploded in the early 1990s, rising from 10 to 50 percent between 1994 and 2004.

---

921 Nomi Prins, *It Takes a Pillage: An Epic Tale of Power, Deceit, and Untold Trillions*, (Hoboken, N.J.: John Wiley & Sons, 2011), 147–49; Charles W. Calomiris and Jason Karceski, "Is the Bank Merger Wave of the 1990s Efficient? Lessons from Nine Case Studies," in *Mergers and Productivity*, ed. Steven N. Kaplan (Chicago: University of Chicago Press, 2000), 97; D'Arista, *Evolution of Finance*, 322.

By the early 2000s, then, Too Big to Fail had become a self-fulfilling prophecy. In the early 1980s, all 10 of the biggest financial companies could have failed without causing much disturbance, at least directly. Just 20 years and a slew of mergers later, the economy was increasingly held captive by a handful of uber-powerful LCFIs. Americans' longstanding fears of concentrated financial power were finally realized but hardly anyone noticed. Capitalist Henry Kaufman made some noises about it, and asked me to investigate (some of the fruits of which I share here), but the rest of the world lumbered onward in oblivion or smug satisfaction with the status quo.[922]

What about the good reasons for LCFI growth, economies of scale and scope and increased X-efficiency? Most studies of scale find "slightly increasing returns to scale among small banks and slightly decreasing returns at large banks."[923] In other words, smaller banks may not have yet achieved minimum efficient scale and would therefore benefit from growing larger. Larger banks, by contrast, may have exceeded maximum efficient scale and hence would benefit from shrinking, or at least holding their size constant. Technological advances may have increased the minimum efficient scale of banks but technology may also reduce efficient scale by reducing transaction and other backroom costs. Consortiums of small banks, for example, achieve cost reductions by using internet business-to-business exchanges and by outsourcing electronic payment platforms and the like.[924]

---

922 Henry Kaufman, *The Road to Financial Reformation: Warnings, Consequences, Reforms*, (Hoboken: John Wiley & Sons, 2009).

923 As quoted in Joseph Hughes and Loretta Mester, "Bank Capitalization and Cost: Evidence of Scale Economies in Risk Management and Signaling," *Review of Economics and Statistics* 80 (1998): 315–325. Another way of stating this is that the "average cost curve has a relatively flat U-shape, with medium-size banks being slightly more cost scale efficient than either large or small banks." Allen Berger, Robert DeYoung, Hena Genay, and Gregory Udell, "Globalization of Financial Institutions: Evidence from Cross-Border Banking Performance," *Brookings-Wharton Papers on Financial Services* (2000), 35.

924 Hanc, "Future of Banking in America," 9; Berger, DeYoung, Genay, and Udell, "Globalization of Financial Institutions," 36; Karlyn Mitchell and Nur Onvural, "Economies of Scale and Scope at Large Commercial Banks: Evidence from the Fourier Flexible Functional Form," *Journal of Money, Credit and Banking* 28 (1996): 178–199; Insurance and Superannuation

Economies of scope and X-efficiency gains are also elusive. One alleged scope advantage, cross-selling a wide variety of financial products via one contact point (like a bank branch teller), is based on the creation of quasi-rents or soft market power, essentially the ability to sell overpriced products to existing customers. Cross-selling doesn't work well, however, when the entire range of products is not competitive or when customers are wary of cross-selling techniques, which they often are. The *Financial Times* put it this way: "Cross-selling is a producer-driven strategy in an increasingly consumer-driven world. It is simply out of touch with the times." Instead of increasing cross-selling by improving its products, for example, Wells Fargo rewarded its employees for signing up customers for products they did not want. It ended up costing the megabank what little remained of its tattered reputation, plus the head of its CEO and at least eight figures of cash.[925]

Commission, "Other Issues: Mergers Amongst Financial Majors and Electronic Commerce," (Australia: 1997); "California Independent Bankers Cautions Fed on NationsBank / B of A Merger," *PR Newswire*, Financial News, 10 July 1998; Joseph Hughes, William Lang, Loretta Mester, and Choon-Geol Moon, "The Dollars and Sense of Bank Consolidation," *Journal of Banking and Finance* 23 (1999): 291–324; Stijn Claessens and Daniela Klingebiel, "Competition and Scope of Activities in Financial Services," *World Bank Research Observer* 16 (2001): 19–40; Group of Ten, "Report on Consolidation in the Financial Sector," (BIS, IMF, and OECD: January 2001), 4; Kenneth D. Jones and Tim Critchfield, "Consolidation in the U.S. Banking Industry: Is the 'Long, Strange Trip' About to End?" (FDIC Working Paper, 2005), 17; Kenneth Carow, Edward Kane, and Rajesh Narayanan, "How Has Financial Modernization Affected Corporate Customers?" NBER Working Paper No. 11256 (March 2005), 5.

George Benston, Gerlad Hanweck, and David Humphrey, "Scale Economies in Banking: A Restructuring and Reassessment," *Journal of Money, Credit and Banking* 14 (1982): 435–456; Group of Ten, "Report on Consolidation," 5; Berger, DeYoung, Genay, and Udell, "Globalization of Financial Institutions," 35–36; Anjan Thakor, "Information Technology and Financial Services Consolidation," *Journal of Banking and Finance* 23 (1999): 697–700; Jonathan Moules, "Happy just to be in business: An online exchange that helps small local banks to gain economies of scale has shown an amazing capacity for survival," *Financial Times*, 13 March 2002; Robert DeYoung and William C. Hunter, "Deregulation, the Internet, and the Competitive Viability of Large Banks and Community Banks," in *The Future of Banking*, ed. Benton Gup (Westport, Conn.: Quorum Books, 2003), 173–201.

925 Ingo Walter, "Strategies in Financial Services, the Shareholders and the System: Is Bigger and Broader Better?" (Hamburg Institute of International Economics Discussion Paper No. 205, 2002), 3–6; Allen Frankel and John Montgomery, "Financial Structure: An International Perspective," *Brookings Papers on Economic Activity* 1991 (1991): 291–292; Charles W. Calomiris and Jason Karceski, "Is the Bank Merger Wave of the 1990s Efficient? Lessons from Nine

Ironically, while the U.S. was radically restructuring its financial regulatory regime, Japan's gut-wrenching experience should have undermined the notion that bigger is always better. In the 1970s and 1980s, Japanese banks, unencumbered by Glass Steagall or branching restrictions and buoyed by a surging economy, became the biggest in the world. In 1982, for example, 15 of the world's 50 biggest banks were Japanese. They controlled $976 billion in assets, almost 30 percent of the total assets of the world's 50 biggest banks. No other country's banks were even close. In the late 1980s, however, the Japanese economy hit a wall from which it has yet to fully recover. Due to epic real estate and stock market crashes, many of its big banks turned into zombies, unable to lend enough to stimulate the economy. They remain moribund to this day, their decaying financial flesh stinking up a Japanese economy that was once thought to be on the brink of exceeding that of the United States. Japan's economy is now only the third largest in the world and only about 40 percent the size of that of the United States.

U.S. policymakers should have learned from the Japanese experience what the whole world figured out in 2008, that big banks can go bankrupt just as easily as small ones can and that the big ones cause much more damage when they go down. After minimum efficient scale has been achieved, what matters is credit quality and asset diversification, not size per se. As economist Joseph Stagg Lawrence pointed out in 1930, "size is

Case Studies," in *Mergers and Productivity*, ed. Steven N. Kaplan (Chicago: University of Chicago Press, 2000), 101–104; D'Arista, *Evolution of Finance*, 108–109; Allen Berger, David Humphrey, and Lawrence Pulley, "Do Consumers Pay for One-Stop Banking? Evidence from an Alternative Revenue Function," *Journal of Banking and Finance* 20 (1996): 1,601–1,621; Gary Hamel, "Wrong merger, wrong logic: Citicorp and Travelers are joining forces for economies of scale but they will be selling their customers short on choice and innovation," *Financial Times*, 15 April 1998; Lucinda Shen, "Wells Fargo's Phony Account Scandal May Not Actually End Up Costing That Much," *Fortune*, 6 December 2016; Stavros Peristiani, "Do Mergers Improve the X-Efficiency and Scale Efficiency of U.S. Banks? Evidence From the 1980s," *Journal of Money, Credit and Banking* 29, no. 3 (1997): 326–37; Allen Berger and David Humphrey, "Efficiency of Financial Institutions: International Survey and Directions for Future Research," *European Journal of Operational Research* 98, no. 2 (1997): 175–212.

not the magic formula of safety. ... Safety is a function of prudence."[926] Instead of encouraging banks to get bigger, regulators should have prevented them from getting too big to fail and worked to make banks of all sizes safer. Call it TSTF: Too Safe (or Solid) to Fail.

LCFIs are paragons of imprudence. Since the rise of the megabanks in the 1990s, the U.S. economy has suffered from three financial crises (1997–98, 2000, and 2008), two recessions (2001 and 2007–8), and an economic funk (2009 to 2017) that crippled the national economy for the better part of a decade. Breaking up the big banks will not necessarily improve the nation's economic outlook, but megabanks are not necessary for recovery and in fact have been impeding it by preventing the sale of houses and depressing consumer demand, much as the mega-zombies in Japan did. And LCFIs may cause another financial meltdown before they are through. The threat they pose is many times that posed by small, self-help institutions created to reduce *de facto* discrimination and predation.

Of course none of this is to say that the problems faced by minorities will cease once entry into the financial system is eased. This is particularly true of Indians, who face a panoply of barriers to economic success, as shown by the rise and demise of Pte Hca Ka, Inc., a bison ranch and processing facility on the Cheyenne River Sioux Reservation. Despite adequate financing, or perhaps because of it, it grew too quickly and, for a variety of cultural and political reasons was unable to adjust quickly enough to a rapidly changing market for bison meat. As shown by the "forced federalism" engendered by the slow retreat of the BIA in recent decades, state bureaucrats can be just as tyrannical as Washington ones while adding yet another layer of complexity to the regulation of Indians' economic affairs. And tribal sovereignty is no answer, either, as some tribal governments are BIA puppets while others are venal and still others incompetent. Were all the problems with Indian Country eliminated,

---

926 Joseph Stagg Lawrence, *Banking Concentration in the United States: A Critical Analysis*, (New York: Bankers Publishing Company, 1930), 13.

over $40 billion in investment would occur there according to one Treasury Department study.[927]

So self-help and free entry and the reduction of financial discrimination and predation it will entail is not a panacea. Some problems simply cannot be solved to everyone's satisfaction, even by government fiat. The cost of small, short-term loans, for example, has always seemed too high to outsiders. No solution has yet to be found and likely one never will be, unless an answer lurks somewhere in new technologies like the distributed ledgers called blockchains. Free entry and self-help, however, is much preferable to government lending or heavy-handed, top-down regulation.[928]

---

927 Sebastian Felix Braun, *Buffalo Inc.: American Indians and Economic Development*, (Norman: University of Oklahoma Press, 2008); Jeff Corntassel and Richard C. Witmer, *Forced Federalism: Contemporary Challenges to Indigenous Nationhood*, (Norman: University of Oklahoma Press, 2008), 16–26, 134–41; Pickering, *Lakota Culture*, 116; Miller, *Reservation "Capitalism"*, 93.

928 Gile, *Farm Credit Situation*, 38; Daily Fintech, "Blockchain Technology Could Revolutionize Small Business Finance," 14 June 2016. Last accessed 26 January 2017: http://bankinnovation.net/2016/06/how-blockchain-technology-could-integrate-financial-physical-supply-chains-and-revolutionize-small-business-finance/.

Bibliography

Archival Sources

American Heritage Center, University of Wyoming, Laramie, Wyoming:
    Pocketbook News, Wilma Soss Papers

Butler Center for Arkansas Studies, Little Rock, Arkansas:
    Union National Bank Records

Federal Writers' Project, Slave Narratives, Washington, D.C.:
    Vol. I, Alabama Narratives
    Vol. X, Missouri Narratives

Georgia Historical Society, Savannah, Georgia:
    Germania Savings Bank, Stockholders Records, 1891–93

Guardian Life Insurance Company of America (GLICA) Archives, New York, New York:
    Circular Letters, Agency Communication and Sales Promotion, Box 212
    Interviews with Executives

Historical Society of Pennsylvania, Philadelphia, Pennsylvania:
    Elizabeth Steele Accounts
    Elizabeth Willing Powel Estate Books
    First Female Beneficial Society of Philadelphia Minutes, 1814–1840
    Hispanic Federation for Social and Economic Development, Administrative Series
    Judith Bogert Memorandum Book, 1843
    Northern Dispensary for the Medical Relief of the Poor
    Pennsylvania Fire Insurance Company Mortgages, 1881, and Claim Book, 1855–1881
    Philadelphia National Bank Signature Book, 1856–1868

National Archives and Records Administration II, College Park, Maryland:
    Records of the Bureau of the Public Debt

New York Historical Society, New York, New York:
  Recoverable Outstanding Debts, 4 November 1763

New York Public Library, New York, New York:
  Staff of the Dunbar National Bank, Harlem, New York City, circa 1930

Pennsylvania State Archives, Harrisburg, Pennsylvania:

Records of the Department of State, Corporation Bureau, Letters Patent,
  1814–1874

Rush Rhees Library, Special Collections, University of Rochester, Rochester,
  New York:
  Barry (Arthur) Papers:
  Agendas/Minutes, Board Meetings Community
  Agendas/Minutes, Exec. Committee East Side/Community
  Business Correspondence, Community Savings
  Business Correspondence East Side Bank
  Correspondence, Savings Bank Association of New York
  Documents: Employee/Public Relations, Community
  Documents: Life Insurance, Community
  Executive Committee Meeting, Agendas/Minutes: Exec. Committee
      Community
  Mortgage Loan Applications, East Side Bank
  Printed Ephemera, East Side and Community Savings
  Real Estate Correspondence, East Side Bank
  Recommendations of the Examining Committee, 1945,
      Recommendations, Exam. Com., East Side/Community
  Stocks, Bonds, Securities, East Side/Community, Agendas/Minutes:
      Exec. Committee Community

State Historical Society of Wisconsin Archives, Madison, Wisconsin:
  "Examination Reports, Domestic Companies, 1908–1910," Insurance
      Department, Examining Division, Box 2, Series 1049.

University of Florida Smathers Libraries, Gainesville, Florida:
  Agreement, Florida Cycle Company and Mercantile Exchange Bank, 20
      July 1900
  Florida Bank & Trust Company Deposit Book, Florida National Bank
      Records, 1887–1989
  Florida National Bank Records, 1887–1989, MS 069
  Scrapbook, Florida National Bank Records, 1887–1989, MS 069
  Statement of Condition and Directory of Officers and Directors, Florida
      National Banks of Florida, Inc., 1983

University of Georgia Libraries, Athens, Georgia:
    Daily Cashier's Settlement Book, Bank of Athens, 1857
    Edward Remington Bank of Savannah Letters, 1860–1862
Virginia Historical Society, Richmond, Virginia:
    James River Company Account Book, 1785–1789

Secondary and Printed Primary Sources

A Reformed Stock Gambler. *Stocks and Stock-Jobbing in Wall-Street, with Sketches of the Brokers, and Fancy Stocks.* New York: New-York Publishing Company, 1848.

Aaron, Henry, Jr. and John B. Shoven. *Should the United States Privatize Social Security?* Cambridge, Mass.: MIT Press, 1999.

Aaronson, Daniel, Daniel Hartley, and Bhashkar Mazumder. "The Effect of the 1930s HOLC 'Redlining' Maps." Federal Reserve Bank of Chicago Working Paper WP 2017–2 (August 3, 2017).

Abbott, Grace. *From Relief to Social Security: The Development of the New Public Welfare Service.* Chicago: University of Chicago Press, 1941.

Abrams, Charles. *Forbidden Neighbors: A Study of Prejudice in Housing.* New York: Harper & Brothers, 1955.

Acharya, Viral and Thomas Cooley. *Regulating Wall Street: The Dodd-Frank Act and the New Architecture of Global Finance.* New York: John Wiley & Sons, 2010.

Ackerman, James M. "Interest Rates and the Law: A History of Usury." *Arizona State Law Journal* (1981): 61–110.

Ackerman, William V. "Indian Gaming in South Dakota: Conflict in Public Policy." *American Indian Quarterly* 33, no. 2 (2009): 253–79.

Adams, Dale W. "Mobilizing Household Savings Through Rural Financial Markets." *Economic Development and Cultural Change* 26, no. 3 (1978): 547–60.

Adams, Sean Patrick. "Soulless Monsters and Iron Horses: The Civil War, Institutional Change, and American Capitalism." In *Capitalism Takes Command: The Social Transformation of Nineteenth-Century America,* edited by Michael Zakim and Gary J. Kornblith. Chicago: University of Chicago Press, 2012.

Adler, Jeffrey, A. *Yankee Merchants and the Making of the Urban West: The Rise and Fall of Antebellum St. Louis.* Cambridge: Cambridge University Press, 1991.

Agarwal, Sumit, Gene Amromin, Itzhak Ben-David. "Loan Product Steering in Mortgage Markets." NBER Working Paper No. w22696 (September 2016).

Alston, Lee J. and Joseph P. Ferrie. "Time on the Ladder: Career Mobility in Agriculture, 1890–1938." NBER Working Paper No. 11231 (March 2005).

Ambuehl, Sandro, B. Douglas Bernheim, Fulya Y. Ersoy, and Donna Harris. "Social Transmission of Financial Decision Making Skills. A Case of the Blind Leading the Blind?" (30 December 2016). Available at SSRN: https://ssrn.com/abstract=2891753

Anand, Bharat N. and Alexander Galetovic. "Relationships, Competition and the Structure of Investment Banking Markets." *Journal of Industrial Economics* 54, no. 2 (2006): 151–99.

Anderson, Dan R. "Commentary." In *Government Risk-Bearing: Proceedings of a Conference Held at the Federal Reserve Bank of Cleveland*, edited by Mark S. Sniderman. Boston: Kluwer Academic, 1993.

Anderson, Elisabeth. "Experts, Ideas, and Policy Change: The Russell Sage Foundation and Small Loan Reform, 1909–1941." *Theory and Society* 37, no. 3 (2008): 271–310.

Anderson, Terry and Bryan Leonard. "Institutions and the Wealth of Indian Nations." In *Unlocking the Wealth of Indian Nations*, edited by Terry Anderson. New York: Lexington Books, 2016.

Anderson, Terry and Dominic Parker. "The Wealth of Indian Nations: Economic Performance and Institutions on Reservations." In *Self Determination: The Other Path for Native Americans*, edited by Terry Anderson, Bruce Benson, and Thomas Flanagan. Stanford: Stanford University Press, 2006.

Anderson, Terry and Steven LaCombe. "Institutional Change in the Indian Horse Culture." In *The Other Side of the Frontier: Economic Explorations into Native American History*, edited by Linda Barrington. New York: Westview Press, 1999.

Anderson, Terry, Bryan Leonard, Dominic Parker, and Shawn Regan. "Natural Resources on American Indian Reservations." In *Unlocking the Wealth of Indian Nations*, edited by Terry Anderson. New York: Lexington Books, 2016.

Anderson, Terry. *Sovereign Nations or Reservations? An Economic History of American Indians*. San Francisco: Pacific Research Institute for Public Policy, 1995.

Anderson, Terry ed. *Unlocking the Wealth of Indian Nations*. New York: Lexington Books, 2016.

Andriotis, AnnaMaria. "Banks Fall Back in Mortgage Lending." *Wall Street Journal*, 3 November 2016.

Anon. "Allan Berube (1946–2007)." *History Workshop Journal* 69 (Spring 2010): 294–96.

Anon. "California Independent Bankers Cautions Fed on NationsBank / B of A Merger." PR Newswire, Financial News, 10 July 1998.

Anon. "Household Ownership of Equities: 2002 and 2005." *The 2006 Statistical Abstract of the United States.* Washington, D.C.: U.S. Census Bureau, 2006.

Anon. "Jumbo Loans Benefit Few Blacks, Hispanics." *Wall Street Journal,* 2 June 2016.

Anon. "Milking Taxpayers: As Crop Prices Fall, Farmers Grow Subsidies Instead." *Economist,* 14 February 2015.

Anon. "Mortgage Lending Discrimination." Field Hearing Before the Committee on Financial Services, U.S. House of Representatives, One Hundred Tenth Congress, 1st Sess., October 15, 2007.

Anon. "Ownership of Mutual Funds, Shareholder Sentiment, and Use of the Internet, 2013." *ICI Research Perspective* 19, 9 (October 2013), 3, 26–27.

Anon. "Regulation and Taxation of House Trailers." *University of Chicago Law Review* 22, no. 3 (1955): 738–51.

Anon. "The Practice of Life Offices in Regard to Assurances on Female Lives." *Journal of the Institute of Actuaries* 29, no. 1 (1891): 75–78.

Anon. "The Underclass." Hearing Before the Joint Economic Committee, Congress of the United States, 100 First Congress, 1st Sess., 25 May 1989.

Anon. *2015 Investment Company Fact Book: A Review of Trends and Activities in the U.S. Investment Company Industry.* New York: Investment Company Institute, 2015.

Anon. *Delaware Gazette and State Journal.* 8 August 1826.

Anon. *First Annual Report of the Provident Loan Society of Rochester, New York.* Rochester: 1914.

Anon. *Proceedings of the Forty-Ninth Annual Meeting of the Life Insurance Association of America.* New York: 1955.

Anon. *The Present Status of Mutual Benefit Associations.* New York: National Industrial Conference Board, 1931.

Antilla, Susan. *Tales from the Boom-Boom Room: The Landmark Legal Battles that Exposed Wall Street's Shocking Culture of Sexual Harassment.* New York: HarperBusiness 2003.

Arbour, Keith. "Benjamin Franklin's First Government Printing: The Pennsylvania General Loan Office Mortgage Register of 1729, and Subsequent Franklin Mortgage Registers and Bonds." *Transactions of the American Philosophical Society* 89, part 5 (1999), 1–89.

Ards, Sheila D. and Samuel L. Myers, Jr., "The Color of Money: Bad Credit, Wealth, and Race." *American Behavioral Scientist* 45, no. 2 (2001): 223–39.

Ariely, Dan. *Predictably Irrational: The Hidden Forces that Shape our Decisions,* rev. ed. New York: Harper, 2010.

Armstrong, Barbara. *Insuring the Essentials: Minimum Wage Plus Social Insurance – A Living Wage Program*. New York: Macmillan Company, 1932.

Arnold, David. "Work and Culture in Southeastern Alaska: Tlingits and the Salmon Fisheries." In *Native Pathways: American Indian Culture and Economic Development*, edited by Brian Hosmer and Colleen O'Neill. Boulder: University Press of Colorado, 2004.

Ashraf, Nava, Colin F. Camerer, and George Loewenstein. "Adam Smith, Behavioral Economist." *Journal of Economic Perspectives* 19, no. 3 (2005): 131–45.

Avery, Robert B., Patricia E. Beeson, and Mark S. Sniderman. "Accounting for Racial Differences in Housing Credit Markets." Federal Reserve Bank of Cleveland Working Paper 9310 (December 1993).

Avery, Robert B., Patricia E. Beeson, and Mark S. Sniderman. "Cross-Lender Variation in Home Mortgage Lending." Federal Reserve Bank of Cleveland Working Paper 9219 (December 1992).

Avery, Robert B., Patricia E. Beeson, and Mark S. Sniderman. "Underserved Mortgage Markets: Evidence from HMDA Data." Federal Reserve Bank of Cleveland Working Paper 9421 (December 1994).

Axilrod, Stephen H. *Inside the Fed: Monetary Policy and Its Management, Martin Through Greenspan to Bernanke*. Cambridge: MIT Press, 2009.

Baar, Kenneth K. "The Right to Sell the 'Im'mobile Manufactured Home in Its Rent Controlled Space in the 'Im'mobile Home Park: Valid Regulation or Unconstitutional Taking?" *The Urban Lawyer* 24, no. 1 (1992): 157–221.

Baradaran, Mehrsa. *How the Other Half Banks: Exclusion, Exploitation, and the Threat to Democracy*. Cambridge: Harvard University Press, 2015.

Baradaran, Mehrsa. *The Color of Money: Black Banks and the Racial Wealth Gap*. Cambridge: Harvard University Press, 2017.

Bair, Frederick H., Jr. "Mobile Homes: A New Challenge." *Law and Contemporary Problems* 32, no. 2 (1967): 286–304.

Baker, George and George D. Smith. *The New Financial Capitalists: Kohlberg Kravis Roberts and the Creation of Corporate Value*. New York: Cambridge University Press, 1998.

Banks, Erik. *Alternative Risk Transfer: Integrated Risk Management Through Insurance, Reinsurance, and the Capital Markets*. Hoboken, N.J.: John Wiley and Sons, 2004.

Banner, Stuart. *How the Indians Lost Their Land: Law and Power on the Frontier*. Cambridge: Belknap Press, 2005.

Baranoff, Dalit. "Shaped by Risk: The American Fire Insurance Industry, 1790–1920." Ph.D. diss., Johns Hopkins University, 2003.

Barrington, Linda. "Native Americans and U.S. Economic History." In *The Other Side of the Frontier: Economic Explorations into Native American History*, edited by Linda Barrington. New York: Westview Press, 1999.

Barrington, Linda. "The Mississippians and Economic Development Before European Colonization." In *The Other Side of the Frontier: Economic Explorations into Native American History*, edited by Linda Barrington. New York: Westview Press, 1999.

Baskin, Jonathan and Paul Miranti. *A History of Corporate Finance*. New York: Cambridge University Press, 1999.

Batchelder, Alan. "Poverty: The Special Case of the Negro." In *The Economics of Poverty: An American Paradox*, edited by Burton Weisbrod. Englewood Cliffs, N.J.: Prentice-Hall, 1965.

Baxter, William. *The House of Hancock*. New York: Russell and Russell, Inc., 1965.

Bayer, Amanda and David Wilcox. "The Unequal Distribution of Economic Education: A Report on the Race, Ethnicity, and Gender of Economics Majors at US Colleges and Universities." Finance and Economics Discussion Series 2017–105. Washington: Board of Governors of the Federal Reserve System, 2017.

Beachy, Robert, Beatrice Craig, and Alastair Owens, eds. *Women, Business and Finance in Nineteenth-century Europe: Rethinking Separate Spheres*. New York: Berg, 2006.

Beaver, Patricia Duane. *Rural Community in the Appalachian South*. Lexington: University Press of Kentucky, 1986.

Becker, Jo, Sheryl Gay Stolberg, and Stephen Labaton. "White House Philosophy Stoked Mortgage Bonfire." *New York Times*, 21 December 2008.

Belangie, Philip and Sue Woodrow. "Turning Equity Into Opportunity: Montana Fund Helps Native Entrepreneurs Enter the Financial Mainstream." *Federal Reserve Bank of Minneapolis Community Dividend* (2008), 1.

Bell, Gregory S. *In the Black: A History of African Americans on Wall Street*. New York: John Wiley & Sons, 2002.

Belth, Joseph. "Discussion." In *The Financial Condition and Regulation of Insurance Companies*, edited by Richard E. Randall and Richard W. Kopcke. Boston: Federal Reserve Bank of Boston, 1991.

Beltramini, Enrico. "Consumer Credit as a Civil Right in the United States, 1968–1976." In *The Cultural History of Money and Credit: A Global Perspective*, edited by Chia Yin Jus, Thomas Luckett, and Erika Vause. New York: Lexington Books, 2016.

Bender, Thomas. *Community and Social Change in America*. Baltimore: Johns Hopkins University Press, 1982.

Benson, David, Aaron Lies, Albert Okunade, and Phanindra Wunnava. "Economic Impact of a Private Sector Micro-Financing Scheme in South Dakota." *Small Business Economics* 36 (2011): 157–68.

Benston, George J. "Savings Banking and the Public Interest." *Journal of Money, Credit and Banking* 4, no. 1 (1972), 131–226.

Benston, George J. *Regulating Financial Markets: A Critique and Some Proposals.* Washington, D.C.: AEI Press, 1999.

Benston, George J., Dan Horky, and H. Marting Weingartner. *An Empirical Study of Mortgage Redlining*, Monograph 1978–5. New York: Salomon Brothers Center, 1978.

Benston, George J., Gerald Hanweck, and David Humphrey. "Scale Economies in Banking: A Restructuring and Reassessment." *Journal of Money, Credit and Banking* 14 (1982): 435–56.

Berger, Allen and David Humphrey. "Efficiency of Financial Institutions: International Survey and Directions for Future Research." *European Journal of Operational Research* 98, no. 2 (1997): 175–212.

Berger, Allen and Gregory Udell. "The Future of Relationship Lending." In *The Future of Banking*, edited by Benton Gup. Westport, Conn.: Quorum Books, 2003.

Berger, Allen, David Humphrey, and Lawrence Pulley. "Do Consumers Pay for One-Stop Banking? Evidence from an Alternative Revenue Function." *Journal of Banking and Finance* 20 (1996): 1,601–21.

Berger, Allen, Rebecca Demsetz, and Philip Strahan. "The Consolidation of the Financial Services Industry: Causes, Consequences, and Implications for the Future." *Journal of Banking and Finance* 23, no. 2 (1999): 135–94.

Berger, Allen, Robert DeYoung, Hena Genay, and Gregory Udell. "Globalization of Financial Institutions: Evidence from Cross-Border Banking Performance." *Brookings-Wharton Papers on Financial Services* (2000).

Bergmann, Barbara. *The Economic Emergence of Women.* New York: Basic Books, 1986.

Berle, Adolf A. and Gardiner C. Means. *The Modern Corporation and Private Property.* New Brunswick, N.J.: Transaction Publishers, 1991.

Berman, Tressa. "'All We Needed Was Our Gardens': Women's Work and Welfare Reform in the Reservation Economy." In *Native Pathways: American Indian Culture and Economic Development*, edited by Brian Hosmer and Colleen O'Neill. Boulder: University Press of Colorado, 2004.

Bernero, Richard. "Second-Generation OTC Derivatives and Structured Products: Catastrophe Bonds, Catastrophe Swaps, and Life Insurance Securitizations." In *Securitized Insurance Risk: Strategic Opportunities for Insurers and Investors*, edited by Michael Himick. Chicago: Glenlake Publishing Co., 1998.

Bernstein, Peter L. *Against the Gods: The Remarkable Story of Risk*. New York: John Wiley & Sons, 1996.

Berube, Allan and Florence Berube. "Sunset Trailer Park." In *White Trash: Race and Class in America*, edited by Matt Wray and Annalee Newitz. New York: Routledge 1997.

Beveridge, Andrew. "Local Lending Practice: Borrowers in a Small Northeastern City, 1832–1915." *Journal of Economic History* 45, no. 2 (1985): 393–403.

Black, Hillel. *Buy Now, Pay Later*. New York: William Morrow and Company, 1961.

Blackmon, Douglas A. *Slavery by Another Name: The Re-Enslavement of Black Americans from the Civil War to World War II*. New York: Anchor Books, 2008.

Blanchard, Ralph. *Liability and Compensation Insurance*. New York: D. Appleton and Co., 1917.

Bodenhorn, Howard. "Were Nineteenth Century Industrial Workers Permanent Income Savers?" NBER Working Paper 23948, October 2017.

Bodie, Zvi. "Commentary." In *Government Risk-Bearing: Proceedings of a Conference Held at the Federal Reserve Bank of Cleveland*, edited by Mark S. Sniderman. Boston: Kluwer Academic, 1993.

Bomey, Nathan. "Promotions Are Mostly a Guy Thing." *USA Today*, 28 September 2016.

Born, Patricia and W. Kip Viscusi. "Insurance Market Responses to the 1980s Liability Reforms: An Analysis of Firm-Level Data." *Journal of Risk and Insurance* 61, no. 2 (1994):192–218.

Boulware, Tyler. *Deconstructing the Cherokee Nation: Town, Region, and Nation Among Eighteenth-Century Cherokees*. Gainesville: University Press of Florida, 2011.

Boynton, Frank D. "Financing the Mobile Home Industry." *Financial Analyst Journal* 16, no. 2 (1960): 87

Brannon, Gerard M. "Public Policy and Life Insurance." In *The Financial Condition and Regulation of Insurance Companies*, edited by Richard E. Randall and Richard W. Kopcke. Boston: Federal Reserve Bank of Boston, 1991.

Branson, Susan. "Women and the Family Economy in the Early Republic: The Case of Elizabeth Meredith." *Journal of the Early Republic* 16, no. 1 (1996): 47–71.

Braun, Sebastian Felix. *Buffalo Inc.: American Indians and Economic Development*. Norman: University of Oklahoma Press, 2008.

Bremner, Robert P. *Chairman of the Fed: William McChesney Martin, Jr. and the Creation of the American Financial System*. New Haven: Yale University Press, 2004.

Brimmer, Andrew F. "Education, Income, and Wealth Accumulation in the Negro Community." Speech by Member of the Federal Reserve System's Board of Governors, (28 May 1970).

Brimmer, Andrew F. "Equal Opportunity in Banking: An Urban Perspective." Speech by Member of the Federal Reserve System's Board of Governors, (11 July 1968).

Brimmer, Andrew F. "Financial Institutions and Urban Rehabilitation." Speech by Member of the Federal Reserve System's Board of Governors, (22 September 1967).

Brimmer, Andrew F. "Recent Developments in Black Banking: 1970–1971." Speech by Member of the Federal Reserve System's Board of Governors, (31 July 1971).

Brimmer, Andrew F. "Small Business and Economic Development in the Negro Community." Speech by Member of the Federal Reserve System's Board of Governors, (25 July 1969).

Brimmer, Andrew F. "Statutory Interest Rate Ceilings and the Availability of Mortgage Funds." Speech by Member of the Federal Reserve System's Board of Governors, (29 May 1968).

Brimmer, Andrew F. "The Black Banks: An Assessment of Performance and Prospects." Speech by Member of the Federal Reserve System's Board of Governors, (28 December 1970).

Brimmer, Andrew F. "The Negro in the American Economy in 1975." Speech by Member of the Federal Reserve System's Board of Governors, (1 April 1966).

Brimmer, Andrew F. and Henry S. Terrell. "The Economic Potential of Black Capitalism." *American Economic Association Annual Meeting* (December 1969): 1–13.

Brodkin, Karen. "How Jews Became White." In *Race, Class and Gender in the United States*, 5th ed. edited by Paula S. Rothenberg. New York: Worth, 2001.

Brooks, John. "Stockholder Season." *New Yorker*, 8 October 1966.

Bubolz, Gordon. *Farmers'-Mutual Windstorm-Insurance Companies*. Washington, DC: Farm Credit Administration, 1938.

Buley, R. Carlyle. *The American Life Convention, 1906–1952: A Study in the History of Life Insurance*. New York: Appleton-Century-Crofts, 1953.

Burne, Katy. "Windfall for Federal Home Loan Banks." *Wall Street Journal*, 24 January 2017.

Butler, John Sibley. *Entrepreneurship and Self-Help Among Black Americans: A Reconsideration of Race and Economics*. Albany: State University of New York Press, 1991.

Calder, Lendol. *Financing the American Dream: A Cultural History of Consumer Credit*. Princeton: Princeton University Press, 1999.

Calloway, Colin G. *First Peoples: A Documentary Survey of American Indian History*, 5th ed. New York: Bedford/St. Martin's 2016.

Calloway, Colin G. *Pen and Ink Witchcraft: Treaties and Treaty Making in American Indian History*. New York: Oxford University Press, 2013.

Calomiris, Charles W. and Jason Karceski. "Is the Bank Merger Wave of the 1990s Efficient? Lessons from Nine Case Studies." In *Mergers and Productivity*, edited by Steven N. Kaplan. (Chicago: University of Chicago Press, 2000.

Calomiris, Charles. "An Economist's Case for GSE Reform." In *Serving Two Masters, Yet Out of Control*, edited by Peter J. Wallison. Washington, D.C.: The AEI Press, 2001.

Calomiris, Charles. *The Postmodern Bank Safety Net: Lesson from Developed and Developing Economies*. Washington, D.C.: The AEI Press, 1997.

Campen, James. "The Struggle for Community Investment in Boston, 1989–1991." In *From Redlining to Reinvestment: Community Responses to Urban Disinvestment*, edited by Gregory D. Squires. Philadelphia: Temple University Press, 1992.

Caplan, Sheri J. *Petticoats and Pinstripes: Portraits of Women in Wall Street's History*. Denver: Praeger, 2013.

Carey, Mark Steven. "Feeding the Fad: The Federal Land Banks, Land Market Efficiency, and the Farm Credit Crisis." Ph.D. Diss., University of California, Berkeley, 1990.

Carlos, Ann and Frank D. Lewis. "Native American Property Rights in the Hudson Bay Region: A Case Study of the Eighteenth-Century Cree." In *Self Determination: The Other Path for Native Americans*, edited by Terry Anderson, Bruce Benson, and Thomas Flanagan. Stanford: Stanford University Press, 2006.

Carlos, Ann and Frank D. Lewis. "Native Americans, Exchange, and the Role of Gift-Giving." In *Unlocking the Wealth of Indian Nations*, edited by Terry Anderson. New York: Lexington Books, 2016.

Carlson, Leonard. "The Economics and Politics of Irrigation Projects on Indian Reservations, 1900–1940." In *The Other Side of the Frontier: Economic Explorations into Native American History*, edited by Linda Barrington. New York: Westview Press, 1999.

Carlson, Leonard. *Indians, Bureaucrats, and Land: The Dawes Act and the Decline of Indian Farming*. New York: Greenwood Publishing, 1981.

Carosso, Vincent. "The Wall Street Money Trust from Pujo through Medina." *Business History Review* 47, no. 4 (1973): 421–37.

Carow, Kenneth, Edward Kane, and Rajesh Narayanan. "How Has Financial Modernization Affected Corporate Customers?" NBER Working Paper No. 11256 (March 2005).

Carter, Sara, Eleanor Shaw, Wing Lam, and Fiona Wilson. "Gender, Entrepreneurship, and Bank Lending: The Criteria and Processes Used by Bank Loan Officers in Assessing Applications." *Entrepreneurship Theory and Practice* 31, no. 3 (2007): 427–44.

Caskey, John P. *Fringe Banking: Check-Cashing Outlets, Pawnshops, and the Poor*. New York: Russell Sage Foundation, 1994.

Cattelino, Jessica. "Casino Roots: The Cultural Production of Twentieth-Century Seminole Economic Development." In *Native Pathways: American Indian Culture and Economic Development*, edited by Brian Hosmer and Colleen O'Neill. Boulder: University Press of Colorado, 2004.

Chamberlain, Kathleen P. *Under Sacred Ground: A History of Navajo Oil, 1922–1982*. Albuquerque: University of New Mexico Press, 2000.

Champagne, Duane. "Tribal Capitalism and Native Capitalists: Multiple Pathways of Native Economy." In *Native Pathways: American Indian Culture and Economic Development*, edited by Brian Hosmer and Colleen O'Neill. Boulder: University Press of Colorado, 2004.

Chapin, Christy Ford. *Ensuring America's Health: The Public Creation of the Corporate Health Care System*. New York: Cambridge University Press, 2015.

Chapin, Christy Ford. "'Going Behind with that Fifteen Cent Policy': Black-Owned Insurance Companies and the State." *Journal of Policy History* 24, no. 2 (2012): 644–74.

Charles, Kerwin Kofi and Jonathan Guryan. "Prejudice and Wages: An Empirical Assessment of Becker's The Economics of Discrimination." *Journal of Political Economy* 116, no. 5 (2008): 773–809.

Chavers, Dean. *Racism in Indian Country*. New York: Peter Lang, 2009.

Chen, Cheryl and Gary Simon. "Actuarial Issues in Insurance on Slaves in the United States South." *The Journal of African American History* 89, no. 4 (2004): 348–57.

Chiappori, Pierre-Andre and Christian Gollier. "Introduction." In *Competitive Failures in Insurance Markets: Theory and Policy Implications*, edited by Pierre-Andrew Chiappori and Christian Gollier. Cambridge: MIT Press, 2006.

Ching, Barbara. "Acting Naturally: Cultural Distinction and Critiques of Pure Country." In *White Trash: Race and Class in America*, edited by Matt Wray and Annalee Newitz. New York: Routledge 1997.

Chute, Carolyn. *The Beans of Egypt, Maine*. New York: Ticknor & Fields, 1985.

Cincotta, Gale and Arthur J. Naparstek. *Urban Disinvestment: New Implications for Community Organization, Research and Public Policy*. Washington, DC: National Center for Urban Ethnic Affairs, 1976.

Claessens, Stijn and Daniela Klingebiel. "Competition and Scope of Activities in Financial Services." *World Bank Research Observer* 16 (2001): 19–40.

Clark, J. P. ed. *Interesting Account of Thomas Anderson, A Slave, Taken from His Own Lips*. 1854?

Clark, Kenneth C. "The Negro in Turmoil." In *The Negro Challenge to the Business Community*, edited by Eli Ginzberg. New York: McGraw-Hill Book Company, 1964.

Clarke, John. "Wingsuit Test Pilot Defies Physics, Has Trouble Getting Life Insurance." *Wall Street Journal*, 6 December 2016.

Clay, Karen. "Intertwining Economies." In *The Other Side of the Frontier: Economic Explorations into Native American History*, edited by Linda Barrington. New York: Westview Press, 1999.

Cleary, Patricia, "'She Will Be in the Shop': Women's Sphere of Trade in Eighteenth-Century Philadelphia and New York." *Pennsylvania Magazine of History and Biography* 119, no. 3 (1995): 181–202.

Clem, Alan. *South Dakota Political Almanac*, 2nd ed. Vermillion: Dakota Press, 1969.

Clune, Henry W. "Remembering Front Street." *Rochester History* 55, no. 3 (1993): 8–17.

Cocheo, Steve. "Justice Department Sues Tiny South Dakota Bank for Loan Bias." *ABA Banking Journal* (January 1994).

Cohen, Jeffrey. "Discussion." In *The Financial Condition and Regulation of Insurance Companies*, edited by Richard E. Randall and Richard W. Kopcke. Boston: Federal Reserve Bank of Boston, 1991.

Coll, Blanche. *Safety Net: Welfare and Social Security, 1929–1979*. New Brunswick, N.J.: Rutgers University Press, 1995.

Collins, William J. and Robert A. Margo. "Race and Home Ownership from the End of the Civil War to the Present." *American Economic Review* 101, no. 3 (2011): 355–59.

Committee on Banking, Housing, and Urban Affairs, U.S. Senate, 103rd Congress, 2nd Sess., "Homeowners' Insurance Discrimination." Washington: GPO, 1994.

Committee on Financial Services, U.S. House of Representatives, 110th Congress, 1st Sess., "Mortgage Lending Discrimination." Washington: GPO, 2008.

Conder, Joseph M. and Gilbert Hopkins. *The Self-Insurance Decision*. New York: National Association of Accountants, 1981.

Connolly, Dennis R. "Government Risk-Bearing: What Works and What Doesn't." In *Government Risk-Bearing: Proceedings of a Conference Held at the Federal Reserve Bank of Cleveland*, edited by Mark S. Sniderman. Boston: Kluwer Academic, 1993.

Corntassel, Jeff and Richard C. Witmer. *Forced Federalism: Contemporary Challenges to Indigenous Nationhood*. Norman: University of Oklahoma Press, 2008.

Costa, Dora. *The Evolution of Retirement: An American Economic History, 1880–1990*. Chicago: University of Chicago Press, 1998.

Cowen, David J. "The First Bank of the United States and the Securities Market Crash of 1792." *Journal of Economic History* 60, no. 4 (2000): 1,041–60.

Cowen, David J. *The Origins and Economic Impact of the First Bank of the United States, 1791–1797*. New York: Garland Publishing, 2000.

Cronon, William. *Changes in the Land: Indians, Colonists, and the Ecology of New England*. New York: Hill and Wang, 1983.

Cropp, Matthew. "The Origins of US Credit Unions." *Financial History* (Spring 2014): 24–27.

Cross, Theodore L. *Black Capitalism: Strategy for Business in the Ghetto*. New York: Atheneum, 1969.

Cummins, J. David and Mary A. Weiss. "The Structure, Conduct, and Regulation of the Property-Liability Insurance Industry." In *The Financial Condition and Regulation of Insurance Companies*, edited by Richard E. Randall and Richard W. Kopcke. Boston: Federal Reserve Bank of Boston, 1991.

Cummins, J. David, ed. *Deregulating Property-Liability Insurance: Restoring Competition and Increasing Market Efficiency*. Washington, DC: AEI-Brookings Joint Center for Regulatory Studies, 2002.

Cunningham, Robert, III and Robert M. Cunningham, Jr. *The Blues: A History of the Blue Cross and Blue Shield System*. Dekalb, Ill.: Northern Illinois University, 1997.

Curl, John. *For All the People: Uncovering the Hidden History of Cooperation, Cooperative Movements, and Communalism in America*. Oakland: PM Press, 2009.

Curry, Leonard P. *The Free Black in Urban America, 1800–1850: The Shadow of the Dream*. Chicago: University of Chicago Press, 1981.

Cutler, David M. and Jonathan Gruber. "Does Public Insurance Crowd Out Private Insurance?" *Quarterly Journal of Economics* 111, no. 2 (1996): 391–430.

D'Arista, Jane W. *The Evolution of Finance, Volume II: Restructuring Institutions and Markets*. Armonk, N.Y.: M.E. Sharpe, 1994.

Dahl, A. E. *Banker Dahl of South Dakota: An Autobiography*. Rapid City: Fenske Book Company, 1965.

Daily Fintech. "Blockchain Technology Could Revolutionize Small Business Finance." (14 June 2016). Last accessed 26 January 2017: http://bankinnovation.net/2016/06/how-blockchain-technology-could-integrate-financial-physical-supply-chains-and-revolutionize-small-business-finance/.

Dannenbaum, Jed. *Drink and Disorder: Temperance Reform in Cincinnati from the Washingtonian Revival to the WCTU*. Urbana: University of Illinois Press, 1984.

Darity, William A., Jr. and Samuel L. Myers, Jr. *Persistent Disparity: Race and Economic Inequality in the United States Since 1945*. Cheltenham: Edward Elgar, 1998.

Davidson, Osha Gray. *Broken Heartland: The Rise of America's Rural Ghetto*. New York: Free Press, 1990.

Davis, Lance E. "The Investment Market, 1870–1914: The Evolution of a National Market." *Journal of Economic History* 25, no. 3 (1965): 355–93.

Davis, Malvin E. *Industrial Life Insurance in the United States*. New York: McGraw-Hill Book Company, 1944.

Dawson, Miles. "Fraternal Life Insurance." *Annals of the American Academy of Political and Social Science* 26 (1905): 128–36.

De Tocqueville, Alexis. *Democracy in America*. Trans. Harvey C. Mansfield and Delba Winthrop. Chicago: University of Chicago Press, 2000.

Dedham, Bill. "Study Discerns Disadvantage for Blacks in Home Mortgages." In *Race, Class and Gender in the United States*, 5th ed., edited by Paula S. Rothenberg. New York: Worth, 2001.

DeYoung, Robert and William C. Hunter. "Deregulation, the Internet, and the Competitive Viability of Large Banks and Community Banks." In *The Future of Banking*, edited by Benton Gup. Westport, Conn.: Quorum Books, 2003.

Di Matteo, Livio and Angela Redish. "The Evolution of Financial Intermediation: Evidence from 19th-Century Ontario Microdata." *Canadian Journal of Economics* 48, no. 3 (2015): 963–87.

Diamond, Neil. *Reel Injun*. Film documentary. 2009.

Dickerson, Mechele. *Homeownership and America's Financial Underclass: Flawed Premises, Broken Promises, New Prescriptions*. New York: Cambridge University Press, 2014.

Dippel, Christian. "Forced Coexistence and Economic Development." In *Unlocking the Wealth of Indian Nations*, edited by Terry Anderson. New York: Lexington Books, 2016.

Douglas, Paul H. "Introduction." In *Buy Now, Pay Later*, by Hillel Black. New York: William Morrow and Company, 1961.

Dunbar, Roxanne A. "Bloody Footprints: Reflections on Growing Up Poor White." In *White Trash: Race and Class in America*, edited by Matt Wray and Annalee Newitz. New York: Routledge 1997.

Dyson, Michael Eric. *Come Hell or High Water: Hurricane Katrina and the Color of Disaster*. New York: Basic Civitas, 2007.

Earling, Peter R. *Whom to Trust: A Practical Treatise on Mercantile Credits*. New York: Rand McNally & Co., 1890.

Ecclesine, Joseph B. *A Compendium of the Laws and Decisions Relating to Mobs, Riots, Invasion, Civil Commotion, Insurrection, &c., as Affecting Fire Insurance*. New York: Grierson and Ecclesine, 1863.

Edwards, Margie L. Kiter. "We're Decent People: Constructing and Managing Family Identity in Rural Working-Class Communities." *Journal of Marriage and Family* 66, no. 2 (May 2004): 515–29.

Edwards, Sebastian. *American Default: The Untold Story of FDR, the Supreme Court, and the Battle Over Gold*. Princeton: Princeton University Press, 2018.

Eisner, Robert. *Social Security: More, Not Less*. New York: Century Foundation Press, 1998.

Embree, Edwin. *Brown Americans: The Story of a Tenth of the Nation*. New York: Viking Press, 1943.

Emery, Herb. "Fraternal Sickness Insurance." In *EH.Net Encyclopedia*, edited by Robert Whaples. (2001).

Ensign, Rachel Louise and Anna Maria Andriotis. "Banks See Low Income Where the Rich Shop." *Wall Street Journal*, 19 May 2017.

Epstein, Abraham. *Insecurity, a Challenge to America: A Study of Social Insurance in the United States and Abroad*, 3rd ed. New York: Random House, 1936.

Ernst, Keith, Deborah N. Goldstein, and Christopher A. Richardson. "Legal and Economic Inducements to Predatory Practices." In *Why the Poor Pay More: How to Stop Predatory Lending*, edited by Gregory D. Squires. Westport, Conn.: Praeger, 2004.

Faulk, Patricia R. "Gender and Power in the Twentieth Century: Mary G. Roebling, Pioneer Woman Banker." Ph.D. Diss., University of Pennsylvania, 1992.

Faulkner, Audrey Olsen, Marsel A. Heisel, Wendell Holbrook, and Shirley Geismar. *When I was Comin' Up: An Oral History of Aged Blacks*. Hamden, Conn.: Archon Books, 1982.

Faure, Michael and Ton Hartlief. *Insurance and Expanding Systemic Risks*. OECD Policy Issues in Insurance No. 5, 2003.

Figart, Deborah M. and Ellen Mutari. "Rereading Becker: Contextualizing the Development of Discrimination Theory." *Journal of Economic Issues* 339, no. 2 (2005): 475–83.

Finnerty, John and Douglas Emery. *Debt Management: A Practitioner's Guide.* Boston: Harvard Business School Press, 2001.

Fishback, Price. "Debt Peonage in Postbellum Georgia." *Explorations in Economic History* 26, 2 (April 1989): 219–36.

Fishback, Price. "How Successful Was the New Deal?: The Microeconomic Impact of New Deal Spending and Lending Policies in the 1930s." *Journal of Economic Literature* 55, 4 (2017): 1,435–85.

Fishback, Price. "Panel Discussion on Saving the Neighborhood, Part III." *Arizona Law Review* 56, 3 (2014): 39–49.

Fishback, Price and Shawn Kantor. *Prelude to the Welfare State: The Origins of Workers' Compensation.* Chicago: University of Chicago Press, 2000.

Fishback, Price, Jonathan Rose, and Kenneth Snowden. *Well Worth Saving: How the New Deal Safeguarded Home Ownership.* Chicago: University of Chicago Press, 2013.

Fisher, Anne B. *Wall Street Women.* New York: Alfred A. Knopf, 1990.

Fisher, Ernest and Chester Rapkin. *The Mutual Mortgage Insurance Fund: A Study of the Adequacy of Its Reserves and Resources.* New York: Columbia University Press, 1956.

Fisher, Melissa S. "Wall Street Women's Herstories." In *Constructing Corporate America: History, Politics, Culture,* edited by Kenneth Lipartito and David B. Sicilia. New York: Oxford University Press, 2004.

Fisher, Melissa S. *Wall Street Women.* Durham: Duke University Press, 2012.

Fite, Gilbert C. "South Dakota's Rural Credit System: A Venture in State Socialism, 1917–1946." *Agricultural History* 21, no. 4 (1947): 239–49.

Fite, Gilbert C. "The History of South Dakota's Rural Credit System." *South Dakota Historical Collections* 45 (1949): 220–75.

Fix, Michael, George C. Galster, and Raymond J. Struyk. "An Overview of Auditing for Discrimination." In *Clear and Convincing Evidence: Measurement of Discrimination in America,* edited by Michael Fix and Raymond J. Struyk. Washington, DC: Urban Institute Press, 1993.

Fleming, Anne. "City of Debtors, Law, Loan Sharks, and the Shadow Economy of Urban Poverty, 1900–1970." *Enterprise & Society* 17, no. 4 (2016): 734–40.

Flynt, Wayne. *Poor But Proud: Alabama's Poor Whites.* Tuscaloosa: University of Alabama Press, 1989.

Foster, William Trufant. *Loan Sharks and Their Victims.* New York: Public Affairs Committee, 1940.

Fowler, Gary L. "The Residential Distribution of Urban Appalachians." In *The Invisible Minority: Urban Appalachians,* edited by William W. Philliber and Clyde B. McCoy. Frankfort: University Press of Kentucky, 1981.

Francisconi, Michael J. *Kinship, Capitalism, Change: The Informal Economy of the Navajo, 1868–1995*. New York: Routledge, 1998.

Frankel, Allen and John Montgomery. "Financial Structure: An International Perspective." *Brookings Papers on Economic Activity* (1991).

Frazier, Ian. *On the Rez*. New York: Farrar, Straus and Giroux, 2000.

Frederiksen, D. M. "Mortgage Banking in America." *Journal of Political Economy* 2, no. 2 (1894): 203–34.

Freeman, Rhoda Golden. *The Free Negro in New York City in the Era Before the Civil War*. New York: Garland Publishing, 1994.

French, Robert Mills and Jeffrey K. Hadden. "Mobile Homes: Instant Suburbia or Transportable Slums?" *Social Problems* 16, no. 2 (1968): 219–26.

Friedberg, Leora and Anthony Webb. "Life Is Cheap: Using Mortality Bonds to Hedge Aggregate Mortality Risk." *The B.E. Journal of Economic Analysis & Policy* (2007) http://www.bepress.com/bejeap/vol7/iss1/art31.

Frye, Dustin and Dominic Parker. "Paternalism versus Sovereignty: The Long-Run Economic Effects of the Indian Reorganization Act." In *Unlocking the Wealth of Indian Nations*, edited by Terry Anderson. New York: Lexington Books, 2016.

Galbraith, Craig, Carlos Rodriguez, and Curt Stiles. "False Myths and Indigenous Entrepreneurial Strategies." In *Self Determination: The Other Path for Native Americans*, edited by Terry Anderson, Bruce Benson, and Thomas Flanagan. Stanford: Stanford University Press, 2006.

Gallay, Alan. *The Indian Slave Trade: The Rise of English Empire in the American South, 1670–1717*. New Haven: Yale University Press, 2002.

Galster, George C. "Use of Testers in Investigating Discrimination in Mortgage Lending and Insurance." In *Clear and Convincing Evidence: Measurement of Discrimination in America*, edited by Michael Fix and Raymond J. Struyk. Washington, DC: Urban Institute Press, 1993.

Garrett-Scott, Shennette. "To Do a Work that Would Be Very Far Reaching: Minnie Geddings Cox, the Mississippi Life Insurance Company, and the Challenges of Black Women's Business Leadership in the Early Twentieth-Century United States." *Enterprise & Society* 17, no. 3 (2016): 473–514.

Gart, Alan. *Regulation, Deregulation, Reregulation: The Future of the Banking, Insurance, and Securities Industries*. New York: John Wiley and Sons, 1994.

Gaumnitz, Jack. "Mobile Home and Conventional Home Ownership: An Economic Perspective." *Nebraska Journal of Economics and Business* 13, no. 4 (1974): 130–43.

Genetin-Pilawa, C. Joseph. *Crooked Paths to Allotment: The Fight over Federal Indian Policy After the Civil War*. Chapel Hill: University of North Carolina Press, 2012.

Geisst, Charles R. *The Last Partnerships: Insider the Great Wall Street Money Dynasties*. New York: McGraw Hill, 2001.

Gerber, Sandy. "Native CDFIs Work Toward a New Economic Reality in South Dakota." *Federal Reserve Bank of Minneapolis Community Dividend* (2008).

Gettler, Brian. "Money and the Changing Nature of Colonial Space in Northern Quebec: Fur Trade Monopolies, the State, and Aboriginal Peoples During the Nineteenth Century." *Social History* 46 (November 2013): 271–93.

Gianaris, Nicholas. *Modern Capitalism: Privatization, Employee Ownership, and Industrial Democracy*. Westport, Conn.: Praeger, 1996.

Gilbert, Abby. "The Comptroller of the Currency and the Freedman's Savings Bank." *Journal of Negro History* 57, no. 2 (1972): 125–43.

Gile, B. M. *The Farm Credit Situation in Southwestern Arkansas, Bulletin No. 237*. Fayetteville: University of Arkansas Agricultural Experiment Station, 1929.

Ginzberg, Lori D. *Women and the Work of Benevolence: Morality, Politics, and Class in the Nineteenth-Century United States*. New Haven: Yale University Press, 1990.

Ginzberg, Eli, ed. *The Negro Challenge to the Business Community*. New York: McGraw-Hill Book Company, 1964.

Goering, Orlando J. and Violet Miller Goering. "Keeping the Faith: Bertha Martinsky in West River South Dakota." *South Dakota History* 25, no. 1 (1995): 37–48.

Goetzmann, William. *Money Changes Everything: How Finance Made Civilization Possible*. Princeton: Princeton University Press.

Goldin, Claudia and Lawrence F. Katz. *The Race Between Education and Technology*. Cambridge: Belknap Press, 2010.

Goldin, Claudia. "The Economic Status of Women in the Early Republic: Quantitative Evidence." *Journal of Interdisciplinary History* 16, no. 3 (1986): 375–404.

Goldstein, Bernard. *A Documentary Guide to Commercial Leasing*. Philadelphia: American Law Institute, 1985.

Goodell, William. *The American Slave Code in Theory and Practice*. London: Clarke, Beeton, and Co., 1853.

Goodwin, Barry K. *The Economics of Crop Insurance and Disaster Aid*. New York: AEI Press, 1995.

Gordon, Sarah Barringer. "The African Supplement: Religion, Race, and Corporate Law in Early National America." *William and Mary Quarterly* 72, no. 3 (July 2015), 385–422.

Graham, Loftin and Xiaoying Xie. "The United States Insurance Market: Characteristics and Trends." In *Handbook of International Insurance: Between Global Dynamics and Local Contingencies*, edited by J. David Cummins and Bertrand Venard. New York: Springer, 2007.

Grant, H. Roger. *Insurance Reform: Consumer Action in the Progressive Era*. Ames: Iowa State University Press, 1979.

Greene, Lance and Mark R. Plane. "Introduction." In *American Indians and the Market Economy, 1775–1850*, edited by Lance Greene and Mark R. Plane. Tuscaloosa: University of Alabama Press, 2010.

Greene, Lance. "Identity in a Post-Removal Cherokee Household, 1838–50." In *American Indians and the Market Economy, 1775–1850*, edited by Lance Greene and Mark R. Plane. Tuscaloosa: University of Alabama Press, 2010.

Gregg, Davis. *Group Life Insurance: An Analysis of Concepts, Contracts, Costs, and Company Practices*. Homewood, Ill.: Richard D. Irwin, 1957.

Grier, Eunice and George Grier. *Privately Developed Interracial Housing: An Analysis of Experience*. Berkeley: University of California Press, 1960.

Grind, Kirsten. "New Loans, Same Old Dangers." *Wall Street Journal*, 11 January 2017.

Gron, Anne. "Capacity Constraints and Cycles in Property-Casualty Insurance Markets." *RAND Journal of Economics* 25 (1994): 110–27.

Group of Ten. "Report on Consolidation in the Financial Sector." BIS, IMF, and OECD: January 2001.

Grout, Paul, William Megginson, and Anna Zalewska. "One Half-Billion Shareholders and Counting: Determinants of Individual Share Ownership Around the World." SSRN Working Paper, (September 2009).

Gunther, John. *Inside U.S.A.* New York: Harper Brothers, 1947.

Gup, Benton E., ed. *Too Big to Fail: Policies and Practices in Government Bailouts*. Westport, Conn.: Praeger, 2004.

Guttentag, Jack M. and Susan M. Wachter. *Redlining and Public Policy Monograph 1980–1*. New York: Salomon Brothers Center, 1980.

Haber, Carole and Brian Gratton. *Old Age and the Search for Security: An American Social History*. (Bloomington: Indiana University Press, 1994).

Haddock, David and Robert Miller. "Sovereignty Can be a Liability: How Tribes Can Mitigate the Sovereign's Paradox." In *Self Determination: The Other Path for Native Americans*, edited by Terry Anderson, Bruce Benson, and Thomas Flanagan. Stanford: Stanford University Press, 2006.

Haeger, John Denis. *The Investment Frontier: New York Businessmen and the Economic Development of the Old Northwest*. Albany: State University of New York Press, 1981.

Hagood, Margaret J. *Mothers of the South: Portraiture of the White Tenant Farm Woman*. Chapel Hill: University of North Carolina Press, 1939.

Hall, Tex G. "Requesting the BIA to Streamline the Title Status Reports and Mutual Help Home Conveyance Process for Indian Housing Programs." National Congress of American Indians Resolution #ABQ-03–012, 21 November 2003.

Hamel, Gary. "Wrong merger, wrong logic: Citicorp and Travelers are joining forces for economies of scale but they will be selling their customers short on choice and innovation." *Financial Times*, 15 April 1998.

Hamermesh, Daniel S. "Ugly? You May Have a Case." *New York Times*, 27 August 2011.

Hamm, John, Frances M. Jones, and Rolf Nugent. *Wage Executions for Debt: Bulletin of the United States Bureau of Labor Statistics No. 622* (1936).

Hanc, Gregory. "The Future of Banking in America: Summary and Conclusions." *FDIC Future of Banking Study*. Washington, D.C.: FDIC, 2004.

Hansmann, Henry. *The Ownership of Enterprise*. Cambridge: Harvard University Press, 1996.

Hardmeyer, Eric. "Why Public Banking Works in North Dakota." *New York Times*, 1 October 2013.

Harkinson, Josh. "How the Nation's Only State-Owned Bank Became the Envy of Wall Street." *Mother Jones*, 27 March 2009.

Harmon, Alexandra. *Rich Indians: Native People and the Problem of Wealth in American History*. Chapel Hill: University of North Carolina Press, 2010.

Harrington, Scott E. "Public Policy and Property-Liability Insurance." In *The Financial Condition and Regulation of Insurance Companies*, edited by Richard E. Randall and Richard W. Kopcke. Boston: Federal Reserve Bank of Boston, 1991.

Harrington, Scott E. "The History of Federal Involvement in Insurance Regulation." In *Optional Federal Chartering and Regulation of Insurance Companies*, edited by Peter J. Wallison. Washington: AEI Press, 2000.

Harrington, Scott E. and Patricia M. Danzon. "Price Cutting in Liability Markets." *Journal of Business* 67 (1994):511–38.

Harris, Abram. *The Negro as Capitalist: A Study of Banking and Business Among American Negroes*. New York: Peter Smith, 1936.

Hartigan, John Jr., "Objectifying 'Poor Whites' and 'White Trash' in Detroit." In *White Trash: Race and Class in America*, edited by Matt Wray and Annalee Newitz. New York: Routledge 1997.

Hartwig, Robert and Claire Wilkinson. "An Overview of the Alternative Risk Transfer Market." In *Handbook of International Insurance: Between Global Dynamics and Local Contingencies*, edited by J. David Cummins and Bertrand Venard. New York: Springer, 2007.

Hensarling, Jeb. "How We'll Stop a Rogue Federal Agency." *Wall Street Journal*, 9 February 2017.

Herera, Sue. *Women of the Street*. New York: John Wiley & Sons, 1997.

Herrick, Kenneth. *Total Disability Provisions in Life Insurance Contracts*. Homewood, Ill.: Richard D. Irwin, 1956.

Hess, Beth B., Elizabeth W. Markson, and Peter J. Stein. "Racial and Ethnic Minorities: An Overview." In *Race, Class and Gender in the United States*, 5th ed., edited by Paula S. Rothenberg. New York: Worth, 2001.

Hetzel, Robert. *The Great Recession: Market Failure or Policy Failure?* New York: Cambridge University Press, 2012.

Hetzel, Robert. *The Monetary Policy of the Federal Reserve: A History.* New York: Cambridge University Press, 2008.

Hickcox, John. *History of the Bills of Credit or Paper Money Issued by New York, from 1709 to 1789.* New York: Burt Franklin, 1866.

Hiltz, Starr Roxanne. "Why Black Families Own Less Life Insurance." *Journal of Risk and Insurance* 38, no. 2 (1971): 225–35.

Hoag, W. Gifford. *The Farm Credit System: A History of Financial Self-Help.* Danville, Ill.: Interstate Printers & Publishers, 1976.

Hochfelder, David. "'Where the Common People Could Speculate': The Ticker, Bucket Shops, and the Origin of Popular Participation in Financial Markets, 1880–1920." *Journal of American History* 93, no. 2 (2006): 335–58.

Hoffman, Beatrix. *The Wages of Sickness: The Politics of Health Insurance in Progressive America.* Chapel Hill: University of North Carolina Press, 2001.

Hollenhorst, Jerome J. "An Analysis of the Federal Land Bank System's Debt Management, 1947–1961." Ph.D. Diss., Iowa State University, 1965.

Holsey, Alson L. "Progress in Industries: Farms, Homes and Business Enterprises." In *Progress of a Race, or the Remarkable Advancement of the American Negro*, edited by J. L. Nichols and William H. Crogman. Naperville, Ill.: J. L. Nichols & Company, 1920.

Holton, Woody. "Abigail Adams, Bond Speculator." *William and Mary Quarterly* 64, no. 4 (2007): 821–38.

Holton, Woody. *Abigail Adams.* New York: Free Press, 2009.

Hosmer, Brian C. *American Indians in the Marketplace: Persistence and Innovation Among the Menominees and Metlakatlans, 1870–1920.* Lawrence: University Press of Kansas, 1999.

Hoyt, G. C. "The Life of the Retired in a Trailer Park." *American Journal of Sociology* 59, no. 4 (1954): 361–70.

Huebner, Solomon. "The Development and Present Status of Marine Insurance in the United States." *Annals of the American Academy of Political and Social Science* 26 (1905): 241–72.

Huffman, James and Robert Miller. "Indian Property Rights and American Federalism." In *Self Determination: The Other Path for Native Americans*, edited by Terry Anderson, Bruce Benson, and Thomas Flanagan. Stanford: Stanford University Press, 2006.

Hughes, James J. and Richard Perlman. *The Economics of Unemployment: A Comparative Analysis of Britain and the United States*. New York: Cambridge University Press, 1984.

Hughes, Joseph and Loretta Mester. "Bank Capitalization and Cost: Evidence of Scale Economies in Risk Management and Signaling." *Review of Economics and Statistics* 80, no. 2 (1998): 314–25.

Hughes, Joseph, William Lang, Loretta Mester, and Choon-Geol Moon. "The Dollars and Sense of Bank Consolidation." *Journal of Banking and Finance* 23, no. 2 (1999): 291–324.

Hunter, J. Robert. "Discussion." In *The Financial Condition and Regulation of Insurance Companies*, edited by Richard E. Randall and Richard W. Kopcke. Boston: Federal Reserve Bank of Boston, 1991.

Hyman, Louis. *Debtor Nation: The History of America in Red Ink*. Princeton: Princeton University Press, 2011.

Iglehart, Calvin and Grant J. Zsofka, eds. *Farming and Farmland in the United States: Changes and Trends, Agriculture Issues and Policies*. New York: Nova Science Publishers, 2012.

Immergluck, Dan. *Credit to the Community: Community Reinvestment and Fair Lending Policy in the United States* New York: M. E. Sharpe, 2004.

Insurance and Superannuation Commission. "Other Issues: Mergers Amongst Financial Majors and Electronic Commerce." Australia: 1997.

Irby, Lee. "Taking Out the Trailer Trash: The Battle Over Mobile Homes in St. Petersburg, Florida." *Florida Historical Quarterly* 79, no. 2 (2000): 181–200.

Isenberg, Nancy. *White Trash: The 400-Year Untold History of Class in America*. New York: Viking, 2016.

James, John A. "Financial Underdevelopment in the Postbellum South." *Journal of Interdisciplinary History* 11, no. 3 (1981): 443–454.

James, Marquis. *The Metropolitan Life: A Study in Business Growth*. New York: Viking, 1947.

Jaremski, Matthew and Price Fishback. "Did Inequality in Farm Sizes Lead to Suppression of Banking and Credit in the Late Nineteenth Century?" *Journal of Economic History* 78, 1 (2018): 155–195.

Jenkins, Holman W. "Terror Insurance Is Here to Stay." *Wall Street Journal*, 8 August 2007.

Jenq, Christina, Jessica Pan, and Walter Theseira. "What Do Donors Discriminate On? Evidence from Kiva.Org." Working Paper, May 2011.

Johansen, Bruce E., ed. *The Encyclopedia of Native American Economic History*. Westport, Conn.: Greenwood Press, 1999.

Johnsen, D. Bruce. "A Culturally Correct Proposal to Privatize the British Columbia Salmon Fishery." In *Self Determination: The Other Path for Native Americans*, edited by Terry Anderson, Bruce Benson, and Thomas Flanagan. Stanford: Stanford University Press, 2006.

Johnsen, D. Bruce. "The Potlatch as Fractional Reserve Banking." In *Unlocking the Wealth of Indian Nations*, edited by Terry Anderson, (New York: Lexington Books, 2016.

Johnson, Paul. "Insurance: Life Insurance." In *The Oxford Encyclopedia of Economic History*, edited by Joel Mokyr. New York: Oxford University Press, 2003.

Joint Economic Committee. *Invest in Women, Invest in America: A Comprehensive Review of Women in the U.S. Economy.* Washington, DC: U.S. Government Printing Office, 2011.

Jones, Jacqueline. *A Dreadful Deceit: The Myth of Race from the Colonial Era to Obama's America.* New York: Basic Books, 2013.

Jones, Jacqueline. *The Dispossessed: America's Underclasses from the Civil War to the Present.* New York: Basic Books, 1992.

Jones, Kenneth D. and Tim Critchfield. "Consolidation in the U.S. Banking Industry: Is the 'Long, Strange Trip' About to End?" FDIC Working Paper (2005).

Jung, Allen F. "Dealer Pricing Practices and Finance Charges for New Mobile Homes." *Journal of Business* 36, no. 4 (1963): 430–39.

Kacy, Howard. *A Unique and Different Company.* Princeton, N.J.: Newcomen Society 1964.

Kaminski, John. *Paper Politics: The Northern State Loan-Offices During the Confederation, 1783–1790.* New York: Garland, 1989.

Kane, Edward J. "Commentary." In *Government Risk-Bearing: Proceedings of a Conference Held at the Federal Reserve Bank of Cleveland*, edited by Mark S. Sniderman. Boston: Kluwer Academic, 1993.

Kantor, Shawn and Price Fishback. "Coalition Formation and the Adoption of Workers' Compensation: The Case of Missouri, 1911 to 1926." In *The Regulated Economy: A Historical Approach to Political Economy*, edited by Claudia Goldin and Gary Libecap. Chicago: University of Chicago Press, 1994.

Karmel, James. "Banking on the People: Banks, Politics, and Market Evolution in Early National Pennsylvania, 1781–1824." Ph.D. dissertation, SUNY Buffalo, 1999.

Kashian, Russell, Fernanda Contreras, and Claudia Perez-Valdez. "The Changing Face of Communities Served by Minority Depository Institutions: 2001–2015." Community Banking in the 21st Century Research and Policy Conference, St. Louis Federal Reserve, St. Louis, Missouri, (September 28–29, 2016).

Kaufman, Frank A. "The Maryland Ground Rent – Mysterious But Beneficial." *Maryland Law Review* 5 (December 1940): 1–72.

Kaufman, Henry. *The Road to Financial Reformation: Warnings, Consequences, Reforms.* Hoboken: John Wiley & Sons, 2009.

Kemmerer, Donald L. "The Colonial Loan-Office System in New Jersey." *Journal of Political Economy* 47, no. 6 (1939): 867–74.

Kiel, Paul and Annie Waldman. "The Color of Debt: How Collection Suits Squeeze Black Neighborhoods." *ProPublica*, 8 October 2015.

Kilbourne, Richard. *Debt, Investment, Slaves: Credit Relations in East Feliciana Parish, Louisiana, 1825–1885.* Tuscaloosa: University of Alabama Press, 1995.

Kilbourne, Richard. *Slave Agriculture and Financial Markets in Antebellum America: The Bank of the United States in Mississippi, 1831–1852.* London: Routledge, 2006.

Kindleberger, Charles. *Manias, Panics, and Crashes: A History of Financial Crises,* 4th ed. New York: John Wiley & Sons, 2000.

King, A. Thomas. *Discrimination in Mortgage Lending: A Study of Three Cities Monograph 1980–4.* New York: Salomon Brothers Center.

Kingston, Christopher. "Marine Insurance in Philadelphia during the Quasi-War with France, 1795–1801." *Journal of Economic History* 71, no. 1 (2011): 162–84.

Kipnis, Laura and Jennifer Reeder. "White Trash Girl: The Interview." In *White Trash: Race and Class in America*, edited by Matt Wray and Annalee Newitz. New York: Routledge 1997.

Kiser, William S. "Navajo Pawn: A Misunderstood Traditional Trading Practice." *American Indian Quarterly* 36, no. 2 (2012): 150–81.

Klein, L. R. and H. W. Mooney. "Negro-White Savings Differentials and the Consumption Function Problem." *Econometrica* 21, no. 3 (1953): 425–56.

Kohn, Meir. *Money, Banking, and Financial Markets,* 2nd ed. New York: Harcourt Brace, 1993.

Kollmann, Trevor. "Housing Markets, Government Programs, and Race During the Great Depression." Ph.D. Diss., University of Arizona, 2011.

Krooss, Herman E. and Martin R. Blyn. *A History of Financial Intermediaries.* New York: Random House, 1971.

Kunkin, Dorothy and Michael Byrne. *Appalachians in Cleveland.* Cleveland: Institute of Urban Studies, 1973.

Kunreuther, Howard. "Ambiguity and Government Risk-Bearing for Low-Probability Events." In *Government Risk-Bearing: Proceedings of a Conference Held at the Federal Reserve Bank of Cleveland*, edited by Mark S. Sniderman. Boston: Kluwer Academic, 1993.

Kusisto, Laura. "Housing Gains Highlight Economic Divide." *Wall Street Journal*, 28 December 2016.

Kuzminski, Adrian. *Fixing the System: A History of Populism, Ancient and Modern*. New York: Continuum, 2008.

La Follette, Robert. *La Follette's Autobiography*. Madison: University of Wisconsin Press, 1911.

Laing, James T. "The Negro Miner in West Virginia." *Social Forces* 14, no. 3 (1936), 416–22.

Lajoux, Alexandra and Dennis J. Roberts. *The Art of Bank M&A: Buying, Selling, Merging, and Investing in Regulated Depository Institutions in the New Environment*. New York: McGraw Hill, 2014.

Lamoreaux, Naomi and William Novak, eds. *Corporations and American Democracy*. Cambridge: Harvard University Press, 2017.

Lawrence, Joseph Stagg. *Banking Concentration in the United States: A Critical Analysis*. New York: Bankers Publishing Company, 1930.

Leavell, R. H., T. R. Snavely, T. J. Woofter, Jr., W. T. B. Williams, and Francis D. Tyson. *Negro Migration in 1916–17*. Washington: U.S. Department of Labor, 1917.

LeFlouria, Talitha. *Chained in Silence: Black Women and Convict Labor in the New South*. Chapel Hill: University of North Carolina Press, 2015.

Lehrman, William G. "Diversity in Decline: Institutional Environment and Organizational Failure in the American Life Insurance Industry." *Social Forces* 73 (1994): 605–35.

Leland, John. "Facing Default, Some Walk Out on New Homes." *New York Times*, 29 February 2008.

Lencsis, Peter M. *Insurance Regulation in the United States: An Overview for Business and Government*. Westport, Conn.: Quorum Books, 1997.

Lennon, Terence. "Discussion." In *The Financial Condition and Regulation of Insurance Companies*, edited by Richard E. Randall and Richard W. Kopcke. Boston: Federal Reserve Bank of Boston, 1991.

Leopold, Alice K. *Highlights, 1920–1960*. Washington: U.S. Department of Labor, 1960.

Levine, Ross. "Finance and Growth: Theory and Evidence." In *Handbook of Economic Growth*, Vol. 1A, edited by Philippe Aghion and Steven N. Durlauf. New York: Elsevier North Holland, 2005.

Levy, Jonathan. *Freaks of Fortune: The Emerging World of Capitalism and Risk in America*. Cambridge: Harvard University Press, 2012.

Lewis, Susan Ingalls. *Unexceptional Women: Female Proprietors in Mid-Nineteenth Century Albany, New York, 1830–1885*. Columbus: Ohio State University Press, 2009.

Liebowitz, Stan J. "Anatomy of a Train Wreck: Causes of the Mortgage Meltdown." In *Housing America: Building Out of a Crisis*, edited by Randall Holcombe and Benjamin Powell. New Brunswick: Transaction Publishers.

Linden, Alexandre, Stefan Bund, John Schiavetta, Jill Zelter, and Rachel Hardee. "First Generation CDPO: Case Study on Performance and Ratings." (28 April 2007). http://www.defaultrisk.com/pp_crdrv141.htm. Accessed 17 May 2016.

Lindsay, Arnett G. "The Negro in Banking." *Journal of Negro History* 14, no. 2 (1929): 156–99.

Listokin, David and Stephen Casey. *Mortgage Lending and Race: Conceptual and Analytical Perspectives of the Urban Financing Problem*. New Brunswick: Center for Urban Policy Research, 1980.

Lockley, Timothy J. "Partners in Crime: African Americans and Nonslaveholding Whites in Antebellum Georgia." In *White Trash: Race and Class in America*, edited by Matt Wray and Annalee Newitz. New York: Routledge 1997.

Lott, Edson. *Pioneers of American Liability Insurance*. New York: United States Casualty Company, 1938.

Lublin, Joann S. "Dozens of Boards Excluded Women for Years." *Wall Street Journal*, 28 December 2016.

Lublin, Joann S. "The More Women in Power, The More Women in Power." *Wall Street Journal*, 27 September 2016.

Lucht, Tracy. *Sylvia Porter: America's Original Personal Finance Columnist*. Syracuse: Syracuse University Press, 2013.

Magid, James. "The Mobile Home Industry," *Financial Analyst Journal* 25, no. 5 (1969), 29–32.

Majewski, John. "Toward a Social History of the Corporation: Shareholding in Pennsylvania, 1800–1840." In *The Economy of Early America: Historical Perspectives and New Directions*, edited by Cathy Matson. University Park: Pennsylvania State University Press, 2006.

Malkin, Jennifer and Johnnie Aseron. *Native Entrepreneurship in South Dakota: A Deeper Look* (CFED, December 2006).

Mandell, Lewis. *The Credit Card Industry: A History*. Boston: Twayne Publishers, 1990.

Mann, Bruce. *Republic of Debtors: Bankruptcy in the Age of American Independence*. Cambridge: Harvard University Press, 2009.

Mantsios, Gregory. "Class in America: Myths and Realities." In *Race, Class and Gender in the United States*, 5th ed., edited by Paula S. Rothenberg. New York: Worth, 2001.

Marceaux, P. Shawn and Timothy K. Perttula. "Negotiating Borders: The Southern Caddo and Their Relationships with Colonial Governments in East Texas." In *American Indians and the Market Economy, 1775–1850*, edited by Lance Greene and Mark R. Plane. Tuscaloosa: University of Alabama Press, 2010.

Mason, David. *From Building and Loans to Bailouts: A History of the American Savings and Loan Industry, 1831–1995*. New York: Cambridge University Press, 2004.

Mayer, Robert. *Quick Cash: The Story of the Loan Shark*. DeKalb: Northern Illinois University Press, 2010.

McCoy, Clyde B. and Virginia McCoy Watkins. "Stereotypes of Appalachian Migrants." In *The Invisible Minority: Urban Appalachians*, edited by William W. Philliber and Clyde B. McCoy. Frankfort: University Press of Kentucky, 1981.

McCulloch, Albert J. "The Loan Office Experiment in Missouri, 1821–1836." *University of Missouri Bulletin* 15, no. 24 (1914).

McDonald, Edward. "Community Reinvestment Is Good for Cities, Good for Lenders." In *From Redlining to Reinvestment: Community Responses to Urban Disinvestment*, edited by Gregory D. Squires. Philadelphia: Temple University Press, 1992.

McDonald, Ian and Liam Pleven. "'Cat Bonds' and Insurer-Inspired Issues Weather the Credit Storm." *Wall Street Journal*, 23 August 2007.

McDonald, Kevin M. "Who's Policing the Financial Cop on the Beat?: A Call for Judicial Review of the Consumer Financial Protection Bureau's Non-Legislative Rules." *Review of Banking and Financial Law* 35, no. 1 (2015–16): 224–71.

McDowall, Duncan. *Quick to the Frontier: Canada's Royal Bank*. Toronto: McClelland & Stewart, Inc., 1993.

McEntire, Davis. *Residence and Race: Final and Comprehensive Report to the Commission on Race and Housing*. Berkeley: University of California Press, 1960.

Meeder, Abbigail A. "Entrepreneurial Activity by Women in Rural South Dakota." M.S., Economics, South Dakota State University, 2007.

Meier, Kenneth J. *The Political Economy of Regulation: The Case of Insurance*. Albany: State University of New York Press, 1988.

Meltzer, Allan. *A History of the Federal Reserve, Vol. 1: 1913–1951*. Chicago: University of Chicago Press, 2003.

Merritt, Carole. *The Herndons: An Atlanta Family*. Athens, Ga.: University of Georgia Press, 2002.

Michelon, L. C. "The New Leisure Class." *American Journal of Sociology* 59, no. 4 (1954): 371–78.

Michener, Ron and Robert E. Wright. "The Real Estate Crash of 1764 and the Coming of the American Revolution." Crisis and Consequence Conference, Hagley Museum & Library, Wilmington, Del., 5 November 2010.

Mihm, Stephen. "Dr. Doom." *New York Times Magazine*, 15 August 2008.

Milanovic, Branko. *The Haves and the Have-Nots: A Brief and Idiosyncratic History of Global Inequality*. New York: Basic Books, 2012.

Miller, Glenn W. *The Problems of Labor*. New York: Macmillan Company, 1951.

Miller, Jr., Thomas W. and Harold A. Black. "Examining Arguments Made By Interest Rate Cap Advocates." In *Reframing Financial Regulation: Enhancing Stability and Protecting Consumers*, edited by Hester Peirce and Benjamin Klutsey. Arlington, Va.: Mercatus Center, George Mason University, 2016.

Miller, Robert J. "Indian Entrepreneurship." In *Unlocking the Wealth of Indian Nations*, edited by Terry Anderson. New York: Lexington Books, 2016.

Miller, Robert J. *Reservation "Capitalism": Economic Development in Indian Country*. Denver: ABC-CLIO, 2012.

Miller, Stephen M. and Geoffrey M. B. Tootell. "Redlining, the Community Reinvestment Act, and Private Mortgage Insurance." Economics Working Papers, DigitalCommons@UConn (2000).

Millis, Harry A. *Sickness and Insurance: A Study of the Sickness Problem and Health Insurance*. Chicago: University of Chicago Press, 1937.

Mills, Quincy. "Black Wall Street." In *Encyclopedia of African American Business History*, edited by Juliet E. K. Walker. New York: Greenwood, 1999.

Miner, H. Craig. *The Corporation and the Indian: Tribal Sovereignty and Industrial Civilization in Indian Territory, 1865–1907*. Norman: University of Oklahoma Press, 1976.

Mintz, Max M. *Seeds of Empire: The American Revolutionary Conquest of the Iroquois*. New York: New York University Press, 1999.

Mitchell, C. Bradford. *A Premium on Progress: An Outline History of the American Marine Insurance Market, 1820–1870*. New York: Newcomen Society, 1970.

Mitchell, Karlyn and Nur Onvural. "Economies of Scale and Scope at Large Commercial Banks: Evidence from the Fourier Flexible Functional Form." *Journal of Money, Credit and Banking* 28 (1996): 178–99.

Moloney, Thomas E. "Discussion." In *The Financial Condition and Regulation of Insurance Companies*, edited by Richard E. Randall and Richard W. Kopcke. Boston: Federal Reserve Bank of Boston, 1991.

Monke, Jim. "Agricultural Credit: Institutions and Issues." In *Agricultural Finance and Credit*, edited by J. M. Bishoff. New York: Nova Science Publishers, 2008.

Monke, Jim. "Farm Credit Services of America Ends Attempt to Leave the Farm Credit System." In *Agricultural Finance and Credit*, edited by J. M. Bishoff. New York: Nova Science Publishers, 2008.

Monke, Jim. "Farm Credit System." In *Agricultural Finance and Credit*, edited by J. M. Bishoff. New York: Nova Science Publishers, 2008.

Moore, W. F. "Liability Insurance." *Annals of the American Academy of Political and Social Science* 26 (1905):319–39.

Moore, Warren. *Mountain Voices: A Legacy of the Blue Ridge and Great Smokies*. Chester, Conn.: Globe Pequot Press, 1988.

Morgan, Gerald. *Public Relief of Sickness*. New York: Macmillan Company, 1922.

Morman, James B. "Cooperative Credit Institutions in the United States." *Annals of the American Academy of Political and Social Science* 87 (January 1920): 172–82.

Moss, David. *When All Else Fails: Government as the Ultimate Risk Manager*. Cambridge: Harvard University Press, 2002.

Moules, Jonathan. "Happy Just to be in Business: An Online Exchange that Helps Small Local Banks to Gain Economies of Scale has Shown an Amazing Capacity for Survival." *Financial Times*, 13 March 2002.

Murphy, Anne L. *The Origins of English Financial Markets: Investment and Speculation Before the South Sea Bubble*. New York: Cambridge University Press, 2009.

Murphy, Sharon Ann. *Investing in Life: Insurance in Antebellum America*. Baltimore: Johns Hopkins University Press, 2010.

Murphy, Sharon Ann. "Life Insurance in the United States through World War I." In *EH.Net Encyclopedia*, edited by Robert Whaples. (2002).

Murphy, Sharon Ann. "Security in an Uncertain World: Life Insurance and the Emergence of Modern America." Ph.D. diss., University of Virginia, 2005.

Murray, David. *Indian Giving: Economies of Power in Indian-White Exchanges*. Amherst: University of Massachusetts Press, 2000.

Murray, J. B. C. *The History of Usury from the Earliest Period to the Present Time … And an Examination into the Policy of Laws on Usury and Their Effect Upon Commerce*. Philadelphia: J. B. Lippincott & Co., 1866.

Murray, John E. *Origins of American Health Insurance: A History of Industrial Sickness Funds*. New Haven: Yale University Press, 2007.

Naisbitt, John and Patricia Aburdene. *Re-inventing the Corporation: Transforming Your Job and Your Company for the New Information Society*. New York: Warner Books, 1985.

National Community Reinvestment Coalition. "The 2005 Fair Lending Disparities: Stubborn and Persistent II." Washington: National Community Reinvestment Coalition, 2006.

Neem, Johann N. *Creating a Nation of Joiners: Democracy and Civil Society in Early National Massachusetts*. Cambridge: Harvard University Press, 2008.

Neiburger, E. J. and Don Spohn. "Prehistoric Money." *Central States Archaeological Journal* 54, no. 4 (2007): 188–94.

Nelson, Scott Reynolds. *A Nation of Deadbeats: An Uncommon History of America's Financial Disasters*. New York: Alfred A. Knopf, 2012.

Newby, I. A. *Jim Crow's Defense: Anti-Negro Thought in America, 1900–1930*. Baton Rouge: Louisiana State University Press, 1965.

Newell, Margaret. *Brethren by Nature: New England Indians, Colonists, and the Origins of American Slavery*. Ithaca: Cornell University Press 2015.

Newitz, Annalee and Matt Wray. "Introduction." In *White Trash: Race and Class in America*, edited by Matt Wray and Annalee Newitz. New York: Routledge 1997.

Newton, Cody. "Business in the Hinterlands: The Impact of the Market Economy on the West-Central Great Plains at the Turn of the 19th Century." In *American Indians and the Market Economy, 1775–1850*, edited by Lance Greene and Mark R. Plane. Tuscaloosa: University of Alabama Press, 2010.

Norberg, Johan. *Financial Fiasco: How America's Infatuation with Homeownership and Easy Money Created the Economic Crisis*. Washington, DC: Cato Institute, 2009.

Norman, Michael. "Wilma Porter Soss, 86, A Gadfly at Stock Meetings of Companies." *New York Times*, 16 October 1986.

Oates, James. *Business and Social Change: Life Insurance Looks to the Future*. New York: McGraw-Hill Book Company, 1968.

Oberly, James W. "Land, Population, Prices, and the Regulation of Natural Resources: The Lake Superior Ojibwa, 1790–1820." In *The Other Side of the Frontier: Economic Explorations into Native American History*, edited by Linda Barrington. New York: Westview Press, 1999.

Obermiller, Phillip J. "The Question of Appalachian Ethnicity." In *The Invisible Minority: Urban Appalachians*, edited by William W. Philliber and Clyde B. McCoy. Frankfort: University Press of Kentucky, 1981.

Olegario, Rowena. *A Culture of Credit: Embedding Trust and Transparency in American Business*. Cambridge: Harvard University Press, 2006.

Olegario, Rowena. *The Engine of Enterprise: Credit in America*. Cambridge: Harvard University Press, 2016.

Olney, Martha L. *Buy Now, Pay Latter: Advertising, Credit, and Consumer Durables in the 1920s*. Chapel Hill: University of North Carolina Press, 1991.

Olney, Martha. "When Your Word Is Not Enough: Race, Collateral, and Household Credit." *Journal of Economic History* 58, no. 2 (1998): 408–31.

Orren, Karen. *Corporate Power and Social Change: The Politics of the Life Insurance Industry.* Baltimore: Johns Hopkins University Press, 1974.

Oviatt, F. C. "Historical Study of Fire Insurance in the United States." *Annals of the Academy of Political and Social Science* 26 (1905):155–78.

Owens, Alastair. "'Making Some Provision for the Contingencies to Which Their Sex Is Particularly Liable': Women and Investment in Early Nineteenth-century England." In *Women, Business and Finance in Nineteenth-century Europe: Rethinking Separate Spheres,* edited by Beatrice Craig, Robert Beachy, and Alastair Owens. New York: Berg, 2006.

Page, Clarence. "Foreword: Loan Sharks in Pinstripes." In *Why the Poor Pay More: How to Stop Predatory Lending,* edited by Gregory D. Squires. Westport, Conn.: Praeger, 2004.

Pak, Susie. *Gentlemen Bankers: The World of J. P. Morgan.* Cambridge: Harvard University Press, 2013.

Parker, Dominic, Randal Rucker, and Peter Nickerson. "The Legacy of United States v. Washington: Economic Effects of the Boldt and Rafeedie Decisions." In *Unlocking the Wealth of Indian Nations,* edited by Terry Anderson. New York: Lexington Books, 2016.

Parker, Henry G. "Discussion." In *The Financial Condition and Regulation of Insurance Companies,* edited by Richard E. Randall and Richard W. Kopcke. Boston: Federal Reserve Bank of Boston, 1991.

Parramore, Thomas C., Peter C. Stewart, and Tommy L. Bogger. *Norfolk: The First Four Centuries.* Charlottesville: University Press of Virginia, 1994.

Partnoy, Frank. *F.I.A.S.C.O.: The Inside Story of a Wall Street Trader.* New York: Penguin Books, 1997.

Patterson, Barbara. *The Price We Pay for Discrimination.* Atlanta: Southern Regional Council, 1964.

Pauly, Mark V. "Commentary." In *Government Risk-Bearing: Proceedings of a Conference Held at the Federal Reserve Bank of Cleveland,* edited by Mark S. Sniderman. Boston: Kluwer Academic, 1993.

Pearson, Robin. "Insurance: Fire Insurance." In *The Oxford Encyclopedia of Economic History,* edited by Joel Mokyr. (2003), 3:90–92.

Pearson, Robin. "Insurance: Historical Overview." In *The Oxford Encyclopedia of Economic History,* edited by Joel Mokyr. (2003), 3:83–86.

Peck, Susan and David Saffert. *Lending on Native American Lands: A Guide for Rural Development Staff.* Washington, DC: Housing Assistance Council, June 2006.

Pehl, Matthew. *The Making of Working-Class Religion.* Chicago: University of Illinois Press, 2016.

Peinado, Carlos J. and Daphne Ross. *Waterbuster.* Film documentary. 2008.

Peirce, Hester and Benjamin Klutsey. "Introduction: Market-Based Financial Regulation." In *Reframing Financial Regulation: Enhancing Stability and Protecting Consumers*, edited by Hester Peirce and Benjamin Klutsey. Arlington, Va.: Mercatus Center, George Mason University, 2016.

Penley, Constance. "Crackers and Whackers: The White Trashing of Porn." In *White Trash: Race and Class in America*, edited by Matt Wray and Annalee Newitz. New York: Routledge 1997.

Peristiani, Stavros. "Do Mergers Improve the X-Efficiency and Scale Efficiency of U.S. Banks? Evidence From the 1980s." *Journal of Money, Credit and Banking 29*, no. 3 (1997): 326–37.

Perkins, Edwin. *American Public Finance and Financial Services, 1700–1815*. Columbus: Ohio State University Press, 1994.

Perkins, Edwin. *The Economy of Colonial America*, 2nd ed. New York: Columbia University Press, 1988.

Perkins, Edwin. *Wall Street to Main Street: Charles Merrill and Middle-Class Investors*. New York: Cambridge University Press, 1999.

Peterson, Richard L. "An Investigation of Sex Discrimination in Commercial Banks' Direct Consumer Lending." *Bell Journal of Economics 12*, no. 2 (1981): 547–61.

Petersson, Tom. "The Silent Partners: Women, Capital and the Development of the Financial System in Nineteenth-century Sweden." In *Women, Business and Finance in Nineteenth-century Europe: Rethinking Separate Spheres*, edited by Beatrice Craig, Robert Beachy, and Alastair Owens. New York: Berg, 2006.

Pettigrew, Thomas. "White-Negro Confrontations." In *The Negro Challenge to the Business Community*, edited by Eli Ginzberg. New York: McGraw-Hill Book Company, 1964.

Pevar, Stephen L. *The Rights of Indians and Tribes*, 4th ed. New York: Oxford University Press, 2012.

Phelps, Clyde William. *The Role of Fleet Leasing in Motor Vehicle Fleet Plans of Business Firms*. Baltimore: Commercial Credit Co., 1969.

Pickering, Kathleen Ann. *Lakota Culture, World Economy*. Lincoln: University of Nebraska Press, 2000.

Pierce, John E. *Development of Comprehensive Insurance for the Household*. Homewood, Ill.: Richard D. Irwin, 1958.

Piketty, Thomas. *Capital in the Twenty-First Century*. Cambridge: Harvard University Press, 2014.

Pinto, Edward J. "Why the 20-Year Mortgage Is the Answer to the Housing Finance Mess." *American Banker*, 5 February 2016.

Pizzo, Stephen. "Minneapolis Fed: Bank Consolidation Won't Cause Economies of Scale." *National Mortgage News*, 7 October 1991.

Plane, Mark R. "'Remarkable Elasticity of Character': Colonial Discourse, the Market Economy, and Catawba Itinerancy, 1770–1820." In *American Indians and the Market Economy, 1775–1850,* edited by Lance Greene and Mark R. Plane. Tuscaloosa: University of Alabama Press, 2010.

Plummer, Wilbur C. "Consumer Credit in Colonial Philadelphia." *Pennsylvania Magazine of History and Biography* 46, no. 4 (1942): 385–409.

Plunz, Richard. *A History of Housing in New York City: Dwelling Type and Social Change in the American Metropolis.* New York: Columbia University Press, 1990.

Pratico, Dominick. *Eisenhower and Social Security: The Origins of the Disability Program.* New York: Writers Club Press, 2001.

President's Appalachia Regional Commission and Committee on Education and Labor. "Regional Poverty: Appalachia and the Upper Great Lakes Region." In *The Economics of Poverty: An American Paradox,* edited by Burton Weisbrod. Englewood Cliffs, N.J.: Prentice-Hall.

Prins, Nomi. *It Takes a Pillage: An Epic Tale of Power, Deceit, and Untold Trillions.* Hoboken, N.J.: John Wiley & Sons, 2011.

Quadagno, Jill. *The Transformation of Old Age Security: Class and Politics in the American Welfare State.* Chicago: University of Chicago Press, 1988.

Rajan, Raghuram G. and Rodney Ramcharan. "Land and Credit: A Study of the Political Economy of Banking in the United States in the Early 20th Century." *Journal of Finance* 66, no. 6 (2011): 1,895–931.

Randall, Richard E. and Richard W. Kopcke. "Insurance Companies as Financial Intermediaries: Risk and Return." In *The Financial Condition and Regulation of Insurance Companies,* edited by Richard E. Randall and Richard W. Kopcke. Boston: Federal Reserve Bank of Boston, 1991.

Randall, Richard E. and Richard W. Kopcke. "The Financial Condition and Regulation of Insurance Companies: An Overview." In *The Financial Condition and Regulation of Insurance Companies,* edited by Richard E. Randall and Richard W. Kopcke. Boston: Federal Reserve Bank of Boston, 1991.

Raper, Arthur and Ira De A. Reid. *Sharecroppers All.* Chapel Hill: University of North Carolina Press, 1941.

Rapone, Anita. *The Guardian Life Insurance Company, 1860–1920: A History of a German-American Enterprise.* New York: New York University Press. 1987.

Regan, Shawn and Terry Anderson. "Unlocking the Energy Wealth of Indian Nations." In *Unlocking the Wealth of Indian Nations,* edited by Terry Anderson. New York: Lexington Books, 2016.

Remini, Robert. *Andrew Jackson and the Bank War: A Study in the Growth of Presidential Power.* New York: W. W. Norton and Company, 1967.

Reséndez, Andrés. *The Other Slavery: The Uncovered Story of Indian Enslavement in America*. New York: Houghton Mifflin Harcourt, 2016.

Ricketts, Erol R. and Isabel V. Sawhill. "Defining and Measuring the Underclass." *Journal of Policy Analysis and Management* 7, no. 2 (1988): 316–25.

Riley, Naomi Schaefer. *The New Trail of Tears: How Washington Is Destroying American Indians*. New York: Encounter Books, 2016.

Rilling, Donna. "Small-Producer Capitalism in Early National Philadelphia." In *The Economy of Early America: Historical Perspectives and New Directions*, edited by Cathy Matson. University Park: Pennsylvania State University Press, 2006.

Ringleb, Al H. and Steven L. Wiggins. (1993) "Institutional Control and Large-scale, Long-term Hazards." In *Government Risk-Bearing: Proceedings of a Conference Held at the Federal Reserve Bank of Cleveland*, edited by Mark S. Sniderman. Boston: Kluwer Academic, 1993.

Rippe, Richard D. "No Savings Crisis in the United States." *Business Economics* 34, no. 3 (1999): 47–55.

Roback, Jennifer. "The Political Economy of Segregation: The Case of Segregated Streetcars." *Journal of Economic History* 46, no. 4 (1986): 893–917.

Robb, George. *Ladies of the Ticker: Woman and Wall Street from the Gilded Age to the Great Depression*. Champaign: University of Illinois Press, 2017.

Robbins, Horace. "'Bigness', the Sherman Act, and Antitrust Policy." *Virginia Law Review* 39 (1953): 907–48.

Roberts, Russell. *The Choice: A Fable of Free Trade and Protectionism*, 3rd ed. New York: Pearson, 2006.

Rock, Howard. *Artisans of the New Republic: The Tradesmen of New York City in the Age of Jefferson*. New York: New York University Press, 1984.

Rockman, Seth. *Scraping By: Wage Labor, Slavery, and Survival in Early Baltimore*. Baltimore: Johns Hopkins University Press, 2009.

Rodriguez, Justine. "Information and Incentives to Improve Government Risk-Bearing." In *Government Risk-Bearing: Proceedings of a Conference Held at the Federal Reserve Bank of Cleveland*, edited by Mark S. Sniderman. Boston: Kluwer Academic, 1993.

Roe, Mark. "A Political Theory of American Corporate Finance." *Columbia Law Review* 91 (1991): 10–67.

Rose, Arnold. *The Negro in America: The Condensed Version of Gunnar Myrdal's An American Dilemma*. New York: Harper & Row, 1948.

Rosenzweig, Mark R. "Savings Behaviour in Low-Income Countries." *Oxford Review of Economic Policy* 17, no. 1 (2001): 40–54.

Rosier, Paul C. "Searching for Salvation and Sovereignty: Blackfeet Oil Leasing and the Reconstruction of the Tribe." In *Native Pathways: American Indian Culture and Economic Development*, edited by Brian Hosmer and Colleen O'Neill. Boulder: University Press of Colorado, 2004.

Ross, Malcolm. *All Manner of Men*. New York: Harcourt, Brace & World, 1948.

Ross, Stephen and John Yinger. *The Color of Credit: Mortgage Discrimination, Research Methodology, and Fair-Lending Enforcement*. Cambridge: The MIT Press, 2002.

Rotella, Elyce and George Alter. "Working Class Debt in the Late Nineteenth Century United States." *Journal of Family History* 18, 2 (1993): 111–134.

Roth, Louise Marie. *Selling Women Short: Gender Inequality on Wall Street*. Princeton: Princeton University Press, 2006.

Rothenberg, Winifred Barr. *From Market-Places to a Market Economy: The Transformation of Rural Massachusetts, 1750–1850*. Chicago: University of Chicago Press, 1992.

Rothstein, Richard. *The Color of Law: A Forgotten History of How Our Government Segregated America*. New York: W. W. Norton, 2017.

Rubinow, I. M. *Standards of Health Insurance*. New York: Henry Holt and Co., 1916.

Rubinow, I. M. *The Quest for Security*. New York: Henry Holt and Co., 1934.

Russ, Jacob and Thomas Stratmann. "Divided Interests: The Increasing Detrimental Fractionation of Indian Land Ownership." In *Unlocking the Wealth of Indian Nations*, edited by Terry Anderson. New York: Lexington Books, 2016.

Ruttenbur, E. M. *History of the Indian Tribes of Hudson's River: Their Origin, Manners and Customs*. Albany: J. Munsell, 1872.

Sander, Kathleen. *The Business of Charity: The Woman's Exchange Movement, 1832–1900*. Chicago: University of Illinois Press, 1998.

Santucci, Larry. "The Secured Credit Card Market." Philadelphia Federal Reserve Discussion Paper, November 2016.

Schafer, Robert and Helen F. Ladd. *Discrimination in Mortgage Lending*. Cambridge: MIT Press, 1981.

Schieber, Sylvester and John B. Shoven. *The Real Deal: The History and Future of Social Security*. New Haven: Yale University Press, 1999.

Schmitz, Amy J. "Promoting the Promise Manufactured Homes Provide for Affordable Housing." *Journal of Affordable Housing and Community Development Law* 13, no. 3 (2004): 384–415.

Schott, Francis. "Disintermediation Through Policy Loans at Life Insurance Companies." *Journal of Finance* 26 (1971):719–29.

Schuck, Peter H. *Why Government Fails So Often and How It Can Do Better*. Princeton: Princeton University Press, 2014.

Schwarzweller, Harry K., James S. Brown, and J. J. Mangalam. *Mountain Families in Transition: A Case Study of Appalachian Migration*. University Park: Pennsylvania State University Press, 1971.

Schweitzer, Mary. *Custom and Contract: Household, Government, and the Economy in Colonial Pennsylvania*. New York: Columbia University Press, 1987.

Scism, Leslie. "Insurance Practice Questioned." *Wall Street Journal*, 17 November 2016.

Scott, Anne Firor. *Natural Allies: Women's Associations in American History*. Urbana: University of Illinois Press, 1992.

Scott, Emmett J. *Negro Migration During the War*. New York: Oxford University Press, 1920.

Sethi, Rita Chaudhry "Smells Like Racism." In *Race, Class and Gender in the United States*, 5th ed. edited by Paula S. Rothenberg. New York: Worth, 2001.

Severson, Robert F., James F. Niss, and Richard D. Winkelman. "Mortgage Borrowing as a Frontier Developed: A Study of Mortgages in Champaign County, Illinois, 1836–1895." *Journal of Economic History* 26, no. 2 (1966): 147–68.

Shalhope, Robert E. *The Baltimore Bank Riot: Political Upheaval in Antebellum Maryland*. Chicago: University of Illinois Press, 2009.

Shammas, Carole. "Re-Assessing the Married Women's Property Acts." *Journal of Women's History* 6, no. 1 (1994): 9–30.

Shaw, Bernard. *Man and Superman: A Comedy and a Philosophy*. Cambridge, Mass.: University Press, 1903.

Shen, Lucinda. "Wells Fargo's Phony Account Scandal May Not Actually End Up Costing That Much." *Fortune*, 6 December 2016.

Shepherd, Pearce. "Principles and Problems of Selection and Underwriting," In *Life Insurance Trends at Mid-Century*, edited by David McCahan. Philadelphia: University of Pennsylvania Press, 1950.

Shirley, Michael. *From Congregation Town to Industrial City: Culture and Social Change in a Southern Community*. New York: New York University Press, 1994.

Silverman, Rachel. "High Finance and Family-Friendly? KKR Is Trying." *Wall Street Journal*, 27 September 2016.

Simon, Ruth and Paul Overberg. "Credit Gap for Black-Owned Firms." *Wall Street Journal*, 10 November 2016.

Simonsen, Jane E. *Making Home Work: Domesticity and Native American Assimilation in the American West, 1860–1919*. Chapel Hill: University of North Carolina Press, 2006.

Slack, Charles. *Hetty: The Genius and Madness of America's First Female Tycoon.* New York: Ecco, 2004.

Smith, Adam. *An Inquiry into the Nature and Causes of the Wealth of Nations.* New York: Modern Library, 1937.

Smith, Dina. "Lost Trailer Utopias: The Long, Long Trailer (1954) and Fifties America." *Utopian Studies* 14, no. 1 (2003): 112–31.

Smith, Kyle. *Predatory Lending in Native American Communities.* Fredericksburg, Va.: First Nations Development Institute, 2003.

Smith, Shanna L. "The Fair-Housing Movement's Alternative Standard for Measuring Housing Discrimination: Comments." In *Clear and Convincing Evidence: Measurement of Discrimination in America,* edited by Michael Fix and Raymond J. Struyk. Washington, DC: Urban Institute Press, 1993.

Smith, Vernon. "Economy, Ecology, and Institutions in the Emergence of Humankind." In *The Other Side of the Frontier: Economic Explorations into Native American History,* edited by Linda Barrington. New York: Westview Press, 1999.

Sniderman, Mark S. "Preface." In *Government Risk-Bearing: Proceedings of a Conference Held at the Federal Reserve Bank of Cleveland,* edited by Mark S. Sniderman. Boston: Kluwer Academic, 1993.

Snowden, Kenneth. "Mortgage Rates and American Capital Market Development in the Late Nineteenth Century." *Journal of Economic History* 47, no. 3 (1987): 671–91.

Snowden, Kenneth. "Mortgage Securitization in the United States: Twentieth Century Developments in Historical Perspective." In *Anglo-American Financial Systems: Institutions and Markets in the Twentieth Century,* edited by Michael Bordo and Richard Sylla. New York: Irwin Professional Publishing, 1995.

Sowell, Thomas. *Black Rednecks and White Liberals.* San Francisco: Encounter Books, 2005.

Sparks, Earl S. *History and Theory of Agricultural Credit in the United States.* New York: Thomas Y. Crowell Co., 1932.

Sparks, Edith. *Capital Intentions: Female Proprietors in San Francisco, 1850–1920.* Chapel Hill: University of North Carolina Press, 2006.

Spiegel, John, Alan Gart, and Steven Gart. *Banking Redefined: How Superregional Powerhouses Are Reshaping Financial Services.* Chicago: Irwin Professional Publishing, 1996.

Squires, Gregory D. "Community Reinvestment: An Emerging Social Movement." In *From Redlining to Reinvestment: Community Responses to Urban Disinvestment,* edited by Gregory D. Squires. Philadelphia: Temple University Press, 1992.

Squires, Gregory D. "The New Redlining." In *Why the Poor Pay More: How to Stop Predatory Lending*, edited by Gregory D. Squires. Westport, Conn.: Praeger, 2004.

Star, David. "Black Dollars Matter." *Atlanta Black Star*, 19 June 2016.

Stein, Charles. *The Maryland Ground Rent System*. Baltimore: Wyman Park Federal Savings and Loan Association, 1952.

Sterner, Richard, Lenoir Epstein, and Ellen Winston. *The Negro's Share: A Study of Income, Consumption, Housing and Public Assistance*. New York: Harper & Brothers, 1943.

Stevens, Mark. *The Big Eight*. New York: Collier Books, 1981.

Stickle, Mark. "The Ohio Life Insurance and Trust Company: Eastern Capital and Mortgage Credit in Ohio, 1834–1845." Unpublished ms., 2011.

Stiglitz, Joseph E. "Perspectives on the Role of Government Risk-Bearing within the Financial Sector." In *Government Risk-Bearing: Proceedings of a Conference Held at the Federal Reserve Bank of Cleveland*, edited by Mark S. Sniderman. Boston: Kluwer Academic, 1993.

Stokes, W. N., Jr., *Credit to Farmers: The Story of Federal Intermediate Credit Banks and Production Credit Associations*. Washington, D.C.: Federal Intermediate Credit Banks, 1973.

Streitmatter, Rodger. *Raising Her Voice: African-American Women Journalists Who Changed History*. Lexington: University Press of Kentucky.

Sullivan, Laura, Tatjana Meschede, Thomas Shapiro, and Maria Fernanda Escobar. "Misdirected Investments: How the Mortgage Interest Deduction Drives Inequality and the Racial Wealth Gap." Institute on Assets and Social Policy and National Low Income Housing Coalition Report, October 2017.

Swarns, Rachel L. "Biased Lending Evolves, and Blacks Face Trouble Getting Mortgages." *New York Times*, 30 October 2015.

Sweeney, Gael. "The King of White Trash Culture: Elvis Presley and the Aesthetics of Excess." In *White Trash: Race and Class in America*, edited by Matt Wray and Annalee Newitz. New York: Routledge 1997.

Sylla, Richard, Robert E. Wright, and David Cowen. "Alexander Hamilton, Central Banker: Crisis Management During the U.S. Financial Panic of 1792." *Business History Review* 83, no. 2 (2009), 61–86.

Syron, Richard. "Administered Prices and the Market Reaction: The Case of Urban Core Property Insurance." *Journal of Finance* 28, no. 1 (1973): 147–56.

Taylor, John, Josh Silver, and David Berenbaum. "The Targets of Predatory and Discriminatory Lending: Who Are They and Where Do They Live?" In *Why the Poor Pay More: How to Stop Predatory Lending*, edited by Gregory D. Squires. Westport, Conn.: Praeger, 2004.

Teackle, Littleton. *An Address to the Members of the Legislature of Maryland, Concerning the Establishment of a Loan Office for the Benefit of the Landowners of the State.* Annapolis, 1817.

Thakor, Anjan. "Information Technology and Financial Services Consolidation." *Journal of Banking and Finance* 23 (1999): 697–700.

Thaler, Richard H. *Misbehaving: The Making of Behavioral Economics.* New York: Norton, 2016.

Thayer, Theodore. "The Land-Bank System in the American Colonies." *Journal of Economic History* 13, no. 2 (1953): 145–59.

Thomasson, Melissa. "Health Insurance in the United States." In *EH.Net Encyclopedia*, edited by Robert Whaples. (2003).

Thomasson, Melissa. "The Importance of Group Coverage: How Tax Policy Shaped U.S. Health Insurance." *American Economic Review* 93, 4 (2003): 1,373–84.

Thompson, Harry F. ed. *A New South Dakota History*, 2nd ed. Sioux Falls: Center for Western Studies, 2009.

Thornton, Tamara. "'A Great Machine' or a 'Beast of Prey': A Boston Corporation and Its Rural Debtors in an Age of Capitalist Transformation." *Journal of the Early Republic* 27, no. 4 (2007): 567–97.

Thorp, Daniel B. "Doing Business in the Backcountry: Retail Trade in Colonial Rowan County, North Carolina." *William and Mary Quarterly* 48, no. 3 (1991): 387–408.

Timiraos, Nick. "Home Buyers Miss Out on Low-Cost Loans: Postcrisis Tightening Curbs Economy as it Hurts Those with Poor Credit." *Wall Street Journal*, 5 December 2016.

Todd, Charles L. and Robert Sonkin. *Alexander Bryan Johnson: Philosophical Banker.* Syracuse: Syracuse University Press, 1977.

Todd, Richard M. "Taking Stock of the Farm Credit System: Riskier for Farm Borrowers." *Federal Reserve Bank of Minneapolis Quarterly Review* 9, no. 4 (1985): 14–24.

Traflet, Janice M. *A Nation of Small Shareholders: Marketing Wall Street After World War II.* Baltimore: Johns Hopkins University Press, 2013.

Treasury Department Study Team. *Credit and Capital Formation: A Report to the President's Interagency Task Force on Women Business Owners*, April 1978.

Tuckett, Harvey G. *Practical Remarks on the Present State of Life Insurance in the United States, Showing the Evils Which Exist, and Rule for Improvement.* Philadelphia: Smith and Peters, 1850.

Turner, Margery, Fred Freiberg, Erin Godfrey, Carla Herbig, Diane K. Levy, and Robin R. Smith. *All Other Things Being Equal: A Paired Testing Study of Mortgage Lending Institutions.* Washington, D.C.: Urban Institute, 2002.

Tursi, Frank. *Winston-Salem: A History*. USA: John F. Blair, 1994.

Twiss, Pamela and Thomas Mueller. "Housing Appalachians: Recent Trends." *Journal of Appalachian Studies* 10, no. 3 (2004): 390–99.

U.S. Commission on Civil Rights. *Mortgage Money: Who Gets It? A Case Study in Mortgage Lending Discrimination in Hartford, Connecticut*. Washington: U.S. Government Printing Office, 1974.

U.S. Department of Labor. *Black Americans: A Chartbook*. Washington: U.S. Government Printing Office, 1971.

U.S. Department of Labor, Women's Bureau. *Negro Women War Workers*. 1945.

U.S. Department of Labor. *Negroes in the United States: Their Employment and Economic Status*, December 1952.

U.S. Department of Labor. *The Negroes in the United States: Their Economic and Social Situation*, June 1966.

U.S. Office of the Comptroller of the Currency. *Annual Report*, 1910.

Usner, Daniel H., Jr., *American Indians in the Lower Mississippi Valley: Social and Economic Histories*. Lincoln: University of Nebraska Press, 1998.

Utgoff, Kathleen P. "The PBGC: A Costly Lesson in the Economics of Federal Insurance." In *Government Risk-Bearing: Proceedings of a Conference Held at the Federal Reserve Bank of Cleveland*, edited by Mark S. Sniderman. Boston: Kluwer Academic, 1993.

Valgren, Victor N. *Farmers' Mutual Fire Insurance in the United States*. Chicago: Chicago University Press, 1924.

Valgren, Victor N. *Reinsurance Among Farmers' Mutual Fire Insurance Companies*. Washington, D.C.: Farm Credit Administration, Bulletin No. 45, 1941.

Vigna, Paul. "'The Prophet of Wall Street' to Retire." *Wall Street Journal*, 13 February 2017.

von Mettenheim, Kurt E. *Federal Banking in Brazil: Policies and Competitive Advantages*. London: Routledge, 2010.

Waciega, Lisa Wilson. "A 'Man of Business': The Widow of Means in Southeastern Pennsylvania, 1750–1850." *William and Mary Quarterly* 44, no. 1 (1987): 40–64.

Wade, Richard C. *The Urban Frontier: The Rise of Western Cities, 1790–1830*. Cambridge: Harvard University Press, 1959.

Wadhwani, R. Daniel. "Protecting Small Savers: The Political Economy of Economic Security." *Journal of Policy History* 18, no. 1 (2006): 126–45.

Wagmiller, Robert. "Debt and Assets Among Low-Income Families." National Center for Children in Poverty. (October 2003).

Wahlstad, Peter P. and Walter S. Johnson, *Credit and the Credit Man*. New York: Alexander Hamilton Institute, 1917.

Wainwright, Nicholas. *A Philadelphia Story: The Philadelphia Contributionship for the Insurance of House from Loss by Fire*. Philadelphia, 1952.

Walker, Juliet E. K. *The History of Black Business in America: Capitalism, Race, Entrepreneurship*, 2nd ed., Vol. 1. Chapel Hill: University of North Carolina Press, 2009.

Walker, Juliet E.K. "White Corporate America: The New Arbiter of Race?" In *Constructing Corporate America: History, Politics, Culture*, edited by Kenneth Lipartito and David B. Sicilia. New York: Oxford University Press, 2004.

Walker, Kenneth. *Guaranteed Investment Contracts: Risk Analysis and Portfolio Strategies*. Homewood, Ill.: Dow Jones-Irwin, 1989.

Walter, Ingo. "Strategies in Financial Services, the Shareholders and the System: Is Bigger and Broader Better?" Hamburg Institute of International Economics Discussion Paper No. 205, (2002).

Wandel, William. *The Control of Competition in Fire Insurance*. Lancaster, Pa.: Art Printing Co., 1935.

Warren, Kees-Jan and Jan Noel. "Not Confined to the Village Clearings: Indian Women in the Fur Trade in Colonial New York, 1695–1732." *New York History* 94, 1–2 (2013): 40–58.

Washburn, Wilcomb E. "Foreword." In *Sovereign Nations or Reservations? An Economic History of American Indians*, by Terry Anderson. San Francisco: Pacific Research Institute for Public Policy, 1995.

Washington, Ebonya. "The Impact of Banking and Fringe Banking Regulation on the Number of Unbanked Americans." *Journal of Human Resources* 41, no. 1 (2006): 106–37.

Weitzman, Phillip. "Mobile Homes: High Cost Housing in the Low Income Market." *Journal of Economic Issues* 10, no. 3 (1976): 576–97.

Welch, Samuel. *Recollections of Buffalo: During the Decade from 1830 to 1840, or Fifty Years Since*. Buffalo: Peter Paul and Bro., 1891.

Weller, Christian E. "Pushing the Limit: Credit Card Debt Burdens American Families." Washington, D.C.: Center for American Progress, 2006.

Wermiel, Sara E. *The Fireproof Building: Technology and Public Safety in the Nineteenth-Century American City*. Baltimore: Johns Hopkins University Press, 2000.

Whaples, Robert and David Buffum. "Fraternalism, Paternalism, the Family, and the Market: Insurance a Century Ago." *Social Science History* 15, no. 1 (1991): 97–122.

Wheeler, Jacob D. *A Practical Treatise on the Law of Slavery, Being a Compilation of all that Decisions Made on That Subject, in the Several Courts of the United States, and State Courts*. New York: Allan Pollock, Jr., 1837.

White, Eugene. "Lessons from the Great American Real Estate Boom and Bust of the 1920s." In *Housing and Mortgage Markets in Historical Perspective*, ed. Eugene White, Kenneth Snowden, and Price Fishback. Chicago: University of Chicago Press, 2014.

White, Leslie. *Modern Capitalist Culture*. Walnut Creek, CA: Left Coast Press, 2008.

White, Richard. *The Roots of Dependency: Subsistence, Environment, and Social Change Among the Choctaws, Pawnees, and Navajos*. Lincoln: University of Nebraska Press, 1983.

White, Shane. *Prince of Darkness: The Untold Story of Jeremiah G. Hamilton, Wall Street's First Black Millionaire*. New York: St. Martin's Press, 2015.

Whiteside, Noel. "Insurance: Health and Accident." In *The Oxford Encyclopedia of Economic History*, edited by Joel Mokyr. (2003), 3:94–98.

Wilder, Craig. *A Covenant with Color: Race and Social Power in Brooklyn*. New York: Columbia University Press, 2000.

Wilkins, Mira. "Multinational Enterprise in Insurance, an Historical Overview." In *Internationalisation and Globalisation of the Insurance Industry in the 19th and 20th Centuries*, edited by Peter Borscheid and Robin Pearson. Zurich: Phillipps-University, Marburg, 2007.

Willis, Lauren E. "The Consumer Financial Protection Bureau and the Quest for Consumer Comprehension." Loyola Law School, Legal Studies Research Paper Series No. 2016–02, August 2016.

Wills, Jocelyn. *Boosters, Hustlers, and Speculators: Entrepreneurial Culture and the Rise of Minneapolis and St. Paul, 1849–1883*. St. Paul: Minnesota Historical Society, 2005.

Winter, Ralph. "The Liability Insurance Market." *Journal of Economic Perspectives* 5 (1991): 115–36.

Winters, R. Y. *Credit Problems of North Carolina Cropper Farmers, Bulletin No. 271*. Raleigh: Experiment Station Library, 1930.

Wishart, David. "Could the Cherokee Have Survived in the Southeast?" In *The Other Side of the Frontier: Economic Explorations into Native American History*, edited by Linda Barrington. New York: Westview Press, 1999.

Witkowski, Rachel. "Banks Are Sprouting Anew in the U.S." *Wall Street Journal*, 9 February 2017.

Woloson, Wendy A. *In Hock: Pawning in America from Independence through the Great Depression*. Chicago: University of Chicago Press, 2009.

Wooldridge, Clifton R. *The Grafters of America*. Chicago: Monarch Book Company, 1906.

Worden, Rolfe A. "Zoning – Townships – Complete Exclusion of Trailer Camps and Parks." *Michigan Law Review* 61, no. 5 (1963): 1010–14.

Wray, L. Randall. "Introduction to an Alternative History of Money." Working Paper No. 717 (May 2012).

Wright, Brian. "Public Insurance of Private Risks: Theory and Evidence from Agriculture." In *Government Risk-Bearing: Proceedings of a Conference Held at the Federal Reserve Bank of Cleveland*, edited by Mark S. Sniderman. Boston: Kluwer Academic, 1993.

Wright, Ivan. *Farm Mortgage Financing*. New York: McGraw-Hill, 1923.

Wright, Kenneth. "The Structure, Conduct, and Regulation of the Life Insurance Industry." In *The Financial Condition and Regulation of Insurance Companies*, edited by Richard E. Randall and Richard W. Kopcke. Boston: Federal Reserve Bank of Boston, 1991.

Wright, Robert E., ed. *Bailouts: Public Money, Private Profit*. New York: Columbia University Press, 2010.

Wright, Robert E. "Banking and Politics in New York, 1784–1829." Ph.D. Diss., SUNY Buffalo, 1997.

Wright, Robert E. "Banking System Stability/Fragility: The Roles of Governance and Supervision in Canada and America." In *Becoming 150: 150 Years of Canadian Business History*, edited by Mark S. Bonham. Toronto: Canadian Business History Association, 2018.

Wright, Robert E. *Corporation Nation*. Philadelphia: University of Pennsylvania Press, 2014.

Wright, Robert E. "Government Bailouts." In *Handbook of Major Events in Economic History*, edited by Robert Whaples and Randall Parker. New York: Routledge, 2013.

Wright, Robert E. "Ground Rents Against Populist Historiography: Mid-Atlantic Land Tenure, 1750–1820." *Journal of Interdisciplinary History* 29, no. 1 (1998): 23–42.

Wright, Robert E. *Hamilton Unbound: Finance and the Creation of the American Republic*. New York: Greenwood Press, 2002.

Wright, Robert E. "Insuring America: Market, Intermediated, and Government Risk Management Since 1790." In *Encuentro Internacional Sobre la Historia del Seguro*, edited by Leonardo Caruana. Madrid: Fundacion MAPFRE, 2010.

Wright, Robert E. *Little Business on the Prairie: Entrepreneurship, Prosperity, and Challenge in South Dakota*. Sioux Falls: Center for Western Studies, 2015.

Wright, Robert E. *Money and Banking*, 3rd ed. Boston: Flat World Knowledge, 2017.

Wright, Robert E. "New Bedford, Massachusetts and the Importance of Local Sources of Capital." *Financial History* 110 (2014).

Wright, Robert E. "On the Economic Efficiency of Organizations: Toward a Solution of the Efficient Government Enterprise Paradox." *Essays in Economic and Business History* 25, no. 1 (2007): 143–54.

Wright, Robert E. *One Nation Under Debt: Hamilton, Jefferson, and the History of What We Owe.* New York: McGraw Hill, 2008.

Wright, Robert E. *Origins of Commercial Banking in America, 1750–1800.* Lanham, Md.: Rowman & Littlefield, 2001.

Wright, Robert E. *The First Wall Street: Chestnut Street, Philadelphia, and the Birth of American Finance.* Chicago: University of Chicago Press, 2005.

Wright, Robert E. *The Poverty of Slavery: How Unfree Labor Pollutes the Economy.* New York: Palgrave Macmillan, 2017.

Wright, Robert E. *The Wealth of Nations Rediscovered: Integration and Expansion in American Financial Markets, 1780–1850.* New York: Cambridge University Press, 2002.

Wright, Robert E. "Women and Finance in the Early National U.S." *Essays in History* 42 (2000) online: www.essaysinhistory.com/articles/2012/100.

Wright, Robert E. and David J. Cowen. *Financial Founding Fathers: The Men Who Made America Rich.* Chicago: University of Chicago Press, 2006.

Wright, Robert E. and George David Smith. *Mutually Beneficial: The Guardian and Life Insurance in America.* New York: New York University Press, 2004.

Wright, Robert E. and Richard Sylla, *Genealogy of American Finance.* Columbia: Columbia University Press, 2015.

Wright, Robert E. and Richard Sylla, eds., *The History of Corporate Finance: Development of Anglo-American Securities Markets, Financial Practices, Theories and Laws,* 6 vols. London: Pickering and Chatto, 2003.

Yenawine, Bruce. *Benjamin Franklin and the Invention of Microfinance.* New York: Routledge, 2010.

Yost, Jeffrey R. *Making IT Work: A History of the Computer Services Industry.* Cambridge, Mass.: MIT Press, 2017.

Young, Kate Porter. "Rural South Carolina: An Ethnographic Study of Homeownership, Home Financing, and Credit." *Cityscape* 3, no. 1 (1997): 13–37.

Zanjani, George. "The Rise and Fall of the Fraternal Life Insurer: Law and Finance in U.S. Life Insurance, 1870–1920." Working paper, 2003.

About the Author:

Robert E. Wright has served Augustana University as the inaugural Nef Family Chair of Political Economy since 2009. After receiving his Ph.D. in economic history from SUNY Buffalo in 1997, Wright taught economics at the University of Virginia and New York University's Stern School of Business. His 18 previous books include *Mutually Beneficial*, *The First Wall Street*, *Financial Founding Fathers*, *One Nation Under Debt*, *Bailouts*, *Fubarnomics*, *Corporation Nation*, *Little Business on the Prairie*, and *The Poverty of Slavery*.

About AIER:

The American Institute for Economic Research in Great Barrington, Massachusetts, was founded in 1933 as the first independent voice for sound economics in the United States. Today it publishes ongoing research, hosts educational programs, publishes books, sponsors interns and scholars, and is home to the world-renowned Bastiat Society and the highly respected Sound Money Project. The American Institute for Economic Research is a 501c3 public charity.

Index

Amherst Holdings, 83
amortization, 31–38, 300
Anasazi, 150
Anderson, Roger, 363
Anderson, Terry, 166
Andress, Mary Vail, 261
Andrews, Bud, 100
Anniston, Alabama, 330
Antebellum period, 42, 93–97, 218, 240–41, 328
Antweiler, Josephine, 217–18
Appalachia, 148, 155, 184, 187, 191, 201–2, 205, 207–8
appraisals (real estate), 77, 104, 120
Ariely, Dan, 3
Arkansas, 21, 245, 280, 301, 303
Armstrong Investigation, 65, 359
Artemis Capital Group, 326
Ashbridge, Anne, 217
Ashbridge, Sarah, 217
Asian-Americans, 4, 133, 255, 322, 339
Ask Computer, 224
Associated Credit Bureaus of America (Consumer Data Industry Association), 50
Association for the Relief of Respectable Aged Indigent Females, 242
Association of Bank Women, 261
Association of Community Organizations for Reform Now (ACORN), 76
Atkinson, Edward, 315
Atlanta Journal/Constitution, 74
Atlanta Life, 260
Atlanta Mutual, 333
Atlanta, Georgia, 108, 135, 333–34
Attic Linen Shop, 29

Australia, 50
automobile finance and insurance, 28, 40, 45–46, 61, 118, 160, 169–70, 195, 209, 211, 230–32, 264, 342
Bable, Elizabeth, 217
Bache & Co., 324–25
Bache, Benjamin Franklin, 215
Bache, Margaret, 215
Bagehot's Rule. *See* Hamilton's Rule
Bailey, Lydia, 238
Baltimore, Md., 90–91, 198, 252, 329, 348
Bank for Cooperatives, 302
Bank of America, 47, 223, 232, 255, 260, 355
Bank of England, 355–56
Bank of Germantown, 217
Bank of Gettysburg, 237–38
Bank of North America, 92, 217, 310, 356
Bank of the Northern Liberties, 242
Bank of the United States (1791–1811), 236–37, 356, 366
Bank of the United States (1816–1836), 301, 357–58, 360–61
Bank of Utica (Miss.), 101
Bank of Utica (N.Y.), 237
BankAmericard, 47
Banking Act of 1933, 361
Banner, Stuart, 154
Baradaran, Mehrsa, 343
Barnett Banks, 168
Barr, Joseph, 6
Bartlett, Armenia, 227
Bateman, Ethel M., 230
Baxter, Margaret H., 237

CPSIA information can be obtained
at www.ICGtesting.com
Printed in the USA
LVHW032002130121
676401LV00008B/939

9 781630 691707